Archaeologies of Cosmoscapes in the Americas

DEDICATION

For F. Kent Reilly III,
a fellow pioneer of ancient cosmoscapes and
navigator for future generations of archaeologists.
A good friend and mentor.

Archaeologies of Cosmoscapes in the Americas

edited by

J. Grant Stauffer,
Bretton T. Giles, and Shawn P. Lambert

Essays in Honor of F. Kent Reilly III

AMERICAN LANDSCAPES

American Landscapes is an imprint of Oxbow Books

Published in the United Kingdom in 2022 by
OXBOW BOOKS
The Old Music Hall, 106–108 Cowley Road, Oxford OX4 1JE

and in the United States by
OXBOW BOOKS
1950 Lawrence Road, Havertown, PA 19083

Paperback Edition: ISBN 978-1-78925-844-8
Digital Edition: ISBN 978-1-78925-845-5

A CIP record for this book is available from the British Library

Library of Congress Control Number: 2022940618

Design and layout by Frabjous Books
Printed and bound in the United Kingdom by Short Run Press

For a complete list of titles, please contact:

UNITED KINGDOM
Oxbow Books
Telephone (01865) 241249
Email: oxbow@oxbowbooks.com
www.oxbowbooks.com

UNITED STATES OF AMERICA
Oxbow Books
Telephone (610) 853-9131, Fax (610) 853-9146
Email: queries@casemateacademic.com
www.casemateacademic.com/oxbow

Oxbow Books is part of the Casemate Group

Front Cover Images (left to right): The Hopewell Site, originally published by Henry Clyde Shetrone in the Ohio Archaeological and Historical Quarterly in 1926 (Vol. 35, pp. 19). Broken ceramic lid knob from a white soul flower cup lid, Burial 23, Yaxuna North Acropolis, Quintana Roo. Image courtesy of David Freidel.
Back Cover Images (left to right): Morning Star pictograph from Picture Cave, Missouri. Image courtesy of Carol Diaz-Granados and Jim Duncan. Aztec calendar stone on display in the Museo Nacional de Antropoloía, Mexico City. Image courtesy of Annabeth Headrick. Map of arranged burials and ritual deposits beneath the Pyramid of the Moon at Teotihuacan (Burial 6), Mexico. Image courtesy of Saburo Sugiyama. Engraved Oneota-style Thunderer engraved on a Tunican bottle from the Lacey site (3PO41), Poinsett County, Arkansas. Image courtesy of Toney Aid.

Contents

Part 2: Place-making and cultivating cosmoscapes

Part 3: Cosmoscapes in perspective

Contributors

Toney Aid
MA Art History, University of Missouri
Independent Scholar
West Plains, MO

Daniel E. Aquino
Director
National Museum of Archaeology and Ethnology of Guatemala
Guatemala City, Guatemala

Madelaine C. Azar
Graduate Student
Department of Anthropology
University of North Carolina at Chapel Hill
Chapel Hill, NC

Steven L. Boles
Senior Research Archaeologist
American Bottom Field Station
Illinois State Archaeological Survey
Fairview Heights, IL

Carol Diaz-Granados
Research Associate
Department of Anthropology
Washington University in St Louis
St Louis MO

James R. Duncan
Independent Anthropological Archaeologist
Former Director of the Missouri State Museum
St. Louis MO

David H. Dye
Professor
Department of Archaeology
University of Memphis
Memphis TN

David A. Freidel
Professor of Archaeology
Department of Anthropology
Washington University in St Louis
St Louis MO

Bretton T. Giles
Fort Riley Archeologist and Collections Manager
Conservation Branch, Environmental Division, DPW
Fort Riley, KS

Annabeth Headrick
Associate Professor and Director
School of Art & Art History
University of Denver
Denver CO

Shawn P. Lambert
Assistant Professor
Department of Anthropology and Middle Eastern Cultures
Mississippi State University
Starkville, MS

Melinda A. Martin
Graduate Student
Department of Archaeology
University of Memphis
Memphis TN

Juan C. Melendez
Pre-Columbian Studies Fellow
Dumbarton Oaks Research Library and Collection
Washington, DC

Joy Mersmann
Graduate Student
Department of Anthropology
University of North Carolina at Chapel Hill
Chapel Hill, NC

Ryan M. Parish
Associate Professor
Department of Earth Sciences
University of Memphis
Memphis, TN

Brian M. Rowe
Graduate Student
Department of Earth Sciences
University of Memphis
Memphis, TN

J. Grant Stauffer
Graduate Student
Department of Anthropology
Washington University in St. Louis
St Louis MO

Vincas P. Steponiatis
Professor of Archaeology and Anthropology
Department of Anthropology
University of North Carolina at Chapel Hill
Chapel Hill, NC

1

Conceptualizing cosmoscapes

J. Grant Stauffer, Bretton T. Giles, and Shawn P. Lambert

Introduction

In this book, we explore how pre-Columbian peoples in the Americas perceived, imagined, and iteratively (re)created dynamic cosmoscapes (cf. Pavel 1981; Berlo 2011; Reichel 2012; Bold 2020), which were entangled in their lifeworlds[1] in distinctly non-modern ways (cf. Latour 1993; Descola 2014a; 2014b). Cosmoscapes constitute "overarching models and templates for the shape and scope of the cosmos" (Reichel 2012, 136–7) or, in other words, ontological landscapes (Pavel 1981, 154; Berlo 2011; Bold 2020). Cultures with shared cosmologies modeled them in innovative ways to create cosmoscapes, the subject matter that our book explores. In other words, cosmoscape is a conceptual tool for understanding the great variety of cosmological models that exist both artifactually and contextually. Along these lines, there has been a tendency to gloss over the way pre-Columbian peoples conceptualized their cosmos as animate and intertwined with the material contexts they inhabited, which, in part, prompts our use of the term cosmoscape(s) (cf. Pavel 1981; Berlo 2010; Reichel 2012; Bold 2020). This material-based approach offers a way of projecting findings across spatial scales to examine nested cosmological models and the symbol systems associated with them, from macrocosm to microcosm (Ellen 1986, 2).

Pre-Columbian Native Americans reconciled their cosmoscapes with the realities they experienced. To do this, aspects of observable realities (objects, plants, animals, peoples, and landmarks) featured prominently in cultural narratives about creating and maintaining order in the cosmos (Hultkrantz 1979, 27–83; Berlo 2011; 2014; Reichel 2012). Because individual experiences varied greatly, this process often resulted in multiple, competing perspectives of shared cosmoscapes, especially when those perspectives held consequences for economic and political interests (Bold 2020). Cosmoscapes tend to emphasize dynamic motion (Boyea 1999; Berlo 2011; 2014) and how proper interpersonal relations emerge from fulfilling reciprocal obligations (Hallowell 1960; Morrison 2000). They often feature narratives about various significant non-human persons and actions during mythopoetic times. Ties to these non-human persons were often cultivated by gifting food, blood, tobacco, songs, prayers, dances, and other performances, as well as consuming drugs that altered human perception, such as tobacco, Datura, balché, and peyote.

Pre-Columbian cosmoscapes in the Americas were typically embedded within relational ontologies (cf. Alberti and Marshall 2009; Olsen 2010; Alberti *et al.* 2011; Alberti 2013; 2016; Kohn 2015; Baltus and Baires 207; Harrison-Buck and Hendon 2018). A common element of some relational ontologies (i.e., analogism) was the way certain parts of complex wholes were believed to mirror or epitome larger structures, often in an exemplary fashion (Ellen 1986, 2–3; cf. Descola 2014a; 2014b). A microcosm can be defined as how something – an object, [human] body, community, place, or situation – encapsulates in miniature the characteristic qualities or features of something much larger (e.g., the macrocosm). The body, house, and settlement (village) are commonly re-occurring cross-cultural symbolic microcosms, but the microcosmic repertoire in various cultures can be more complex and culturally specific (Ellen 1986). Microcosms and macrocosms can also be relative, interpenetrating, multidimensional codes, since at the same time the body may condense the house, the house can conversely condense the body (*sensu* Ellen 1986, 3; Williamson 2007). Similarly, objects, representations, settlements/villages, and other architectural features can constitute important dimensions of cosmoscapes. Some representational imagery portrayed aspects of pre-Columbian cosmoscapes and we argue that this imagery can spur archaeological thought, analogous to how paintings inspired landscape perspectives (Ingold 1993; 2012; Cosgrove 1998).

This volume's contributors explore these issues in more depth and provide detailed, well-contextualized case studies that examine the ways pre-Columbian peoples perceived, imagined, and iteratively (re)created dynamic cosmoscapes. In this introduction, we tackle four topics that contextualize and provide background for the case studies. The first section is *Cosmoscapes as ontological landscapes*, which examines how the roots of cosmoscapes are tied to the literature on landscapes, relational ontologies, and art history/iconography. *Objects as cosmoscapes* constitutes the second section that discusses how highly ritualized objects and iconography can create horizontal linkages between peoples, landscapes, environments, and material culture; as well as vertical linkages connecting nonhuman persons and worlds through material, sociopolitical, and religious dynamics. The third section, *Placemaking and cultivating landscapes*, explores how landscapes were modified and encoded to fit experiences of the world, reflecting different peoples' cosmoscapes in culturally specific ways. The final section summarizes the subsequent case studies in the volume.

Cosmoscapes as ontological landscapes

The cosmoscape concept has developed in recent literature as a way of exploring how communities produce and model different ontological realities in their lifeworlds (cf. Pavel 1981; Berlo 2011; 2014; Reichel 2012; Slater 2014; Bold

2020). Its emerging formulation derives from landscape theory and relational ontologies (Pavel 1981; Berlo 2011; Slater 2014; Bold 2020), as well as art history and iconography (Berlo 2011; 2014). Accordingly, we explore how cosmoscapes are rooted in landscape theory, the ontological turn, and iconography (art history). In particular, we discuss how F. Kent Reilly's iconographic and symbolic analyses of pre-Columbian representational imagery and symbols provide inspiration for our approaches.

Recent use of the term cosmoscape(s) builds upon developments in landscape theory. Sauer's (1926, 46) initial definition of landscape was formulated in the early 20th century (Peet 1985) to counteract the popularity of environmental determinism (*sensu* Ratzel 1896). Sauer's (1926) perspective was influenced by social psychology, exemplified by Durkheim's (1960, 79) notion of a collective conscience as "the totality of beliefs and sentiments". Durkheim's debates with Ratzel drew greater attention to the role of human agency in landscape transformations and subsequent discussions exposed several concerns about the relationships among members of past societies, their connections to the environment, and the means of studying them (Hirsch 1995). Despite the extensive scholarly literature on landscapes, a focus on cosmoscape(s) offers a novel alternative and fresh perspective on certain tensions and ambiguities within landscape theory.

One tension in landscape theory is its focus: is the landscape concept purely a "synthetic abstraction" that captures the immaterial perceptions of one's surroundings (Anschuetz *et al.* 2001, 163) or does it also refer to the ways that past cultures transformed their surroundings (Norton 1989, 37)? Moreover, this dichotomy ignores how Native American peoples create and use objects and features as cosmological models, which blur the boundaries between the perception and transformation of their surroundings. For example, the four large architectural supports in the Navajo hogan (the traditional polygonal dwelling) relate to the four sacred mountains that circumscribe their homeland – *Dinétah* (Berlo 2011, 11). Archaeological approaches focused strictly on human-environment interactions also tend to underplay the ways that the objects and places endowed with cosmological significance are approached as animate social agents (*sensu* Appadurai 1988; Cochrane 2007). These interactions often include ritual oblation and gift-giving to create/promote mutual obligations and relations with non-human persons – including important places like mountains and caves – but violent events can also be interpreted as a backlash if the person is believed to have acted exploitatively or disrespectfully (cf. Hallowell 1960; Morrison 2000; Dye and King 2007; Berlo 2011; 2014; Slater 2014; Bold 2020; Skaanes 2021).

The second tension is that traditional landscape studies are rooted in 17th century landscape painting in Western traditions (Cosgrove 1998, 20–1; Ingold 1993; Skaanes 2021, 224). It is therefore problematic that archaeological perspectives on Native American landscapes are often deeply rooted in Euro-centric ways of conceptualizing the use/meaning of various objects, spaces, and places. For example, relatively little attention has focused on the implications of creating ephemeral and cosmologically charged compositions intended to be dispersed on the wind like Navajo sandpaintings (Berlo 2011; 2014) or mounded over like the Great Mortuary and Spirit Lodge within the Craig Mound at Spiro, Oklahoma (Lambert 2018; Brown *et al.* 2020). Equally significant are the ways that various objects were killed or removed from circulation throughout the pre-Columbian Americas, practices typical of sacrificial economies (cf. Kűchler 1997; Penney 2004; Giles 2010). Evidence for the episodic re-enactment of creation [cosmogonic] events that established novel orders of existence (Boyea 1999; Cobb and King 2005; Hultkrantz 1979; Lewis and Stout 1998) also emphasizes dynamic motion, rather than moments of stasis analogous to landscape paintings (Berlo 2011, 10–11; see also Ingold 1993; Cosgrove 1998; Skaanes 2021).

Cosmoscapes are also a product of the ontological turn, which consist of a range of approaches related to peoples' perception and beliefs about reality and their actual ontological commitments – the way they recreate realities through their actions (cf. Alberti and Marshall 2009; Olsen 2010; Alberti *et al.* 2011; Alberti 2013; 2016; Kohn 2015; Skousen and Buchanan 2015; Baltus and Baires 2017; Harrison-Buck and Hendon 2018). This theoretical turn is often associated with Philippe Descola's (2014a; 2014b), Eduordo Viveiros de Castro's (1998; 2004), and Bruno Latour's (1993; 1999) work, but considerable variability exists in these approaches, touchstones, and trajectories. One important trajectory relates to Native American perspectives on being, becoming, and worlding – typically referred to as relational ontologies. We argue that a comparative perspective that explores how past peoples had similar and/or different ontologies should be a crucial element of these approaches.

For example, Descola (2014a; 2014b) proposes a fourfold schema of ontologies that he labels: animism, totemism, analogism, and naturalism. Animism describes how certain Native Americans conceptualize a "continuity of souls and a discontinuity of bodies" (Descola 2014a, 129–43; 2014b, 275; see also Bird-David 1999; Viveiros de Castro 1998; 2004), although we would replacing the term "souls", as the animating lifeforce/power, with various culturally specific concepts, like mana, orenda, wakan, manitou, and teotl (Hewitt 1902; La Flesche 1932; Fogelson and Adams 1977; Hultkrantz 1979; Vail 2000; van der Grijp 2014). Totemism relates to groups "where some beings in the world share sets of physical and moral attributes that cut across the boundaries of species", as exemplified by totemic moieties like the Nungar of Southwest Australia (Descola 2014a, 144–71; 2014b, 275–6). Analogism is predicated on the idea that all entities in the world are composed of a "multiplicity of essences, forms and substances" that organized and recombined as a result of "dense networks of analogies" (Descola 2014a, 201–31; 2014b, 276). Conversely, naturalism refers to our own modern Western ontology that incorporates an idea of nature as the physical world that collectively includes plants, animals, the landscape, and other features and products of the earth as opposed to humans or human creations (Latour 1993; Descola 2014a, 172–200; 2014b, 276–7). Descola (2014b, 277) also acknowledges that while some ontologies fit neatly into these categories; complex combinations or "hybrid" ontologies are very common.

The ontological complexity and diversity present in various societies emphasize the myriad of ways that cosmoscapes were perceived, imagined, and iteratively (re)created by pre-Columbian peoples in the Americas. In this vein, our book's contributors describe in their case studies how the cosmoscapes of many pre-Columbian groups reflect complex combinations of animism and analogism. Yet the analogism that occurs in many pre-state societies is more scalar and emphasizes how complex wholes (or collectives) at different scales mirror and are organized into larger structures; a perspective akin to fractal personhood (cf. Descola 2014a; 2014b; see also Strathern 1988; 1991; Fowler 2004; Giles 2010). Additionally, the metaphors employed by different groups can vary from bundles in Mesoamerica and the Eastern Woodlands (Hall 1997; Guernsey and Reilly 2006; Zendeño 2008; 2009; Pauketat 2013; Skousen and Buchanan 2015; Reilly 2021) to boxes on the Northwest Coast (MacDonald 1981; Seguin 1984; Kan 1989) and knotworks in the Pacific (Küchler 2003). These metaphors were typically rich, complex interpenetrating analogies that vary in subtle ways but are often related to ideas about the person/body, a cross-culturally common microcosm (Wayman 1982; Ellen 1986).

The cosmoscape literature has also examined shifting and competing ontologies, as well as "ontological fusions" (Pavel 1981; Bold 2020). For instance, Thomas Pavel (1981) examines how the shifts and conflicts occurred during a transition in 18th century Europe from a Christian ontology to a scientific one, as well as how lifeworlds divided into sacred and profane domains create multilevel ontologies in which certain sacred objects, places, and/or times can belong to multiple worlds (see also Bold 2020). In multilevel ontologies, sacred objects, places, and/or times serve as "articulation points where the two worlds meet, in what one could call an ontological fusion" (Pavel 1981, 5). These ontological fusions can vary from complete to partial, depending on how the sacred and profane are divided and parceled into domains (Pavel 1981, 7–8). In this vein, most of the objects and places that manifest cosmoscapes signify ontological fusions of multiple worlds or, in other words, *axis mundi*. In turn, Rosalyn Bold (2020, 195) analyzes how animist and modern ontologies "contest and converse with one another to compose a shifting cosmoscape in a community in highland Bolivia". Her discussion examines how ontological understandings can be complex and circumstantial, especially in negotiating animist perspectives and the exploitation of the earth or "natural environment" (Bold 2020).

Art historical and iconographic approaches provide a third touchstone for the cosmoscape literature. Accordingly, art historians and iconographers' contributions to understanding pre-Columbian imagery and cosmology of Central and North America research is so vast that it is impossible to summarize here. Yet it is worth highlighting the long-term contributions of Kent Reilly – both in terms of his scholarly work and organizing scholars into interdisciplinary collectives. During his long career, Reilly extensively contributed to ancient Olmec, Maya, and Mississippian understandings of representational imagery, symbolism, and placemaking. His work provides impressive examples of how objects – including their ritual treatment and representational imagery – served as cosmological models, as well as how past peoples cultivated and perceived sacred places as bridging worlds in ways that produced rich, interwoven cosmoscapes. Kent and his work's influence on this volume's contributors is one of the threads that binds (or bundles) us together.

Reilly's work offers multiple examples of how objects were entangled with cosmological models and narratives about cosmogonic events. One prominent example is Reilly's research on bundles and bundling in Mesoamerica (Guernsey and Reilly 2006; Reilly 2006) and North America (Reilly 2021). For example, Guernsey and Reilly (2006) tackled the ceremonial associations of bundles in Mesoamerica, including their links to lineage continuity, ancestor veneration, and positions of authority. Similarly, the bundles identified by Reilly (2006) in Formative period, Olmec imagery provide important antecedents for later Maya imagery. This work's importance lies not only in identifying bundles but also how the process of wrapping, containing, and opening bundles was central to Mesoamerican rituals. Another notable contribution is Reilly's (2004) argument that many Mississippian representations probably correspond to a tripartite cosmic model, consisting of an Above World, Middle World, and Beneath World (Fig. 1.1). Alternately, he has worked extensively on the associations of important Mississippian themes and narrative characters, such as the Great Serpent (Reilly 2011), Hightower style anthropomorphic imagery (King and Reilly 2011), and locatives – like eye surrounds and petaloids (Reilly 2004; 2007).

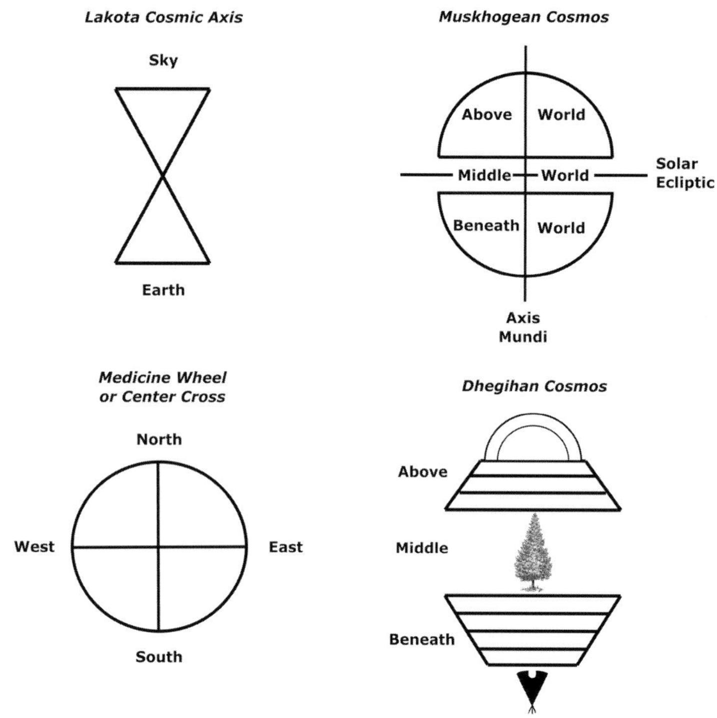

Fig. 1.1. Common motifs representing the structure of the cosmos in Native American societies (adapted from Swanton 1928; Goodman 1992; Reilly 2004; Duncan 2011, fig. 2.2).

Reilly has contributed ideas about how Mesoamerican and Eastern Woodland peoples produced and perceived their sacred places as bridges between worlds, creating vibrant, sophisticated cosmoscapes. Building on David Stuart's (1996) insight that many Maya stellae were probably wrapped or bundled, Reilly argues (2006) that the process of unwrapping and rewrapping these (stellae) bundles was probably a dominant plaza ritual. In turn, Reilly (2006) illustrated how representation of cords, ropes, knots, ties, and bundles on Olmec and Maya imagery, monumental statues, and architecture was closely associated with positions of authority (including Maya kingship). Conversely, his detailed analysis of Complex A at La Venta showed how it materialized the Maya underwater realm – Xibalbá (Reilly 1989a). Additionally, Reilly (1986) has illustrated how Maya architectural features and occupations were actively folded into pre-existing Olmec landscapes, as well as the way that crafting objects recombined the animating forces of people and things.

Objects as cosmoscapes

This section of our volume explores how cosmoscapes are manifested through the creation, use, and deposition of ritualized objects in the Americas. There are important insights to consider when analyzing how objects can manifest cosmoscapes. First, objects have relatedness to the world (Buchanan and Skousen 2015). The ontologies of objects as entangled beings fundamentally involved networks of human and non-human beings, constantly connecting and interacting with different lifeworlds (Harrison-Buck 2015). Second, objects relate and experience lifeworlds not only as active agents but also as physical objects. As Olsen (2010, 67) explains, they are "being-in this world as a concrete existence of involvement that unites [things] with the world". Third, objects as cosmoscapes challenge traditional archaeological conceptions of the spatiality and directionality of objects. Traditional archaeological views commonly employ a human-centered perspective of how objects influence people, places, and other things (Tilley 2004). According to Tilley (1994, 16), an understanding of this space takes its "starting point with the upright human body looking out on the world". In this spirit, directionality and spatiality should be the universal basis for comprehending objects and how people experience objects within space, place, and time. We do not emphasize the centrality of human causality but the centrality of things and how objects impact space, place, people, and history. Objects have independent agency, whether they are represented or not.

How iconography adorned ritualized objects to construct and evoke cosmoscapes is another focal point of this section. Archaeological, iconographic, ethnographic, ethnohistorical, and philosophical materials are used to foster a more nuanced understanding of how movement, bodily experiences, and relational things form the basis of animistic cosmoscapes. Harrison-Buck's (2015) study of Maya iconography and religion called these relational ontologies "meshworks" (see also Ingold 2007; 2011). Iconography in well understood archaeological and historical contexts is what Jean Molesky-Poz (2006, 154–68) describes as a distinct way of knowing that reflects "the profound sense of relatedness rooted in the perception of a shared [cosmoscape] in all creation".

How objects act is another important aspect of objects as cosmoscapes. As Heidegger (1971, 179) posited, these acts are objects "gathering and staying qualities, as something evoking the 'nearness' of (or embeddedness in) a lifeworld set apart [from] something that unites, not as property but as a work: the thingness of things". Accordingly, objects can independently act as microcosms that allow people to create, maintain, communicate, and transform lifeworlds. Framing objects as comsoscapes signifies that objects are no longer viewed as peripheral to the world but are in fact things being-in-the-world. Therefore, we highlight entanglements of objects with everything and everyone they encounter during their life histories. We concern ourselves with how objects manifest these cosmoscape lifeworlds and the people who take part in their creation, use, distribution, and deposition.

Cosmoscapes can be created as portable artifacts that exercise agency to fulfill reciprocal obligations. Native Americans even identified naturally occurring, unmodified objects as cosmoscapes, like the *Busycon* whelk shell (Helms 1979; 1993; Kelly and Brown 2012). Reilly (pers. comm. 2018) likens the *Busycon* whelk shell's shape to the Klein bottle, a non-orientable surface and mathematical model of interconnected spaces (González-Díaz and Garay 1999, fig. 1). The whelk's spiral direction reflects the dynamic motions of cosmic forces in space-time and informs the organization of Muskhogean "rotundas" where similarly directed dance movements historically occurred (Marquardt and Kozuch 2016, 8–11, figs 10 and 11). In North America, the richest concentration of iconographically laden *Busycon* whelk shell fragments and cups has been recovered from the Craig Mound's Spirit Lodge, where elaborate mortuary rituals took place (Phillips and Brown 1984; Brown *et al.* 2020). Its innately special qualities made the marine whelk shell a desirable crafting medium throughout eastern North America and inspired the creation of shell effigy pottery (Kozuch 2013, 34–5, figs 3–4). Beads crafted from *Busycon* sp. whelk shells may have functioned as an early form of "currency", according to Prentice (1987, 199). The symbolism of *Busycon* whelk shells and replications of their common form demand attention to multiscalar relationships that collectively embody cosmoscape.

Some artifacts can be described as cosmoscapes that intertwine cosmological information with representations of specific people and other-than-human-persons (*sensu* Morrison 2000). Tracing the origins of Maya iconographic themes and motifs to the Olmec of Tabasco, Mexico, Reilly (1986; 1990) pioneered the idea that cosmic models were carved onto stone statues like the Las Limas monument that personified absent ruler(s). Iconographically, the monument's political charter is encoded by motifs that transform it into the sacred world tree, a metaphorical *axis mundi* (Reilly 1990, 22). Smith and Miller (2009) examine several Mississippian statues that likely had similar functions. Etowah's Mound C, Georgia, provides an archaeological example of violence carried out through the desecration of mound-top ancestral temples and painted marble statues (Dye and King 2007). Brown (2013a, 363–5) argues that ancestral cult veneration at Spiro and Cahokia was expressed through burial arrangements that solidified group claims to valuable properties and highlights the use of tableaux to intertwine the animated dead with their accoutrements. The variety of funerary figurines and statues crafted from wood, bone, ceramic, and stone in the Eastern Woodlands thus provide examples of animated objects whose social lives were intertwined with living people in journeys across cosmoscapes.

Artifacts that embody cosmoscapes often include finely decorated pottery. In the American Bottom region, Pauketat and Emerson (1991, 931–5) interpret incised motifs on Ramey Incised pottery as representations of the cosmos, fitting for our present application of the cosmoscape concept. Mindful of the Muskhogean cosmogram that resembles two, superimposed pots (Swanton 1928, 478) – one being inverted and the other upright – they view the act of reaching down and into the pot as establishing "the user's relation to earth, fertility, the disorder of an Under World, and feminine life forces, but only as mediated by cosmological order" (Pauketat and Emerson 1991, 934). Like Gibson's (2006) comparison of earthen mounds in the Lower Mississippi River Valley to "navels of the earth" where humanity first emerged, Pauketat and Emerson (1991, 933–4) interpret pot orifices as representations of primordial emergence places. They add that Ramey Incised pots were involved in rites of intensification that resembled the Muskhogean Green Corn Ceremony (*sensu* Witthoft 1949). The widespread circulation of Ramey Incised pottery with distinctive, "calling card" motifs beyond the Cahokia site thus evidence direct contact between different sociopolitical entities in ceremonial situations, perhaps identifying specific families or individuals (Emerson 1989; 1997; Hall 1991).

The embedded symbol systems of cosmoscapes permit the identification of their parts, as well as the entangled roles of objects, people, and practices (Reilly 2004, 127). Consequently, vessels crafted into cosmoscapes billboard the qualities of their contents, such as libations that activated shamanic transformations (Reilly 1989b, 11; 2004, 132; Freidel *et al.* 1993, 33; Dye 2007; 2011, 108). The association of specific substances, locatives, and cosmic places may also communicate information about the social groups responsible for making certain medicinal substances, the ecological settings of their ingredients, and the proper settings for their use. For example, Mississippian compound vessels often consist of strainers and stackable bottles, jars, and beakers (Luer 1996). Compound vessels are often iconographically laden and whole examples convey a complete cosmoscape; perhaps facilitating a sequence of medicinal preparation stages (Lambert 2018). Especially if compound vessel components belong to distinct social groups like crafting tools among Osage clans (*sensu* Kelly 2006, 241–2), compound vessel assembly likely symbolizes an assembled culture. Sampled for residues left by their contents, Arkansas River Valley examples provided Datura signatures (King *et al.* 2018; Lambert *et al.* 2021). Remarkably, these Native American Antikythera mechanisms navigate their operators through cosmoscapes symbolically and experientially (Lambert 2018). With this example in mind, we consider how a cosmoscape perspective reveals large-scale assemblies that inextricably embed cultures with their homelands as a means of placemaking.

Placemaking and cultivating cosmoscapes

This section examines how architectures create, landscapes are transformed, and settlements are organized to reinforce, mirror, and intertwine aspects of cosmoscapes. Centered on *axes mundi*, cosmoscapes envelope microcosms, fulfilling what objects arranged in tableaux accomplish in smaller contexts (Eliade 1957; Ellen 1986; Chappell 2002). As kinds of cosmograms (*sensu* Smith 2005), cosmoscapes encode co-existing ontologies in a multiplicity of arrangements, across physical and imagined spaces (Pavel 1981; Ellen 1986, 2, 16; Marquardt and Crumley 1987, 5–7). As ontological landscapes, cosmoscapes are distinct, multiscalar lifeworlds that supply complex, rich, and interpenetrating analogies (Pavel 1981, 152). Cosmoscapes can host dynamic, complex systems that articulate potent objects (Machner and Bentley 2003; Lansing 2009; Kohler 2012). If people develop self-consciousness by making meaningful objects and those objects supply meaning to the crafter in turn (*sensu* Marx 1844, xxii; Olsen 2010), then perhaps cosmoscapes likewise involve collective consciences, "common traditions, the memory of their great ancestors, [and] the collective ideal of which they are incarnation" (Durkheim 1971, 348).

As landscapes and settlements, cosmoscapes structure society and channel the forces that animate them. Consequently, cosmoscapes can be as ephemeral as Navajo sandpaintings (*sensu* Berlo 2011; 2014) and as enduring as earthen mounds (*sensu* Miller 2015; Ingold 1993). Investigations of Native American folklore and iconography make clear that such forces animate primordial ancestors, other-than-human-persons, and their settings (Reilly 2004; Lankford 2007; Bold 2020). Globally, cosmoscapes define the human body or even a specific person as the *axis mundi* (*sensu* Wayman 1982), but New World cultures see persons and things as indistinguishable parts of larger wholes (DeLanda 2006, 3; Giles 2010, 74). For example, mana (Polynesia), orenda (Haudenosaunee), and Wako^{n}da (Osage) are culture-specific referents to an animating force all things possess (Hewitt 1902, 37; La Flesche 1932, 193; Hultkrantz 1979; van der Grijp 2014, 51). Aztec illustrations in the Borgia Codex show that animating forces are heavily concentrated in sacred bundles containing ritual objects, faunal material, and human remains (Díaz and Rodgers 1993, pl. 36; Guernsey and Reilly 2006, vii, fig. 1). In many cases, these forces are only visible to ritual specialists who exclusively access distant places of the cosmoscape (colour Pl. 1) (Briggs 2003; Reichel 2012, 129–36). Appeals to animating forces were often restricted to special purpose buildings organized as microcosms, where a shaman could depart on journeys to otherworldly locations (Hoffman 1891; Fortune 1932; Dewdney 1975; Freidel *et al.* 1993; Reichel 2012, fig. 9.2; Lambert *et al.* 2021).

Common focal points of cosmoscapes and anthropological discourse in general include houses and "house societies" (Beck 2007; Kahn and Kirch 2013; Joyce and Gillespie 2017). Cross-culturally, houses bear strong associations with the human body, animating forces, and directionality (Wayman 1982; Thybony 1998; Williamson 2007). The Tlingit consider the human body a "house for the spirit" (Kan 1989, 49–50; Giles 2010, 77), and the Osage organized their House of Mysteries to reflect the universe's organization (La Flesche 1925, 84). Northwest Coast societies generally view body and house as intertwined microcosms (MacDonald 1981; Thybony 1998). The Berber House's famously inverted internal and external spaces, directing one's movements within it (Bourdieu 1970, 167). The Creek rotunda's resemblance to the *Busycon* shell likewise facilitates dancing in spiraling directions, connecting the rotunda microcosm to a specific object and their enveloping macrocosm (Bartram 1995, 175; Marquardt and Kozuch 2016, 9). North American earthworks were often arranged as multistage, nested microcosms, containing potent pots, sacred bundles, hearths, poles, bodies, and houses (Fowler *et al.* 1999; Sherwood and Kidder 2011; Kidder and Sherwood 2017; Lambert 2018; Sawyer and King 2021). At Spiro, the Craig Mound encapsulated a Caddoan Spirit Lodge that housed a tableau of mortuary furniture, altogether situated atop the Great Mortuary's cribwork with human remains (Brown *et al.* 2020). This diorama concluded a world renewal ceremony, bridging worlds of the living and the spirits (Brown et al. 2020, 112–13). Thus, cosmoscapes contain nested microcosms that articulate with each other in ritual performances to satisfy dire needs with animating force and divine assistance (Boyea 1999).

The placement of microcosmic architectures within villages and cities facilitated a dynamo of intended (and unintended) behaviors. Some architectural site arrangements emanate bodily metaphors like houses do (Palka 2002; Tate 2008, 38). Their layouts reflect the nature of reciprocal obligations and encode cosmological narratives, pooling critical resources in common spaces (Lewis and Stout 1998; Headrick 2007, 51; Sassaman *et al.* 2020). The arrangement of Osage villages reflected their division into sky and earth moieties, and reciprocal obligations to each other (La Flesche 1921, 50–1). The distribution of essential knowledge between them cemented an ontological reality: the union of sky (father) and earth (mother) is the source of all life (Bailey 1995, 31; Hall 1997, 193–4; Brown and Kelly 2015, 222–3). Cahokia's layout has been analogously interpreted with this Osage village model that could also apply to American Bottom settlement patterns as a whole (Fowler 1978; Kelly 1996; Milner 2006; Kelly and Brown 2014).

Cosmoscapes that structure ontological realities at the scale of settlement patterns also organize complex systems (*sensu* Kohler 2012). Like the division of Osage society, Balinese farming villages are arranged between Mt Batur's crater lake, the source of purity and clean water, and the sea, chaos incarnate and the ultimate destination of the island's water supply. In accordance with calendars provided by water temple priests, the obligations villages fulfill for the rice goddess at diversion canal water shrines between sea and summit collectively ensure successful harvests (Lansing 2009). Perhaps Native American agricultural settlements along the Mississippi likewise cooperated to maintain their cosmoscape (see Fritz 2019; Hall 1991). One way or another, these cases illustrate how cosmoscape perspectives dissolve the liminal boundaries between natural, social, and spiritual lifeworlds.

The intertwining of patterned settlements with sanctified natural features is another salient feature of cosmoscapes. Landscapes are saturated with collective memories and modified to project ontological realities (Mallery 1893; Diaz-Granados and Duncan 2000; Brown 2013b; Henry 2017; 2020). For example, Choctaw mound sites cluster around the location of Nanih Wayah, "the mother mound", where their ancestors first emerged (Gibson 2006). Likewise, stories about bear's migration across the Great Lakes and deliverance of the Midē'wiwin's founding rituals has been related to distributions of late pre-Columbian, earthen enclosures (Howey and O'Shea 2006). Over time, natural and human-made features articulate and intertwine within overarching cosmoscapes.

Experiences that reinforce personal commitments to Native American ontologies certainly include quests for visions and sacred objects from distant places (Helms 1979; 1993; Kelly and Brown 2012). Strategically placed on the landscape, stone alignments like the Fort Smith Medicine Wheel, exhibit cosmological layouts and serviced vision quests (Lowie 1918, 436). Likewise, the Columbia Plateau's Scratched Style petroglyphs mark places where "ritual gashing" rites took place, transforming the participants' bodies and surrounding rock faces (Keyser and Taylor 2006,

216–17). Picture Cave, Missouri, displays a spectacular creation story in total darkness (Diaz-Granados *et al.* 2015), while Mesoamerican caves and mountains embody earth-monsters and rain-giving other-than-human persons (Reilly 1993; Brady and Prufer 2005). Marking concentrations of animating forces, historical event sites, or sacred object sources was a means of ensnaring the fundamental pieces of cosmoscapes.

Cosmoscapes are multiplicitous, multi-scalar assemblages of microcosms that encode ontologies across all dimensions of societies. In the Black Hills of Montana, the Lakota related their home physiography to their cosmology, creating star and earth maps that paired ageless natural features and night-sky constellations (Goodman 1992; Sundstrom 1996). Their villages' strategic locations on the landscape prioritized cone-shaped tipis whose sacred bundle contents pointed to corresponding constellations above (Goodman 1992, 9, 16–17). When in their proper place at the right time, sacred bundles occupied the axes connecting mirrored earth-sky dimensions of the Lakota cosmoscape and sinched their microcosmic realities together (Good 1989; Goodman 1992, 12–15, 29; Sundstrom 1996; Hall 1997, 24–30). In sum, the material and immaterial culture of the Lakota – their homes, their homelands, and their kindred spirits – embody a complex and interconnected cosmoscape. Our book provides similar case studies that highlight bundled aspects of cosmoscapes.

Organization of the volume

The book's organization reflects a scalar division of cosmoscapes into microcosms and macrocosms (Ellen 1986). In the first section titled *Objects as cosmoscapes*, the contributing authors share perspectives about the complexity of artifactual microcosms and their influences on past peoples' lifeworlds. These case studies examine how objects and their imagery reveal and encode cosmoscapes in specific contexts (Bold 2020). These discussions tackle how diverse arrays of objects can be intertwined with cosmoscapes, including Mississippian ceramic effigy bowls (Azar and Steponaitis), figurines (Boles), bottles (Lambert), and calumet pipes (Dye and Aid) in Southeastern North America, as well as Maya greenstone mosaic masks in the Guatemalan lowlands (Melendez *et al.*) and Aztec calendar stones in Central Mexico (Headrick).

The second section titled *Placemaking and cultivating cosmoscapes* contains chapters that examine how pre-existing landscapes were modified and encoded to create dynamic cosmoscapes. In this regard, rock art and earthworks were strategically positioned across ancestral landscapes to mark potent places (Duncan and Diaz-Granados); post features established sightlines and marked monuments that correspond with an *a priori* cosmological order (Mersmann and Stauffer); and tornados, whirlwinds, and other wind-related phenomena became icons for the edification of others (Martin); while the ritual deposits covered by mounds offered glimpses of richly, interwoven Native American cosmoscapes (Giles *et al.*). Significant overlap exists between both sections of the book as artifactual tools for navigating and participating in overarching cosmoscapes were used to enact historic change across geographic space and cultural boundaries (Dye).

Azar and Steponaitis examine how effigy bowls in the central Mississippi River Valley portray animal and human subjects from distinct places in the Mississippian cosmoscape. They also explore how the vessels' colored slips and decorative qualities inform their users about whom the pots and their contents belong to, as well as the nature of their contents. Additionally, Azar and Stepontaitis discuss how these vessels facilitated important interactions through the way they functioned during specific ritual events.

Lambert's chapter investigates how compound vessels from the central Arkansas River Valley were used in processing medicines from *Datura*, a toxic hallucinogen that grows in some parts of southern North America. While considering the vessels' form and decorative qualities, Lambert explains how *Datura*-infused medicines allowed shamanic specialists to access visions of a beneath world in the Mississippian cosmoscape that was otherwise inaccessible.

Dye and Aid examines calumet ceremonialism between the Oneota and Tunica who became entangled after the former's long and violent journey through the Mississippi River Valley. Given these two groups distinct cultural histories and different cosmoscape perspectives, Dye and Aid argue that calumet ceremonies likely fostered dialogues that facilitated their co-existence and permitted political and ideological negotiations. Moreover, they contend that sustained interactions and negotiations in ritual forums resulted in a novel Siouan–Tunican appreciation of the cosmoscape that both groups embraced, respected, and understood.

Boles employs a rediscovered female limestone figurine from Ohio as an entry point into an examination of the form and decorative qualities of "Cahokian" style female figurines. He argues that, despite being made from limestone, the female figurine is identical in all other respects to the Cahokian flint clay suite; an association reinforced by its St Louis formation source. Additionally, Boles discusses the growing number of Cahokia style female figurines recovered outside Greater Cahokia and re-evaluates their role in Cahokian religion. He argues that they evoke the mythical personage "Earth Mother", and draws on rich ethnographic records to explore their symbolism and regional significance.

Melendez, Freidel, and Aquino examine greenstone mosaic masks found across the Maya lowlands in the burials of deified rulers. Their analysis assesses the materials used to produce these masks and their referents. Following detailed examinations of snakes' faces and heads, they argue that the tesserae of greenstone mosaic masks could represents snakes' scales. They also suggest that these masks served as idealized insignias of the *Kaanul* "snake" regime, represented by the head of a snake in ancient Maya glyphs. Similarly, Melendez *et al.* contend that individually carved blocks in the massive, buried pavements at the Olmec site of La Venta also symbolized snake scales, composing larger mosaic masks that represent snake faces. These examples show how pre-Columbian mosaic technique could have been inspired by scales and scuta of snakes, crocodiles, and turtles.

Headrick examines symbolic associations of Aztec calendar stones, not only including how the Aztec sacrificed individuals on calendar stones but also these objects' links to auto-sacrifice and iconographic precedents of their imagery.

Moreover, she employs ethnohistoric records to examine how the imagery of calendar stones connects to acts of human sacrifice, as well as why this imagery was deemed appropriate for these acts. Headrick's analysis also extends to how calendar stones were closely intertwined with the symbolism of auto-sacrifice, identifying iconographic precedents for the imagery on the Aztec Calendar Stone and illustrating that intimate relationship between rulers and solar-related sacrifice was part of its intended symbolism.

Mersmann and Stauffer examine the spatial layout and alignments of center poles at the Cahokia site. They make the case that center poles functioned as important personages associated with "First Man" from Dhegihan beliefs that embodied the Sun and attracted lightning strikes from above world forces. Mersmann and Stauffer also identify site-wide patterns among the tallest poles that conform to a cross-shaped pattern from bird's eye view, which marked the site's location atop an *axis mundi* and connected activity areas to their cosmoscape. They discuss, as well, how cross motifs independently fulfilled a similar centering function in Mesoamerica.

Duncan and Diaz-Granados re-examine the Braden Style, a widespread art tradition, which is often considered to have originated at the Cahokia site. However, they argue that the Braden Style developed earlier than Cahokia and was centered in the Lower Missouri River Valley, where this style provides a bridge between the terminal Late Woodland and the Emergent Mississippian periods. Duncan and Diaz-Granados also examine the symbolic content of representations in the Braden Style, arguing that they follow specific cultural sanctions and parameters. They then offer explanations for some Braden symbols and suggest that this imagery relates to spiritual, hierarchical, and military tropes, indicative of complex Western Mississippian behaviors.

Martin explores through an ethnohistoric and iconographic analysis of Earth Mother narratives and Mississippian imagery discernable patterns and potential connections between swirls, portals, and serpents, as well as whether this imagery was associated with agriculture, rain, renewal, and tornadoes. She focuses attention on the potent forces that animate cosmoscapes, by examining the significance Native American peoples placed on tornadoes, whirlwinds, and other wind-borne phenomena, as well as how they might have been represented in Mississippian imagery. Additionally, Martin relates how these natural phenomena and Native American ontologies can become interwoven in cosmoscape perspectives, as well as the way that they incorporate important narratives to personages like the "Earth Mother".

Giles, Rowe, and Parish explore how the lower floor below Mound 2 at the Hopewell site illustrates a Middle Woodland cosmoscape perspective. They begin by suggesting similarities between Hopewell Mound 2 and the ephemerality, symbolism, and ritual intent of Navajo sandpaintings, before delving into how its burials and features materialized a cosmological model. Their iconographic analysis serves as an entry point into how Middle Woodland avian-anthropomorphic imagery was associated with these Mound 2 burials, charnel facilities, and biface caches. Accordingly, Giles *et al.* argue that the appearance of headless figures and decapitated heads in Middle Woodland avian-anthropomorphic imagery could be connected to treatment of certain burials, while continuities and differences between the Middle Woodland, Late Woodland, and Mississippian patterning guides their subsequent discussion.

Freidel brings his understanding of Yaxuna and Teotihuacan's elaborate architectures to compare with the elaborate burial contexts in Cahokia's Mound 72 and the Craig Mound at Spiro, proposing that all four contexts functioned as portals to distant places in Mayan, Teotihuacano, and Mississippian cosmoscapes. These insights build upon his landmark works with Linda Schele and Joy Parker in *Forest of Kings* and *Maya Cosmos,* incorporating new insights from Spiro and existing hypotheses from Cahokia.

The book concludes with a synthetic perspective of cosmoscapes and how it advances Native American studies, by the editors. Reflecting on the insights provided by the volume's contributors, Lambert *et al.* contextualize the marriage of archaeology, iconography, and Native American ethnohistory in the cosmoscape perspective. They conclude that these interdisciplinary studies can better interpret the material record of the ancient past by recognizing nuanced perspectives of cosmos that see landscapes and objects as being endowed with animating forces, interacting with other-than-human persons, and saturated with meaning from complex analogies.

Note

1 Lifeworld refers to the ways that people engage with objects, places, and landscapes to create, experience, and conceive shared understandings of their universe and how they fit within it (Husserl 1970; see also Olsen 2010, 64–7).

References

Alberti, B. (2013) Relational ontologies. In *Archaeology after Interpretation: Returning materials to archaeological theory*, eds B. Alberti, A.M. Jones and J. Pollard, 37–42. Routledge, New York.

Alberti, B. (2016) Archaeologies of ontology. *Annual Review of Anthropology* 45, 163–79.

Alberti, B., Fowles, S., Holbraad, M., Marshall, Y. and Witmore, C. (2011) 'Worlds otherwise' archaeology, anthropology, and ontological difference. *Current Anthropology* 52, 896–912.

Alberti, B. and Marshall, Y. (2009) Animating archaeology: Local theories and conceptually open-ended methodologies. *Cambridge Archaeological Journal* 19.3, 344–56.

Anschuetz, K.F., Wilhusen, R.H. and Scheick, C.L. (2001) An archaeology of landscapes: Perspectives and directions. *Journal of Archaeological Research* 9, 157–209.

Appadurai, A. (1988) *The Social Life of Things: Commodities in cultural perspective.* Cambridge University Press, Cambridge.

Bailey, G.A. (1995) *The Osage and the Invisible World: From the works of Francis La Flesche.* University of Oklahoma Press, Norman OK.

Baltus, M. and Baires, S. eds (2017) *Relational Engagements of the Indigenous Americas: Alterity, ontology, and shifting paradigms.* Lexington Books, Lexington KY.

Bartram, W. (1995) *William Bartram on the Southeastern Indians*, eds G.A. Waselkov and K.E. Holland Braund. University of Nebraska Press, Lincoln.

Beck, R.A. (ed.) (2007) *The Durable House: House Society models in archaeology.* Center for Archaeological Investigations Occasional Paper 35, Carbondale, IL.

Berlo, J.C. (2011) Navajo cosmoscapes – up, down, within. *American Art* 25, 10–13.
Berlo, J.C. (2014) Navajo sandpainting in the age of cross-cultural replication. *Art History: Journal of the Association of Art Historians* 37, 688–707.
Bird-David, N. (1999) 'Animism' revisited: Personhood, environment, and relational epistemology. *Current Anthropology* 40, S67–S91.
Bold, R. (2020) Constructing cosmoscapes: Cosmological currents in conversation and contestation in contemporary Bolivia. *HAU: Journal of Ethnographic Theory* 10, 195–208.
Bourdieu, P. (1970) The Berber house or the world reversed. *Social Science Information* 9, 151–70.
Boyea, A. (1999) Native American music and curriculum: Controversies and cultural issues. *Philosophy of Music Education Review* 7, 105–17.
Brady, J.E. and Prufer, K.M. eds (2005) *In the Maw of the Earth Monster: Studies of Mesoamerican ritual cave use.* University of Texas Press, Austin TX.
Briggs, J. (2003) The invisible rendered visible: The art of seeing through the shaman's eye. *Nexus* 16, 8–26.
Brown, J.A. (2013a) Archaeological study of mortuary practices in the Eastern United States. In *The Oxford Handbook of the Archaeology of Death and Burial*, eds S. Tarlow and L.N. Stutz, 359–73. Oxford University Press, Oxford.
Brown, J.A. (2013b) On ceremonial landscapes. In *Early and Middle Woodland Landscapes of the Southeast*, eds A.P. Wright and E.R. Henry, 237–46. University Press of Florida, Gainesville FL.
Brown, J.A. and Kelly, J.E. (2015) Surplus labor, ceremonial feasting, and social inequality at Cahokia: A study in social process. In *Surplus: The politics of production and the strategies of everyday life*, eds C.T. Morehart and K. De Lucia, 221–44. University Press of Colorado, Boulder CO.
Brown, J.A., Barker, A.W. and Sabo, G. III (2020) The Spirit Lodge, Spiro ritual, and cosmic renewal. In *Recovering Ancient Spiro: Native American art, ritual, and cosmic renewal*, eds E. Singleton and F.K. Reilly III, 92–112. National Cowboy & Western Heritage Museum, Oklahoma City OK.
Buchanan, M.E. and Skousen, B.J. (2015) *Tracing the Relational: The archaeology of worlds, spirits, and temporalities.* University of Utah Press, Salt Lake City UT.
Chappell, S.A. (2002) *Cahokia: Mirror of the cosmos.* University of Chicago Press, Chicag IL.
Cobb, C.R. and King, A. (2005) Re-inventing Mississippian tradition at Etowah, Georgia. *Journal of Archaeological Method and Theory* 12, 167–92.
Cochrane, A. (2007) We have never been material. *Journal of Iberian Archaeology* 9, 137–57.
Cosgrove, D.E. (1998) *Social Formation and Symbolic Landscape.* University of Wisconsin Press, Madison WI.
DeLanda, M. (2006) *A New Philosophy of Society: Assemblage theory and social complexity.* Continuum Books, New York.
Descola, P. (2014a) *Beyond Nature and Culture.* University of Chicago Press, Chicago IL.
Descola, P. (2104b) Modes of being and forms of prediction. *HAU: Journal of Ethnographic Theory* 4, 271–80.
Dewdney, S. (1975) *The Sacred Scrolls of the Southern Ojibway.* University of Toronto Press, Toronto.
Diaz-Granados, C. and Duncan, J.R. (2000) *The Petroglyphs and Pictographs of Missouri.* University of Alabama Press, Tuscaloosa AL.
Diaz, G. and Rodgers, A. (1993) *The Codex Borgia: A full-color restoration of the ancient Mexican Manuscript*, Dover Publications, Mineola NY.
Diaz-Granados, C., Duncan, J.R. and Reilly, F.K. III (eds) (2015) *Picture Cave: Unraveling the mysteries of the Mississippian cosmos.* University of Texas Press, Austin TX.
Durkheim, E. (1960) *The Division of Labor in Society* (trans. G. Simpson), The Free Press, Glencoe IL.

Durkheim, E. (1971) *Elementary Forms of Religious Life* (trans. J.W. Swain, Original publication 1912). Free Press, New York.

Duncan, J.R. (2011) The Cosmology of the Osage. In *Visualizing the Sacred: Cosmic visions, regionalism, and the art of the Mississippian world*, eds G.E. Lankford, F. K. Reilly III and J.F. Garber, 18–36. University of Texas Press, Austin TX.

Dye, D.H. (2007) Ritual, medicine, and the war trophy iconographic theme in the Mississippian Southeast. In *Ancient Objects and Sacred Realms: Interpretations of Mississippian Iconography*, eds F.K. Reilly III and J.F. Garber, 289–320. University of Texas Press, Austin TX.

Dye, D.H. (2011) Mississippian ceramic art in the Lower Mississippi Valley. In *Visualizing the Sacred: Cosmic visions, regionalism, and the art of the Mississippian world*, eds G.E. Lankford, F.K. Reilly III and J.F. Garber, 99–117. University of Texas Press, Austin TX.

Dye, D.H. and King, A. (2007) Desecrating the sacred ancestor temples: Chiefly conflict and violence in the American Southeast. In *North American Indigenous Warfare and Ritual Violence*, eds R.J. Chacon and R.G. Mendoza, 160–181. University of Arizona Press, Tucson AZ.

Eliade, M. (1957) *The Sacred and the Profane: The nature of religion.* Harcourt, Brace & World, New York.

Ellen, R. (1986) Microcosm, macrocosm and the Nuaulu house: concerning the reductionist fallacy as applied to metaphorical levels.' *Bijdragen tot de taal-, land-en volkenkunde* 142, 1–30.

Emerson, T.E. (1989) Water, serpents, and the underworld: An exploration into Cahokia Symbolism. In *Southeastern Ceremonial Complex: Artifacts and analysis*, ed. P.K. Galloway, 45–95. University of Nebraska Press, Lincoln NE.

Emerson, T.E. (1997) Elite ideology and the Mississippian cosmos. in *Cahokia: Domination and Ideology in the Mississippian World*, eds T.R. Pauketat and T.E. Emerson, 190–228. University of Nebraska Press, Lincoln NE.

Fogelson, R. and Adams, R.N. eds (1977) *The Anthropology of Power: Ethnographic studies from Asia, Oceania, and the New World.* Academic Press, New York.

Fortune, R.F. (1932) *Omaha Secret Societies*. Columbia University Contributions to Anthropology 14, Columbia University Press, New York.

Fowler, C. (2004) *TheAarchaeology of Personhood: An anthropological approach.* Routledge, New York.

Fowler, M.L. (1978) Cahokia and the American Bottom: Settlement archaeology. In *Mississippian Settlement Patterns*, ed. B.D. Smith, 455–78. Academic Press, New York.

Fowler, M.L., Rose, J.C., Vander Leest, B. and Ahler, S.R. eds (1999) *The Mound 72 Area: Dedicated and sacred space in early Cahokia.* Illinois State Museum, Reports of Investigations 54, Illinois State Museum, Springfield IL.

Freidel, D.A., Schele, L. and Parker, J. (1993) *Maya Cosmos: Three thousand years on the shaman's path.* William Morrow & Company, New York.

Fritz, G. (2019) *Feeding Cahokia: Early agriculture in the North American heartland*, University of Alabama Press, Tuscaloosa AL.

Gibson, J.L. (2006) Navels of the earth: Sedentism in early mound-building cultures in the lower Mississippi Valley. *World Archaeology* 38, 311–29.

Giles, B.T. (2010) Sacrificing complexity: Renewal through Ohio Hopewell rituals. In *Ancient Complexities: New perspectives in pre-Columbian North America*, ed. S.M. Alt, 73–95. University of Utah Press, Salt Lake City UT.

González-Díaz, P.F. and Garay, L.J. (1999) Nonorientable spacetime tunneling. *Physical Review D*59, 1–11.

Good, D.L. (1989) *Birds, Beads, & Bells: Remote sensing of a Pawnee medicine bundle.* Anthropological Series 5, Kansas State Historical Society, Topeka KS.

Goodman, R. (1992) *Lakota Star Knowledge: Studies in Lakota stellar theology.* Siŋte Gleska University, Mission SD.

Guernsey, J. and Reilly, F.K. III (2006) Introduction. in *Sacred Bindings of the Cosmos: Ritual acts of bundling and wrapping in ancient Mesoamerica*, eds J. Guernsey and F.K. Reilly III, 1–12. Ancient America Special Publication 1, Bundary End Archaeology Research Center, Barnardsville NC.

Hall, R.L. (1991) Cahokia identity and interaction models of Cahokia Mississippian. In *Cahokia and the Hinterlands: Middle Mississippian cultures of the Midwest*, eds T.E. Emerson and R.B. Lewis, 3–34. University of Illinois Press, Urbana IL.

Hall, R.L. (1997) *An Archaeology of the Soul: North American Indian belief and ritual.* University of Illinois Press, Urbana IL.

Hallowell, A.I. (1960) Ojibwa ontology, behavior, and world view. In *Culture in History: Essays in Honor of Paul Radin*, ed. S. Diamond, 19–52. Columbia University Press, New York.

Harrison-Buck, E. (2015) Maya religion and gods: Relevance and relatedness in the animic cosmos. In Buchanan and Skousen (eds), 113–30.

Harrison-Buck, E., and J.A. Hendon eds (2018) *Relational Identities and Other-than-human Agency in Archaeology*. University Press of Colorado, Boulder CO.

Headrick, A. (2007) *The Teotihuacan Trinity: The Sociopolitical Structure of an Ancient Mesoamerican City.* University of Texas Press, Austin TX.

Heidegger, M. (1971) *Poetry, Language, Thought*. Harper and Row, New York.

Helms, M.W. (1979) *Ancient Panama: Chiefs in search of power.* University of Texas Press, Austin TX.

Helms, M.W. (1993) *Craft and the Kingly Ideal: Art, trade, and power.* University of Texas Press, Austin TX.

Henry, E.R. (2017) Building bundles, building memories: Processes of remembering in Adena–Hopewell societies of Eastern North America. *Journal of Archaeological Method and Theory* 24, 88–228.

Henry, E.R. (2020) Documenting ceremonial situations and institutional change at Middle Woodland geometric enclosures. *Midcontinental Journal of Archaeology* 45, 203–25.

Hewitt, J.N.B. (1902) Orenda and the definition of religion. *American Anthropologist* 4, 33–46.

Hirsch, E. (1995) Landscape: Between place and space. In *The Archaeology of Landscape: Perspectives on place and space*, eds E. Hirsch and M. O'Hanlon, 1–30. Clarendon Press, Oxford.

Hoffman, W.J. (1891) The Midē'wiwin or 'Grand Medicine Society' of the Ojibway. *Seventh Annual Report of the Bureau of Ethnology 1885-1886*, 149–299. Smithsonian Institution, Washington DC.

Howey, M.C.L. and O'Shea, J.M. (2006) Bear's journey and the study of ritual in archaeology. *American Antiquity* 71, 261–82.

Hultkrantz, Å. (1979) *The Religions of the American Indians.* University of California Press, Berkeley CA.

Husserl, E. (1970) *The Crisis of European Sciences and Transcendental Philosophy.* Northwestern University Press, Evanston IL.

Ingold, T. (1993) The temporality of landscape. *World Archaeology* 25, 152–4.

Ingold, T. (2007) Materials against materiality. *Archaeological Dialogues* 14, 1–16.

Ingold, T. (2011) *Being Alive: Essays on movement, knowledge and description.* Routledge, London.

Ingold, T. (2012) The Shape of the Land, in *Landscapes Beyond Land: Routes, Aesthetics, Narratives*, eds A. Árnason, N. Ellison, J. Vergunst, and A. Whitehouse, 197–208. Berghahn Books, New York.

Joyce, R.A. and Gillespie, S.D. (2017) *Beyond Kinship: Societal and material reproduction in house societies.* University of Pennsylvania Press, Philadelphia PA.

Kahn, J.G. and Kirch, P.V. (2013) Residential landscapes and house societies of the late prehistoric society islands. *Journal of Pacific Archaeology* 4, 50–72.

Kan, S. (1989) *Symbolic Immortality: The Tlingit potlatch of the nineteenth century.* Smithsonian Institution Press, Washington DC.

Kelly, J.E. (1996) Redefining Cahokia: Principles and elements of organization. *Wisconsin Archaeologist* 6, 97–119.

Kelly, J.E. (2006) The ritualization of Cahokia: The structure and organization of early Cahokia crafts. In *Leadership and Polity in Mississippian Society*, eds B.M. Butler and P.D. Welch, 73–90. Center for Archaeological Investigations Southern Illinois University Occasional Paper 33, Carbondale IL.

Kelly, J.E. and Brown, J.A. (2012) In search of cosmic power: Contextualizing spiritual journeys between Cahokia and the St. Francois Mountains. In *Archaeology of Spiritualities*, eds K. Rountree, C. Morris, and A.D. Peatfield, 107–29. Springer, New York.

Kelly, J.E. and Brown, J.A. (2014) Cahokia: The processes and principles of the creation of an early Mississippian city. In *Making Ancient Cities*, eds A.T. Creekmore III and K.D. Fisher, 292–336. Cambridge University Press, Cambridge.

Keyser, J.D. and Taylor, M.W. (2006) The blade cuts two ways: Using ethnographic analogy to interpret the Columbia Plateau Scratched Style. In *Talking with the Past: The ethnography of rock art*, eds J.D. Keyser, G. Poetschat and M.W. Taylor, 200–24. Oregon Archaeological Society, Portland OR.

Kidder, T.R. and Sherwood, S.C. (2017) Look to the earth: The search for ritual in the context of mound construction. *Archaeological and Anthropological Sciences* 9, 1077–99.

King, A., Powis, T.G., Cheong, K.F., Deere, B., Pickering, R.B., Singleton, E. and Gaikwad, N.W. (2018) Absorbed residue evidence for prehistoric *Datura* use in the American Southeast and Western Mexico. *Advances in Archaeological Practice* 6, 312–27.

King, A. and Reilly, F.K. III (2011) Raptorial imagery at Etowah: The raptor is the path to power. In *Visualizing the Sacred: Cosmic visions, regionalism, and the art of the Mississippian world*, eds G.E. Lankford, F.K. Reilly III and J.F. Garber, 313–20. University of Texas Press, Austin TX.

Kohler, T. (2012) Complex systems and archaeology. Santa Fe Institute working paper 2011-06-023, 93-123. Electronic document. http://sfi-edu.s3.amazonaws.com/sfi-edu/production/uploads/sfi-com/dev/uploads/filer/00/f1/00f13507-a54a-46c1-9e3a-d8e169e5be1b/11-06-023.pdf, accessed 9.25.2021.

Kohn, E. (2015) Anthropology of ontologies. *Annual Review of Anthropology* 44, 311–27.

Kozuch, L. (2013) Ceramic shell cup effigies from Illinois and their implications. *Southeastern Archaeology* 32, 29–45.

Küchler, S. (1997) Sacrificial economy and its objects: Rethinking colonial collecting in Oceania. *Journal of Material Culture* 2, 39–60.

Küchler, S. (2003) Imaging the body politic: The knot in pacific imagination. *L'Homme* 165, 205–22.

La Flesche, F. (1921) The Osage Tribe: Rite of chiefs, sayings of the Ancient Men. In *Thirty-Sixth Annual Report of the Bureau of Ethnology*, 35–604. Smithsonian Institution, Washington DC.

La Flesche, F. (1925) The Osage Tribe: Rite of vigil. In *Thirty-Ninth Annual Report of the Bureau of Ethnology*, 31–630. Smithsonian Institution, Washington DC.

La Flesche, F. (1932) *A Dictionary of the Osage Language*. Bureau of American Ethnology Bulletin 109, Washington DC.

Lambert, S.P. (2018) Addressing the cosmological significance of a pot: A search for cosmological structure in the Craig Mound. *Caddo Archaeological Journal* 28, 21–37.

Lambert, S.P., Perttula, T.K. and Gaikwad, N.W. (2021) Production matters: Organic residue evidence for Late Precolumbian *Datura*-making in the Central Arkansas River valley. *Advances in Archaeological Practice,* 1–11. https://www.cambridge.org/core/journals/advances-in-archaeological-practice/article/abs/production-matters/8767998261B84066BA893CAF80133288, accessed 1.4.2022.

Lankford, G.E. (2007) The "Path of Souls": Some death imagery in the Southeastern ceremonial complex. In *Ancient Objects and Sacred Realms: Interpretations of Mississippian Iconography*, eds F.K. Reilly III and J.F. Garber, 174–212. University of Texas Press, Austin TX.

Lansing, S. (2009) *Priests and Programmers: Technologies of power and the engineered landscapes of Bali.* Princeton University Press, Princeton NJ.

Latour, B. (1993) *We Have Never Been Modern.* Harvard University Press, Cambridge MA.
Latour, B. (1999) *Pandora's Hope: Essays on the reality of science studies.* Harvard University Press, Cambridge MA.
Lewis, R.B. and Stout, C. eds (1998) *Mississippian Towns and Sacred Spaces: Searching for an architectural grammar.* University of Alabama Press, Tuscaloosa AL.
Lowie, R.H. (1918) *Myths and Traditions of the Crow Indians*, Anthropological Papers 25.1, American Museum of Natural History, New York.
Luer, G.M. (1996) Mississippian ceramic jars, bottles, and gourds as compound vessels. *Southeastern Archaeology* 15, 181–91.
MacDonald, G.F. (1981) Cosmic equations in Northwest Coast Indian art. In *The World is as Sharp as a Knife: An anthology in honor of Wilson Duff*, ed D.N. Abbot, 225–38. British Columbia Provincial Museum, Victoria BC.
Machner, H. and Bentley A. (2003) The power law of rank and household on the north Pacific. In *Complex Systems and Archaeology*, eds A. Bentley and H. Machner, 47–60, University of Utah Press, Salt Lake City UT.
Mallery, G. (1893) *Picture-Writing of the American Indians.* Tenth Annual Report of the Bureau of American Ethnography to the Secretary of the Smithsonian Institution, Government Printing Office, Washington, DC.
Marquardt, W.H. and Crumley, C.L. (1987) Theoretical issues in the analysis of spatial patterning. In *Regional Dynamics: Burgundian landscapes in historical perspective*, eds C.L. Crumley and W.H. Marquardt, 1–18. Academic Press, New York.
Marquardt, W.H. and Kozuch, L. (2016) The lightning whelk: An enduring icon of Southeastern North American spirituality. *Journal of Anthropological Archaeology* 42, 1–26.
Marx, K. (1844) *Estranged Labor, Economic-Philosophical Manuscripts.* Electronic document. https://www.marxists.org/archive/marx/works/1844/manuscripts/labour.htm, accessed on 9.25.2021.
Miller, J. (2015) *Ancestral Mounds: Vitality and volatility of Native America.* University of Nebraska Press, Lincoln NE.
Milner, G.R. (2006) *The Cahokia chiefdom: The archaeology of a Mississippian society* (revised edn). University Press of Florida, Gainesville FL.
Molesky-Poz, J. (2006) Cacao in Ancient Maya religion: First fruit from the maize tree and other tales from the underworld. In *Chocolate in Mesoamerica: A cultural history of Cacao*, ed C. McNeil, 154–83. University Press of Florida, Gainesville FL.
Morrison, K.M. (2000) The cosmos as intersubjective: Native American other-than-human persons. In *Indigenous Religions: A companion*, ed G. Harvey, 23–36. Cassel, New York.
Norton, W. (1989) *Explorations in the Understanding of Landscape: A cultural geography.* Contributions in Sociology 77, Greenwood Press, New York.
Olsen, B. (2010) *In Defense of Things: Archaeology and the ontology of objects.* Rowman & Littlefield, Altamira MD.
Palka, J.W. (2002) Left/right symbolism and the body in ancient Maya iconography and culture. *Latin American Antiquity* 31, 419–43.
Pauketat, T.R. (2013) *An Archaeology of the Cosmos: Rethinking agency and religion in ancient America.* Routledge, New York.
Pauketat, T. and Emerson, T (1991) The ideology of authority and the power of the pot. *American Anthropologist* 93, 919–41.
Pavel, T.G. (1981) Fiction and the ontological landscape. *Studies in 20th Century Literature* 6, 149–63.
Peet, R. (1985) The Social origins of environmental determinism. *Annals of the Association of American Geographers* 75, 309–33.
Penney, D. (2004) The archaeology of aesthetics. In *Hero, Hawk and Open Hand: American Indian art of the ancient Midwest and Southeast*, eds R.F. Townsend and R.V. Sharp, 43–55, Art Institute of Chicago and Yale University Press, New Haven CO and London.

Phillips, P. and Brown, J.A. (1984) *Pre-Columbian Shell Engravings from the Craig Mound at Spiro*, Vol. 1. Peabody Museum Press, Cambridge MA.

Prentice, G. (1987) Marine shells as wealth items in Mississippian societies. *Midcontinental Journal of Archaeology* 12, 193–223.

Ratzel, F. (1896) *History of Mankind* (trans A.J. Buler). Macmillan, London.

Reichel, E. (2012) The landscape in the cosmoscape, and sacred sites and species among the Tanimuka and Yukuna Amerindian tribes (north-west Amazon). In *Sacred Species and Sites: Advances in biocultural conservation*, eds G. Pungetti, G. Oviedo, and D. Hooke, 127–51. Cambridge University Press, Cambridge.

Reilly, F.K. III (1986) Olmec iconographic influences on the symbols of Maya rulership: An examination of possible sources. In *Sixth Palenque Round Table*, ed. V. Fields, 151–66. Palenque Round Table Serie 8. University of Oklahoma Press, Norman OK.

Reilly, F.K. III (1989a) Enclosed ritual spaces and the watery underworld in formative period architecture: New observations on the function of La Venta Complex A. In *Seventh Palenque Round Table*, eds M.G. Robertson and V. Fields, 125–35. Pre-Columbian Art Research Institute, San Francisco CA. Electronic document. https://www.precolumbia.org/pari/publications/RT09/EnclosedSpaces.pdf, accessed on 1.4.2022.

Reilly, F.K. III (1989b) The shaman in transformation pose: A study of the theme of rulership in Olmec Art. *Record of the Art Museum, Princeton University* 48, 4–21.

Reilly, F.K. (1990) Cosmos and rulership: The function of Olmec-style symbols in Formative Period Mesoamerica. *Visible Language* 24, 12–37.

Reilly, F.K. III (1993) The lazy-S: A formative period iconographic loan to Maya hieroglyphic writing. *Eighth Palenque Round Table*, eds M.J. Macri and J. McHargue, 413–424. Palenque Round Table Serie 10, Pre-Columbian Art Research Institute, San Francisco CA.

Reilly, F.K. III (2004) People of Earth, People of Sky: Visualizing the Sacred in Native American Art of the Mississippian Period' in *Hero, Hawk, and Open Hand: American Indian Art of the Ancient Midwest and South*, eds R.F. Townsend and R.V. Sharp, The Art Institute of Chicago in association with Yale University Press, New Haven, 125–138.

Reilly, F.K. III (2006) Middle formative origins of the Mesoamerican ritual act of bundling. In *Sacred bindings of the cosmos: Ritual acts of bundling and wrapping in ancient Mesoamerica*, eds J. Guernsey and F.K. Reilly III, 13–34. Ancient America Special Publication 1, Bundary End Archaeology Research Center, Barnardsville NC.

Reilly, F.K. III (2007) The petaloid motif: A celestial symbolic locative in the shell art of Spiro. In *Ancient Objects and Sacred Realms: Interpretations of Mississippian iconography*, eds F.K. Reilly III and J.F. Garber, 40–55. University of Texas Press, Austin TX.

Reilly, F.K. III (2011) The Great Serpent in the lower Mississippi Valley. In *Visualizing the Sacred: Cosmic visions, regionalism, and the art of the Mississippian world*, eds G.E. Lankford, F.K. Reilly III and J.F. Garber, 118–34. University of Texas Press, Austin TX.

Reilly, F.K. III (2021) Ritual languages of the Southeast: Sacred bundles in the memory theaters of Mississippian period ritualism. In *Mississippian Culture Heroes, Ritual Regalia, and Sacred Bundles*, ed. D.H. Dye, 57–80. Lexington Books, Lanham MD.

Sassaman, K.E., Blessing, M.E., Goodwin, J.M., Jenkins, J.A., Mahar, G.J., Boucher, A., Barbour, T.E. and Donop, M.C. (2020) Maritime ritual economies of cosmic synchronicity: Summer solstice events at a civic-ceremonial center on the northern Gulf Coast of Florida. *American Antiquity* 85, 22–50.

Sawyer, J.A. and King, A. (2021) Nested bundles within Etowah's Mound C. In *Mississippian Culture Heroes, Ritual Regalia, and Sacred Bundles*, ed. D.H. Dye, 81–106. Lexington Books, Lanham MD.

Sauer, C. (1926) Recent developments in cultural geography. In *Recent Developments in the Social Sciences*, eds E.C. Hayes and L.P. Lippincott, 154–212. Lippincott Series in Sociology, Lippinscott, Philadelphia PA and London.

Seguin, M. (1984) Lest there be no salmon: Symbols in traditional Tsimshian potlatch. In *The Tsimshian. Images of the Past: Views for the present*, ed. M. Seguin, 99–109. University of British Columbia Press, Vancouver BC.

Sherwood, S.C. and Kidder, T.R. (2011) The DaVincis of dirt: Geoarchaeological perspectives on Native American mound building in the Mississippi River basin. *Journal of Anthropological Archaeology* 30, 69–87.
Skaanes, T. (2021) Mapping materiality – social relations with objects and landscapes. In *Mapping the Unmappable?*, ed U. Dieckmann, 223–60. Transcript Press, Bielefeld.
Skousen, B.J. and Buchanan, M.E. (2015) Advancing an archaeology of movements and relationships. In Buchanan and Skousen (eds), 1–19.
Slater, D.A. (2014) Into the Heart of the Turtle: Caves, ritual, and power in ancient Central Yucatan, Mexico. Unpublished Doctoral Dissertation, Department of Anthropology, Brandeis University.
Smith, M.E. (2005) Did the Maya build architectural cosmograms?, *Latin American Antiquity* 16, 217–24.
Smith, K. and Miller, J., (2009) *Speaking with the Ancestors: Mississippian stone statuary of the Tennessee-Cumberland Region.* University of Alabama Press, Tuscaloosa AL.
Strathern, M. (1988) *The Gender of the Gift*, University of California Press, Berkeley CA.
Strathern, M. (1991) One man and many men. In *Big Men and Great Men: Personifications of power in Melanesia*, eds M. Godelier and M. Strathern, 197–214. Cambridge University Press, Cambridge.
Stuart, D. (1996) Kings of stone: A consideration of stelae in ancient Maya ritual and representation. *RES: Anthropology and Aesthetics* 29/30, 148–71.
Sundstrom, L. (1996) Mirror of Heaven: Cross-cultural transference of the sacred geography of the Black Hills. *World Archaeology* 28, 177–89.
Swanton, J.R. (1928) Religious beliefs and medical practices of the Creek Indians. *Forty-Second Annual Report of the Bureau of American Ethnology*, 477–684, Washington DC.
Tate, C.E. (2008) Landscape and a visual narrative of creation and origin at the Olmec ceremonial center of La Venta. In *Pre-Columbian Landscapes of Creation and Origin*, ed J. Staller, 31–65. Springer, New York.
Tilley, C. (1994) *A Phenomenology of Landscape: Places, paths, and monuments.* Berg, Oxford.
Tilley, C. (2004) *The Materiality of Stone: Explorations in landscape phenomenology.* Berg, Oxford.
Thybony, S. (1998) *The Hogan: The traditional Navajo home.* Western National Parks Association, Tucson AR.
Vail, G. (2000) Pre-hispanic Maya religion: Conceptions of divinity in the Postclassic Maya codices. *Ancient Mesoamerica* 11, 123–47.
Van der Grijp, P. (2014) *Manifestations of Mana: Political power and divine inspiration in Polynesia.* Lit Verlag, Zürich.
Viveiros de Castro, E. (1998) Cosmological deixis and Amerindian perspectivism. *Journal of the Royal Anthropological Institute* 4, 469–88.
Viveiros de Castro, E. (2004) Perspectival anthropology and the method of controlled equivocation. *Tipití* 2, 3–22.
Wayman, A. (1982) The human body as microcosm in India, Greek cosmology, and sixteenth-century Europe. *History of Religions* 22, 172–90.
Witthoft, J. (1949) *Green Corn Ceremonialism in the Eastern Woodlands.* Museum of Anthropology, University of Michigan Press Occasional Paper 13, Ann Arbor MI.
Williamson, R. (2007) 'Otinontsiskiaj ondaon' ('The House of Cut-Off Heads'). In *The Taking and Display of Human Body Parts as Trophies by Amerindians*, eds R.J. Chacon and D.H. Dye, 190–221. Springer, New York.
Zedeño, M.N. (2008) Bundled worlds: The roles and interactions of complex objects from the North American Plains. *Journal of Archaeological Method and Theory* 15, 362–78.
Zedeño, M.N. (2009) Animating by association: Index objects and relational taxonomies. *Cambridge Archaeological Journal* 19, 407–17.

Part I

Objects as cosmoscapes

2

Modeling the cosmos: Rim-effigy bowl iconography in the Central Mississippi Valley

Madelaine C. Azar and Vincas P. Steponaitis

The Central Mississippi Valley (CMV), extending southward along the Mississippi River from the mouth of the Ohio River to the mouth of the Arkansas River, was home to a vibrant potting tradition dating to the Late Mississippian period (AD 1350–1600), a time characterized by intense population nucleation and heightened conflict. From the mid-14th century until Hernando de Soto's arrival in AD 1541, communities in northeast Arkansas, southeast Missouri, western Tennessee, and northwest Mississippi consolidated into large, palisaded towns marked by monumental earthen mounds and ceremonial plazas. It is within this milieu that artistic achievement flourished. Potters crafted a wide array of fine ceramic wares depicting diverse religious symbolism, including abstract motifs referencing the cosmos as well as representational images of powerful otherworldly beings, spirit persons, and culture heroes (Morse and Morse 1983, 271–301; P. Morse 1981; D. Morse 1989, 107; O'Brien and Dunnell 1998; Cobb and Drake 2008).

Among the variety of decorated ceramics dating to the Late Mississippian period, rim-effigy bowls are perhaps the CMV's most prevalent and ubiquitous form. In fact, Phillips, Ford, and Griffin described rim-effigy bowls as "one of the most constant features of the Middle Mississippi vessel complex" (1951, 161) in their seminal survey of the Lower Mississippi River Valley. These vessels are characterized by the presence of appliqué rim adornments depicting the head and tail of an animal or human. The subject matter of rim-effigy bowls can vary greatly, making the corpus ripe for iconographic analysis. However, while many attempts have been made to identify recurring animal species or human figures represented by these vessels, their broader iconographic significance within the context of Mississippian cosmology and ritual has not been adequately explored.

This chapter provides one of the first systematic iconographic analyses of CMV rim-effigy bowls, combining visual analysis and ethnographic analogy to produce a model that relates vessel imagery to potential cosmological referents and ritual customs once recognized by CMV Mississippians. In particular, we first offer a more careful classification of both the stylistic and thematic elements of these vessels, rather than relying on previous studies of rim-effigy bowls that tend to classify imagery arbitrarily. To better understand the iconographic significance of rim-effigy bowls to their users we also look to the oral traditions of American Indian communities descended from Mississippian peoples. These traditions provide insight into the legendary characters and fundamental cosmic principles that may have been reflected in this vessel form. Ultimately, this iconographic analysis not only serves to clarify the meaning of rim-effigy bowls to CMV communities, but also situates the region within larger understandings of Mississippian cosmology and ritual across the American South.

The corpus

Formally, rim-effigy bowls in the CMV are characterized by the presence of a modeled-clay effigy head and tail affixed to opposite sides of the vessel's rim, although bowls sometimes exhibit a second head effigy in place of a tail. The body of the vessel can occasionally exhibit incised motifs like swirl crosses or festoons. Effigy heads usually face outward but inward facing effigy heads are also common (D. Morse 1989, 108). Occasionally, effigy heads are hollow, containing a single ceramic rattle. Vessel x-rays indicate that this feature is intentional not a consequence of wear or deterioration (Howell 2011). Tail effigies are either tabular, coiled, or curved. Tabular forms may feature a "tail rider," or miniature modeled figure that sits atop the tail adorno. Tail riders most often represent animals such as birds, turtles, or panthers. Viewed in totality, rim-effigy bowls constitute three-dimensional renderings of living creatures – usually serpents, birds, or humans.

Within the scope of scholarship on Mississippian art and iconography, including discussions of the Southeastern Ceremonial Complex (SECC), the CMV's rim-effigy bowl corpus has been largely overlooked. Despite their omnipresence throughout the region and the fact that Antonio Waring and Preston Holder (1945, 30) posited a Middle Mississippi Valley origin for the SECC, CMV rim-effigy bowls rarely factor into broader discussions of Mississippian ritual art found across the American South. This is unfortunate because, while the CMV rim-effigy bowl corpus dates to a later period than most other SECC material, many of the motifs and images that appear across vessels are clearly related to canonical SECC iconography (Rands 1956; Dye 2014; 2017a; 2018).

Fortunately, more recent discussions of these vessels are now beginning to explore the possibility that rim-effigy bowl imagery may reference transcendental beings, culture heroes, and otherworldly realms that were integral to the Mississippian cosmovision (Bomar 2011; Lankford and Dye 2014; Azar 2020). This insight is consistent with the placement of these vessels in burials (House 2003) and indicates that they held symbolic significance. However, as we have mentioned, the iconography of the corpus has been neither subjected to a comprehensive visual analysis nor interpreted within the context of American Indian belief and ritual.

Methodology

To begin our visual analysis, we assembled a sample of whole rim-effigy bowls from published photographs (Phillips 1939; Perino 1967a; 1967b; O'Brien 1994; Gannon 1999; Morse 1981; Hathcock 1983; 1988; D. Morse 1989; Meltzer and Dunnell 1992; Brown 2005; House 2005; Lankford and Dye 2014; Bogg and Bogg 2016). The bowls derive from the CMV's four best-defined Late Mississippian ceramic phases: Nodena, Parkin, Kent, and Walls (Fig. 2.1) (Morse and Morse 1983, 271–302; Mainfort 2003; 2005). In total, we reviewed 245 rim-effigy bowls from 38 sites and localities across the region (Azar 2020).

We sought out a methodology that would allow us to analyze systematically the imagery within our sample. We ultimately turned to the work of Knight (2013), who offers a stepwise approach to iconographic analysis in pre-contact New World art corpora. Broadly, this methodology includes (1) assembling a sample of the corpus in question, (2) identifying styles of execution, (3) defining subject matter themes within these styles, and (4) connecting imagery to referents through ethnographic analogy. These lines of inquiry should lead to an iconographic model which Knight defines as a description of representational imagery according to emic perceptions of meaning (2013, 165).

Visual analysis: Style and theme

Following Knight's approach, we divided our visual analysis into two parts. We first performed a stylistic analysis and then a thematic analysis of the sample. This order of operations allows style and theme to be reviewed as separate elements where style reflects aesthetic rules of vessel execution and theme refers to the subject matter of the bowls and their effigies. Stylistic analysis is an essential preliminary step in this process because it limits conjecture and provides a degree of control over the process (Knight 2013, 23). Specifically, the identification of different visual styles within an art corpus can expose the range of variation in the appearance of particular subject matter themes, preventing the misclassification of themes based on their stylistic execution.

With this in mind, we ultimately defined ten rim-effigy bowl styles based on bowl form, effigy size and shape, and aspects of decoration (Azar 2020). Because we treated theme and style as independent analytical entities, a single style could, and often did, include multiple effigy themes. In particular, we identified four major recurring themes that were distributed widely across the Nodena, Parkin, Kent, and Walls phases in the CMV within the ten designated styles. These themes included (1) crested birds resembling woodpeckers or wood ducks, (2) serpents, (3) raptors, and (4) humans with cone-shaped head adornments, called "coneheads" for short (Fig. 2.2). Other non-recurring bowl themes were present, mostly consisting of humans with a variety of different head coverings and hairstyles. However, more than 85% of the sample consisted of the four themes discussed here.

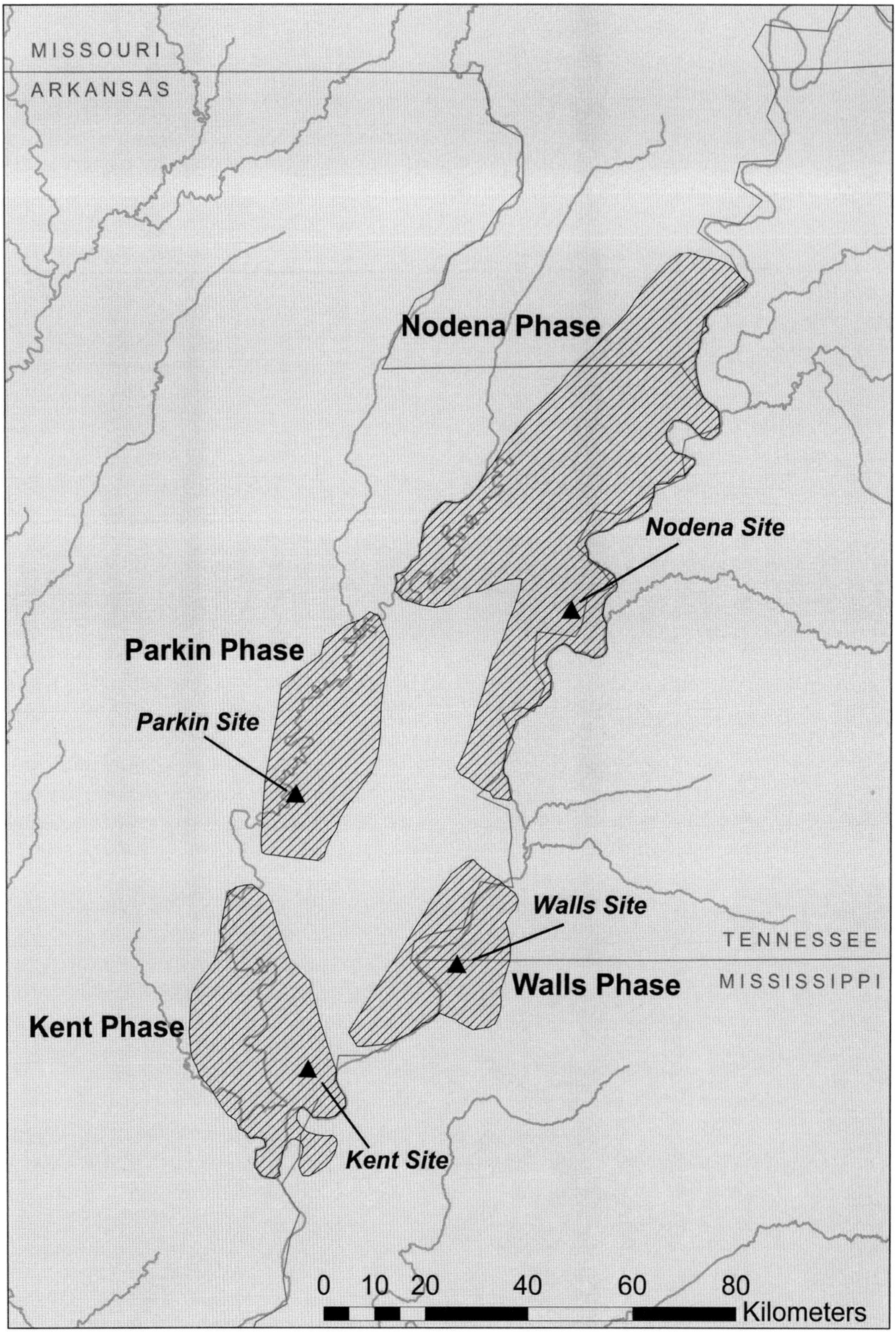
MISSOURI
ARKANSAS
Nodena Phase
Nodena Site
Parkin Phase
Parkin Site
Walls Site
TENNESSEE
MISSISSIPPI
Walls Phase
Kent Phase
Kent Site
0 10 20 40 60 80
Kilometers

Fig. 2.1. (opposite) Late Mississippian ceramic phases in the CMV (adapted from Morse and Morse 1989, fig. 12.1).

Ethnographic analogy: From themes to referents

To explore the broader significance of rim-effigy bowls and approximate their emic meaning, we relied on ethnographic analogies derived from reports and observations of historic American Indian groups of the Great Plains and South, as a contemporaneous written record does not accompany the corpus. A number of American Indian groups from these regions have been linked, either culturally or historically, to Late Mississippian societies. Ethnographic descriptions of these descendant groups, specifically those recounting oral traditions, cultural practices, and ceremonial activities, have been used to interpret the iconography of major Mississippian ritual art corpora, including material from Moundville, Etowah, and Spiro (Reilly and Garber 2007; Lankford *et al.* 2011; Steponaitis *et al.* 2019).

These ethnohistoric records have also been used to clarify how Mississippians may have perceived the structure and scope of their universe. Based on these sources, it appears that the Mississippian cosmos was likely understood as a tripartite universe, consisting of a watery Beneath World and celestial Above World separated from each other by an Earth Disk (Fig. 2.3) (Emerson 1997; Lankford 2007d; Duncan 2011). Within this model, the Above and Beneath Worlds – although multilayered themselves – existed in structural and spiritual opposition to one another.

The Beneath World was envisioned as a dark and watery abyss, home to snakes, serpents, and other formidable water beings. Consequently, it is closely associated

Fig. 2.2. Rim-effigy bowl themes: a. serpent from Beck (LMS 13-O-07); b. crested bird from Bradley (LMS 11-P-02); c. raptor from Middle Nodena (LMS 10-Q-04); d. human conehead from Walls (LMS 13-P-01) (courtesy of the University of Arkansas Museum Collections).

Fig. 2.3. The Mississippian cosmos (illustration by Jack Johnson in Reilly 2004, fig. 2).

with death, chaos, and the afterlife (Hudson 1976; Emerson 1989). In contrast, the Above World, or sky vault, engendered order, light, and purity, serving as a home for weather spirits and great avian beings (Hudson 1976; Duncan 2011; King and Reilly 2011). Floating atop the waters of the Beneath World, the Earth Disk – also referred to as the earthly plane or Middle World – sat between these two mirrored realms. Finally, connecting these cosmic layers was a great *axis mundi*, or centering entity, often conceptualized as a tree, pole, or sacred fire (Lankford 2007d; 2011b). Thus, the Mississippian universe was typified by a series of dualistic oppositions between Above and Beneath world forces. However, these forces did not exist as mutually exclusive, value-laden binaries, as good and evil often operate in Christian conceptions of Heaven and Hell. Rather, Above and Beneath world forces likely existed as two sides of the same coin, often acting simultaneously within the same context as essential, interacting parts of a larger balanced whole (Lankford 2008, 94–6).

As part of this balanced whole, a variety of human and non-human beings resided within each realm of the Mississippian cosmos. In this sense, it was a "peopled" universe. Beyond relatively mundane humans and animals, cosmic realms were populated and even traversed by a variety of human and non-human characters, including powerful heroes, enchanted objects, and chimeric monsters in addition to giants, cannibals, and tricksters (see Dorsey 1904a; 1904b; 1904c; 1906; Swanton 1929; Sumner 1951; Lankford 1987; Reilly 2011). These were often the subjects of Mississippian art (Knight *et al.* 2001).

To explore the possibility that CMV rim-effigy bowls may depict some of these cosmic characters, we searched for ethnographic analogies in the Native oral traditions of Great Plains and South. Indeed, we were able to identify several recurring characters in these oral traditions that may have served as referents for the figures depicted in rim-effigy bowls. Notably, upon studying the stories and legends that recount the deeds and exploits of these characters, we observed that they all share a common trait – cosmic duality. This trait is manifest in their ability to transcend the earthly plane and move throughout the upper and lower realms of the cosmos, highlighting the foundational principle of oppositional tension. Each of these figures is discussed in turn below.

Serpents

Consistently associated with the watery Beneath World, death, and the afterlife, the Great Serpent monster appears in many Native oral traditions in the Great Plains and South (Dye 2018). This being can take on many different forms, including a snake-like water monster with horns or antlers as well as an underwater panther with a long, serpentine tail. Regardless of form, this figure is always formidable, capable of churning up lakes, streams, and rivers and causing harm to humankind. Even so, this netherworld being is also known to offer cosmic power and protection to individuals brave enough to seek passage into the depths of the Beneath World (see Lankford 2011b, 87–8; Reilly 2011, 119).

The image of this serpent being is found frequently across all forms of Mississippian art. However, in addition to its horned or antlered underwater form, the Mississippian serpent monster is also occasionally depicted with wings – with the most notable corpus of such images originating from Moundville (Steponaitis and Knight 2004). Previous studies of Mississippian iconography have concluded that these winged serpent images may reference the ability of the Great Serpent to move from the Beneath World to the Above World. Notably, George Lankford has suggested that this movement might actually be manifest in the constellation Scorpio, which not only resembles a serpent but also rises just above the southern horizon during the summer months in the Northern Hemisphere (Lankford 2007b; 2007c).

This Above/Beneath World duality of the Great Serpent was central to the mortuary beliefs of many historic Native groups in the Great Plains and South (Lankford 2007b, 179–80). Specifically, the Great Serpent's ascension into the Above World reflects its guardianship over the "Path of Souls" to the afterlife, which was visible in the night sky as the Milky Way. Like the Great Serpent, the Path of Souls had an astronomical cognate. Along this path, the deceased journey to "Realm of the Dead" (Reilly and Garber 2011, 119). Thus, the Great Serpent was at once both underwater antagonist and celestial guardian, posing great threat to humanity while also guiding souls from one life to the next. In this sense, the Great Serpent embodies the polar tension that epitomizes the Mississippian cosmos.

Crested birds

Crested bird effigies in the CMV generally resemble two distinct natural prototypes – wood ducks and woodpeckers. Both these birds make noteworthy appearances in American Indian legends recounting the origins of the Earth. There are two primary creation stories among historic groups in the Great Plains and South, namely the Flood and Earth Diver stories. While many variations of these legends exist – sometimes even blending elements of each – all appear to work upon the same basic premise: prior to the origin of the Earth, the world was flooded. Only the Above World (sky) and Beneath World (water) existed.

Across Earth Diver stories, different animals are enlisted to dive beneath the primal waters and retrieve a clump of mud or sand from the bottom, which is then spread to form the Earth Disk (Dorsey 1904b, 11; Kongas 1960; Lankford 1987, 106–17). In the Central Plains, specifically among the Crow, Skidi Pawnee, and Arikara, it is a duck that successfully completes this task. While other protagonists (e.g., a muskrat or crawfish) also occur in these legends, the essential element of the Earth Diver story is the ability of the animal to penetrate the waters of the Beneath World from above (Kongas 1960). This trait is inherently dualistic, as the animal must be able to traverse the boundary between the Above and Beneath worlds in order to create the Earth Disk. The duck is a particularly apt embodiment of this duality because it has the ability to both fly and swim.

Woodpeckers exhibit a similar cosmic duality in several Native origin stories. According to the Creek version of the Flood/Earth-Diver legend, the world in the beginning was inhabited only by "two red-headed woodpeckers, which hung to the clouds, with their tails awash in the waters" (Swanton 1928, 488). The Alabama version of the Flood story is similar (Swanton 1929, 121). Ethnohistoric sources often note that these stories were used to explain woodpeckers' tail markings (see Swanton 1928; 1929). However, it is also notable that the woodpeckers in these stories are essentially straddling cosmic realms – existing simultaneously in the sky and the water. In this sense, they act as a physical connection between the Above World and Beneath World, similar to an *axis mundi*.

Reinforcing this dualistic understanding of woodpeckers within the Mississippian cosmos is a shell engraving from Spiro Mounds (Lankford 2007a, fig. 2.9). The engraving depicts several crested birds – potentially woodpeckers – flying among the branches of a stylized tree. A strikingly similar scene is described in an Alabama allegory wherein a woodpecker harnesses the world's water when he discovers "a cane as big as a tree ... [lights] upon it, and [begins] pecking". Water pours forth from the hole and "all the creeks [are] overflowed" (Swanton 1929, 124). Lankford (2007a) interprets the tree in the Spiro engraving as an *axis mundi* that binds cosmic realms together. Thus, the tree in the Alabama water story may also be interpreted as a centering entity – specifically one that can channel the waters of the Beneath World into the realms above. When considered together, the Alabama water story and the Spiro shell engraving suggest that woodpeckers may have indeed been perceived as dualistic cosmic beings, able to fly throughout the Above World but also access the Beneath World via the *axis mundi* – sometimes even acting as connecting entities themselves.

Conehead humans

Many of the human effigies in the CMV corpus are distinctive for their cone-shaped heads or head coverings. This "conehead" figure appears to be largely unique to the CMV and adjacent regions. Lankford and Dye (2014) have suggested that these effigies may reference the wild brother of the legendary Hero Twin duo. The Twins, also widely known as "Lodge-Boy" and "Thrown-Away", appear in nearly every Native oral tradition throughout the Americas (Sumner 1951). The story of the Twins is often told in sequential episodes recounting their life histories.

The Twins' origin story generally begins with the unnatural death of a pregnant woman at the hands of a cannibal or monster. The Twins are ripped or cut from her womb. One of the brothers, known as Lodge-Boy, is raised by the boys' father while the other, known as Thrown-Away, is cast out along with the afterbirth following their mother's murder. One day Thrown-Away suddenly appears, revealing himself to his brother and coercing him into a series of rebellious escapades. The boys' father eventually discovers their mischievous antics and plots to catch Thrown-Away, making several attempts before he is finally successful (Sumner 1951; Lankford and Dye 2014).

Having been discarded after birth, Thrown-Away is always portrayed as a wild and untamed figure with mysterious origins. He often spawns from his mother's placenta or emerges from the depths of lake, river, or spring (Dorsey 1904a; 1904b; 1904c; Sumner 1951; Lankford 1987). He is frequently described as having sharp teeth, long hair, and sly or sneaky behavior (Dorsey 1906, 144; Lankford and Dye 2014). For these reasons, Thrown-Away must always be captured or domesticated. These characteristics have obvious links to the themes of chaos and death ascribed to the watery Mississippian Beneath World.

Distinctive cone-shaped heads among human rim effigies in the CMV may specifically reference Thrown-Away's appearance in several origin stories. Stories from the Central Plains recount that Lodge-Boy and his father catch – or tame – Thrown-Away by tying up his long hair in an inflated animal bladder, preventing him from returning to the bottom of the lake, pond, or stream from which he emerged. Lankford and Dye (2014) posit that CMV conehead effigies depict Thrown-Away as he appears in this particular scene with his hair tied up in a bladder.

In every version of the Twins' story, the boys embark on a series of cosmic adventures recounted in many subsequent legendary episodes. The two work together to conquer monsters, giants, and cannibals – often killing their mother's murderer as well. They steal antlers from underwater serpents and plunder eggs from the nests of the great Thunderbirds (Sumner 1951; Lankford 1987, 162). Their success in these adventures often becomes essential to the welfare or restoration of mankind (Sumner 1951, 79). As a result of these victories, the Twins eventually ascend to the Above World as Thunderers (i.e., Lightning Boy and Thunder Boy), or weather spirits (Sumner 1951, 65; Dye 2014; 2017a; Duncan and Diaz-Granados 2000).

It is significant that Thrown-Away is constantly portrayed as a dualistic character in Native lore. Early in his life history he is strongly associated with the forces of the Beneath World. However, through his domestication, he becomes a culture hero, battling formidable foes to maintain cosmic balance. Notably, his final apotheosis brings him into the Above World, contrasting directly with his origins. Thus, Thrown-Away's life history, in addition to his literal existence as a twin, typifies the oppositional tension of the Mississippian cosmos.

Raptors

Like conehead effigies, some raptor effigies may also reference dualistic Twin lore. As noted, several Native oral traditions recount the Twins' battle with Thunderbirds, powerful raptors associated with the powers of the Above World (Sumner 1951, 19, 35, 66). Notably, many raptor rim-effigy bowls exhibit inward facing heads accompanied by a pair of talons in place of a tail, depicting the bird as "belly up" or otherwise incapacitated (Fig. 2.2c) – perhaps a reference to its defeat by the Twins. Some traditions even maintain that the boys ascend to the Above World as raptors themselves (Sumner 1951, 59–79). Ethnohistoric accounts of Native groups indicate that war clubs, feathers, and falcon pelts were viewed as symbols of the Twins and/or the Thunderers. The Tunica, Omaha, and Creek often included these items in the ritual bundles of sodalities dedicated to the veneration of the Thunderers (Dye 2017a; 2017b; Duncan and Diaz-Granados 2000).

An iconographic model

The identification of cosmic referents among CMV rim-effigy bowls provides the foundation for an iconographic model of the vessel form itself. As described above, rim effigies in the CMV appear to reference several dualistic cosmic beings. In particular, this duality, or slipperiness of cosmic classification, reflects the intricate balance of cosmic forces that is integral to Native belief systems throughout the Great Plains and South (Lankford 2008, 95). Beyond the effigies themselves, the broader rim-effigy bowl form also alludes to this oppositional tension. Specifically, the placement of rim effigies and the use of decorative motifs and design elements appear to constitute a holistic, three-dimensional rendering of the tripartite Mississippian cosmos. In this sense, CMV rim-effigy bowls may be interpreted as miniature *cosmoscapes* (Fig. 2.4).

Cosmoscapes

A cosmoscape is a template for understanding the structure and extent of a particular universe. This not only includes realms such as land, water, or sky and the

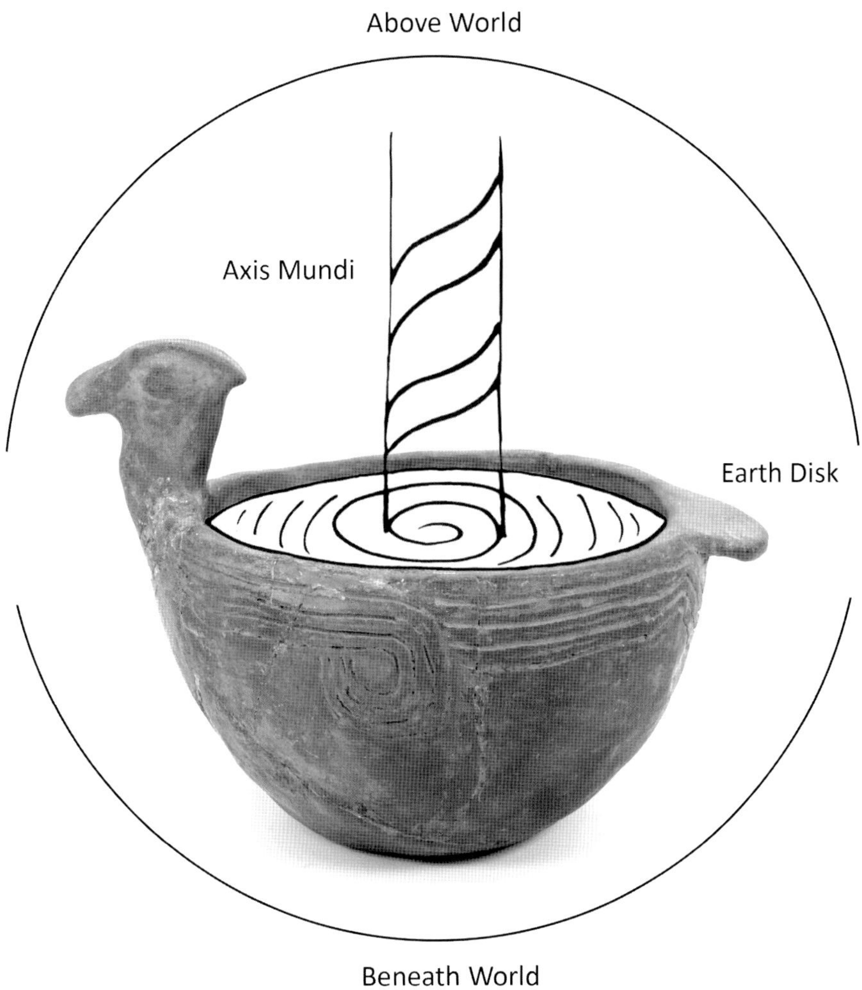

Fig. 2.4. A rim-effigy bowl as a cosmogram. A conceptual *axis mundi* is created by swirling the contents of the vessel. Note the presence of a looped square motif at the rim. Vessel from Chickasawba Mound (LMS 9-Q-2) (courtesy of the University of Arkansas Museum Collections).

beings that inhabit them, but also the cosmic planes and otherworldly beings that may lie beyond. Put simply, a cosmoscape is a more expansive conceptualization of a landscape, which is often concerned only with the humans, plants, animals, or built features within an earthly realm. Cosmoscape is an ideal concept for characterizing indigenous American templates of the universe – including the ancient Mississippian template – because these models often eschew binary distinctions between natural and supernatural entities. Rather, the cosmos is viewed as an integrated whole where generative dualities may exist within a place, time, or being – but not as mutually exclusive dichotomies (e.g., natural/supernatural, person/thing, good/bad, life/death) (Norton-Smith 2010, 82–6; Bloch 2021).

A growing number of scholars studying indigenous cultures in the Americas have opted to frame their work within the context of cosmoscapes to achieve more accurate representations of Native beliefs, practices, and worldviews (Berlo 2011;

Reichel 2012; Slater 2014; Bold 2020). For example, the concept of cosmoscape, when used in American contexts like the Mississippian Valley, more aptly captures the ubiquitous indigenous belief in an animated cosmos. That is, non-human entities, such as animals, plants, otherworldly beings, and even geological features like lakes, caves, and mountains, are often viewed as having human-like agency (Slater 2014, 8–15; Bold 2020). This agency, or personhood, is inherent to the cosmos itself and, by animating sacred non-human entities, connects all planes of the universe to create a complex whole (Reichel 2012, 138).

Beyond recognizing widespread presence of cosmic animacy in their surroundings, indigenous cultures in the Americas often recreate their cosmoscapes on a smaller scale. Many built environments have been identified as "maps" of the cosmos. For example, the Navajo create ritual sandpaintings that serve as cosmic diagrams (Berlo 2011). Similarly, tribes in the Colombian Amazon build communal roundhouses to mirror the structural elements of their cosmos (Reichel 2012, 130). By interacting with these entities, humans are able to connect with and conceptualize the cosmos on a smaller scale. This allows them to absorb, harness, or consult with the forces of the universe.

Rim-effigy bowls as cosmoscapes

Among rim-effigy bowls, the three layers of the Mississippian cosmos are present both in the bowl itself as well as the larger space it occupies. Broadly, this space consists of a sphere bisected by a horizontal plane. The plane flush with the rim of the bowl can be interpreted as the Earth Disk. This is highlighted by the occasional appearance of incised looped square or festoon motifs directly below the rim of some bowls, a design that has been interpreted as a symbol of the four corners of the Earth (Lankford 2007a, 24). The equivalence of this horizontal plane with the Earth Disk is also apparent in the use of "tail riders" – modeled birds, panthers, or turtles that are perched upon a tabular tail effigy. Tail riders appear to sit atop the horizontal plane of the rim, creating the image of an animal dwelling upon the Earth Disk.

The body of the effigy figure, or the bowl itself, may double as a receptacle for the waters of the Beneath World, as indicated by the occasional presence of scroll or swirl cross designs encircling the vessel body (see O'Brien 1994, fig. 1.1). These motifs have previously been recognized as representations of portals to the Beneath World (Lankford 2007c, 24; 2011b). This interpretation of the bowl, or body, as a cosmic container is supported by documentation of historic American Indian cosmology. Specifically, as Lankford (2007c) posits, the Earth Diver and Flood stories in the Great Plains and South suggest that the waters of the Beneath World are enclosed in a solid container, the bottom of which holds the soil or mud that is used to create the Earth. Similarly, the Muskogeans believe that a stone bowl rotates through the horizon from the Above World to the Beneath World as day turns to night (Reilly 2011, 119).

Sitting atop the Earth Disk is a conceptual reflection of the bowl itself, forming the vault of the Above World or night sky of the Beneath World. The notion that

a

b

Fig. 2.5. a. Examples of Hixon-style gorgets from the Hixon and Etowah sites (from Lankford 2007a, fig. 2.7); b. crested bird rim-effigy bowl from Neeley's Ferry (LMS 11-N-04) (from Phillips 1939, pl. 58, vessel D2).

an intangible celestial realm lies above the bowl is indicated by the occasional presence of beaded rims. This beading is very similar to the petaloid borders that surround incised designs on shell cups from Spiro. Reilly (2007) has suggested that petaloid motifs serve as celestial locatives. Thus, the placement of beaded rims at the junction between the spaces above and below the Earth Disk could symbolize a transition between cosmic realms.

Most importantly, however, this cosmoscape is "peopled" or animated by the beings depicted by the effigies themselves. The head – and sometimes tail – of a cosmic character extend into the space above the bowl's orifice, while its body lies below. This creates a sense of simultaneous existence both above and below the Earth Disk – a possible reference to the character's cosmic duality and the importance of balancing Above and Beneath world forces.

This type of structural configuration appears in other Mississippian art forms. Specifically, Hixon style gorgets provide an apt model for interpreting the iconography of rim-effigy bowls. Within Hixon-style design fields, two crested birds appear to be standing upon a horizontal bar separated by a vertical striped pole. Beneath the horizontal bar is often a set of parallel lines that resemble the upper contours of a ceramic pot. Lankford (2007a) interprets this design field as a cosmic model, where the vertical pole symbolizes an *axis mundi*, the stylized pot acts as the Beneath World, and the horizontal bar, doubling as the pot's rim, represents the Middle World. Much like the *axis mundi*, the crested birds – perched upon the rim of a pot – seem to connect the Beneath World (the pot) to the Above World (the semicircular space above the pot). In this way, Hixon-style gorgets exhibit imagery very similar to CMV rim-effigy bowls. Notably, Hixon-style crested birds bear a striking resemblance to several crested-bird effigies on bowls recovered from the region (Fig. 2.5).

Unlike Hixon gorgets, rim-effigy bowls do not depict an obvious *axis mundi*. However, it should be remembered that rim-effigy heads were occasionally hollow, containing a single ceramic rattle. To limit spillage, the most reasonable way to "rattle" a full rim-effigy bowl would be to swirl it in a circular motion. Interestingly, this motion not only creates a watery vortex symbolic of the Beneath World (Nowak 2018), but also figurative vertical axis comparable to the striped pole depicted in Hixon-style gorgets. Although a physical axis is not present, this movement creates an axis of sound (Lankford 2007a), suggesting that – when maneuvered – rim-effigy bowls may have become interactive cosmoscapes.

Studies of other Mississippian ritual ceramic vessels, including Ramey Incised pots from Cahokia and burial vessels from the Craig Mound at Spiro, support this reading of CMV rim-effigy bowls (Pauketat and Emerson 1991; Lambert 2018). Nor were such cosmic references confined to Mississippian time. During the Late Woodland period in the Lower Mississippi Valley, pots of the Coles Creek culture were commonly decorated with multiple parallel lines at the rim, a three-dimensional version of the "centering" theme that symbolically defined the vessel's orifice as an *axis mundi* (compare vessels in Ford 1951, 74–9 to stone palettes and copper gorgets bearing the same theme in Knight and Steponaitis 2011, 219–26, 236).

Discussion: Rim-effigy bowls in context

Overall, rim-effigy bowls appear to represent animated Mississippian cosmoscapes, reinforcing the concept of Above World/Beneath World tension or cosmic balance. But who used these vessels? A previous study of the spatial distribution of the rim-effigy bowl styles and themes used in this study indicates that these vessels were likely produced and used locally (Azar 2020). Bowls of a certain style not only tend to come from the same geographical area but also tend to depict a single theme, suggesting that communities throughout the CMV were producing or commissioning particular vessels for local use.

To characterize the communities who may have used rim-effigy bowls, we again turned to the recorded traditions of historic Native groups. In the late 19th and early 20th centuries, ritual sodalities were prevalent among the Ponca, Pawnee, Iowa, Osage, Caddo, Tunica, and Omaha (Fletcher and LaFlesche 1911; Murie 1914; Skinner 1915; Fortune 1932; Bailey 1995; Huffman and Earley 2014; Dye 2018). As elite social collectives, sodalities practiced esoteric and proprietary forms of ritual activity, often worshiping specific animal spirits, culture heroes, or other otherworldly characters. Part of this ritual activity included the maintenance of sacred bundles containing cosmologically charged items (e.g., animal pelts, rattles, maces, pipes, or feathers) that aided in conjuring a totemic spirit or cosmic being (see Dye 2017b for a broad review of historic sodalities). Sodalities also owned other forms of ritual sacra, like finely crafted ceramic vessels. These items were often manufactured in limited numbers by skilled sodality members that were commissioned based on their reputation within the group (Bailey 1995, 47; Dye 2019, 11). Ritual sacra produced in these contexts essentially served as inalienable possessions (Weiner 1985; 1992).

Given these historic period examples, David Dye (2017b; 2018; 2019) has previously argued for the presence of prestigious ritual sodalities or collectives in the Late Mississippian CMV, identifying ceramic vessels – including rim-effigy bowls – as inalienable possessions reflecting group identity. However, all rim-effigy bowls in the CMV – regardless of their effigies – seem to act as handheld cosmoscapes. This shared form seems to likewise indicate a shared function throughout the region, hardly reflecting a form of esoteric cosmic knowledge belonging *only* to sodality members.

Contrasting use wear patterns across vessels support the notion that rim-effigy bowls were not strictly elite wares but rather a regionally recognized ceramic form that transcended social or ritual boundaries. In particular, while many rim-effigy bowls in the CMV are finely crafted, others are not. Some bowls are highly burnished and well formed with intricate effigy features and painted or incised designs, indicating production by especially skilled potters. These higher-quality rim-effigy bowls rarely show signs of use wear beyond basal abrasion. In contrast, many other rim-effigy bowls in the region feature simple effigies, plain surfaces, and a lack of overall symmetry. These vessels also tend to have interior carbonization and/or exterior sooting indicating use during cooking. These two distinct patterns of use wear suggest that some rim-effigy bowls may have indeed been produced by skilled potters for exclusive religious collectives who used them as ritual serving vessels. Others may have been manufactured by less skilled potters at the household or general community level, sometimes functioning as cooking vessels (see Steponaitis *et al.* 2019, 20–1 for a similar argument with reference to pipes).

Importantly, we posit that more simply executed rim-effigy bowls, namely those lacking incised or painted designs, likely held the same religious meaning as more finely crafted rim-effigy bowls, which were often bedecked with incised cosmic symbolism and detailed effigies. That is, regardless of the relative simplicity or complexity of rim-effigy bowl designs, all acted as miniature animated cosmoscapes. The presence of cooking residues on some lower quality rim-effigy bowls does not necessarily indicate a utilitarian or non-ritual function but may be related to the preparation of ritual medicines, as we discuss further below. The difference between high- and low-quality vessels instead lies in the context of production and use (e.g., elite vs domestic). This phenomenon may have been similar in some ways to the simultaneous display of Christian crosses in communal church buildings, private household settings, and even restricted spaces reserved for trained clergy.

Based on our identification of rim-effigy bowls as cosmic models referencing universal balance and powerful cosmic beings, it is possible that people across the CMV deployed rim-effigy bowls during rites related to healing, regeneration, or the restoration of cosmic harmony by acknowledging the generative tension between cosmic forces and channeling important cosmic beings. Ritual activity focused on cosmic harmony was common among historic American Indian groups descended from pre-contact Mississippians. For example, communal green-corn ceremonialism, which celebrates the renewal of life in the form of a successful crop, was vital to the restoration of cosmic wholeness and harmony among many Southern groups (Howard 1968; Waring 1968; Fairbanks 1979; Hudson 1979). Further, the healing, renewal, and revitalization of people, spaces, and sacred objects was often achieved by Native shamans through supplication to tutelary spirits or transcendental cosmic beings in both the Great Plains and South (Murie 1914; Benedict 1923; Fortune 1932; Dye 2020). Again, because the principles of balance and wholeness were fundamental to the Mississippian cosmovision, rituals involving rim-effigy bowls could have occurred domestically, communally, or within the context of more exclusive social collectives. In all cases, particular effigy themes may have been chosen based on ancestral identity or local tradition, somewhat like the veneration of particular patron saints across the Catholic world.

Based on ethnographic reports of historic American Indian renewal ceremonies and shamanic practices, Mississippian ritual practices likely involved the frequent preparation and consumption of hallucinogenic or stimulant medicines, such as those made from holly (*Ilex*) or jimsonweed (*Datura*) (Fletcher and La Flesche 1911; Murie 1914; Skinner 1915; Fairbanks 1979; Hudson 1979; Lankford 2012; 2014; Dye 2017b). Indeed, residue analyses indicate that Mississippian ritual ceramics – including some rim-effigy bowls – were likely used to prepare or serve herbal medicines (Crown *et al.* 2012; Miller 2015; King *et al.* 2018). These medicines would have been ingested by supplicants seeking to achieve renewal or restoration via ritual cleansing or purification (Milanich 1979). In addition, some medicines, especially those made from *Datura*, may have been used to initiate hallucinogenic trances in order to conjure a particular spirit or culture hero that could restore cosmic balance or wholeness (King *et al.* 2018; Steponaitis *et al.* 2019; Dye 2020).

Evidence of cooking among lower quality rim-effigy bowls indicates that these vessels may have been used to prepare – not only serve – ritual medicines or other comestibles. As discussed, a brewed decoction would have been ideal for swirling a rim-effigy bowl, both to produce a rattling noise and to create a figurative *axis mundi*. In this way, the user of the bowl would have for a brief time become the central, motivating force of the cosmos, perhaps providing them access the cosmic power of the effigy figure in order heal, regenerate, or restore balance.

Perhaps bolstering this interpretation of rim-effigy bowls as widely used ritual sacra are archaeological depictions and ethnohistoric descriptions of Native shamans in eastern North America. In a discussion of figural stone pipes from the Lower Mississippi Valley, Steponaitis and colleagues (2019) argue that anthropomorphic pipes depict shamans in the midst of ceremonial activity – perhaps even in trance states fueled by ritual medicines. They suggest that the complex and distinctive hairstyles, hats, and caps donned by these individuals – as rendered in the pipes – would have indicated their role in society as skilled ritual practitioners.

These head coverings may have also conferred special power to their users. Native historic period ritual practitioners received cosmic abilities through communication with and supplication to otherworldly beings or spirits. Distinctive headwear was thought to facilitate this bond. For example, the medicine societies of the Iowa, Pawnee, Ponca, and Omaha incorporated specific headwear – namely hide or animal-pelt caps – into their practices. These caps, which were often adorned with horns, antlers, or feathers, were thought to possess the shamanistic powers that allowed for the invocation of specific cosmic beings (see Dye 2017b for a deeper discussion). Similarly, hairstyles with crests or coiled braids atop the head, sometimes called "horns," were worn by Native religious practitioners in the Great Plains and western Great Lakes as signs of spiritual power (Steponaitis *et al.* 2019: 17, fig. 9).

Notably, aside from the conehead human effigies, many rim-effigies from the CMV depict humans with elaborate head coverings, hairstyles, or caps. For instance, many don what may be animal pelts resembling serpent monsters and birds (Hathcock 1983, fig. 11; Dye 2017b). Many more of the human effigies exhibit intricate hairstyles and head coverings that were completely unique. It may be that these effigies depict ritual practitioners consuming medicines and performing rites meant to heal or renew balance. Nor is it coincidence that many of the non-human beings depicted on rim effigies – crested birds, raptors, and antlered serpents – are creatures who have prominent crests or other "headgear."

Conclusions

Based on the iconographic model presented here, we posit that communities throughout the Late Mississippian CMV– regardless of social status – may have utilized rim-effigy bowls during rituals emphasizing the structure and wholeness of the cosmos. Each bowl makes layered references to the vital balance between cosmic forces, a concept that has previously been highlighted as a guiding principle in the Mississippian worldview (Hudson 1976; Lankford 2008). The cosmic beings embodied by the effigies themselves, combined with their orientation within a handheld cosmoscape, create a readable object laden with meaningful references to foundational oral stories (Reilly 2011, 120). And in turn, through the production and utilization of these vessels – perhaps in medicine preparation or consumption – CMV Mississippians actively recreated and reinforced the structure of their cosmos.

More broadly, our analysis of CMV rim-effigy bowls extends the scope of current research in Mississippian iconography. The CMV rim-effigy bowl corpus constitutes a significant body of ritual paraphernalia that should not be overlooked in future discussions of representational imagery found across the Mississippian world. In addition, many other finely crafted ceramics were produced during the Late Mississippian period in the CMV that have not yet been subjected to systematic iconographic analysis. To further broaden our understanding of how Mississippians perceived, recreated, and interacted with their cosmos, these ceramics should be recognized as meaningful art objects alongside Spiro's shell cups, Etowah's copper plates, and Moundville's engraved pots.

References

Azar, M. (2020) Making heads or tails: An iconographic analysis of Late Mississippian rim-effigy bowls in the Central Mississippi River Valley. Unpublished Master's thesis, Department of Anthropology, University of North Carolina at Chapel Hill. Chapel Hill NC.

Bailey, G. (1995) *The Osage and the Invisible World: From the Works of Francis La Flesche*. University of Oklahoma Press, Norman OK.

Benedict, R. (1923) *The Concept of the Guardian Spirit in North America*. American Anthropological Association Memoir 29, American Anthropological Association, Washington DC.

Berlo, J. (2011) Navajo cosmoscapes – up, down, within. *American Art* 25, 10–13.

Bloch, L.J. (2021) No gods, no masters: Indigenous environmental knowledge in Mississippian art. *Southeastern Archaeology* 40, 248–65.

Bogg, R. and Bogg, L. (2016) *Cat Serpents: Underwater spirits in Mississippian pottery*. Longbranch Books, Longbranch WA.

Bold, R. (2020) Constructing cosmoscapes: Cosmological currents in conversation and contestation in contemporary Boliva. *Journal of Ethnographic Theory* 10, 195–208.

Bomar, B. (2011) The Moundville duck bowl. *Alabama Heritage* 100, 8–9.

Brown, T.L. (2005) Ceramic *Variability within the Parkin Phase: A Whole Vessel Metric Analysis from Northeast Arkansas*. Arkansas Archaeological Survey, Research Series No. 32. University of Arkansas, Fayetteville.

Cobb, C. and Drake, E. (2008) The colour of time: Head pots and temporal convergences. *Cambridge Archaeological Journal* 18, 85–93.

Crown, P., Emerson, T., Gu, J., Hurst, W.J., Pauketat, T. and Ward T. (2012) Ritual black drink consumption at Cahokia. *Proceedings of the National Academy of Sciences* 109, 13944–9.

Dorsey, G. (1904a) *Traditions of the Arikara*. Publication 17, Carnegie Institution of Washington, Washington DC.

Dorsey, G. (1904b) *Traditions of the Skidi Pawnee*. Memoirs of the American Folklore Society 3. American Folklore Society, Boston, New York.

Dorsey, G. (1904c) *Traditions of the Osage*. Publication 88, Anthropological Series 7(1). Field Columbian Museum, Chicago IL.

Dorsey, G. (1906) *The Pawnee Mythology (Part 1)*. Publication 59. Carnegie Institution of Washington, Washington DC.

Duncan, J. (2011) The cosmology of the Osage: The Star People and their universe. In Lankford *et al.* (eds), 18–33.

Duncan, J. and Diaz-Granados C. (2000) Of masks and myth. *Midcontinental Journal of Archaeology* 25, 1–26.

Dye, D. (2014) Lightning Boy face mask gorgets and Thunder Boy war clubs: Ritual organization of Lower Mississippi Valley Warfare. Unpublished paper presented at the 71st annual meeting of the Southeastern Archaeological Conference, Greenville SC.

Dye, D. (2017a) Lightning Boy and Thunder Boy: The Hero Twins in the Lower Mississippi Valley. Manuscript on file, Anthropology Department, University of Memphis, Memphis TN.

Dye, D. (2017b) Animal pelt caps and Mississippian ritual sodalities. *North American Archaeologist* 38.1, 63–97.

Dye, D. (2018) Ceramic wares and water spirits: Identifying religious sodalities in the Lower Mississippi Valley. In *Ceramics of Ancient America: Multidisciplinary approaches*, eds Y. Huntington, D. Arnold and J. Minich, 29–61. University Press of Florida, Gainesville FL.

Dye, D. (2019) Head pots and sodalities in the Lower Mississippi Valley. In *Shaman, Priest, Practice, Belief: Materials of ritual and religion in Eastern North America*, eds S. Carmody and C. Barrier, 208–34. University of Alabama Press, Tuscaloosa AL.

Dye, D.H. (2020) Anthropomorphic pottery effigies as guardian spirits in the Lower Mississippi Valley. In *Cognitive Archeology: Mind, ethnography, and the past in South Africa and beyond*, eds D.S. Whitley, J.H.N. Loubser, and G. Whitelaw, 201–23. Routledge, London.

Emerson, T.E. (1989) Water, serpents, and the Underworld: An exploration into Cahokian symbolism. In *The Southeastern Ceremonial Complex: Artifact and analysis*, ed. P. Galloway, 45–92. University of Nebraska Press, Lincoln NE.

Emerson, T. (1997) Cahokian elite ideology and the Mississippian cosmos. In *Cahokia: Domination and ideology in the Mississippian world*, eds T. Pauketat and T. Emerson, 190–228. University of Nebraska Press, Lincoln NE.

Fairbanks, C. (1979) The function of black drink among the Creeks. In Hudson (ed.), 120–49.

Fletcher, A. and La Flesche, F. (1911) *The Omaha Tribe*. Twenty-Seventh Annual Report of the Bureau of American Ethnology. Government Printing Office, Washington DC.

Ford, J. (1951) *Greenhouse: A Troyville-Coles Creek period site in Avoyelles Parish, Louisiana*. Anthropological Papers 44. American Museum of Natural History, New York.

Fortune, R. (1932) *Omaha Secret Societies*. Columbia University Contributions to Anthropology 14. Columbia University Press, Columbia NY.

Gannon, T. (1999) A Mortuary Analysis of the Vernon Paul Site (3CS25): Sociopolitical organization at a Late Mississippian site in Cross County, Arkansas. Unpublished Ph.D. dissertation, Department of Anthropology. University of Arkansas, Fayetteville AR.

Hathcock, R. (1983) *The Quapaw and Their Pottery*. Hurley, Camden AR.

Hathcock, R. (1988) *Ancient Indian Pottery of the Mississippi River Valley*. Walsworth Publishing, Marceline MO.

House, J. (2003) *Gifts of the Great River: Arkansas effigy pottery from the Edwin Curtiss Collection*. Peabody Museum of Archaeology and Ethnology, Harvard University, Cambridge MA.

House, J.H. (2005) *Gifts of the Great River: Arkansas effigy pottery from the Edwin Curtiss Collection*. Peabody Museum of Archaeology & Ethnology, Harvard University, Cambridge MA.

Howard, J. (1968) *The Southeastern Ceremonial Complex and Its Interpretation*. Missouri Archaeological Society Memoir 6. University of Missouri, Columbia MO.

Howell, M. (2011) Sonic-iconic examination of Adorno rattles from the Mississippian-era Lake George site. *Music in Art* 36, 231–44.

Hudson, C. (1976) *The Southeastern Indians*. University of Tennessee Press, Knoxville TN.

Hudson, C. (1979) *Black Drink: A Native American tea*. University of Georgia Press, Athens GA.

Huffman, T. and Earley, F. (2014) Caddoan archaeology on the High Plains: A conceptual nexus of bison, lodges, maize, and rock art. *American Antiquity* 79, 655–78.

King, A. and Reilly, F.K. III (2011) Raptor imagery at Etowah: The raptor is the path to power. In Lankford *et al.* (eds), 313–48.

King, A, Powis, T., Cheong, K., Deere, B., Pickering, R., Singleton, E. and Gaikwad, N. (2018) Absorbed residue evidence for prehistoric *Datura* use in the American Southeast and Western Mexico. *Advances in Archaeological Practice* 6, 312–27.

Knight, V.J. (2013) *Iconographic Method in New World Prehistory*. Cambridge University Press, New York.

Knight, V.J. and Steponaitis, V. (2011) A redefinition of the Hemphill Style in Mississippian art. In Lankford *et al.* (eds), 201–39.

Knight, V.J., Brown, J. and Lankford G. (2001) On the subject matter of Southeastern ceremonial complex art. *Southeastern Archaeology* 20, 129–41.

Kongas, E. (1960) The Earth Diver (Th. A 812). *Ethnohistory* 7, 151–80.

Lambert, S. (2018) Addressing the cosmological significance of a pot: A search for cosmological structure in the Craig Mound. *Caddo Archaeological Journal* 28, 21–37.

Lankford, G. (1987) *Native American Legends: The Southeast*. August House, Atlanta GA.

Lankford, G. (2007a) Some cosmological motifs in the southeastern ceremonial complex. In Reilly and Garber (eds), 8–38.

Lankford, G. (2007b) The Great Serpent in Eastern North America. In Reilly and Garber (eds), 107–35.

Lankford, G. (2007c) The "Path of Souls": Some death imagery in the Southeastern ceremonial complex. In Reilly and Garber (eds), 174–212.

Lankford, G. (2007d) *Reachable Stars: Patterns in the ethnoastronomy of Eastern North America.* University of Alabama Press, Tuscaloosa AL.

Lankford, G. (2008) *Looking for Lost Lore: Studies in folklore, ethnology, and iconography*. University of Alabama Press, Tuscaloosa AL.

Lankford, G. (2011a) Regional approaches to iconographic art. In Lankford *et al.* (eds), 3–17.

Lankford, G. (2011b) The swirl cross and the center. In Lankford *et al.* (eds), 251–78.

Lankford, G. (2012) Weeding out the noded. *Arkansas Archeologist* 50, 50–68.

Lankford, G. (2014) Following the noded trail. *Arkansas Archeologist* 53, 51–68.

Lankford, G. and Dye, D. (2014) Conehead effigies: A distinctive art form of the Mississippi Valley. *Arkansas Archeologist* 53, 37–50.

Lankford, G., Reilly F.R., III, and Garber, J. eds (2011) *Visualizing the Sacred: Cosmic visions, regionalism, and the art of the Mississippian world.* University of Texas Press, Austin TX.

Mainfort, R. (2003) Assessing Late Period phases in the Central Mississippi Valley. *Southeastern Archaeology* 22, 17.

Mainfort, R. (2005) A K-means analysis of Late Period ceramic variation in the Central Mississippi Valley. *Southeastern Archaeology* 24.1, 59–69.

Meltzer, D. and Dunnell, R. eds (1992) *The Archaeology of William Henry Holmes.* Smithsonian Institution Press, Washington DC.

Milanich, J. (1979) Origins and prehistoric distributions of black drink and the ceremonial shell drinking cup. In Hudson (ed.), 83–119.

Miller, J. (2015) Interior carbonization patterns as evidence of ritual drink preparation in Powell Plain and Ramey Incised vessels. *American Antiquity* 80, 170–83.

Morse, D. (1989) *Nodena: An Account of 90 Years of Archaeological Investigation in Southeast Mississippi County, Arkansas.* Arkansas Archeological Survey Research Series 30. University of Arkansas, Fayetteville AR.

Morse, P. (1981) *Parkin.* Arkansas Archaeological Survey Research Series 13. University of Arkansas, Fayetteville AR.

Morse, D. and Morse, P. (1983) *Archaeology of the Central Mississippi Valley* (2nd edn). University of Alabama Press, Tuscaloosa AL.

Murie, J. (1914) *Pawnee Indian Societies.* Anthropological Papers 11.7, 543–644. American Museum of Natural History, New York.

Norton-Smith, T.M. (2010) *The Dance of Person and Place: One interpretation of American Indian philosophy,* Suny Press, Albany NY.

Nowak, J. (2018) Iconography beyond sight. An object-oriented approach to prehistoric Southeastern ceramics. Unpublished paper presented at the 75th Annual Meeting of the Southeastern Archaeological Conference, Augusta GA.

O'Brien, M. ed. (1994) *Cat Monsters and Head Pots: The archaeology of Missouri's Pemiscot Bayou.* University of Missouri Press, Columbia MO.

O'Brien, M. and Dunnell, R. (1998) A brief introduction to the archaeology of the Central Mississippi River Valley. In *Changing Perspectives on the Archaeology of the Central Mississippi River Valley*, eds M. O'Brien and R. Dunnell, 1–30. University of Alabama Press, Tuscaloosa AL.

Pauketat, T. and Emerson, T. (1991) The ideology of authority and the power of the pot. *American Anthropologist* 93, 919–41.

Perino, G. (1967a) *The Banks Village Site, Crittenden County, Arkansas.* Memoir 4, Missouri Archaeological Society, Springfield MO.

Perino, G. (1967b) *The Cherry Valley Mounds and Bands Mound 3*, Memoir 1, Central States Archaeological Societies Maxville IN.

Phillips, P. (1939) Introduction to the archaeology of the Mississippi Valley. Unpublished Ph.D. dissertation, Department of Anthropology, Harvard University, Cambridge MA.

Phillips, P., Ford, J. and Griffin, J.B. (1951) *Archaeological Survey in the Lower Mississippi Alluvial Valley, 1940–1947*. Papers of the Peabody Museum of Archaeology and Ethnology 25. Harvard University, Cambridge MA.

Rands, R. (1956) Southern cult motifs on Walls-Pecan Point pottery. *American Antiquity* 22, 183–6.

Reichel, E. (2012) The landscape in the cosmoscape, and sacred sites and species among the Tnaimuka and Yukuna Amerindian Tribes (northwest Amazon). In *Sacred Spaces and Sites: Advances in biocultural conservation*, eds G. Pungetti, G. Oviedo and D. Hooke, 127–51. Cambridge University Press, Cambridge.

Reilly, F.K. III (2004) People of earth, people of sky: Visualizing the sacred in Native American art of the Mississippian Period. In *Hero, Hawk, and Open Hand: American Indian Art of the Ancient Midwest and South*, eds R.F. Townsend and R.V. Sharp, 125–37. Yale University Press, New Haven CO.

Reilly, F.K. III (2007) The petaloid motif: A celestial symbolic locative in the shell art of Spiro. In Reilly and Garber (eds), 39–55.

Reilly, F.K. III (2011) The Great Serpent in the Lower Mississippi Valley. In Lankford *et al.* (eds), 118–33.

Reilly, F.K. III and Garber, J. eds (2007) *Ancient Objects and Sacred Realms: Interpretations of Mississippian iconography*. University of Texas Press, Austin TX.

Reilly, F.K. III and Garber, J. (2011) Dancing in the Otherworld: The human figural art of the Hightower Style revisited. In Lankford *et al.* (eds), 294–312.

Skinner, A. (1915) *Societies of the Iowa, Kansa, and Ponca Indians*. Anthropological Paper 11.9, 679–801. American Museum of Natural History, New York,

Slater, D. (2014) Into the Heart of the Turtle: Caves, ritual, and power in ancient Central Yucatan, Mexico. Unpublished Ph.D. dissertation, Department of Anthropology, Brandeis University, Waltham MA.

Steponaitis, V. and Knight V.J. (2004) Moundville art in historical and social context. In *Hero, Hawk, and Open Hand: American Indian art of the ancient Midwest and South*, eds by R. Townsend and R. Sharp, 167–81. Art Institute of Chicago and Yale University Press, New Haven CO.

Steponaitis, V., Knight, V.J. and Lankford, G. (2019) Effigy pipes of the Lower Mississippi Valley: Iconography, style, and function. *Journal of Anthropological Archaeology* 55, 101070 [DOI:10.1016/j.jaa.2019.101070].

Sumner, M. (1951) Lodge-Boy and Thrown-Away: An analytic study of an American Indian folktale. Unpubished Ph.D. dissertation, Department of Anthropology, Stanford University CA.

Swanton, J. (1928) *Religious Beliefs and Medical Practices of the Creek Indians*. Bureau of American Ethnology Bulletin 43, Government Printing Office, Washington DC.

Swanton, J. (1929) *Myths and Tales of the Southeastern Indians*. Bureau of American Ethnology Bulletin 88, Government Printing Office, Washington DC.

Waring, A. (1968) The southern cult and Muskhogean ceremonial: General considerations. In *The Waring Papers*, ed. S. Williams, 30–69. Papers of the Peabody Museum of Archaeology and Ethnology 58. Harvard University, Cambridge MA

Waring, A. and Holder, P. (1945) A prehistoric ceremonial complex in the Southeastern United States. *American Antiquity* 47, 1–34.

Weiner, A. (1985) Inalienable wealth. *American Ethnologist* 12, 210–27.

Weiner, A. (1992) *Inalienable possessions: The paradox of keeping-while-giving*. University of California Press, Berkeley CA.

3

Cahokia's wandering supernaturals: What does it mean when the Earth Mother leaves town?

Steven L. Boles

After decades of exploring the beginnings of Mississippian culture at Cahokia, scholars in recent years have begun to look more closely at its demise. More specifically, attention has been focused less on causes for abandonment and more on dispersal and integration of Cahokian emigrants (Emerson and Lewis 1991; Boles 2017, 2020; Baltus and Baires 2020; Baltus *et al.* 2020; Emerson *et al.* 2020; McNutt and Parish 2020; Mehta and Connaway 2020; Watts Malouchos 2020; Wilson *et al.* 2020). The coalescence of immigrants with native Late Woodland groups created Cahokia ca. AD 1050. Population peaked in the mid-12th century with an estimated 20,000 residents for Cahokia proper combined with its East St Louis precinct (Pauketat and Lopinot 1997; Brennan *et al.* 2018). The decline of Cahokia was drawn out over a span of roughly 200 years although a marked depopulation is archaeologically visible after the early 13th century (Pauketat and Lopinot 1997; Milner 1998). Data on droughts in the Cahokia region show that severe droughts began during the early Stirling phase (AD 1100–1200) and dominated the late Stirling phase (Benson *et al.* 2009). Although not suggested as the sole reason for the eventual abandonment of Cahokia, such conditions would have surely had profound effects on both the dietary needs as well as the social fabric of an agrarian society, especially one on the scale of Cahokia.

In spite of the exodus of thousands upon thousands of Cahokians over time, looking for and identifying relocated Cahokians via the archaeological record is a challenging task. While there are various aspects of cultural manifestations to explore, lithic items are well suited for this undertaking as they were durable, highly portable, many necessary for everyday tasks, have known and generally limited raw material sources, and the relative ease in recognizing exotic lithic materials and material culture (Boles 2020). Even so, while there are a number of lithic items associated with Cahokia, only the Cahokia-style flint clay figurines can confidently be stamped with *Made at Cahokia* and, given their religious nature, were arguably items that were the most likely to remain in possession of Cahokians (Boles 2016; 2020).

Through the work of Thomas Emerson and colleagues, we know that iconic

Cahokian figurines were made almost exclusively from Missouri flint clay, a material sourced to the Cahokia region (Emerson and Hughes 2000; Emerson *et al.* 2002). Flint clay deposits are found in the karstic region of the Ozark Highland (Chapman 1975) and within the Missouri flint clay district (Keller *et al.* 1954). Here, flint clay formed as pockets in old sinkholes and are exposed as layers under sandstone rimrock (McQueen 1943, 139–45; Keller 1944, 380–1). According to research by Emerson and Hughes each sinkhole deposit appears to be unique and the flint clay layer usually ranges from white to gray, dark gray, light tan, or various shades of red if stained by iron deposits (2000, 92–3). Although their comparative flint clay sample was limited, they felt that it was likely that Cahokians quarried one or perhaps a few closely spaced sources in western St Louis County, roughly 30–40 km from the site (Emerson and Hughes 2000, 90). It is widely accepted that earth openings represented portals to the Underworld in Native American mythology and this may have factored into the choice of using flint clay to portray otherworldly beings (Emerson and Hughes 2000, 93). The Missouri Ozark region in addition to being imbued with spiritual or religious aspects also provided other important resources for Cahokian culture. Examples of such resources include Burlington chert from the Crescent Quarries, galena and hematite for pigment production, basalt for axe-head production, and ortho-quartzite for discoidal manufacture (Pauketat 1997a; 1997b; 1998; Pauketat and Emerson 1997). The control of this symbolical and economically rich resource area perhaps also added to the allure of using flint clay to carve religious sacra (Emerson and Hughes 2000, 84, 93).

The figurines were carved with great attention to anatomical detail and proportional balance and the suite contains human male and female figures as well as various animal types (Emerson 1982; 1983; Boles 2020, table 3.1a). The creation of the figurines at Greater Cahokia appears to have occurred during the Stirling phase (AD 1100–1200) based on depositional contexts from temples or special use features at civic-ceremonial sites (Emerson and Boles 2010; Emerson 1989). Cahokian figurines have also been recovered from sites scattered across the Midcontinent, Southeast, Southwest, and Deep South regions (Emerson *et al.* 2002; 2003; Emerson and Girard 2004; Boles 2017; 2020).

Of note, the incredible detail depicted in the flint clay figurines appears to have developed out of nowhere and rather rapidly at Cahokia. There are no known highly detailed carved stone human or animal figurines in the preceding Early Mississippian Lohmann phase or the earlier Late Woodland period in the Greater Cahokia region. Within the Midcontinent, one has to go back to the Middle Woodland period to find anatomically correct and detailed human and animal figures; these were produced from both clay and various pipestones. Conversely, after the Stirling phase, detailed human and animal imagery is no longer carved three-dimensionally from stone in the Cahokia region. At this time, the creation of such imagery shifts to two dimensional figures on other media such as engraved marine shell cups and repoussé copper plates, the level of production or even the production of either at Cahokia is, however, poorly understood. Notable too is the absence or near absence of female imagery on these media.

Dimensions for the Cahokia figurines range from roughly 8 cm to 20 cm in height and can weigh up to 2.7 kg (Boles 2020, table 3.1a). The female figurines are typically depicted in a kneeling stance and placed on a circular platform or pedestal. Most appear to be wearing a skirt and all have at least one item depicted with them while some have numerous items. Common motifs include baskets, packs or pouches, serpents, sunflowers, maize, and other vegetative plants. Symbolically, these motifs reference the Upper and Lower Worlds, common in Native American cosmology (Lankford 2007). The ever-present circular disk the figures kneel upon could be referencing the Earth Disk of the Middle World.

Although interpretations vary on who or what the flint clay figurines depict, it is broadly assumed that these figurines represent Cahokian supernaturals. The female figurines in general can be interpreted as representations of an Earth Mother persona who is typically regarded as the mother of all life, vegetation, representative of the cycle of life, often associated with the Underworld and a death goddess, and also identified as a lunar deity (Prentice 1986, 249–50). In essence, the female imagery depicted in the Cahokia style represents other-than-human persons associated with creation (Reilly 2020). It has also been suggested that these female figurines were associated with a fertility cult, used during renewal ceremonies and served as conveyers of the Cahokian cosmos to the populace (Emerson 1997a, 216–28).

At present, six female effigy figurines have been recovered from Cahokia and at least six have been recovered from outside Cahokia proper (area in and around Cahokia and East St Louis precincts). Of the outliers, four are made from flint clay and one each from sandstone and limestone (Table 3.1). The use of other than flint clay materials for the production of figurines might suggest that these two were either made before the source for flint clay was discovered or after it was either exhausted or perhaps no longer controlled by Cahokians circa shortly before or after AD 1200, when centralized power at Cahokia was being threatened or greatly diminished.

Table 3.1. Cahokia female figurines

Name	*Site*	*Reference*
Cahokia		
Birger	BBB Motor	Emerson and Jackson 1984
Keller	BBB Motor	Emerson and Jackson 1984
Sponemann	Sponemann	Jackson *et al.* 1992
Willoughby	Sponemann	Jackson *et al.* 1992
West	Sponemann	Jackson *et al.* 1992
Exchange	East St Louis	Emerson and Boles 2010
Outside Cahokia		
Schild	Schild	Perino 1971
Westbrook	Desha Co., AR	Perino 1971
New Madrid	New Madrid Co., MO	Boles 2014; 2017
Bostrom	Madison Co., IL	Emerson 1983
McBeth	Pickaway Co., OH	Boles and Lewis 2019
Woman with mortar	Spiro, OK	Hamilton 1952

There are two other non-flint clay Cahokia-style figurines from the Cahokia region that I am aware of. One is clearly a male effigy figurine made from red sandstone and recovered near the Schild site in Greene County, Illinois (Boles 2014) and the other is a kneeling figure pipe of indeterminate gender made from limestone and recovered from a stone box burial near Fenton, Missouri (Emerson 1982). The limestone figure is heavily eroded and the only discernable accouterment is a series of bracelets on the right arm. Neither figure directly pertains to the topic of this chapter but they are mentioned to show that Cahokian artisans used lithic materials other than flint clay on occasion. Also, some limestones and sandstones will redden to varying degrees when heated. Emerson and Hughes suggested that Cahokians might have selected flint clays that were red or perhaps even turned from white, tan, or gray to red during ceremonial burning (2000, 89). If the desired ceremonial end color was red, for what that may have symbolized, then the use of heat-sensitive/heat-altering limestone and sandstone is less problematic.

In this chapter I focus on the Cahokian female figurines found outside of Cahokia and touch on the possibilities of what it may mean when the Earth Mother leaves town. In doing so I employ an investigative method advocated by Prentice in his interpretation of the Birger figurine (1986, 263) and build on the works of Kent Reilly and members of his Mississippian Iconography Workshop. In so doing I use various lines of study including iconography and ethnohistorical accounts and incorporate depositional contexts as well (Knight 2012).

Depositional context is paramount in determining the timing of the distribution of female flint clay figurines outside Cahokia and is a key factor in discussing why they left. If they left at the time of manufacture and use at Cahokia, this might infer that they were part of sacred bundles associated with missionizing entourages and expectations for deposition would be in special use structures or related features; if they left after manufacture/use at Cahokia, this could be interpreted as emigrants from Cahokia taking with them sacred objects and relocating to new homes with outside groups. Thus their deposition would likely be in sacred bundles buried with individual bundle-keepers. Unfortunately, most of these figurines were discovered without the benefit of scientific methods. In order to develop any sense of chronology related to their departure and deposition, I incorporate data from the recovery of Cahokia flint clay male and animal figures as well. However, in spite of timing, my main argument is that these sacred objects left with Cahokians and were not traded, exchanged, or gifted to outsiders and were in turn buried with either original emigrants or their descendants (Boles 2020).

Suite of Cahokian Earth Mother figures not recovered at Cahokia proper

McBeth figurine

The most recent discovery or rather rediscovery of a female figurine was brought to my attention in 2018 (Boles and Lewis 2019). It was immediately clear upon inspection that this limestone pipe was of Cahokian manufacture. The broken figurine weighs over 2.3 kg and is 14.5 cm tall. It was carved in a kneeling position and placed on a circular disc-shaped platform (Colour Pl. 2). A skirt is visible above the knees and three strapped pouches are draped from her lower arms and another strapped pouch is grasped in the right hand. All the pouches have a single row of rectangular depressions below the openings. Her left hand is cradling a shallow circular basket or plate filled with six objects that resemble sunflower heads or perhaps lotus heads. Most of her upper body and head is missing. The figurine was drilled from the back for pipe use. In addition to breakage, the figurine was altered by heat as evidenced by reddened areas. There are also some raised reddish-orange areas that may be red ochre residue. Zak Lasemi, Senior Geologist with the United States Geological Survey, identified the limestone as coming from the St Louis formation and indicated that outcrops of this formation are present along the west bank of the Mississippi River below St.Louis (Zak Lasemi pers. comm. 2019).

The limestone figure-pipe had resided in a private collection in the East St Louis area for roughly 40 years. Although it bore a catalog number, the owner at that time did not have any provenience information. Given the intrigue and importance of this pipe a determined effort was made to learn more about its discovery. After nine months of research, the pipe's catalog number was tracked to an Ohio collector who purchased the pipe from the finder's family in 1944. His detailed journal entry included a well-drawn sketch of the figure-pipe and also revealed that it was found ca. 1935 near the Scioto River in Pickaway County, Ohio. This was an unexpected find spot as little evidence of interactions between Cahokia and upper Ohio Valley Fort Ancient groups have been reported (Cook 2015; Boles and Lewis 2019). Unfortunately, additional details of the figurine's discovery were not recorded.

Spiro figurine

The other non-flint clay female figurine found outside Cahokia is made from sandstone and was recovered in the 1930s by collectors at Spiro Mounds in Oklahoma. Hamilton (1952) referred to this figure pipe as the Woman with Mortar. This figurine is also kneeling on a circular platform (Fig. 3.1). There is a tall basket with vertical lines placed in front of her and she clutches what looks to be a strapped pouch in her right hand and a large shucked ear of maize in her left hand. She has an unusual, strapped pouch on her back with the straps extending down from circular projections on her shoulders. Judging from pictures, the circular projections may represent sunflower heads. The basket was drilled for use as a pipe; it is not clear if this was a post-manufacture conversion or part of the original design. I have not had the opportunity to examine this figurine first hand but, judging from a picture, it is clear that the left arm was broke in three places and a crack is visible spreading around the waist, both front and back. It is not clear however if this represents a complete break or just the beginning of one (see Brown *et al.* 2020, 98). The figurine also has numerous areas with black specks. These may be pigment residue, possibly the results of burning, or may merely be a natural deposit.

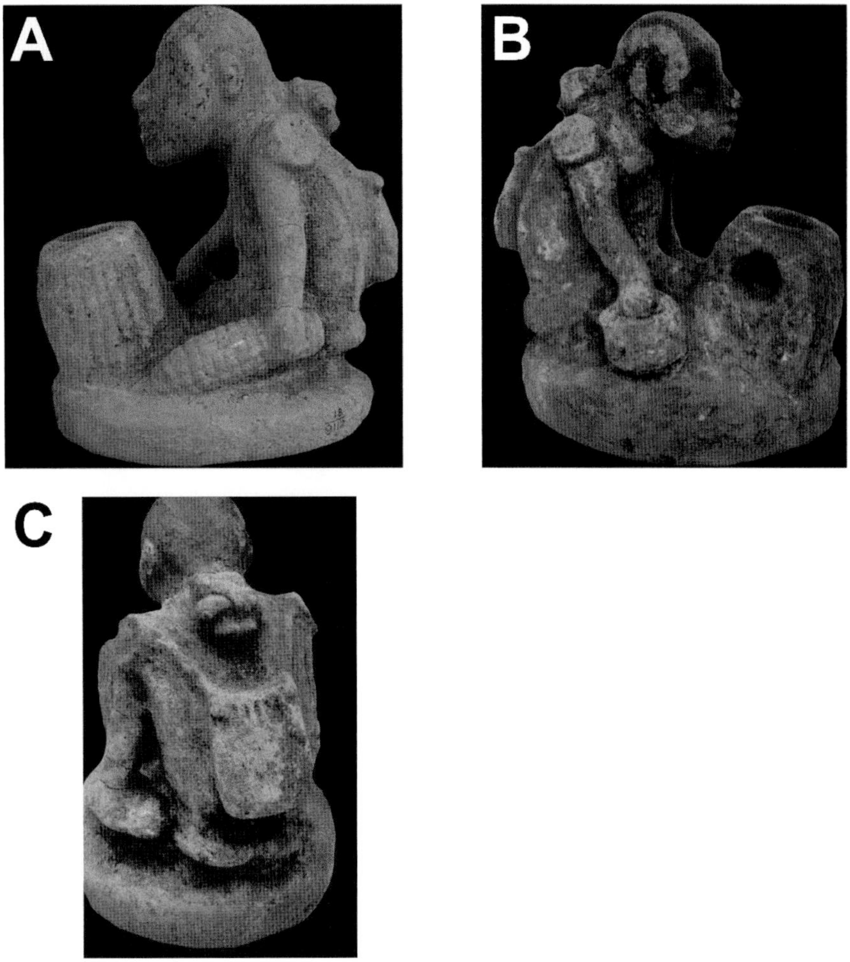

Fig. 3.1. Spiro female, LeFlore County, Oklahoma (sandstone).

This figure was recovered from inside what has been recently interpreted as the Spirit Lodge at Spiro in Le Flore County, Oklahoma. The Spirit Lodge was a hollow chamber inside the conical-shaped Craig Mound and was constructed directly over an earlier decommissioned ossuary (Brown *et al.* 2020). The hollow chamber was breached by a group of individuals known as the Pocola Mining Company in the early 1930s for the sole purpose of looting and selling artifacts. While much important contextual information was lost, various researchers have been able to reconstruct the placement of many of the artifacts taken from the hollow chamber. This important reconstruction has allowed for informed speculation on the unique nature of the deposit (Brown *et al.* 2020).

According to Brown *et al.* (2020) the Earth Mother figure was placed in the center of the hollow chamber feature and next to the curated human remains of a single individual that likely represents a sacred bundle. Numerous elaborate artifacts including woven baskets and other figurines made from both stone and wood were also placed in the hollow chamber (Brown *et al.* 2020, 102). One of the figurines, a male figure with elaborate paraphernalia, was made from Missouri flint

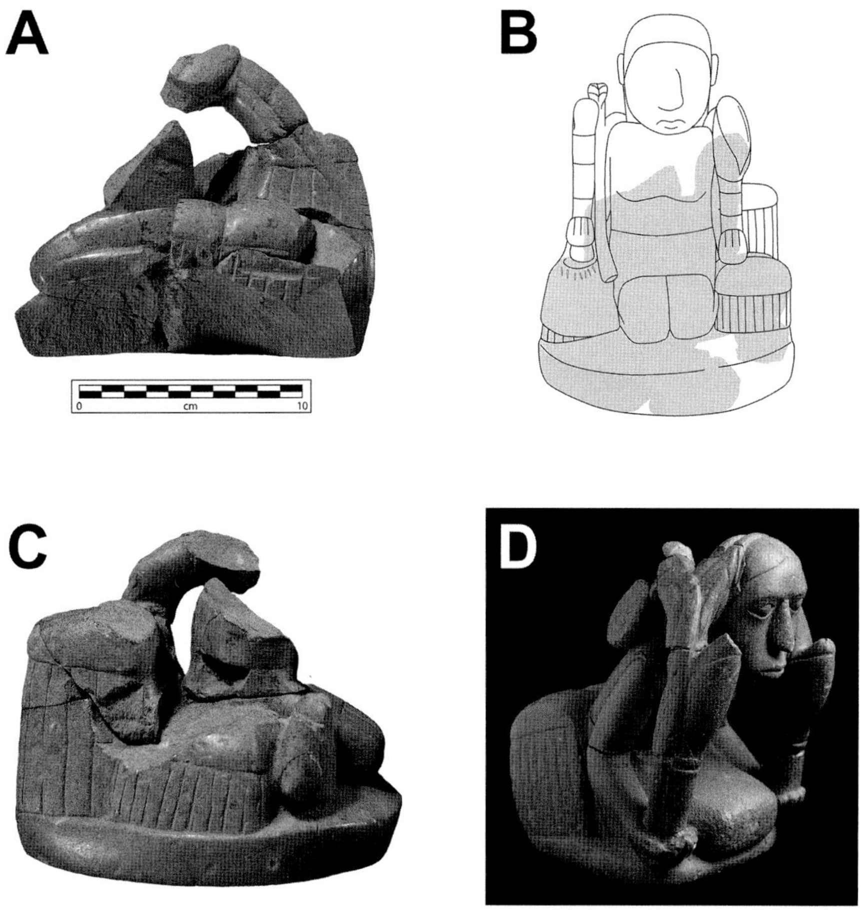

Fig. 3.2. A. Westbrook figurine, Desha County, Arkansas, flint clay; B–D. New Madrid figurine, New Madrid County, Missouri, flint clay.

clay and also carved in the Cahokia-style. Several other Cahokia flint clay figurines along with elite status items were recovered from burial contexts in the ossuary below the hollow chamber. The ossuary, often referred to as the Great Mortuary, was located in a 10 ft (3.05 m) high platform mound. Use of this mound began ca. AD 1200 with a crematory basin off one corner of the mound and a large central pit excavated to accommodate human remains. Closure of the ossuary has been placed at ca. AD 1400, which is when the construction of the hollow chamber commenced; closure of this chamber is suggested shortly after completion.

Westbrook figurine

The Westbrook figurine is made from flint clay and was recovered by two collectors, Harvey McGehee and Leon Tucker, at the Opossum Bayou site in Desha County, Arkansas in 1969 (Perino 1971; Boles 2014). The figurine depicts a kneeling figure on top of a large circular platform (Fig. 3.2A). A large, lidded basket is behind the figure and she appears to be emerging from it. She has both sunflower and probable maize stalks sprouting from her upturned hands that arch over her back.

The figurine was found with a single individual that McGehee identified as an adult female. She was buried in an intrusive shaft tomb burial ca. 9 ft (2.74 m) below the mounds surface (J.T. Ross, McGehee's son-in-law, pers. comm. 2018). The Westbrook figurine was smashed, possibly by a large, worked piece of galena found adjacent to it. Other grave goods included a discoidal, marine shell beads, two wooden copper covered bear canine effigy ear adornments, a copper pin and two Caddo Gahagan chert knives. The individual was also placed on top of a slab of white kaolin clay. The skull had been removed at the time of burial and replaced with a large conch shell dipper (Boles 2014). Incidental support of McGehee's evaluation on the sex of the individual may be inferred by de Bry's depiction of females serving males the black drink with conch shell cups (Fundaburk 2006, pl. 29). Additionally, the Exchange Avenue female flint clay figurine recovered from recent investigations at the East St Louis site is also depicted with a shell cup tilted on its side as if pouring its content (Emerson and Boles 2010; Boles *et al.* 2018).

New Madrid figurine

Another flint clay figurine was found in New Madrid County, Missouri (Boles 2014; 2017). The first fragments of this figurine were found in 2002. Since that time, a local surface collector has recovered additional pieces each year from a small-farmed site located in the floodplain roughly 4.4 miles (7 km) from the Mississippi River. At present 33 pieces have been recovered with 15 fitted together to form the bulk of the figure, the remaining pieces are clearly part of the same figurine but pieces are missing that would allow attachment to the main body. The figure is depicted in a kneeling position on a large circular disk (Fig. 3B–D). She is wearing a skirt and is surrounded by five lidded baskets, identical to the those depicted with the Westbrook and Spiro figures. Like the Westbrook figure, she appears to be emerging from the large basket behind her and also has what looks to be maize stalks sprouting from her hands. On her right side she also has a strapped pouch decorated with a row of rectangular depressions below the opening, again similar to the pouches depicted on the other figurines. At present, the upper chest and shoulder area as well as the head have not been recovered. Without excavation of the site, it's not clear if the figurine is coming from a special use/temple structure or possibly a disturbed burial. Hints of the latter may be inferred from the lack of additional ceremonial objects or even common everyday tools and debris in this small area; the only other artifacts reported in the vicinity of the figurine and assumed associated are four marine shell beads and two marine shell pendants.

Schild figurine

The last two female flint clay figurines were recovered in Illinois. Greg Perino recovered one of the figurines from a young female burial (20–35 years of age) at the Schild site in 1962 (Perino 1971, 25–6, 117; Goldstein 1980; Emerson 2003, 147). The Schild site is in Greene County, Illinois and approximately 50 miles (80.5 km) north of Cahokia Mounds. The figurine is depicted in a kneeling position on

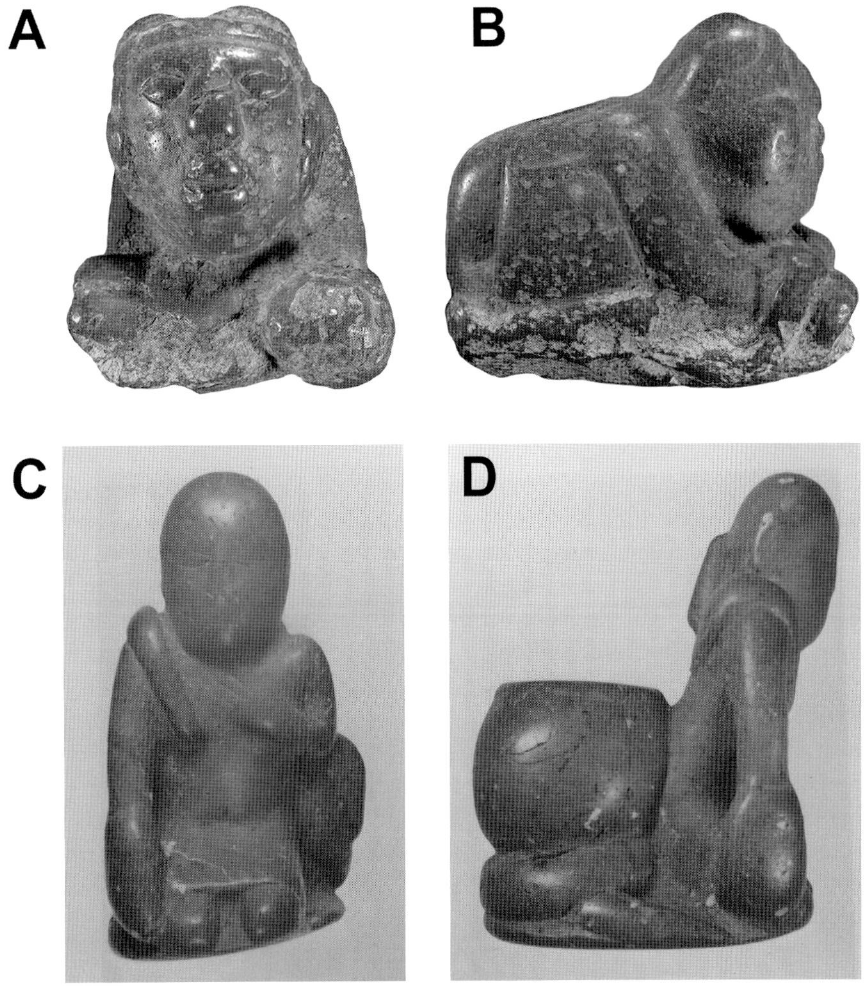

Fig. 3.3. Bostrom figurine, flint clay (A, B), Schild figurine, flint clay (C, D).

a circular platform or disk and is seated in front of a large bowl and seems to be emerging from it (Fig. 3.3D). The figurine shows extensive handling wear and much of the detail has been obscured. However, it is clear that a serpent is wrapped around the jar-shaped pipe bowl, an object is draped over her right shoulder, and her right hand is immersed in a pouch-like object or possibly morphing into a squash or gourd similar to the squash on the back of the Birger figure. Her left hand is placed over the left breast and she is clearly wearing a skirt that rest above the knees. Perino states that the pipe had been burned and fractured although he does not elaborate on the breakage. Judging from his photos it is clear that the pipe bowl had been broken off along with part of the snake coiled beneath it and it also appears that the left arm had been broken off. Prentice reported on a pattern of symbolic breakage or "killing" to Mississippian human effigies and noted that quite often one or both arms would be broken off or damaged (Prentice 1986, 242, 247–8).

Other associated grave goods include a Stirling phase Ramey incised jar, a frog effigy hooded water bottle, bone and shell tools, and skull parts from two weasels. Robert Hall suggested that the weasel skulls might represent a pair of weasel skin medicine bags (Emerson 2003a, 145). With this in mind, it is possible that the object draped over the figures shoulder is a medicine bag rather than a short-handled hoe as has been suggested (Emerson 1997b, 207). Based on the context and associated grave items, Emerson (2003) suggested that this individual may have been a shaman or healer.

Bostrom figurine

Two construction workers discovered the last figurine in this discussion. The Bostrom figure-pipe was reportedly found in 1955 from a disturbed burial along with numerous marine shell beads and an exceptionally crafted perforated Cahokia-style discoidal (Bob Simons pers. comm. 2017). The burial was located on a bluff top roughly 3 miles (4.8 km) northeast of Cahokia Mounds and very near the Kane Mounds (Emerson and Hargrave 2000). This figurine was carved to serve as a pipe and has a block-shaped body (Fig. 3.3B). The figure is kneeling and holds a smaller human figure in its out-stretched arms. Aside from hair ornaments or buns, the only other trapping is a strapped bag or pouch resting on the figures right side. This pouch has the row of rectangular depressions and is identical to the pouches depicted on three other figurines. The figure appears to have been heat-altered as evidenced by pot lids. The pot lids have been polished over from handling although it is not clear if this was done prehistorically or from recent handling. Flint clay is actually very soft and will polish within seconds when rubbed with just fingertips. The pipe also has what appears to be calcium carbonate deposits in various places; this is consistent with a mortuary deposit. Finally, the bowl is blackened from use.

Emerson (1983) originally interpreted the Bostrom figure as a male based on possible ear ornaments and the side pouch rather than a backpack as depicted on other female figurines. While it is true that only male figures have been depicted with ear ornaments, I would argue that the possible ear ornaments on this heavily worn figure may simply be protruding ears and that the pouch was placed on the side rather than the back to accommodate the pipe bowl. I know of no other male figure with a side pouch or backpack. This pipe is an excellent example that illustrates that Cahokian artisans produced figure-pipes as well as figurines. Therefore, figurines that were later drilled for smoking use was just as likely to have been done by Cahokians regardless of the widespread deposition of these figures (Boles 2020, 84).

Emerson later suggested that the Bostrom figure might also represent a shaman engaged in the retrieval of a lost soul as represented by the subordinate figure displayed in its outstretched arms. Emerson points out that shamans are often 3rd or 4th gendered individuals and it appeared that biological males more commonly took on women's roles or dress. He concluded that a baseline, male and female genders were being portrayed while identifying sex of the figures were generally unknown unless male genitals were depicted (Emerson 2003 146). With this in mind, the Bostrom figure displays both a male gender based on the headdress or possible ear ornaments and also a woman's gender with the bag on its side. The biological sex of this figure is not depicted and thus it may represent a male or female displaying both male and female accouterments. I include the Bostrom figure in this discussion as representing a female Earth Mother role based on the pouch or seed bag.

Summary

As is evident by the pictures and descriptions, the female figurines share a number of motifs. Four of the six figurines are depicted with sacred containers (baskets and ceramic vessels) and all appear to be emerging from or physically conjoined with them. Four of the six figurines have similarly decorated pouches or backpacks and are also depicted with sunflowers, probable maize, or both. Stand-alone motifs or depictions include a serpent with one figurine and a smaller second human figure with another. Collectively, the six outliers share a common fertility and regenerative theme and as mentioned earlier, have been interpreted as various representations of a general Earth Mother persona (Prentice 1986).

Depositional details as noted earlier are known for four of the six outlying female figurines. Three were recovered from mortuary contexts and a fourth associated with human remains at Spiro. The Spiro deposition is unique and the associated human remains appear to have been curated remains that were likely encased in a sacred bundle rather than representative of an individual interment. Unfortunately, sexes of the individuals interred are only known for two, Schild and Westbrook, both determined to be females.

Similarities in decommissioning rituals for the figurines are also noteworthy as five of the six were intentionally broken and three were heat-altered (Perino 1971, 120; Emerson and Boles 2010). Likewise, the female figurines from Cahokia proper were also heat-altered and often broken (Emerson and Boles 2010). Five of the six from Cahokia were broken, three of the five were also exposed to heat, and the one from East St Louis was just heat-altered.

A number of the burials containing Cahokia figurines also shared similar grave goods. Excluding Spiro, four with known items other than the pipes contained beads (Bostrom, New Madrid, Schild, and Westbrook) and two contained discoidals (Bostrom and Westbrook). Of interest, near the Bostrom find spot, one of the burials from Kane Mound #1 contained a burial episode with four adults and two children buried with two discoidals and 42 whelk beads. Another burial in Mound #1 contained an adult and child along with a flint clay tube pipe (Melbye 1963). This pipe is similar to the sucking tube inserted in the flint clay frog effigy pipe depicted with the human shaman figure referred to as the Frog Smoker found at Spiro (Emerson and Hargrave 2000; Emerson 2015). Although the Westbrook burial contained numerous other items not found in the other burials, the grave goods from all three burials may well have been incorporated into bundles. Assuming that the pipes were part of shaman/healer's paraphernalia, these pipes would've likely been incorporated into medicine bundles.

Discussion

Thematically, all 12 of the Cahokia-style female figures (from Cahokia proper and outliers) could be characterized as representations of a general Earth Mother persona based on shared accoutrements. However, several researchers have argued for a specific identity for the female figures such as the Old-Woman-Who-Never-Dies or Grandmother from ethnohistorical correlates of Hidatsa and Mandan mythology (Colvin 2012; Mueller and Fritz 2016; Fritz 2019). The link with the Old-Woman-Who-Never-Dies is her strong association with sunflowers and snakes, both commonly depicted on the female figurines. Sunflowers are depicted on the Westbrook, Sponemann, Birger, and possibly the McBeth and Spiro figurines and snakes/serpents are depicted on the West, Schild, and Birger figurines. The Old-Woman-Who-Never-Dies is also strongly associated with fertility and vegetation. Figurines depicted with probable maize representations include Westbrook, Sponemann (Fortier 1992), Spiro, and New Madrid. Although there is some disagreement on whether maize is being depicted (Mueller and Fritz 2016, 121; Fritz 2019, 110), I agree with Doug Jackson's assertion that until the "maize ears" are identified as some other plant, he is willing to allow the carvers some artistic license in depicting maize (Jackson 2017, 158; see also Fritz 2019, 110). In support of maize depictions, the ear in the hand of the Spiro female certainly looks to be maize (Prentice 1986, 260; Brown *et al.* 2020, 98) and the top of the left stalk on the New Madrid figurine is tasseled as seen on the basket behind the female (Boles 2017, 132).

Figurines with other vegetative elements include the Birger figurine with squash (Emerson 1984; Fritz 2019). As mentioned earlier, the Schild female may also have a squash or gourd depicted at the bottom of her right hand. Baskets and pouches have been interpreted as sacred bundles (Brown 2007, 55–6) and figurines depicted with lidded baskets include Westbrook, Spiro (I interpret what was originally identified as a mortar as actually being a basket, see Hamilton 1952, 36), New Madrid, and Keller. The Keller figurine not only has a basket with vertical lines in front of her, but also in my opinion here, is kneeling on top of small baskets with vertical lines that have been turned upside down (Emerson 1984, 260, pl. 8). If my interpretation is correct, she is in essence emerging from the sacred bundles similar to the Westbrook and New Madrid figures. Several figurines are depicted with pouches and include Spiro, New Madrid, McBeth, Bostrom, and Birger. Those with pouches are also reminiscent of other Earth Mother personas such as Corn Mother and Snake Woman, both of whom carried pouches of seeds to give to humankind (Dorsey 1905, 18). Additionally, three figures also have small hand-held strapped bags and include New Madrid, McBeth, and Spiro.

In addition to sharing a common theme it appears that most, if not all, the female figurines were decommissioned by fire, breakage, or both. This also holds true for most male and animal figurines as well (Prentice 1986; Emerson and Boles 2010; Boles 2020). Colvin (2012) also discussed this pattern and looking to ethnographic accounts for possible correlates noted that decommissioning rituals associated with Old-Woman-Who-Never-Dies images in Mandan and Hidatsa Goose societies revealed that during some ceremonies, the "Holy Women" would heat up the image and then douse it with water causing it to explode (Colvin 2012, 57, 62). Colvin also noted that the origin of the Old-Woman-Who-Never-Dies as related in the Hidatsa Sacred Arrow myth involved a woman being killed with a strike to the head by a rock from the heavens (Colvin 2012, 70). He points out that this mode of "ritual death" can be observed on the Birger, Keller and Westbrook figurines. I would add to the list the Spiro, New Madrid, and McBeth figurines (Boles 2017; Boles and Lewis 2019).

As suggested earlier, the figurines/figure pipes were likely incorporated into some type of bundle. Although the contents of bundles varied many were historically known to have included pipes (Dorsey 1904; Bowers 1965; Chamberlin 1982; Radin 1990). For instance, the Mandan Old-Woman-Who-Never-Dies bundle included a corn basket (representing the Old Woman) covered with an antelope hide, sacred arrows, a human scalp, a wooden pipe, two clay pots, a snakeskin, a foxskin, white sage, a gourd rattle, elkskin, a deer skull and horns, a piece of bearskin, blackbird heads, corn, beans, pumpkins, and sunflowers (Bowers 1965, 345). As for the inclusion of Cahokian figurines with human interments, a brief review of Historic period bundle transfers shows that bundle transfers were often purchased by initiates within the same clan and if there were no worthy initiates, the bundles were buried with last bundle keeper (Dorsey 1904, xx–xxii; Bowers 1965, 171, 201; Bailey 1995, 18; Hall 1997, 69). The Mandan and Hidatsa examples of women cults associated with Old-Woman-Who-Never-Dies bundles offer a notion that such bundles might be interred with female bundle practioners, bringing to mind the female burials at Schild and Opossum Bayou.

However, in direct contrast, the female figurines at Cahokia proper were used and decommissioned via fire and breakage at Stirling phase (AD 1100–1200) temples or special use areas near the mound centers in the bottomland. These locales were active use areas and ritual decommissioning's were part of ceremonial events, whether public displays or more intimate for a select audience or participants. In my opinion, this depositional contrast between use of female figurines at Cahokia and their inclusion in mortuary associations outside of Cahokia strongly infers that these figurines were not given, traded, or transferred to outsiders. After all, decommissioning via fire and breakage is consistent for these figurines whether at Cahokia or far away. This consistency would seem to suggest that those who possessed these female figurines outside of Cahokia knew the proper ritual for decommissioning even if they were to be placed in the burial of the last bundle keeper. It is also of no small consequence that an equal number of female figurines have been recovered from outside of Cahokia as in Cahokia proper. This is noteworthy when one considers the amount of excavation that has taken place at Greater Cahokia compared to other regions and that we know of five of the six outsider female figures based solely upon avocational or collector chance discoveries.

The downside of these unscientific discoveries is that we are largely left without datable contexts for the deposition of Cahokian female flint clay figurines. The only dated depositions are for Schild and Spiro. The Schild figure was interred with a female burial along with a Stirling phase Ramey Incised jar. Given the contemporaneity of production and use of flint clay figurines at Cahokia and the timing of deposition, it is possible that the female in the burial was the original figurine owner and Cahokian emigrant. As for the Spiro figure, deposition is placed at roughly AD 1400. This is some 200 years after the production and use of such figures at Cahokia appears to have ceased. At present, neither flint clay figurines of any gender or type nor production debris has been recovered from post Stirling phase features at Cahokia. This indicates that by ca. AD 1200, flint clay figurines/ figure pipes were no longer produced or actively used at Cahokia. Assuming that these figures were associated with bundles and related to ceremonial events no longer being performed, it seems doubtful that they would have been curated for any length of time at Cahokia, at least none has been found there to indicate otherwise. The temporal gap between their production and use at Cahokia and the deposit in the hollow chamber at Spiro entailed ten generations of curation. Other flint clay figurines recovered from the Great Mortuary contexts include seven males figures and one frog effigy (Boles 2020, table 3.1a). The timing for the onset of the Great Mortuary is placed at ca. AD 1250 (Livingood *et al.* 2020, 47), which provides the earliest date for deposition of the other flint clay figures. The only AMS dated context for a flint clay figurine found outside Cahokia was recovered at the Gahagan site in northwestern Louisiana.

Excavations at Gahagan by Moore and later by Webb, yielded two flint clay figures, one a frog effigy carved in the Cahokia style and the other an unusual male figure not carved in the Cahokia style. AMS dating was taken from two wooden artifacts and one leather object associated with the flint clay burials. A calibrated weighted average from the three samples provided a date range of cal. AD 1021–1160 at the two-sigma level (Emerson and Girard 2004, 62). Given the timing of flint clay figurine production at Cahokia during the Stirling phase (AD 1100–1200), the Gahagan flint clay burials would post-date AD 1100 and fall possibly near the mid-century mark. Regardless, the deposition of flint clay figurines with human interments bespeaks of bundle keepers as opposed to ceremonial use and deposition in special-use structures or related features as was carried out at Cahokia.

As mentioned earlier, Emerson has suggested that the female figurines at Cahokia were utilized in renewal ceremonies. Also noted earlier was the lack of pre-Stirling phase carved stone fertility figures and the post-Stirling shift to two dimensional male figures. The creation of and later cessation of female fertility figurines at Cahokia appears to coincide with the intensification of maize production ca. AD 1050 and the later onset of severe and persistent droughts ca. AD 1150–1200 (Benson *et al.* 2009). A similar scenario has been suggested for the use and deposition of the Spiro female figure. Brown and colleagues have interpreted the complex sequence of events at Spiro and suggest that the sacred objects within the Spirit Lodge were placed in diorama-fashion and representative of a stage whereby human and spirit interaction could take place (Brown *et al.* 2020, 98–9). Furthermore, they suggest that the Earth Mother figure was placed in the center of the Spirit Lodge and served as the conceptual *axis mundi* connecting the cosmological Upper, Middle, and Lower worlds. This ritual performance was to perhaps instigate a cosmic renewal that would evoke the rain-making deities to provide rain and thus end persistent droughts in the Lower Arkansas Valley and subsequently restore Caddoan political, religious, and social order (Brown *et al.* 2020, 122; Burnette *et al.* 2020).

Given the reverence and symbolic placement of the Cahokian Earth Mother in the Spirit Lodge at Spiro, it is relevant to ask how and why this figurine ended up in a seemingly foreign context. I would argue that it is perhaps not as much of a mystery as it might seem. Although some might suggest that the exotic nature of the figurine would have made it desirable, to the Caddoan in this case (*sensu* Helms 1988; 1993), I find it more plausible that this figurine and others from Cahokia ended up at Spiro and other locales with Cahokians who emigrated back to an ancestral homeland (Boles 2020, 78–9). Strontium isotope analysis of Cahokian burial populations revealed that as much as a third of the population at any point in Cahokia's history was non-local (Slater *et al.* 2014). Recent investigations at Cahokia's East St Louis Precinct revealed that as much as 13% of the early Mississippian arrow point assemblage was non-local as was roughly 3%t of the ceramic assemblage (Boles *et al.* 2018: Brennan *et al.* 2018). Much of these assemblages originated from the Caddoan region. Also of note, the Earth Mother persona was a commonly recorded mythological being among many Native American agrarian groups although specific names and creation stories varied for this persona (Hultkrantz 1957, 101–2; Prentice 1986, 249–62; Mueller and Fritz 2016, 114–17). The Caddo for instance referred to this being by various names including Mother Corn, Mother Moon, and Spider Woman (Dorsey 1905, 59; Prentice 1986, 254–5). It seems reasonable that the use of a Cahokian depiction of this persona by the Spiro Caddoan would have been acceptable given the likelihood of a shared mythology and ancestry (Boles 2020, 78–9).

In closing, the two Cahokia female figurines that have come to light in the last decade (McBeth and New Madrid) along with an often-overlooked figurine from Spiro and a reinterpretation of the Bostrom figurine have been important discoveries and revelations. Collectively they refine earlier notions that the female figurines generally stayed or were not allowed to leave Cahokia versus the male figurines that were sought by outsiders and allowed to leave under some form of exchange (Alt and Pauketat 2007, 244; Emerson 2015, 57–8; Pauketat 2009, 117). These new discoveries/revelations have also allowed for a re-evaluation of how and why these figurines ended up in faraway places.

We know that people began departing Greater Cahokia in the early to mid-AD 1100s and seemingly associated to some extent by the onset and intensification of droughts during that century. Over several generations, thousands of Cahokians emigrated to new locales in all directions. These emigrants took with them items needed for everyday survival as well as various bundles and religious sacra. Assuming the figurines discussed here represented Cahokian supernaturals, embodied spiritual power, and were incorporated into sacred, religious, or medicine bundles, it seems unlikely that these potent objects would have been traded, gifted, or transferred to outsiders (Bailey 1995, 18; Hall 1997, 69; Boles 2020, 80–6). Excluding the Spiro figure with unique context, three of the five remaining outlying female figurines were recovered from documented mortuary contexts. This would suggest that these items were personal possessions as opposed to community property and as such, likely buried with the last bundle keeper, two of whom were female religious leaders or healers. In some cases, Cahokian religious sacra may have been interred with original Stirling phase Cahokian emigrants such as Schild and Gahagan or passed down through numerous Cahokian descendants such as Spiro.

Finally, the brief argument presented here offers a reasonable explanation for migration and bundle constraints to account for Cahokian sacra in distant lands and with that, insight on what it may have meant when the Earth Mother left town.

References

Alt, S.M. and Pauketat, T.R. (2007) Sex and the Southern cult. In *Southeastern Ceremonial Cult: Chronology, Content, Context*, ed. A. King, 232–50. University of Alabama Press, Tuscaloosa AL.

Bailey, G.A. (1995) *The Osage and the Invisible World: From the works of Francis La Flesche.* University of Oklahoma Press, Norman OK.

Baltus, M.R. and Baires, S.E. (2020) Creating and abandoning "Homeland": Cahokia as place of origin. *Journal of Archaeological Method and Theory* 27, 111–27.

Baltus, M.R., Baires, S.E., Malouchos, E. and Mehta, J.M. (2020) Diasporic connections: Cahokia and the greater Southeast. *Journal of Archaeological Method and Theory* 27, 1–6.

Benson, L.V., Pauketat, T.R. and Cook, E.R. (2009) Cahokia's boom or bust in the context of climate change. *American Antiquity* 74, 467–83.

Boles, S.L. (2014) Supernaturals in the Confluence Region. Unpublished paper presented at the 71st Annual Meeting of the Southeastern Archaeological Conference, Greenville SC.

Boles, S.L. (2016) Cahokian Diaspora: Tracking migration through material culture. Unpublished paper presented at the Mid-South Archaeological Conference, Memphis TN.

Boles, S.L. (2017) Earth-Diver and Earth-Mother: Ancestral flint clay figurines from Cahokia. *Illinois Archaeology* 29, 129–48.

Boles, S.L. (2020) Tracking Cahokians through material culture. In McNutt and Parish (eds), 49–86.

Boles, S.L. and Lewis, M. (2019) Solving the McBeth figurine mystery: Professional and avocational collaboration and the importance of documentation. *Prehistoric American* 53, 36–9.

Boles, S.L., Ely, J.M., Poling, A.I., Holschen, M.S. and Kitchen, C.H. (2018) Lithics from the East St. Louis Precinct. In *Revealing Greater Cahokia, North America's First Native City: Rediscovery and Large-Scale Excavations of the East St. Louis Precinct*, eds T.E. Emerson, B.H. Koldehoff, and T.K. Brennan, 387–444. Studies in Archaeology 12, Illinois State Archaeological Survey, Prairie Research Institute, University of Illinois at Urbana-Champaign IL.

Bowers, A.W. (1965) *Hidatsa Social and Ceremonial Organization.* U.S. Government Printing Office, Washington DC.

Brennan, T.K., Betzenhauser, A.M., Lansdell, M.B., Plocher, L.A., Potter, V.E. and Blodgett, D.F. (2018) Community organization of the East St. Louis Precinct. In *Revealing Greater*

Cahokia, North America's First Native City: Rediscovery and Large-Scale Excavations of the East St. Louis Precinct, eds T.E. Emerson, B.H. Koldehoff, and T.K. Brennan, 147–202. Studies in Archaeology 12, Illinois State Archaeological Survey, Prairie Research Institute, University of Illinois at Urbana-Champaign IL.

Brown, J.A. (2007) On the identity of the Birdman within Mississippian period art and iconography. In *Ancient Objects and Sacred Realms: Interpretations of Mississippian iconography*, eds F. Kent Reilly and J.F. Garber, 56–106. University of Texas Press, Austin TX.

Brown, J.A., Barker, A.W., and Sabo, G. III (2020) The Spirit Lodge, Spiro ritual, and cosmic renewal. In *Recovering Ancient Spiro: Native American art, ritual, and cosmic renewal*, eds E.D. Singleton and F.K. Reilly III, 92–113. National Cowboy and Western Heritage Museum, Oklahoma City OK.

Burnette, D.J., Dye, D.H. and Hill, A.A. (2020) Climate change, ritual practice, and weather deities at Spiro. In *Recovering Ancient Spiro: Native American art, ritual, and cosmic renewal*, eds E.D. Singleton and F.K. Reilly III, 76–89. National Cowboy and Western Heritage Museum, Oklahoma City OK.

Chamberlin, V.D. (1982) *When the Stars Came Down from Heaven: Cosmology of the Skidi Pawnee Indians of North America.* Ballena, Los Altos CA.

Chapman, C.H. (1975) *The Archaeology of Missouri I.* University of Missouri Press, Columbia MO.

Colvin, M.H. (2012) Old-Woman-Who-Never-Dies: A Mississippian survival in the Hidatsa world, Unpublished M.A. thesis, Department of Anthropology, University of Texas, San Marcos TX.

Cook, R. (2015) Mississippians in a foreign land. In *Medieval Life in America's Heartland*, eds T.R. Pauketat and S.M. Alt, 54–60. School for Advanced Research Press, Santa Fe NM.

Dorsey, G.A. (1904) *Traditions of the Skidi Pawnee*, American Folk-Lore Society, Boston and New York.

Dorsey, G.A. (1905) *Traditions of the Caddo.* Carnegie Institution of Washington, Washington DC.

Emerson, T.E. (1982) *Mississippian Stone Images in Illinois*, Illinois Archaeological Survey, University of Illinois Urbana-Champaign IL.

Emerson, T.E. (1983) The Bostrom figure pipe and the Cahokian effigy style in the American bottom. *Midcontinental Journal of Archaeology* 8, 257–67.

Emerson, T.E. (1984) Stirling Phase occupation. In *The BBB Motor Site*, eds T.E. Emerson and D.K. Jackson, 197–321, American Bottom Archaeology FAI-270 Site Reports 6, University of Illinois Press, Urbana IL.

Emerson, T.E. (1989) Water, serpents, and the underworld: An exploration into Cahokian symbolism. In *The Southeastern Ceremonial Complex: Artifacts and analysis*, ed. P. Galloway, 45–92, University of Nebraska Press, Lincoln NE.

Emerson, T.E. (1997a) Cahokian elite ideology and the Mississippian cosmos. In *Cahokia: Domination and ideology in the Mississippian world*, eds T.R. Pauketat and T.E. Emerson, 190–228. University of Nebraska Press, Lincoln NE.

Emerson, T.E. (1997b) *Cahokia and the Archaeology of Power.* University of Alabama Press, Tuscaloosa AL.

Emerson, T.E. (2003) Materializing Cahokia shamans. *Southeastern Archaeology* 22, 135–54.

Emerson, T.E. (2015) Goddesses, priests, and ancestors: The Earth Goddess cult at Cahokia. In *Medieval Life in America's Heartland*, eds T.R. Pauketat and S.M. Alt, 54–60. School for Advanced Research Press, Santa Fe NM.

Emerson, T.E. and Boles, S.L. (2010) Contextualizing flint clay Cahokia figures at the East St. Louis Mound Center. *Illinois Archaeology* 22, 473–90.

Emerson, T.E. and Girard, J.S. (2004) Dating Gahagan and its implications for understanding Cahokia–Caddo interactions. *Southeastern Archaeology* 23, 57–64.

Emerson, T.E. and Hargrave, E. (2000) Strangers in paradise? Recognizing ethnic diversity on the fringes of Cahokia. *Southeastern Archaeology* 19, 1–23.

Emerson, T.E. and Hughes, R.E. (2000) Figurines, flint clay sourcing, the Ozark Highlands, and Cahokian acquisition, *American Antiquity* 65, 79–101.
Emerson, T.E. and Jackson, D.K. eds (1984) *The BBB Motor Site.* American Bottom Archaeology, FAI-270 Site Reports 6, University of Illinois Press, Urbana IL.
Emerson, T.E. and Lewis, R.B. eds (1991) *Cahokia and the Hinterlands: Middle Mississippian cultures of the Midwest,.*University of Illinois Press, Urbana IL.
Emerson, T.E., Hughes, R.E., Hynes, M.R. and Wisseman, S.U. (2002) Implications of sourcing Cahokia-style flint clay figures in the American Bottom and the Upper Mississippi River Valley, 309–38. *Midcontinental Journal of Archaeology* 27.
Emerson, T.E., Hughes, R.E., Hynes, M.R. and Wisseman, S.U. (2003) The sourcing and interpretations of Cahokia-style figurines in the trans-Mississippi south and southeast. *American Antiquity* 68, 287–313.
Emerson, T.E., Hedman, K.M., Brennan, T.K., Betzenhauser, A.M., Alt, S.M. and Pauketat, T.R. (2020) Interrogating diaspora and movement in the greater Cahokian world. *Journal of Archaeological Method and Theory* 27, 54–71.
Fortier, A.C. (1992) Stone figurines. In *The Sponemann Site 2: The Mississippian and Oneota Occupations*, eds D.K. Jackson, A.C. Fortier and J.A. Williams 277–304. American Bottom Archaeology FAI–270 Site Reports 24, University of Illinois Press, Urbana,
Fritz, G.J. (2019) *Feeding Cahokia: Early agriculture in the North American heartland.* University of Alabama Press, Tuscaloosa AL.
Fundaburk, E.L. (ed.) (2006) *Southeastern Indians Life Portraits: A Catalogue of Pictures, 1564–1935.* University of Alabama Press, Tuscaloosa.
Goldstein, L.G. (1980) Mississippian mortuary practices: A case study of two cemeteries in the Lower Illinois Valley. Northwestern University Archaeological Program, Scientific Papers 4, Northwestern University Archaeological Program, Evanston IL.
Hall, R.L. (1997) *An Archaeology of the Soul: North American Indian belief and ritual.* University of Illinois Press, Urbana IL.
Hamilton, H.W. (1952) The Spiro Mound. *Missouri Archaeologist* 14, 17–86.
Helms, M.W. (1988) *Ulysses' Sail: An ethnographic odyssey of power, knowledge, and geographic distance.* Princeton University Press, Princeton NJ.
Helms, M.W. (1993) *Crafts and the Kingly Ideal: Art, trade, and power.* University of Texas Press, Austin TX.
Hultkrantz, Å. (1957) *The North American Orpheus Tradition.* Ethnological Museum Monograph Series 2, Stockholm.
Jackson, D.K. (2017) Notes on the Birger and other flint clay figurines. *Illinois Archaeology* 29, 149–64.
Jackson, D.K., Fortier, A.C. and Williams, J.A. (1992) *The Sponemann Site 2: The Mississippian and Oneota occupations.* American Bottom Archaeology FAI-270 Site Reports 24, University of Illinois Press, Urbana IL.
Keller, W.D. (1944) The clays of Missouri. In *Geology of Missouri*, ed. E.B. Branson, 376–84. University of Missouri Studies 19.8.
Keller, W.D., Westcott, J.F. and Bledsoe, A.O. (1954) The origin of flint clays. *Proceedings of the Second Clay Minerals Conference* Publication 325, 7–46. National Academy of Science, Washington DC.
Knight Jr., V.J. (2012) *Iconographic Method in New World Prehistory.* Cambridge University Press, Cambridge.
Lankford, G.E. (2007) Some cosmological motifs in the Southeastern ceremonial complex. In *Ancient Objects and Sacred Realms: Interpretations of Mississippian iconography*, eds F.K. Reilly and J.F. Garber, 3–38. University of Texas Press, Austin TX.
Livingood, P., Regnier, A. and Hammerstedt, S. (2020) Spiro and surrounding sites. In *Recovering Ancient Spiro: Native American art, ritual, and cosmic renewal*, eds E. Singleton and F.K. Reilly, 36–53. National Cowboy and Western Heritage Museum, Oklahoma City OK.

McNutt, C.H. and Parish R.M. eds (2020) *Cahokia in Context: Hegemony and diaspora.* University of Florida Press, Gainsville FL.

McQueen, H.S. (1943) *Geology of the Fire Clay Districts of East Central Missouri.* Second Series 28. Missouri Geological Survey and Water Resources, Rolla MI.

Mehta, J.M. and Connaway, J.M. (2020) Mississippian culture and Cahokian identities as considered through household archaeology at Carson, a monumental center in north Mississippi. *Journal of Archaeological Method and Theory* 27, 28–53.

Melbye, F.J. (1963) *The Kane Burial Mounds*, Archaeological Salvage Report 15. Southern Illinois University Museum, Carbondale IL.

Milner, G.R. (1998) *The Cahokia Chiefdom: The archaeology of a Mississippian society*. Smithsonian Institution Press, Washington DC.

Mueller, N.G. and Fritz, G.J. (2016) Woman as symbols and actors in the Mississippi Valley: Evidence from female flint-clay statues and effigy vessels. In *Native American Landscapes: An engendered perspective*, ed. C. Claassen, 109–50. University of Tennessee Press, Knoxville TN.

Pauketat, T.R. (1997a) Cahokian political economy. In *Cahokia: Domination and ideology in the Mississippian world*, eds T.R. Pauketat and T.E. Emerson, 30–51. University of Nebraska Press, Lincoln NE.

Pauketat, T.R. (1997b) Specialization, political symbols, and the crafty elite of Cahokia. *Southeastern Archaeology* 16, 1–15.

Pauketat, T.R. (1998) Refiguring the archaeology of greater Cahokia. *Journal of Archaeological Research* 6, 45–89.

Pauketat, T.R. (2009) *Cahokia: Ancient America's great city on the Mississippi.* Penguin Books, London.

Pauketat, T.R, and Emerson, T.E. (1997) Conclusions: Cahokia and the four winds. In *Cahokia: Domination and ideology in the Mississippian world*, eds T.R. Pauketat and T.E. Emerson, 30–51. University of Nebraska Press, Lincoln NE.

Pauketat, T.R. and Lopinot, N.H. (1997) Cahokian population dynamics. In *Cahokia: Domination and ideology in the Mississippian world*, eds T.R. Pauketat and T.E. Emerson, 103–23. University of Nebraska Press, Lincoln NE.

Perino, G.H. (1971) The Mississippian component at the Schild Site (No. 4), Greene County, Illinois. In *Mississippian Site Archaeology in Illinois*, ed J.A. Brown, 1–141. Archaeological Survey, Urbana IL.

Prentice, G. (1986) An analysis of the symbolism expressed by the Birger figurine. *American Antiquity* 51, 239–66.

Radin, P. (1990) *The Winnebago Tribe.* University of Nebraska Press, Lincoln NE.

Reilly, F.K. III (2020) Foundational and cosmological themes in Braden-syle art. In *Recovering Ancient Spiro: Native American art, ritual, and cosmic renewal.* eds E. Singleton and F.K. Reilly, 220–33. National Cowboy and Western Heritage Museum, Oklahoma City OK.

Slater, P.A., Hedman, K.M. and Emerson, T.E. (2014) Immigrants at the Mississippian polity of Cahokia: Strontium isotope evidence for population movement. *Journal of Archaeological Science* 44, 117–27.

Watts Malouchos, E. (2020) Angel ethnogenesis and the Cahokian diaspora. *Journal of Archaeological Method and Theory* 27, 128–56.

Wilson, G.D., Bardolph, D.N., Esarey, D. and Wilson, J.J. (2020) Transregional social fields of the Early Mississippian Midcontinent. *Journal of Archaeological Method and Theory* 27, 90–110.

4

Altered states and cosmoscapes: The production and consumption of *Datura* in the Central Arkansas River Valley

Shawn P. Lambert

Throughout history, people have made, used, and combined special-purpose containers, iconography, and psychoactive plant materials from their surrounding landscapes to alter their daily lives and reach or communicate with something or someone beyond "normal" daily lived experiences. I refer to this combination as a hallucinogenic bundle. Hallucinogenic bundles occupy key roles in ceremonial practices and discourse and can alter or enhance behavioral practices and cosmological understandings when they are consumed for their mind-altering qualities (Schultes *et al.* 2001; Sayre 2018). In many ancient societies, hallucinogenic bundles were used to manifest specific visions, but also used for a variety of medicinal purposes (Rafferty and Mann 2004; Sayre and Bruno 2017). Ritual practitioners that used hallucinogenic bundles undoubtedly harbored special knowledge about different levels of plant toxicity to enter into altered states of consciousness and had the ability to decipher the meanings of the materials, imagery, and visions they experienced. The manipulation and use of these materials and iconography gave ritual practitioners particular resonance and power within their society (Rafferty 2018; Lambert *et al.* 2021).

The containers from which these psychoactive concoctions were consumed, associated imagery, and the plant intoxicants themselves have quotidian and ritual manifestations. However, these hallucinogenic bundles traditionally have been assumed to be simple attempts to flee the social realm (Sayre 2018), over-consumption (Dietler 2006), or temporary escape from everyday life and primarily used for informal events (Douglas 1987). Yet, the specific ritual contexts in which these bundles are discovered in the archaeological record in eastern North America show that they appear to be continually codified and mandated within local practices and traditions (Rafferty 2018; Lambert 2021). This chapter incorporates the idea of entanglement, lifeworlds, and cosmoscapes to understand how ritual practitioners used hallucinogenic ceramic bundles in the Central Arkansas Valley. I demonstrate that a hallucinogenic bundle can be theorized as a microcosmic conduit that ritual practitioners use to produce a kind of cosmoscape to enter and communicate with other worldly realms.

The hallucinogenic bundle I analyze here is the production and use of *Datura* from the Central Arkansas River Valley. *Datura* (*D. stramonium*) is a member of a family of flowering plants that contain potent alkaloids, scopolamine, and atropine, which can induce powerful hallucinations (Rafferty 2018). Many Native American cultures have used *Datura* for various medicinal and hallucinogenic purposes (Rafferty 2007; 2018). Direct botanical evidence of *Datura* use in preColombian times in eastern North America is limited. However, recent applications of organic residue analyses on preColumbian materials in North America have shown promising results, which indicate the widespread use and consumption of *Datura* (King *et al.* 2018; Robinson *et al.* 2020). For instance, research conducted by King *et al.* (2018) identified specific ceramic and marine shell vessels as containers from which Native people consumed a *Datura* hallucinogenic concoction. However, until now, archaeologists have not determined how indigenous communities in the Southeast prepared *Datura*.

Specifically, this chapter expands on recent research that identified a key *Datura* alkaloid (atropine) in residue samples collected from two unique polychrome-painted ceramic composite bottles with internal clay "filters" found in Late Mississippian contexts (AD 1400–1700) in the Central Arkansas River valley (Lambert *et al.* 2021). This research showed that ritual practitioners used specialized ceramic containers to produce and prepare *Datura* tea-like beverages and utilized the vessels' *Datura*-specific imagery during production and consumption to interact with cosmological forces. I will show how the Arkansas hallucinogenic bundles were "in-the-moment" events of cosmological understanding and transformation. These consciousness altering moments were important events when ritual practitioners re-affirmed or altered the understandings of their historical trajectories.

Datura research in eastern North America and beyond

Throughout the Americas, it appears that an essential cultural practice was (and still is) the use of hallucinogenic plants that induce a variety of altered states of consciousness, each of which affects human physiology and cognition in specific ways (Litzinger 1981; Benitez *et al.* 2018). Through recent research, archaeologists have become more aware of the importance of hallucinogenic plants in a variety of social, communal, religious, and ritual practices by Native Americans in eastern North America (Lankford 2014; King *et al.* 2018) as well as elsewhere in North America (Rafferty 2018). One of the most widely distributed of these plants used during the late pre-Columbian period in the Americas was the genus *Datura* (Geeta and Gharaibeh 2007). *Datura* is a member of the family Solanaceae, which includes plants such as nightshade (*Atropa belladonna*) and tobacco (*Nicotiana tabacum*). *Datura* is a flowering plant that contains intoxicant compounds known as alkaloids. The alkaloids that produce powerful hallucinogenic effects include atropine, scopolamine, and hyoscyamine, and an overdose of the alkaloids is potentially lethal (Lester *et al.* 1991). These alkaloids are also present in other genera of the Solanaceae family including angel's trumpet (*Brugmansia*) and mandrake (*Mandragora*), etc (Benitez *et al.* 2018).

Datura is a common wild plant found throughout the world, from North and

South America to Asia, Europe, and Africa (King *et al.* 2018). Specifically, *Datura* occurred locally throughout the American Southwest and eastern North America during pre-Columbian times (Litzinger 1981; Geeta and Gharaibeh 2007; Rafferty 2018). The preparation, use, and consumption of *Datura* are still poorly understood in the eastern North America. However, recent organic chemical, stylistic, and iconographic studies are beginning to shed new light on the cultural significance of *Datura* before the appearance of Europeans (Stahl 1985; Baker 1994; King *et al.* 2018; Robinson *et al.* 2020).

The presence of *Datura* has been confirmed at Mississippian period (AD 1000–1600) sites. One of the more significant discoveries of *Datura* was in the American Bottom at the BBB Motor Site near Cahokia. There, archaeologists discovered carbonized *Datura* seeds in context with a ceremonial feature inside a special-purpose structure (Emerson and Jackson 1984; Emerson 1989; see also Parker and Simon 2018, 139–42 for other Mississippian sites with archaeobotanical evidence of *Datura*). The presence of carbonized *Datura* seeds in a ceremonial feature indicates that the plant was in some way associated with ritual practices in late pre-Columbian societies in eastern North America (Wagner 2000; Rafferty 2018). Brown (1997, 474) discussed evidence that pre-Columbian ritual practitioners along the Atlantic coast used *Datura* to induce hallucinogenic experiences and male initiation rites, which "has lent further support to the belief that hallucinogenic experiences was once more commonplace in the Eastern Woodlands."

The use and cultural significance of *Datura* has also been proposed based on specific ceramic design attributes whereby potters chose to decorate primarily

Fig. 4.1. Noded Vessels from the central Mississippi Valley (adapted from Lankford 2012).

simple bowls with spiked/noded exteriors. Lankford (2012; 2014) studied 32 noded vessels from 21 late pre-Columbian sites in the CMV (Fig. 4.1). Lankford proposed that the form and arrangement of the nodes on these vessels represent the spikey fruit pod of the *Datura* plant. His findings were developed from previous research conducted by Litzinger (1981). He argued that there was a widespread *Datura* tradition from Mesoamerica through the Southwest. Litzinger also associated similar spiked/noded vessels with the use of *Datura* in the Southwest. In both cases, Litzinger and Lankford suggested that noded vessels were effigies of the *Datura* spiked fruit. Lankford argued that the Southwest *Datura* tradition and the use of noded ceramics passed from the Southwest to the Central Mississippi Valley, symbolic of a broadly shared "prehistoric shamanic complex" (Lankford 2012, 60). One way to associate the noded vessels directly with *Datura* use/consumption is to conduct organic residue analysis of this distinctive vessel form to detect alkaloids present in *Datura*. To our knowledge, archaeologists have not conducted this research.

In their significant contribution to *Datura* research in eastern North America, King *et al.* (2018) completed organic residue and iconographic analyses on several late pre-Columbian Mississippian/Caddo ceramic vessels and marine shell cups. This was the first time archaeologists used organic residue analysis to locate *Datura*-specific alkaloids preserved in ceramic and shell vessels from Caddo and Mississippian contexts. The residue analysis detected *Datura* alkaloids in several ceramic vessels and engraved shell cups. Their iconographic analysis correlated the use of *Datura* and the Beneath World, one of the three layers to the world conceived by many Native Americans. This multifaceted study has provided a better understanding of the rituals that involved *Datura* use, consumption, and imagery in the pre-Columbian world.

Preparation and use of Datura

To understand *Datura* preparations and its possible uses, it is important to look beyond the Eastern Woodlands where more research has been done. In many historical accounts, especially among the Chumash people, *Datura* preparation required specific people who possessed great knowledge of the plant, its hallucinogenic properties, and how to control concentration levels for medicinal and hallucinogenic purposes (Applegate 1975). All parts of the plant (e.g., seeds, petals, leaves, roots, and stems) contain hallucinogenic alkaloids, but studies have shown that its seeds and roots contain the highest alkaloid concentrations (Benitez *et al.* 2018). In several Hopi, Maya, and Aztec accounts of *Datura* preparation, seeds were commonly ground and added into liquid or animal fat mixtures for external and internal use (Litzinger 1981; Vanpool 2009; Robinson *et al.* 2020). *Datura* producers also boiled leaves and seeds, sometimes by mixing *Datura* with tobacco or fermented liquids in special ceramic jars to produce a hallucinogenic-inducing brew (Litzinger 1981; Guerra-Doce 2015). Roots were commonly roasted and boiled before consumption (Robinson *et al.* 2020). Recent studies have shown that *Datura* could be consumed by ingesting raw parts of the plant, chewing or sucking on plant parts, smoking leaves, or inhaling its vapors (Baker 1994; Benitez *et al.* 2018; Robinson *et al.* 2020). Practitioners used *Datura* for a wide range of medicinal and psychoactive purposes and the plant was used mainly in spiritual, ritual, and supernatural contexts (Robinson *et al.* 2020).

Arkansas composite bottles

The ceramic vessels used in this study are two Late Mississippian composite bottles held in the Harry J. Lemley collections of the Gilcrease Museum at the Thomas Gilcrease Institute of American History and Art in Tulsa, Oklahoma (Colour Pl. 3). Lemley was a Federal Judge in Arkansas during the first half of the 20th century, and during that time, he amassed a collection of over 3500 Mississippian ceramic vessels primarily from Arkansas and Missouri. After Lemley's death, the collection was donated to the Gilcrease Museum. Unfortunately, these vessels, along with the rest of Lemley's collection, have limited, if any, provenience information due to the likely less than standard recovery methods employed by collectors who recovered these many vessels. The two composite bottles' only contextual information are the counties in Arkansas from where they were discovered.

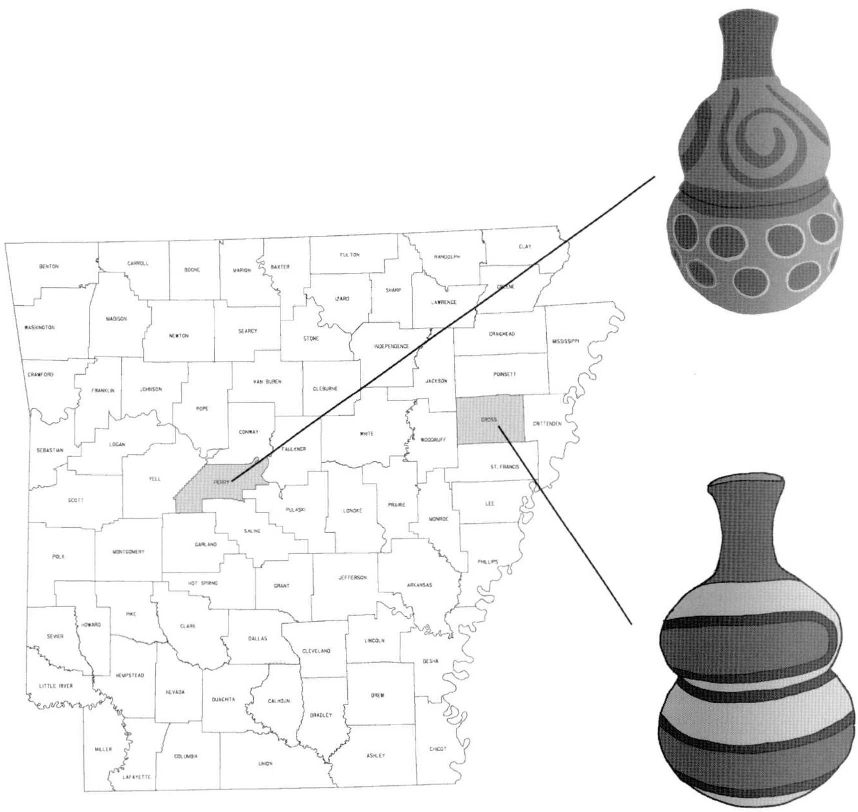

Fig. 4.2. Map of the locations where vessels may have been recovered.

The two ceramic bottles sampled are from Mississippian sites in Arkansas (Fig. 4.2). By studying the vessels' forms and polychrome painted decorations, both vessels are typed as Avenue Polychrome, dating between AD 1400 and 1700 (Phillips 1970). Avenue Polychrome painted vessels are usually well-represented in Carden Bottoms phase (AD 1400–1600) assemblages in the Central Arkansas River Valley (Jeter and Mintz 1990; Wiewel 2014). Avenue Polychrome bottles are primarily tempered with shell, have polished surfaces, out-flaring rims, flattened or slightly rounded lips, and constricted necks that are usually painted red. Most potters painted these vessels with red, white, and black pigments in curvilinear and rectilinear designs (Phillip 1970, 41).

Recently, Lambert *et al.* (2021) selected these two vessels to conduct organic residue analysis because of their unusual internal construction. Inside each bottle is a very thin internal clay shelf with a series of concentric perforated holes that has been incorporated below the juncture of the bottleneck with the globular portion of the body (Fig. 4.3). The only way potters could have placed the internal clay shelfs or filters in the bottles was during their initial construction. Both filters were joined to the interior walls when the clay was still wet. Lambert *et al.* (2021) argued that the internal perforated disks served as a filter or strainer that allowed the ritual practitioners to develop a concentrated brewed concoction from plant materials like *Datura*. According to Bell (1980, 95), the "presence of strainers in bottles is very rare and there are hundreds of bottles which do not have this device present." Bell also proposed that these internal clay disks were associated with the overall vessel form and may have functioned as a complex filtering device. There are a total of only four vessels from the Lemley Collection at the Gilcrease Museum that have internal clay filters. Lambert *et al.* (2021) were granted permission from the Gilcrease Museum to sample two of the vessels because parts of the internal clay filters were broken on them, allowing access to the base of the bottle to obtain a residue sample without damaging the intact filters.

Vessel #21

Vessel #21 is a shell-tempered composite bottle 25 cm in height with two globular sections, a constricted neck, and an out-flaring rim (Colour Pl. 3). The globular area just below the bottle neck has a red-painted spiral motif repeated four times around the body. The scrolls are zoned with faint residues of black paint. The constricted area in the middle portion of the bottle has a red-painted band outlined with black paint. The lower globular section is comprised of two rows of red-painted circles outlined with white paint. The internal clay filter is below the juncture of the bottleneck and the upper globular portion. In this vessel, there are three concentric circles of perforations and a large purposeful perforation in the middle.

Vessel #22

Vessel #22 is a shell-tempered composite bottle that also has an upper and lower globular section. The vessel, 23 cm in height, has a red-painted constricted neck

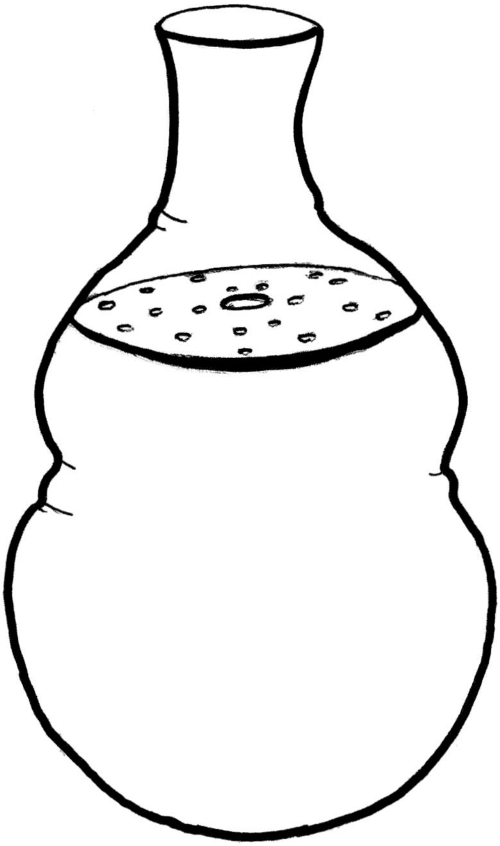

Fig. 4.3. Drawing of vessel with the location and design of internal clay filter.

with an out-flaring rim (Colour Pl. 3). The motif is a red and white interlocking scroll design outlined with black paint. This motif is repeated on the upper and lower globular sections. Like Vessel #21, the internal clay filter is below the juncture of the bottleneck and the upper globular portion. The filter also has a series of three concentric perforations. Due to damage, however, it is difficult to say if the filter also had a larger perforation in the center.

Defining hallucinogenic bundles as a microcosm

The archaeological record of eastern North America is scarce with examples of ancient communities expending significant amounts of labor to craft objects and procure organic materials to invoke consciousness-altering events, especially regarding the production and use of *Datura* (Spielmann 2008; King *et al.* 2018; Rafferty 2018; Lambert *et al.* 2021). Therefore, when these are found in restricted archaeological contexts, I assert they can be considered as hallucinogenic bundles or microcosms that ritual practitioners used to enact and interact with a cosmoscape. Because there is a strong relationship between special-purpose objects, like the bottles in this study, and relations between the ritual practitioners who made and used them, it is not uncommon for the objects to exhibit physical and symbolic manifestations of the individual(s) who constructed and used them and the world or worlds in which they represent. These constructs express the ceremonial, political, and/or social segmentation of a particular community, and the resulting creation is referred to by Spielmann (2008, 47) "as a microcosm or sociogram of the community." Here, the term "microcosm" generally refers to larger landscape features such as political centers, state capitals, and smaller landscape features such as kin groups and Hopewell earthworks (Spielmann 2008). However, I argue that single objects and the specialized ways in which people made and used them can also be regarded as microcosms. I adopt Ellen's (1986, 2) definition of microcosm as objects "constituting a little world in itself." In this vein, the associated iconography and objects and the ways people use them are fundamental parts of cosmological perceptions. Thus, a ceramic bottle could be a cosmologically compressed, complex symbolic network of all life's fundamental relations and important devices to interpret and reinterpret the worlds around people – a Rosetta Stone of reality. "Microcosms are therefore the middle-range incorporation of various complex symbolic registers in terms of a much smaller set of relations based on an aspect of experiential reality" (Ellen 1986, 3).

For objects to be considered microcosms, they need to be (1) produced, used, or deposited in ritual contexts, (2) ritual practitioners are the primary users of the crafted objects, and (3) restricted and viewed by only specific members of a community (Ellen 1986; Spielmann 2008). The unusually constructed Arkansas ceramic bottles appear to have been produced and used in ritual contexts. First, both bottles were found in mound contexts, likely in mortuary contexts but due to limited provenience their exact depositional contexts are uncertain. Archaeologists have argued that mound centers represent microcosms (Bernardini 2004; Carr and Case 2005; Spielmann 2008). Knight (1998) has used the concept of a microcosm to understand the spatial arrangement of the mounds at Moundville. Knight suggested that because the mounds are permanent fixed features on the landscape, they became a blueprint of important social distinctions of reality and ensured intergenerational stability through time and space. In this sense, mound centers are microcosms that re-affirmed the social memory of people who occupied that space (Wilson 2010). But what about the objects that people ritually deposited in the mounds? Archaeologists tend to focus primarily on the arrangement of large earthworks as the "fixed points" of a microcosm. While archaeologists who study these sites do not necessarily imply that all mound arrangements have microcosmic status, there seems to be a universality to its pervasive presence. What I am skeptical of are the implicit assumptions of mounds as fixed features on the landscape that represent a single microcosm, as though they are frozen in time. I believe this assumption produces a historically static view of the complex practices and traditions that occurred during mound construction, including specific local and non-local objects deposited during mound construction. In this light, ever-evolving mound centers can be theorized as an amalgamation of different microcosmic events, from accretionally built mound stages to the construction of on-mound structures and the use and deposition of ritualized objects. This concept in which specific objects have their own microcosmic presence in the construction of a communal ritual place, may aid us in understanding the true complexity of the roles that they played in pre-Columbian societies. Specifically, how ritual practitioners entangled themselves with ritualized objects to enact and interact with different cosmological lifeworlds.

In this spirit, I argue that we need to begin to recognize that objects deposited in mound contexts can also be distinct microcosmic events that expand site histories. Once we recognize that an object can be viewed as a microcosm, there are some questions that need to be answered. First, for whom are they a microcosm? Are they restricted for the ritual practitioners who made, used, and deposited them or were they intended to be seen by the entire community? During these microcosmic events, do ritual practitioners arrange the objects and imagery in some overall symmetrical pattern that is esoteric in nature or arranged in a manner that others can decode their meanings? In my experience with collaborating with several Native American groups, what is most interesting (probably to the chagrin of many archaeologists) is the inherent malleability of meaning of objects with microcosmic significance. Contemporary Native American artists who have revitalized ancient ceramic practices have looked at their own histories and maintain that objects and imagery have their own orders, understood in many ways to different people through time and space, and meaning can easily be transformed, distorted, or hidden (Earles 2015; Redcorn 2015). Furthermore, what is not always clear in such studies is whether or not the community conceived of an object in the same way as the ritual practitioners who wielded their powers as a cosmoscape.

These are the only composite bottles known to exist in eastern North America with internal clay filters that were used to produce *Datura* beverages. If they were available on a community-level, I would expect that they would have been recovered in domestic contexts as well. Their rarity of form and function also suggest that they were made by ceramic specialists. The fact that both were used to produce *Datura* also showcase their use in ritual contexts by ritual specialists.

Entanglement, lifeworlds, and cosmoscapes

How do we perceive the significance of ritual practitioners producing and using these ceramic bottles to enact and interact with different lifeworlds? First, objects and humans are constantly engaged with one another (Olsen 2010). According to Hurssel 1982, 214–15) "During moments people produce and use objects become a meaningful object of or for something." This type of intentionality and entanglement does not need to correspond to any "real" object or "real" event. Rather ritual practitioners can utilize objects as a means to create and interact with consciously experienced objects, non-human beings, and other related imagery that cannot be seen or experienced by others.

This ontological entanglement between objects, people, and places is what Husserl (1970) called lifeworlds and emphasizes the importance of life experiences with objects as fundamental for our understanding of the world and how we experience different lifeworlds (Olsen 2010, 60). Humans and objects are engaged things that are actively involved in the different lifeworlds they experience. This way, lifeworlds are not about how the world exists "in us" but how objects, people, and places "are in the world" as active agents (Matthews 2002, 28–9). Thus, interaction with specific objects allows people to experience and communicate with different lifeworlds as being-in-the-world.

Ritual practitioners' use of specialized containers to make and consume hallucinogenic properties is an entangled existence – they are tightly joined to the world in which they seek to understand and used to manifest different lifeworlds. To conceptualize the nature of these interacting lifeworlds in ritual practitioners' experiences of the objects, imagery, and altered states of consciousness in which they use to understand them, we can turn to the notion of cosmoscapes. A cosmoscape "is a reference of the complex whole within which [people] define their existence; it is also a model that portrays in its structure and functioning their social organization, shamanism, ranking, and gender relations" (Reichel 2012, 138). Reichel (2012) studied the cosmoscape of the Tanimuka and Yukuna people and how they use cosmoscapes to define their existence. Special purpose objects, imagery of sacred guardians, and important features on the mountainous landscape are dynamic parts of how they enact and experience their cosmoscape. Important here, with respect to this study, is the critical connection of sacred plant species and their use to open and communicate with different lifeworlds. Tanimuka and Yukuna ritual practitioners or shamans process and consume a variety of sacred hallucinogenic plants, like tobacco and other mind-altering plants, that not only represent the origins of their tribes, but also, they use them in "sacred centres" to connect to different cosmological realms (Reichel 2012, 142).

Potters across the Mississippian world, from Oklahoma to Florida, made a variety of composite bottles to understand the interactions and connections between their differing lifeworlds (Luer 1996; Lambert 2018). Archaeologists have suggested, since many are recovered from mound contexts and burned special purpose structures, ritual elites made and used composite bottles for specific ritual activities (Pauketat 1987). For example, composite bottles recovered from the Banks Village site in Arkansas may have been used to heat a liquid concoction for ritual consumption (Luer 1996). Prentice (1986, 112–13) argued that ritual practitioners used gourd-shaped composite bottles to make and serve hallucinogenic and medicinal beverages in several Southeast Native American groups. In Florida, during the contact period, gourd-shaped vessels with holes were used to produce the black drink (Fairbanks 1979, 131; Andrews and Andrews 1981, 24–5). One ethnohistorical account in the late 18th century documented an initiation ritual of a Creek war chief. During the initiation, a shaman and two warriors carried a red-painted gourd-shaped bottle that contained a brew made from a powerful plant (Milfort (1959, 138–40). The *Datura* plant may have been what was used during this initiation ritual, and the gourd-shaped vessel described sounds remarkably like the vessels in this study.

If ritual practitioners made and used the vessels as straining devices to produce a concentrated *Datura* compound to visualize and experience a cosmoscape, how did it operate? Lambert *et al.* (2021) proposed that this involved a three-step process to produce a concentrated *Datura* concoction. The first step for *Datura* makers would have been to procure, dry, and grind the *Datura* flowers, leaves, roots, and/or seeds before putting them into the filtering vessels. We also need to determine how the practitioners inserted the *Datura* plant remains through the filter. One possible way is through the large central hole in the strainers. *Datura* producers could have used this opening to insert the larger elements, like parts of the *Datura* flower, to rest at the bottom of the vessels. The next step may have been to add a liquid, like water, or some other liquid mixture. At this point, the large, dried elements and liquid are combined. Then, the mixture may have been put over a fire and heated. Lankford (2012; 2014) suggested that the *Datura* plant parts needed to be heated to release the highest concentration of hallucinogenic alkaloids (Lankford 2012; 2014). This has been shown in recent research into making other pre-Columbian beverages, such as cacao and yaupon (King *et al.* 2018). Therefore, the incorporation of dried *Datura* elements, liquids, and heat would have provided the required conditions to produce a concentrated *Datura* beverage. An experimental archaeology study could be conducted on vessel replicas to better understand the *Datura* drink-making process. Finally, to separate the hallucinogenic compound from the heavy organic materials, a simple tilt of the vessel would allow the liquid contents to escape, while the large materials would be unable to pass through the filter. These leftovers may have been used again or emptied by using a simple utensil.

A key summary point here is that a few combined things, like ceramic vessels, sacred plants, imagery, and the human body, can be used to experience an entire cosmoscape (Reichel 2012; Bold 2020). These hallucogenic bundles are used for ritualized thinking and perceiving powerful forces and nonhuman beings that maintain life, the world, and the universe. Likewise, the use of the Arkansas hallucinogenic bundles allowed ritual practitioners and perhaps other solicited participants to become a part and make sense of spiritual networks of powerful imagery, beings, and lifeworlds – giving a heightened awareness of the connections of people, places, and things of the universe.

Iconographic evidence of hallucinogenic bundles

Iconographic representations are another source of evidence to understand how ritual practitioners made and used *Datura* to produce a comsoscape. Some of the most illustrating depictions of *Datura* brewing and use associated with ritual practices are found in California and the American Southwest. For instance, Robinson *et al.* (2020) studied pinwheel pictographic imagery in a cave in California that they argue represents a blooming *Datura* flower. In context with the pinwheel imagery were several chewable 'quids' (small lumps of fibrous materials) that contained *Datura* prepared and chewed by shamans to enter altered states of consciousness. Likewise, in northeast Arizona, Malotki (1999) researched rock art imagery that he argued to be motifs resembling *Datura* as well as several anthropomorphic "shaman" figures holding Datura. Vanpool (2009) employed a cross-cultural comparative approach that highlighted the importance of *Datura* use in shamanistic practices and emphasized the common co-occurrence of *Datura* and imagery as an important ritual process to contact other cosmological realms. In the Mimbres region of the American Southwest, potters embellished ceramic bowls with *Datura* imagery and various geometric shapes that may have been the result of hallucinogenic-related visions (Berlant *et al.* 2018).

These examples show that it may have been a common ritual practice for *Datura* practitioners to combine the production and use of *Datura* concoctions with related imagery on different mediums to connect, manipulate, and record their cosmological journeys (Vanpool 2009; Dye 2012; Robinson *et al.* 2020). It is reasonable to suggest that the ritual practitioners utilized the bottles' imagery during *Datura* brew production to interact with their cosmological universe. Many southeastern Native American groups used special containers to produce and consume concentrated brewed beverages to induce altered states of consciousness as a way to connect with other cosmological realms (Luer 1996; Brown 1997; Loubser *et al.* 2018).

Fig. 4.4. Illustration showing the noded vessel (bottom right), the Datura spiked seed pod (upper right) and the polychrome vessel with Datura-like motifs (left).

The ritual specialists who made and used the Arkansas hallucinogenic bundles likely visualized a cosmoscape similar to other late pre-Columbian or Mississippian groups at that time. The Mississippian cosmos is based on opposing layers or three linked cosmological levels. Several locatives or visual keys have been identified that are characteristic of each cosmological realm (Reilly 2004; Reilly and Garber 2007). The layers include (1) the Beneath World comprised of water and underwater creatures, (2) the Above World of the sky, sun, and flying creatures, and (3) the Middle World of people, land, animals, and other natural elements (Lankford 2011; Dye 2012). People occupying the Middle World were in a constant battle to keep the two opposing worlds in balance. Religious practitioners wielded this sacred power to connect, communicate, and stabilize the cosmological realms through ritual propitiation and iconographic representation (Reilly 2004, 126). Surmising that specific imagery and consumption of *Datura* was a common practice to help reach another realm, the imagery embellished on the two Arkansas stacked vessels with *Datura* may have been used to help stimulate similar otherworldly experiences.

In this study, the vessels with internal clay filters also have configurations of motifs that may be cosmologically charged and associated with the four cardinal directions. The imagery on Vessel #21 was only analyzed because we believe it has complex representational imagery of *Datura*. The combination of motifs on Vessel

#21 is particularly noteworthy since the bottom portion and imagery may represent Mississippian cosmological precepts and *Datura* seed pods. The iconography on the lower globular portion of this vessel – a series of red-painted circles and outlined in white – is perhaps indicative of the spiked fruit of the *Datura* plant (Fig. 4.4). This interpretation is similar to Lankford's (2012, 2014) identification of a series of noded vessels from the CMV and Caddo areas as effigies pots that portray the *Datura* plant's spiky fruit. The bottom portion of composite bottle #21 has a similar form to Lankford's noded vessels, and the painted circles may be a two-dimensional representation of the circular *Datura* seed pods.

Recent analyses suggest that *Datura* use and motifs can be associated directly with Mississippian cosmologies. For example, David Dye (2015) has suggested that a series of female effigy bottles may be associated with the use of *Datura* in the Lower Mississippi Valley. Specifically, Dye (2015, 14) likened the posture and "vacant look about the face" as a stylized depiction of a trance-like state, perhaps during the ritualized use of *Datura*. King *et al.* (2018) also sampled one of these female effigy bottles and the residue results were positive for *Datura*, supporting Dye's (2015) argument. Several Native American groups in eastern North America consider the female to represent the night sky, a known reference to the Beneath World (Duncan and Diaz-Granados 2004). In this context, female effigy bottles of this type may represent the Beneath World and the powers that women brought to their communities (King *et al.* 2018). Lankford (2014) has suggested that the green pigments, such as glauconite, found on ceramic containers may have represented the blue/green spit of the nocturnal sphinx moth, who is known as the pollinator of the *Datura* flower. Spiral and winged motifs on Moundville bottles and the famous Moundville Willoughby disk have also been attributed as representations of the sphinx moth (Knight and Franke 2007).

These interpretations could have implications for the interpretation of the four spiral motifs located on the upper globular portion of Vessel #21 under the bottleneck. An overhead view of the spirals in relation to the opening of the bottle shows that they are in quadripartite configuration, connected to the four cardinal directions in the Mississippian cosmos (Reilly 2007). According to Lankford's (2007) research on Cox Mound gorgets, the location of the spirals may specify a specific cosmological direction that reflects the directional powers of the Middle World. Thus, the spirals that make up the motif at the top portion of the bottle may represent the Middle or This World. However, the spiral motifs could also be indicative of the sphinx moth's proboscis (*sensu* Knight and Franke 2007). If this is true, the vessel could also have Beneath World associations, similar to research findings by Lankford (2012; 2014) and King *et al.* (2018). Recent research of stacked bottles from Caddo ceremonial mound centers (e.g., Lambert 2017; King *et al.* 2018) has shown that the vessel form is just as important as the motifs. The form of the bottles may represent layers of the cosmos, and by pouring the *Datura* tea from the bottom of the bottle, *Datura* makers and consumers were also taking powers from the Beneath World bringing them into the Middle World (see also Reilly 2011). Whatever the meanings were hundreds of years ago, the iconography, form, and construction of these bottles leads to a confident conclusion that ritual practitioners used the objects, imagery, and *Datura* to enact a cosmoscape of one or more lifeworlds that connected them in some way to a broader understanding of their cosmological universe.

For *Datura* research, there are several questions that remain unanswered that can help us understand the lifeworlds of past people. Can we use stylistic and iconographic research to understand *Datura* use? Can finding *Datura* archaeobotanical evidence in ceremonial contexts and comparing archaeological evidence with early written texts help us determine its use in ritualized practices? Was *Datura* use and consumption available to all members of a society or was its use restricted to ritual specialists? Is there any evidence of *Datura* use in domestic contexts? Can evidence be found of *Datura* use in earlier (pre-AD 1400) Caddo/Mississippian contexts? How was Datura prepared and ingested by pre-Columbian groups: by filtering it into a tea-like drink, smoking it, or both? The evidence obtained from the study of organic residues in unique composite Mississippian bottles from the CMV is a beginning point to answer (1) how did pre-Columbian people prepare *Datura* using a unique set of ceramic vessels, (2) what does the imagery on the vessels mean with respect to *Datura* production and consumption, and (3) how does *Datura* consumption construct cosmoscapes in different ritual contexts? It is fair to say that collaboration with contemporary Native American groups will also be critical to understand how their ancestors were entangled with people, places, and objects and how they experienced and defined cosmoscapes.

Conclusions

The material, temporal, and cosmological being-in-the-world is always a hybrid experience and is the moment when people can use ritualized objects to create connections between different times, pasts, and places. This is as much the case for the Arkansas hallucinogenic bundles. This chapter indicates how ritual practitioners may have utilized the Arkansas hallucinogenic bundles as part of a cosmoscape to better understand their lifeworlds, where their vertical cosmological realms of the Above, Middle, and Beneath Worlds are as crucial as the horizontal linkages that connect people, objects, and places together. Ritual practitioners used these ritualized bundles to enter altered states of consciousness to experience and communicate with other cosmological temporalities. Exactly what, we may never know. From the evidence presented in the study, they may have used the bundles to negotiate human existence or to monitor and balance their opposing lifeworlds. Lastly, ritual practitioners may have used mind altering events to maintain the worldviews of their communities from the information they obtained, decoded, and communicated.

References

Andrews, E.W. and Andrews, C.M. eds (1981) *Jonathan Dickinson's Journal or God's Protecting Providence*. Southeastern Printing, Stuart FL.

Applegate, R.B. (1975) The Datura cult among the Chumash. *Journal of California Anthropology* 2, 6–17.

Baker, J.R. (1994) The Old Woman and her gifts: Pharmacological bases of the Chumash use of *Datura*. *Curare* 17, 253–76.

Bell, R.E. (1980) *Oklahoma Indian Artifacts*. Contribution from the Stovall Museum, University of Oklahoma, Norman OK.

Benitez, G., March-Salas, M., Villa-Kamel, A., Chaves-Jimenez, U., Hernandez, J., Montes-Osuna, N., Moreno-Chocano, J. and Carinanos, P (2018) The genus *Datura L.* (Solanaceae) in Mexico and Spain – ethnobotanical perspective at the interface of medical and illicit uses. *Journal of Ethnopharmacology* 219, 133–51.

Berlant, T., Maurer, E. and Burtenshaw, J. (2018) *Decoding Mimbres Painting: Ancient ceramics of the American South*. Prestel, New York.

Bernardini, W. (2004) *Hope Oral Tradition and the Archaeology of Identity*. University of Arizona Press, Tucson AZ.

Bold, R. (2020) Constructing cosmoscapes: Cosmological currents in conversation and contestation in contemporary Bolivia. *Journal of Ethnographic Theory* 10, 195–208.

Brown, J.A. (1997) The archaeology of ancient religion in the eastern Woodlands. *Annual Review of Anthropology* 26, 465–85.

Carr, C. and Case, D.T. (2005) The gathering of Hopewell. In *Gathering Hopewell*, eds C. Carr and D.T. Case, 19–50. Springer, Boston MA

Dietler, M. (2006) Alcohol: Anthropological/archaeological perspectives. *Annual Review of Anthropology* 35, 229–49.

Douglas, J.E. (1987) Late prehistoric archaeological remains in the San Bernardino Valley southeastern Arizona. *Kiva* 53, 35–51.

Duncan, J.R. and Diaz-Granados, C. (2004) Empowering the SECC: The "Old Woman" and oral tradition. In *The Rock Art of Eastern North America: Capturing images and insight*, eds C. Diaz-Granados and J.R. Duncan, 190–215. University of Alabama Press, Tuscaloosa AL.

Dye, D.H. (2012) The Duck River Cache and Middle Mississippian Ritual Performance. Unpublished paper presented at the 23rd Annual Meeting of Current Research in Tennessee Archaeology, Nashville TN.

Dye, D.H. (2015) Earth Mother Cult Ceramic Statuary in the lower Mississippi Valley. Unpublished paper presented at the 72nd Annual Southeastern Archaeological Conference, Nashville TN.

Earles, C.K. (2015) Traditional Caddo potter. *Journal of Northeast Texas Archaeology* 54,101–10.

Ellen, R. (1986) Microcosm, macrocosm and the Nuaulu house: Concerning the reductionist fallacy as applied to metaphorical levels. *Bijdraden tot de Taal - en Volkenkunde* 142, 1–30.

Emerson, T.E. (1989) Water, serpents and the Underworld: An exploration into Cahokia symbolism. In *The Southeastern Ceremonial Complex: Artifacts and analysis*, ed, P. Galloway, 45–92. University of Nebraska Press, Lincoln NE.

Emerson, T.E., and Jackson, D.K. (1984) *The BBB Motor Site*. University of Illinois Press, Urbana IL.

Hursserl, E. (1970) *The Crisis of European Sciences and Transcendental Philosophy* III. Northwestern University Press, Evanston IL.

Hursserl, E. (1982*) Ideas Pertaining to a Pure Phenomenology and to a Phenomenological Philosophy.* Kluwe Academic, Dordrecht.

Fairbanks, C.H. (1979) The function of black drink among the Creeks. In *Black Drink, A Native American Tea*, ed. C. M. Hudson, 120–49. University of Georgia Press, Athens GA.

Geeta, G.R. and Gharaibeh, W. (2007) Historical evidence for a pre-Columbian presence of *Datura* in the Old World and implications for a first millennium transfer from the New World. *Journal of Bioscience* 32, 1227–44.

Guerra-Doce, E. (2015) The origins of inebriation: Archaeological Evidence of the consumption of fermented beverages and drugs in prehistoric Eurasia. *Journal of Archaeological Method and Theory* 22, 751–82.

Jeter, M.D., and Mintz, J.J. (1990) Ceramics from the Goldsmith Oliver 2 Site. In *Goldsmith Oliver 2 (3PU306): A protohistoric archeological site near Little Rock, Arkansas*, Vol. I, eds M.D. Jeter, K.H. Cande, and J.J. Mintz, 255–316. Report submitted to the Federal Aviation Administration by Arkansas Archeological Survey.

King, A., Powis, T.G., Cheong, K.F., Deere, B., Pickering, R.B., Singleton, E. and Gaikwad, N.W. (2018) Absorbed residue evidence for prehistoric *Datura* use in the American Southeast and Western Mexico. *Advances in Archaeological Practice* 6, 312–27.

Knight, V. (1998) Moundville as a diagrammic ceremonial center. In *Archaeology of the Moundville Chiefdom*, eds V.J. Knight and V.P. Steponaitis, 44–62. Smithsonian Institution Press, Washington DC.

Knight, V.J. and Franke, J.A. (2007) Identification of a moth/butterfly supernatural in Mississippian art. In Reilly and Garber (eds), 136–51.

Lambert, S.P. (2017) Alternative Pathways to Ritual Power: Evidence for centralized production and long-distance exchange between northern and southern Caddo communities. Unpublished PhD dissertation, Department of Anthropology, University of Oklahoma, Norman OK.

Lambert, S.P. (2018) Addressing the cosmological significance of a pot: A search for cosmological structure in the Craig Mound. *Caddo Archaeology Journal* 28, 21–37.

Lambert S. P. (2021) Imagery in motion: Object itineraries of Spiro Engraved vessels. In *New Methods and Theories for Analyzing Mississippian Imagery*, eds B.T. Giles and S.P. Lambert, 219–245. University of Florida Press, Gainsville FL.

Lambert, S.P., Perttula, T.K. and Gaikwad, N.W. (2021) Production matters: Organic residue evidence for late pre-Columbian *Datura*-making in the Central Arkansas River Valley. *Advances in Archaeological Practice* 10(2), 1–11.

Lankford, G.E. (2007) Some cosmological motifs in the Southeastern ceremonial complex. In Reilly and Garber (eds), 8–38.

Lankford, G.E. (2011) The swirl-cross and the center. In *Visualizing the Sacred: Cosmic visions, regionalism, and the art of the Mississippian world*, eds G.E. Lankford, F.K. Reilly III and J.F. Garber, 251–78. University of Texas Press, Austin TX.

Lankford, G.E. (2012) Weeded out the noded. *Arkansas Archaeologist* 50, 50–68.

Lankford, G.E. (2014) Following the noded trail. *Arkansas Archaeologist* 53, 51–68.

Lester, R.N., Nee, M. and Estrada, N. (1991) Solanaceae III – taxonomy, chemistry, evolution. In *Proceedings of Third International Conference on Solanaceae*, ed. J.G. Hawkes, 197–210. Royal Botanic Gardens, Kew.

Litzinger, W. (1981) Ceramic evidence for prehistoric Datura use in North America. *Journal of Ethnopharmacology*. 4, 57–74.

Loubser, J., Ashcraft, S. and Wettstaed, J. (2018) Betwixt and between: The occurrence of petroglyphs between townhouses of the living and townhouses of spirit beings in northern Georgia and western North Carolina. In *Transforming the Landscape: Rock art and the Mississippian cosmos*, eds C. Diaz-Granados, J. Simek, G. Sabo III and M. Wagner, 200–41. American Landscapes 4. Oxbow Books, Oxford

Luer, G.M. (1996) Mississippian ceramic jars, bottles, and gourds as compound vessels. *Southeastern Archaeology* 15, 181–91.

Malotki, E. (1999) The use of hallucinogenic plants by the archaic-basketmaker rock art creators of the Palavayu, northeast Arizona: The case for *Datura*. *American Indian Rock Art* 25, 101–20.

Mathews, E. (2002) *The Philosophy of Merleau-Ponty*. McGill-Queen's University Press, Montreal.

Milfort, L. (1959) *Memoirs, or a Quick Glance at My Various Travels and My Sojourn in the Creek Nation*. Trans and ed. B.C. McCary. Continental Book, Kennesaw GA.

Olsen, B. (2010) *Archaeology and the Ontology of Objects.* AltaMira Press, Lanham CA.

Parker, K.E. and Simon, M.L. (2018) Magic plants and Mississippian ritual. In *Archaeology and Ancient Religion in the American Midcontinent*, eds B.H. Koldehoff and T.R. Pauketat, 117–66. University of Alabama Press, Tuscaloosa AL.

Pauketat, T.R. (1987) A functional consideration of a Mississippian domestic vessel assemblage. *Southeastern Archaeology* 6, 1–15.

Phillips, P. (1970) *Archaeological Survey in the Lower Yazoo Basin, Mississippi, 1949-1955.* Papers of the Peabody Museum of Archaeology and Ethnology 60. Cambridge MA.

Prentice, G. (1986) Origins of plant domestication in the eastern United States: Promoting the individual in archaeological theory. *Southeastern Archaeology* 5, 103–19.

Rafferty, S.M. (2007) The archaeology of alkaloids. In *Theory and Practice of Archaeological Residue Analysis*, eds H. Barnard and J.W. Eerkens, 179–88. British Archaeological Report S1650, Archaeopress, Oxford.

Rafferty, S.M. (2018) Prehistoric intoxicants of North America. In *Ancient Psychoactive Substances*, ed. S.M. Fitzpatrick, 112–27. University of Florida Press, Gainesville FL.

Rafferty, S.M. and Mann, R. (2004) Smoking pipes and culture. In *Smoking and Culture: The archaeology of tobacco pipes in Eastern North America*, ed. S.M. Rafferty, xi–xix. University of Tennessee Press, Knoxville TN.

Redcorn, J. (2015) Traditional Caddo potter. *Journal of Northeast Texas Archaeology*, 54, 101–10.

Reichel, E. (2012) The landscape in the cosmoscape, and sacred sites and species among the Tanimuka and Yukuna Amerindian tribes (northwest Amazon). *Sacred Species and Sites: Advances in Biocultural Conservation*, eds G. Pungetti, G. Oviedo and D. Hooke, 127–51. Cambridge University Press, Cambridge.

Reilly, F.K. III (2004) People of earth, people of sky: Visualizing the sacred in native art of the Mississippian period. In *Hero, Hawk, and Open Hand: American Indian art of the ancient Midwest and South*, eds R. Townsend and R.V. Sharp, 125–38. Yale University Press, New Haven CO..

Reilly, F.K. III (2007) The petaloid motif: A celestial symbolic locative in the shell art of Spiro. In Reilly and Garber (eds), 39–55.

Reilly, F.K. III (2011) The Great Serpent in the lower Mississippi Valley. In *Visualizing the Sacred: Cosmic visions, regionalism, and the art of the Mississippian world*, eds G.E. Lankford, F.K. Reilly III and J.F. Garber, 118–36. University of Texas Press, Austin TX.

Reilly, F.K. III and Garber, J.F. eds (2007) *Ancient Objects and Sacred Realms: Interpretations of Mississippian Iconography*. University of Texas Press, Austin TX.

Robinson, D.W., Brown, K., McMenemy, M., Dennany, L., Baker, M.J., Allan, P., Cartwright, C., Bernard, J., Sturt, F., Kotoula, E., Jazwa, C., Gill, K.M., Randolph-Quinney, P., Ash, T., Bedford, C., Gandy, D., Armstrong, M., Miles, J. and Haviland, D. (2020) *Datura* quids at Pinwhel Cave, California, provide unambiguous confirmation of the ingestion of hallucinogens at a rock art site. *Proceedings of the National Academy of Sciences* 117, 31026–37.

Sayre, F. (2018) The politics of the anthropogenic. *Annual Review of Anthropology* 41, 57–70.

Sayre, M.P. and Bruno, M.C. (2017) *Social Perspectives on Ancient Lives from Paleoethnobotanical Data*. Springer, New York.

Schultes, D., Close, T.J., Graner, A., Langridge, P., Matsumoto, T., Muehlbauer G., Kazuhiro S., Schulman A.H., Waugh R., Roger P. W. and Stein, N. (2001) The International Barley Sequencing Consortium: At the threshold of efficient access to the barley genome. *Plant Physiology* 149, 142–7.

Spielmann, K. (2008) Crafting the sacred. *Research in Economic Anthropology*, 27, 37–72.

Stahl, P.W. (1985) The hallucinogenic basis of early Valdivia Phase ceramic bowl iconography. *Journal of Psychoactive Drugs* 17, 105–23.

Vanpool, C.S. (2009) The signs of the sacred: Identifying shamans using archaeological evidence. *Journal of Anthropological Archaeology* 28, 177–90.

Wagner, G.E. (2000) Tobacco in prehistoric eastern North America. In *Tobacco Use by Native Americans: Sacred smoke and silent killer*, ed. J.C. Winter, 185–201. University of Oklahoma Press, Norman OK.

Wiewal, R. (2014) Constructing Community in the Central Arkansas River Valley: Ceramic compositional analysis and collaborative archaeology. Unpublished PhD dissertation, Department of Anthropology, University of Arkansas, Fayetteville AR.

Wilson, G.D. (2010) Community, identity, and social memory at Moundville. *American Antiquity*, 75, 3–18.

5

Oneota and Tunican cosmoscapes in the Lower Mississippi Valley

David H. Dye and Toney Aid

Studies of iconography and ritual institutions are witnessing a resurgence in archaeology. For example, an iconographic approach to Mississippian ritual objects and sacra is increasingly seen as an indispensable perspective in ongoing arguments, debates, and interpretations that further our appreciation and understanding of cosmoscapes and their denizens (Townsend and Sharp 2004; King 2007; Reilly and Garber 2007; Lankford *et al.* 2011; Knight 2013; Diaz-Granados *et al.* 2015; Carmody and Barrier 2020). Cosmoscapes are envisioned as animate, dynamic, and multiscalar, encompassing networks of human and other-than-human beings sedimented in reciprocal obligations (Pavel 1981; Berlo 2011; Bold 2020). Objects created as agentic images of cosmoscapes may act as microcosms, to which people may appeal, conjure, supplicate, and transform (Lankford 2004). Likewise, recent interest has focused on the nature of Mississippian institutional entanglements and interconnections among people, their cosmoscapes, and other-than-human beings (Lankford 2008; Pauketat 2013; Holland-Lulewicz *et al.* 2020). In addition, studies of Mississippian ritual have become central to contemporary theoretical and methodological discussions of entanglements, negotiations, and political power (Baires 2017; Alt 2018; Diaz-Granados *et al.* 2018; Koldehoff and Pauketat 2018; Singleton and Reilly 2020; Dye 2021c).

Negotiations within the framework of social institutions underlie webs of connections among humans, other-than-human beings, and things within the seen and unseen worlds (Donnellan 2020). People with differing ontologies, however subtle, endure, reach agreements, resist, and transform the multiple pathways to power, prestige, and wealth through material goods and their myriad employments in ritual practice and protocols. In this sense, exotic goods as inalienable objects may be deployed within political and ritual economies with performative sacra and ritual paraphernalia included as a vital component of dialogues, mediations, negotiations and power brokering. We draw upon ethnographic and ethnohistoric accounts of ritual sodality membership, sacra circulation, and social boundaries to illustrate how people create ritual institutions to further opportunities for affiliations and negotiations. For example, Calumet-like ceremonies and ritual sodalities as communities of practice bring people together as congregations to discharge cosmic debts and supplicate other-than-human beings.

Following Miriam Stark's (1998) work on social boundaries, we ask how style may be evaluated in the archaeological record by presenting a case study for evaluating stylistic engraved imagery that is alien to the resident ceramic production of the northern Lower Mississippi Valley (nLMV). This region is the homeland of Mississippian Tunican-speakers, who lived along the Mississippi River between the confluences of the Arkansas and Ohio rivers. We recognize two stylistic traditions of engraving: 1) an indigenous nLMV Tunican engraving and 2) an Eastern Prairie or Midwestern Oneota engraving. Despite differences in style however, shared cosmological themes are evident. When found in the nLMV, both engraving traditions are generally restricted to Tunican ceramic bottles. We envision these engraved ceramic bottles, and associated ritual goods, as portable boundary objects that cross social boundaries rather than demarcating them (Star 1989; Star and Griesemer 1989; Wenger 1998; 1999). Such objects facilitate the transmission process when potters as social brokers, often with differing agendas and divergent backgrounds, histories, and identities come into contact (Mills 2018). In this sense the unit of analysis for engagements in social practice is the ritual communities of practice that people form through social participation as individuals within the intersection of social institutions as they pursue negotiated mutual enterprises.

We argue that nLMV engraved imagery reflects the active roles of identity, meaning, social practice, and ritual negotiations among distant and politically distinct populations: nLMV Tunicans and Midwestern Oneota. Mississippian and Oneota interactions were frequently violent, often resulting in intercommunity conflict, loss of life, population displacement, and trophy taking, especially in the thirteenth and fourteenth centuries (Hollinger 2005; 2018; Milner *et al.* 1991). In the late sixteenth century, mechanisms for cooperation gain ascendancy, promoting greater flows of iconographic imagery and ritual goods. After reviewing distinctions in Mississippian and Oneota artistry, we turn to a brief discussion of Oneota and Tunican ritual entanglements and negotiations. Next, we examine the material evidence for Oneota and Tunican interactions. And finally, we draw some conclusions concerning Oneota imagery appearing on Tunican bottles between the mid-16th century Hernando de Soto expedition and the mid-17th century Tunican population collapse and subsequent migration down the Mississippi River and out of the nLMV.

Cosmoscapes, entanglements, and negotiations

Archaeologists have recently focused their attention on investigating ritual as a means to contest and negotiate reciprocal power relationships among people and other-than-human beings within broader shifting and unbounded cosmoscapes (Barber and Joyce 2018; Bold 2020; Howey 2020). Iconography provides an important focal point for insights into these web-like ritual interactions and interconnections among ethnically distinct polities, focusing our attention on the ways disparate groups negotiate multiple pathways to political and social agendas through the depiction of celestial realm beings. Such social fields are dynamic and continually in motion, being collectively constituted, with other-than-human beings, people, and things collaborating and entangled in myriad relations (Latour 2005). Beliefs in animate cosmoscape relationships stem from the interplay of agency, political power, and ritual efficacy (Berlo 2011; Reichel 2012; Slater 2014). Thus, cosmoscapes produce different ontological realities shared at multiple scales and negotiated among individuals with differing histories through ritual practice (Berlo 2011; 2014; Pavel 1981; Reichel 2012; Slater 2014; Bold 2020).

Oneota and Tunican artisans recorded their cosmological conceptions on ceramic bottles and stone, leaving an important corpus of iconographic imagery. These depictions of other-than-human beings draw our attention to cosmopolitical entanglements and negotiations among artisans and ritual practitioners at a time of encroaching European colonialism. We envision such interactions as sedimented in the agency of actors who actively negotiate political, and social roles, creating opportunities for community interaction and culture contact (Nordine 2000). Here, interactions possess ritual components in which connections with other-than-human beings are made paramount and permanent. Such cosmopolitical conversations, discourse, and negotiations among Oneota and Tunica artisan ritual practitioners reflect the mutual flows of ideas, things, and values, resulting in the creation of animistic depictions and engravings on ceramic bottles, disk pipes, human remains, stone slabs, and symbolic weaponry. Isabelle Stengers (2005, 995) characterizes cosmopolitics as "the unknown constituted by multiple divergent worlds, and to the articulation of which they would eventually be capable". We perceive Oneota and Tunican political agency as concentrated in the engravings of cosmological motifs and other-than-human beings and undertaken as components of mutually beneficial negotiations within ritual contexts.

Animistic figural motifs on ceramic bottles reflect the divergent and multiple worlds of Oneota-Tunica interactions and the entanglements of ideas, images, things, and values. Rather than static or timeless ritual forms, we propose the engravings encapsulated a historical trajectory of ancestral and non-human agency embodied in an iconographic corpus of Oneota figural imagery engraved on Tunican ceramic bottles (Fig. 5.1). These engraved vessels and their artistic production, political agency, and ritual practice instill a sense of cosmic transformations, rather than mute imagery to the craftsperson, engraver, and practitioner. Thus, cosmoscapes and their conceptualizations are contested and negotiated by ritual practitioners engaged in contrasting ontologies that reflect competing cosmological perspectives and cultural narratives. Mississippian artisans created dynamic cosmoscapes through engraved and painted symbolic microcosms on cave walls, ceramic vessels, marine shell, and rock art.

Figural imagery embodies complex cosmoscapes, which ritual specialists map or replicate in terms of humans, other-than-human persons, and embedded or enmeshed cosmic realms. For Oneota and Tunican ritual practitioners the world is not anthropocentric, but rather, humans are but one component of complex webs of interconnected relationships conjoining animals, humans, landscapes, and other-than-human beings into dynamic, entangled, and ongoing cosmoscapes.

Fig. 5.1. Engraved Oneota-style Thunderer engraved on a Tunican bottle, Lacey site (3PO41), Poinsett Co. AR (photograph: Toney Aid).

The ceramic vessel thus becomes the embodiment of the world created by transcendental beings at the dawn time. As is the case with Navajo sandpaintings, ceramic vessels conceptually diagram the motions of an animate and dynamic universe existing in the "mythopoetic context of layered time, space, and meaning" (Griffin-Pierce 1992, 7).

Rituals conducted within animate landscapes provide access and linkages to socio-religious based power and privilege. Mississippian plazas, for example, served as arenas where rituals could be publicly enacted to construct, contest, and negotiated (Kidder 2004; Cobb and Butler 2017), while medicine lodges and temples provide space for legerdemain theatrics that showcased powers bestowed and transferred to ritual practitioners by other-than-human beings (Dye 2020). To tap into the inherent powers of the cosmoscape, ritual specialists not only accessed the dawn time, but also performed and recounted its creation and the beginning of human existence (Morphy 1995; Staller 2008). Through rituals involving magical drugs, medicinal drinks, and purifying emetics, Mississippians created and maintained connections with spiritual entities at the ideological moment of creation through reciprocal obligations and cosmic debts (Cobb and Stephenson 2017).

Eastern North American indigenous cosmoscapes, comprised of horizontal partitions and vertical layers, include the Above World, This World, and the Beneath World as well as the cardinal directions. Each realm and its denizens could be accessed or conjured through offerings, performances, prayers, rituals, and supplications. In these cosmoscapes spiritual and socio-political power overlap, as the religious practices of diverse congregations and constituencies are bolstered, contested, negotiated, resisted, and undermined (Joyce 2018). Individuals understood to have demonstrated particular spiritual powers emerge as ritual practitioners, their efficacy deriving from transfers of powers from guardian spirits and other-than-human beings that reside in the surrounding cosmoscape.

Ritual engagements promote the resolution of conflicting cosmological currents, premising ontological landscapes where interacting cosmopolitical understandings manifest an actor's experiences of the world (Pavel 1981). Oneota and Tunica ritual programs within which contestation, negotiation, and resistance play out are materialized through these engraved ceramics depicting other-than-human beings. Politically strategic decisions may be predicated on cosmopolitical conversations among ritual practitioners where reality is "fragmented, and many worlds can be at play in the same moment, contesting each other for relevance, or complementing one another's perspectives" (Bold 2020, 197). We envision Oneota figural art on Tunican bottles as exhibiting cosmological beliefs in which conflicting or contrasting worldviews may be created, negotiated, resisted, and resolved.

Oneota and Tunican worlds: AD 1550–1650

The Oneota world underwent significant changes in the 15th and 16th centuries (Henning 1970; Green 1995; Hollinger and Benn 1998; Berres 2001; Brown and Sasso 2001; Hollinger 2005; Shirar 2019). People began moving into large regional centers, creating vast distances between not only Oneota groups, but also Oneota and non-Oneota populations. For example, some 560 km separate the Oneota Chariton locality on the Lower Missouri River from their Tunican neighbors to the south along the nLMV. Inter-regional interactions between such groups began to thrive, implementing and transforming ritual protocols and relationship building, such as the Calumet ceremony, which became widely established throughout eastern North America (Blakeslee 1981; Gunderson 1993; Hollinger 2005; 2018). Archaeologists have noted how the Calumet ceremony was central to establishing peaceful relationships and creating ritual partnerships between individuals in the early contact period (Brown 1989; 2006; Hall 1997).

After AD 1500, eastern prairie polities took on a relative uniformity in material culture that was to characterize them until well into the 17th century (Brown and Sasso 2001, 212). Oneota Siouan speakers, who had had long-term connections with the Upper Mississippi Valley (Springer and Witkowski 1982), began moving westward into the Great Plains. At the same time, Algonquian speakers migrated westward from the Great Lakes and Central Ohio Valley into the eastern prairies. In the early 17th century small amounts of European items appear in the southern Great Lakes area as trade in and competition for these goods began to increase interpolity contact. To facilitate these transactions, to forge alliances, and to safeguard traders and travelers, the Calumet ceremony drew upon earlier, pre-existing rituals (Fletcher 1904; Blakeslee 1975; 1981; Brown 1989; 2006; Hall 1997).

Large trading centers emerged, often located at strategic points along major rivers connecting Oneota groups with distant areas. At the Utz site in the Chariton region, for example, nLMV and Southwestern ceramics, Minnesota pipestone, and southern Appalachian face mask gorgets are evident (Bray 1991), in addition to European trade goods (Bray 1978; Mason 2006). Oneota contact and exchange with non-Oneota groups peaked during this "classic" period as evidenced by Oneota figural imagery, motifs, and objects in non-Oneota contexts such as the Lower Ohio (Pollack 2004), Middle Ohio (Griffin 1943; Drooker 1997), Middle Missouri (Warren 2007), and nLMV (Jolly 1983) areas.

Oneota site clusters in the Chariton region of central Missouri were comprised of Chiwere and Dhegihan Siouan speakers (Yelton 1998): the Missouria appearing in the early 15th century and the Osage migrating into the area in the 16th century (McMillan 2014). While violent conflict characterized by long-distance, small-scale raiding continued, new territories were neither gained nor existing ones lost. Warfare now emphasized the fulfillment of individual interests in war honors and personal prestige (Hollinger 2005). Although inter-community conflict continued, inter-regional exchange began to thrive as ritual peacemaking mechanisms and alliance building, such as the Calumet ceremony, became necessary to maintain communication and trade. By the early 1600s, mid-continent populations were being destabilized by indirect but nevertheless increasing effects of European contact. In response, leaders employed Calumet-like rituals to establish fictive kin relationships with traditional enemies to build alliances, establish peace, and promote exchange (Hollinger 2005).

The Tunican world also became fundamentally and irrevocably transformed with the influx of people into extreme southeastern Missouri and northeastern Arkansas from the Mississippi-Ohio rivers confluence region (MORCR) in the late fourteenth century (Burnette *et al.* in press; Morse and Morse 1983). New towns and polities arose as the nLMV witnessed a crowded and heavily fortified landscape, resulting in cosmoscape and ritual transformations due to competition, negotiations, resistance, social conflict, and warfare. For example, ritual sodalities that supplicated specific other-than-human beings may have suffered membership loses due to new alignments with the cosmoscape. While Tunican contacts with Oneota populations are not evident in MORCR in the thirteenth and fourteenth centuries, interactions appear in the new social landscape of the late sixteenth to early seventeenth century, a time when the ramifications of European colonization reach deep into eastern North America (Fig. 5.2).

Tunican speakers as a linguistic isolate had been deeply entrenched in the nLMV well to the south of Oneota settlements, constituting a region of culturally diverse polities (Haas 1940; Anderson and Maxwell 2019; Kaufman 2019). The entrance of the Hernando de Soto expedition in May 1541 provides a critical window into the Tunican world. The expedition chroniclers document considerable animosity among regional rulers, often erupting in warfare (Dye 1994), with alliances typically brokered through marriages and rituals (Lankford 2008, 115–35). By the late 16th century pan-regional ritual goods had undergone an expansion throughout the nLMV, evidencing strong ties with Oneota groups to the north and Mississippians to the east.

Competition among polities over European goods in the mid-continent began

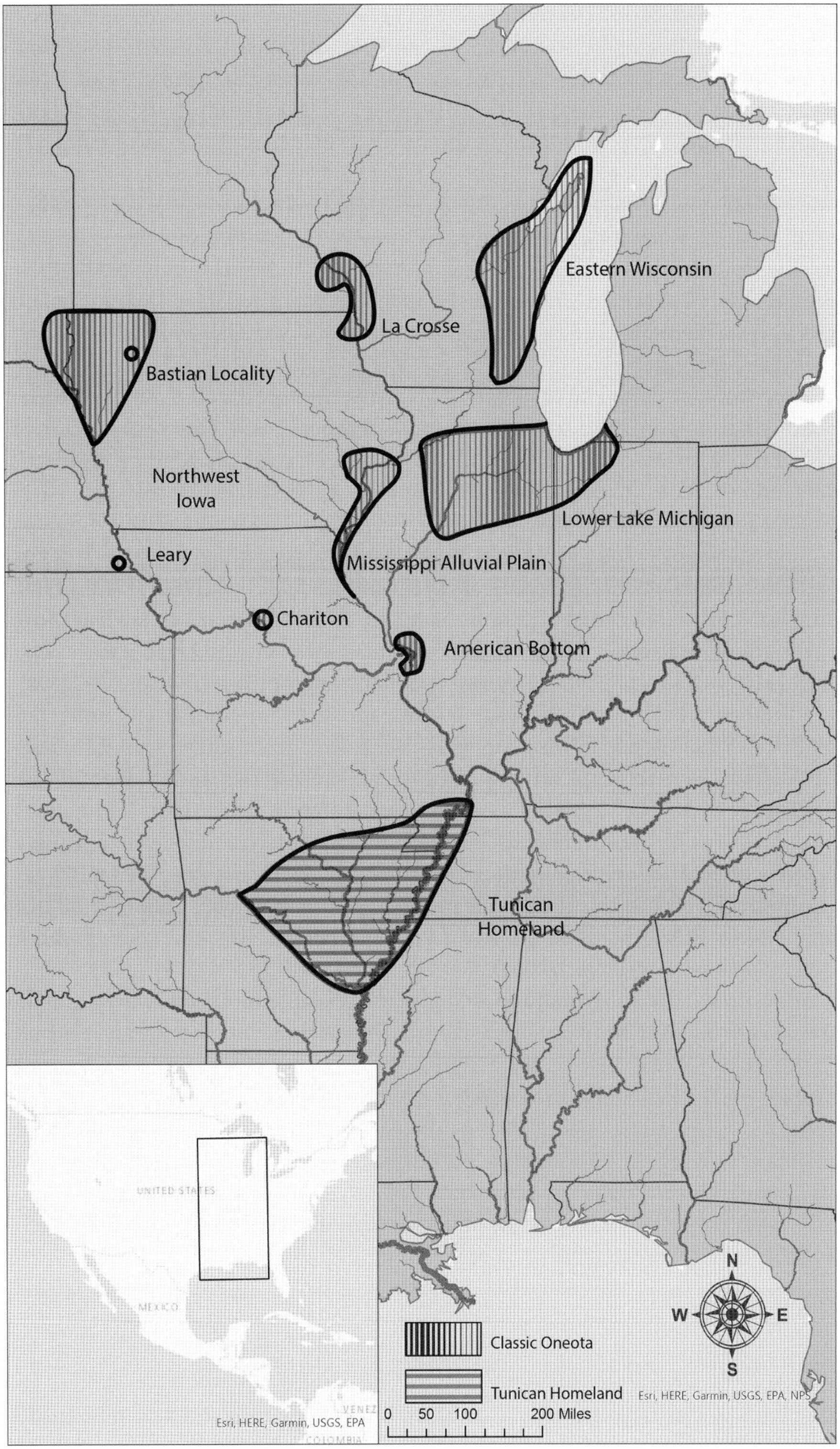

Fig. 5.2. Map of the Oneota and Tunican worlds (adapted from Dye 2017, fig. 6.1 and Henning 1998, fig. 3; drawing: Berkay Tok).

escalating in the early 17th century, when nLMV polities became engaged, albeit distantly and marginally, in the fur, pelt, and perhaps slave trade. While the flow of European goods into the interior was limited, consisting primarily of a few brass and iron objects, along with small numbers of glass beads, trade goods both indigenous and European appear in the nLMV as evidence of the developing and emerging exchange networks. Oneota (Siouan) and Illinois (Algonquian) sites in northern Illinois reveal a similar suite of early 17th century exchange goods, which occur in limited quantities (Mazrim and Esarey 2007, 185–6). As further evidence of new exchange networks, face mask gorgets and nLMV ceramic vessels have been recovered at the Anker site at Lake Michigan's southwestern tip (Bluhm and Liss 1961), which suggest direct linkages of the nLMV with the Great Lakes during the early fur trade.

Early contact period sites in the nLMV have also produced distinctive hide-processing tools in the form of snub-nose scrapers; reflecting the pursuit of diversified peltries: beaver, fox, mink, otter, and raccoon, in addition to bison, deer, and elk hides. These hide processing tools are restricted to the same early contact sites as those with indigenous ritual sacra, as well as conservative numbers of European goods. The Tunica in the 18th century were noted for their roles as extractors, middlemen, and processors in the salt trade (Brown 1980, 9; Brain 1988; Ellis 2017). Sixteenth century accounts mention traders in the nLMV, such as those encountered at Pacaha, where the de Soto expedition encountered people who traveled from polity to polity carrying copper and salt for trade (Hudson 1997, 306).

Ritual goods circulation between Oneota and Tunican populations, reflected in shared ritual items, flowing along Midwestern Oneota interaction networks throughout the Mississippi Valley, Northeast, northern Plains, and Upper Midwest (Delâge 1993, 88). Colin Betts (2006, 252), for example, notes that "indigenous trade patterns in the seventeenth century are characterized by an increasingly eastern orientation as a consequence of the fur trade and the availability of European objects." At this time Tunicans began interacting with Caborn-Welborn populations to the northeast; Caborn-Welborn people also had contacts with Oneota populations (Pollack 2004).

In contrast, there is virtually no evidence of Tunican interactions with Caddoan speakers to the west, Muskogean speakers to the southeast, or Natchezan speakers to the south. Unlike Oneota interactions with Caborn-Welborn and Fort Ancient people, which resulted in Oneota motifs on local (Caborn-Welborn) jars, Tunican domestic wares (nLMV jars), do not display Oneota motifs. The presence of Oneota engraving on Tunican-style bottles, and the absence of Oneota motifs on jars, suggest interactions between these two linguistic groups was not based on marriages but rather was sporadic and seemingly limited to ritual formats, such as Calumet-like ceremonies.

Oneota and Tunican iconography

Engraved bottles from the nLMV Tunican homeland are distinctive and easily distinguished from Oneota jars. William H. Holmes (1886a; 1886b; 1903) noted these differences in the late 19th century based on his work with museum collections of Mississippi Valley vessels. The predominant Tunican engraved ceramic ware, Walls Engraved, often features intertwined swirl motifs (guilloches) (Phillips 1970), while Oneota jars have chevron and linear motifs (Hollinger and Benn 1998). Engraved images of other-than-human beings that appear in the nLMV are almost exclusively found on ceramics, which is the preferred durable media for artistic imagery due to the lack of easily carved stone. In contrast, Oneota engravers preferred disk pipes, human bones, rock facings, and stone tablets.

We note the close similarity of Oneota figural imagery found in the Oneota world, with similar depictions engraved on Tunican bottles. The four primary themes Oneota engravers employed on Tunican pottery center on birdmen, "dancing" figures, Thunderers, and watery realm spirits (also known as cat serpents, underwater panthers). Oneota artisans creating these images often superimposed design motifs and figural imagery, creating multiple overlain images, as if the act of engraving was as important as the creation of the images; being overwritten to the extent that multiple images, often impossible to separate, are found on a single bone or lithic surface.

Oneota ceramics, typically globular jars, exhibit carefully arranged motifs trailed in the soft paste of vessel shoulders and sometimes lips and interior rim surfaces (Benn 1989, 243). Most motifs are represented by less than half a dozen subjects rendered in many design variations. Nested chevrons, for example, are thought to represent stylized Thunderbird wings, while abstract hawk motifs are depicted as bodies, tails, and wings. Pendant triangles are also placed on bird tails, as well as occupying the central design of ceramic motifs or within the body of birdmen. Engraved images on stone tablets depict other-than-human beings, often composed of elements from various "natural" species, as well as supernatural beings.

Tunican engraved wares are virtually limited to the nLMV, and are characterized by fine, dry paste engraving on fine, polished, shell-tempered bottles. The engraving depicts a wide variety of designs in which bands and zones filled with cross-hatching play a major role (Phillips *et al.* 1951, 127–9). Tunican artists employed balanced, oppositional symmetry in both geometrical and figural imagery. Many of the design motifs and themes are closely related to Moundville's Hemphill-style engraved wares, with their center bands and symbols, crested birds, human body parts or trophies, raptors, and winged serpents (Steponaitis and Knight 2004; Knight 2007; Phillips 2012). Tunican artistry possesses dynamic symmetry and motion, especially with emphasis on conventionalized images of other-than-human beings and serpents. Unlike Oneota engravers, Tunican pottery engravers avoided superimposing their imagery. Tunicans also modeled other-than-human beings in ceramic media as three-dimensional ceramic "effigies".

We present examples of Oneota figural imagery from the Midwest followed by essentially the same images engraved on Tunican ceramic bottles. Four other-than-human beings are discussed as iconographic themes employed by Oneota engravers who depict their representations on Tunican bottles: Thunderers, "dancing" figures, Birdmen, and watery realm spirits. We argue that many if not most of the Tunican bottles engraved with Oneota-like figures and motifs were done by Oneota ritual practitioners, with the bottles being found in nLMV contexts. However,

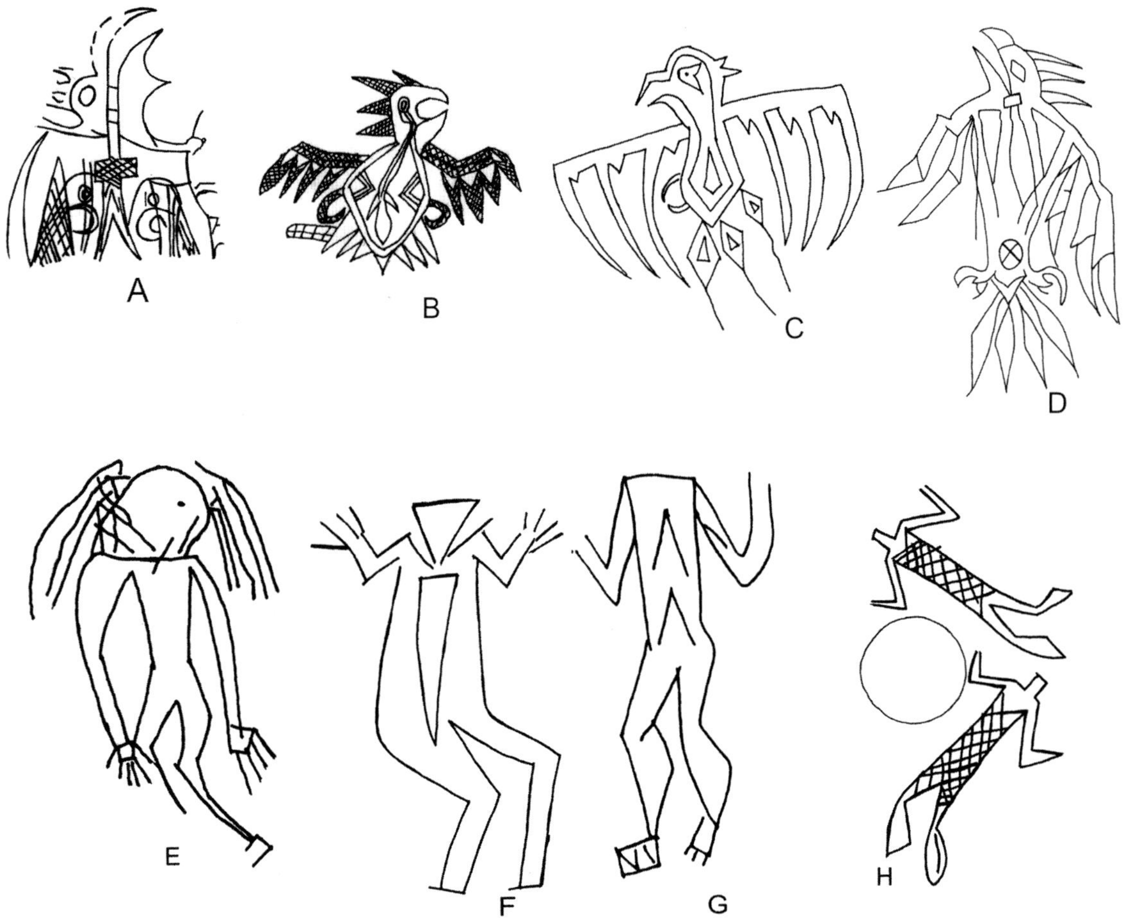

the location where the bottles were engraved remains unknown; they may have been transported to Oneota communities by Tunicans, or Oneota ritual specialists may have traveled to the nLMV to engrave local Tunican bottles. Either way, we suggest that the engraving was undertaken within ritual contexts among Oneota and Tunicans to cement relationships based on negotiated cosmoscape ontologies.

Thunderers

Thunderers dwell in the Upper World of the cosmoscape (Bender 2020) and, as raptors, they are depicted with curved beaks, claws or talons, crested heads, eyes, forked tails, and wings. The Irvine tablet, found at the Utz site (23SA2) in Saline County, MO (Bray 1963, fig. 8) (Fig. 5.3A), is engraved on a hematite slab and exemplifies Oneota conceptions and their theme of Thunderer beings. We identify three examples of Thunderers engraved on Tunican ceramic bottles from the nLMV that exhibit strong similarities to the Irvine tablet. The first figure is

Fig. 5.3. (opposite) Birdmen and "Dancing" figures: A. engraved birdman, New Albin tablet, Allamakee Co. IA (from Bray 1963, fig. 23; B. engraved birdman on Tunican bottle, Bradley Site (3CT7), Crittenden Co; C. engraved birdman on female figure, Fletcher pipe, Mississippi Co AR; D. abstract human figure with birdman attributes, including a raptor's head and talon claws, Notgrass Site (3MS15), Mississippi Co AR; E. engraved "dancing" figure, Oneota Stiles Tablet #9, Bastian Site (13CK28), Cherokee Co IA (after Bray 1963, fig. 20; F. one of four dancers engraved on a Tunican bottle from northeast Arkansas (based on Holmes 1886a, fig. 410; G. headless dancer engraved on a bottle from Mississippi Co AR; H. two headless dancers engraved a Tunican bottle, Wildy Site (3MS10), Mississippi Co AR (drawing by Toney Aid, except C. David H. Dye).

from a bottle from the Lacey site (3PO41) in Poinsett County, Arkansas, which is engraved with three full-figured raptors and a decapitated raptor head (Fig. 5.3B). A birdman with a bifurcated tail is also engraved on the bottle's base. The second example is one of three Thunderers engraved on a flared-rimmed beaker from the Parkin site (3CS29), Cross County, Arkansas (Fig. 5.3C). This depiction illustrates three images of half suns separating the raptors just below the perforated rim. The final bottle depicts one of ten raptors engraved on a bottle from an unknown site in Mississippi County, Arkansas (Jolly 1983, fig. 1) (Fig. 5.3D).

Dancing figures

Anthropomorphic engraved "dancing" figures are often shown lacking hands, heads, and feet, as if they represent humans subject to body part removal, perhaps as legerdemain ('slight of hand') demonstrations or war trophies, their bodies depicted by angular lines. When heads are engraved they are usually triangular or square, while feet are rectangular and hands consist of lines for fingers. We illustrate one example from Oneota contexts, and three Tunican examples engraved on bottles. The Oneota Stiles Tablet #9, engraved on a catlinite slab, was found at the Bastian site (13CK28) in Cherokee County, Iowa (Bray 1963, fig. 20) (Fig. 5.3E). The Stiles figure has a distinctive dome-shaped head with flowing lines at the sides of the head. Similar angular forms have been found in the nLMV. For example, a bottle engraved with four dancers is reported by William H. Holmes (1886a, fig. 410) from an unknown site in Arkansas (Fig. 5.3F). One of the four engraved dancers is illustrated here. The second example is a headless dancer engraved on a bottle from an unknown site in Mississippi County, Arkansas (Fig. 5.3G). The third bottle, from the Wildy site (3MS10), Mississippi County, Arkansas, portrays two headless dancers (Fig. 5.3H).

Birdmen

Stylized avian beings identified as birdman are denoted by avian heads, belts and kilts, chevrons, forked tails, speech symbols, and wing-like arms (Benn 1989, 245). In some instances only one motif may be present. These birdmen may be anthropomorphic images of people transformed into other-than-human thunder spirits (Brown 2007). The New Albin catlinite tablet from Allamakee County, Iowa (Orr 1922; Bray 1963, fig. 23; Benn 1995, fig. 17E; Roberson 2020a) has two figures that exhibit the characteristic Oneota features of birdmen with bifurcated tail-like legs, triangular-shaped wing-like arms, and crested, raptor heads (Fig. 5.4A). As part of this composition additional beings are depicted: an upside-down dancing human displayed across the birdman's upper torso, a partial image of a dancer in the field to the right, and a small headless birdman between the legs of the main image. These four figures seem to comprise one composition but stone tablets, often catlinite, generally received multiple engravings by Oneota engravers over time (Bray 1963; Hollinger 2005).

Engravings on Tunican bottles closely resemble the New Albin birdman images. We present three examples of Tunican bottles engraved with birdman figures. One engraved birdman is found on the body of a bottle from the Bradley site (3CT7) in Crittenden County, AR (Fig. 5.4B). The belt and chevron design on the torso are characteristic of birdman imagery. A raptor claw also appears on the neck of the vessel. A second engraved figure is from an unknown site in Mississippi County, Arkansas. The ceramic bowl-holder female figure pipe has a birdman engraved on her left side (Tolan *et al.* 2021) (Fig. 5.4C). The final birdman example, from the Notgrass site (3MS15), Mississippi County, Arkansas, is an abstract human figure with birdman attributes, including a raptor's head and talon claws (Fig. 5.4D). This composite birdman/Thunderer is further identified by the zig-zag lines at the sides, an Oneota motif identified as lightning. These anthropomorphic raptors may represent ritual practitioners who have transformed into birdmen/Thunderers, gaining other-than-human aid, powers, and protection.

Fig. 5.4. (opposite) Raptors and watery realm spirits: A. Oneota engraved Thunderer, Irvine tablet, Utz Site (23SA2), Saline Co MO (based on Bray 1963, fig. 8); B. engraved Thunderer on bottle, Lacey Site (3PO41), Poinsett Co AR; C. this raptor is one of three engraved on a flared rimmed beaker from the Parkin Site, 03CS029, Cross Co AR (private collection), three images of half suns separate the raptors just below the perforated rim; D. one of ten engraved raptors on a Tunican bottle, Mississippi Co AR (based on Jolly 1985, fig. 1); E. engraved water spirit, Stiles Tablet #1, Bastian Site (13CK28), Cherokee Co IA (based on Bray 1963, fig. 11); F. Head of a water spirit engraved on bottle, Notgrass Site (3MS15), Mississippi Co AR; G. engraved water spirit on Tunican bottle, Friends Mound Site (3MS6), Mississippi Co AR; H. engraved water spirit on Tunican bottle, Crosskno Site (3MS18), Mississippi Co AR (drawings by Toney Aid).

Watery realm spirits

Watery realm spirits are often composites of avians, canines, felines, and serpents, combined to create other-than-human beings extolled in mythic narratives as cat serpents or underwater panthers. Watery realm spirits are depicted in both Oneota and Tunican engraving, but Oneota figures are stylistically distinct based on their antler-like horns, curved bodies, sharp teeth, and feathered crests. The Stiles Tablet #1, from the Bastian site (13CK28) in Cherokee County, Iowa, portrays an Oneota watery realm figure with what appears to be crested feathers; however, they face forward like horns rather than feathers, which usually extend backwards (Bray 1963, fig. 11; Henning and Hollinger 2015; Roberson 2020b) (Fig. 5.4E). The figure displays circular eyes, fang-like teeth, a pronounced rounded head, and a short snout, characteristic of watery realm spirits. These features match other-than-human beings related in eastern North American charter myths (Swanton 1929; Lankford 1987).

Beneath World or watery realm, other-than-human beings may exhibit antlers, distinctive eye surrounds, horns, forward facing plumes, sharp fangs or teeth (Lankford 2007; Reilly 2011; Dye 2018). The three Tunican examples illustrated are engraved with Oneota-style watery realm spirits. The first example is the head of a Beneath World, underwater spirit from the Notgrass site (3MS15), Mississippi County, Arkansas (Fig. 5.4F). Like the Stiles tablet, the Notgrass image displays an amalgam of features including avian crosshatched feathers, mammalian pointed ears and snout, and reptilian clawed and pointed feet. In the second nLMV example, an engraved bottle from the Friend site (3MS6), Mississippi County, Arkansas (Fig. 5.4G), the being faces the viewer and displays antlers placed atop its head; the characteristic ears, mouth, and nose at the side of the face, and eyes are typical of nLMV engraved "monster-face" bottles from extreme southeastern Missouri (Hathcock 1988, 145). The addition of antlers in our example distinguishes it from the "monster-face" figures. We suggest both views represent two perspectives of a watery realm being. Finally, a watery realm spirit figure is engraved on a bottle from the Crosskno site (3MS18), Mississippi County, Arkansas (Fig. 5.4H).

Oneota and Tunican engraving share key themes such as avians, birdmen, and serpents, but the ways in which these other-than-human beings are depicted are

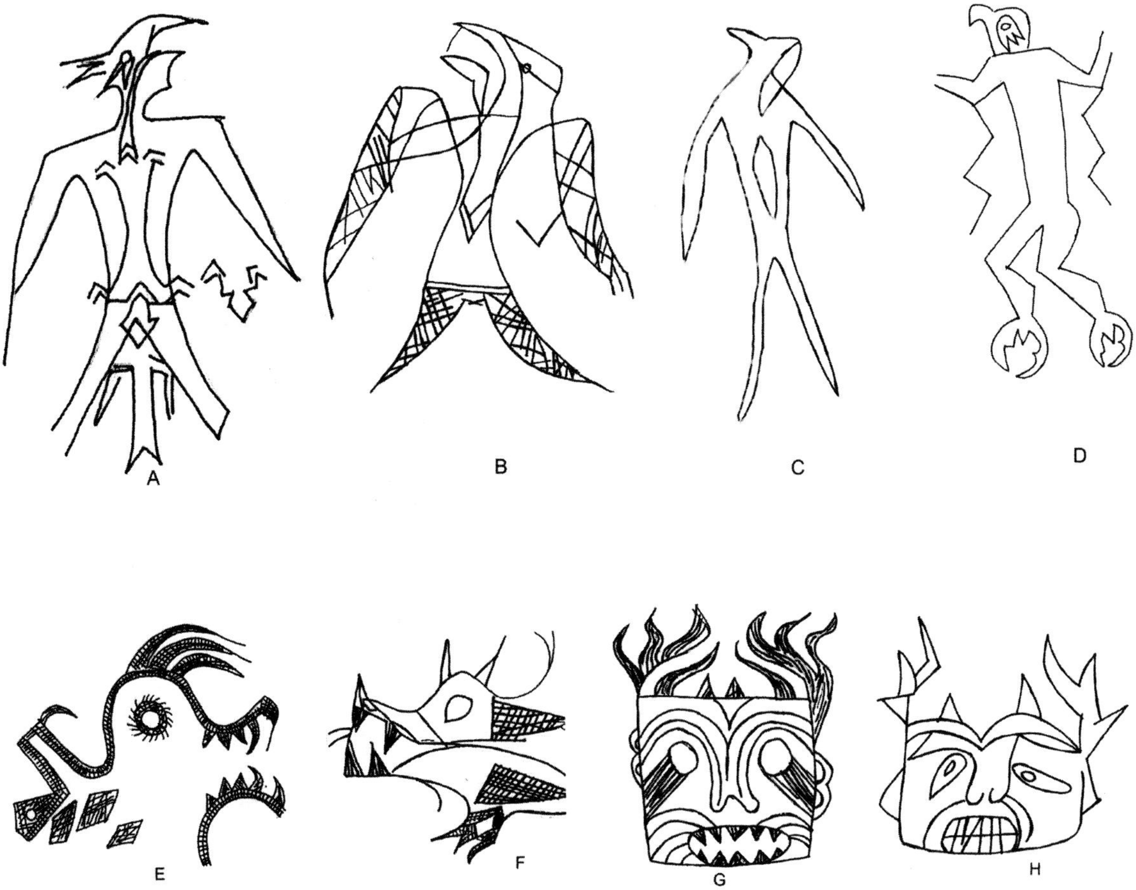

fundamentally different. They differ not only in stylistic approach but also in the preferred media. While Oneota engravers eschewed ceramics for bone and stone surfaces, Tunicans chose to concentrate their efforts on ceramic bottles. When Oneota potters depict transcendent beings, especially avian forms, they usually depict stylized body parts, including bodies, tails, and wings.

Guardian spirits and ritual sodality transfers

While we can argue that interconnections existed between Oneota and Tunican groups, the vexing issue lies in assessing the ritual and social relationships that cemented entanglements prompting the presence of Oneota figural depictions on Tunican ceramics. The close correspondence of Oneota-style other-than-human beings engraved on Tunican bottles in addition to a female effigy pipe, draws our attention to the close and interconnected relationships among ritual practitioners and their cosmology comprised of culture heroes, guardian spirits, and other transcendental beings residing in the indigenous cosmoscape. In eastern

North America ritual practice often requires the presence of guardian spirits and other-than-human beings. For example, in 1673 Father Jacques Marquette (1899, 133), while visiting the Illini, noted a Calumet ceremony and the presence of an other-than-human figure. He observed that ritual practitioners placed upon a large mat the "God of the person who gives the Dance; for each has his own god, which they call their Manitou. This is a serpent, a bird, or similar thing, of which they have dreamed while sleeping, and in which they place all their confidence for the success of their war, their fishing, and their hunting." The presence of other-than-human beings at ritual events would have been paramount for its success.

Ritual adoption in the presence of a "manitou" was key to such ceremonies, but we suggest the nature of adoption has been largely misunderstood. Rather than adoption into a kin group (a family, phratry, lineage, or clan), we argue that ritual goods such as ceramic bottles and disk pipes circulated as part of the adoption process into ritual sodalities, following a basic ritual pattern in the Midwest and northern Plains. Purchase into a ritual sodality and the acquisition of inalienable goods, secretive knowledge, and theatrical performances was predicated on adoption by a ritual "father". For example, Hidatsa ritual purchases of medicine societies took the form of transfers to acquire supernatural power (Bowers 1965). Ritual sellers as "fathers" sold their rights to the society to their ritual "sons". In friend to friend purchases society members selected a friend to whom they would supply a duplicate set of the society equipment, i.e., ritual goods (Bowers 1965, 92). Thus, father–son and friend–friend relations created and furthered intertribal relationships and ritually crafted bundle elements, paraphernalia, and regalia. The production of sodality-related sacra, based on ritual transfers, would have taken place through crafting apprenticeships in which the members of a ritual sodality would constitute a community of practice. In this sense ritual relationships enabled engravers and potters to learn from each other and to create negotiated repertoires of ceramic practice.

Alfred Bowers (1965, 95) notes that in every situation of a sacred character, there existed a ritual kinship relationship between the "sacred characters and objects on the one hand and the bundle owner and purchaser on the other". While these are referred to as father-son relations, they are clearly ritual nonkin relationships. Mutual purchases of ritual sodalities by Oneota and Tunicans may have resulted in Tunican potters producing characteristically Mississippian bottles and Oneota artisans engraving Oneota motifs on these bottles as part of the sodality transfers. Whether the production and transaction took place in the Oneota world or the Tunican world may have been immaterial to the outcome of ritual sodality purchase. Clearly, people and goods were moving throughout these interconnected social landscapes in the midst of cosmoscape negotiations.

Additional evidence for ritual interactions among Tunicans and Oneota is found in distinctive inalienable goods. For example, catlinite disk pipes from Oneota quarries in the upper Midwest are found among northern Tunican polities (Brown, 1989; 2006), the same towns in which Mississippian bottles with Oneota engraved motifs and European goods are located. Important Tunican ritual centers, such as the Campbell site (23PM5) in southeastern Missouri and the Chickasawba (3MS5) site in northeastern Arkansas, possess the largest number of catlinite disk pipes and early colonial goods found in the nLMV. The Campbell site produced a brass book binder fragment, glass chevron beads, iron knife fragments, and metal bells (O'Brien, 1994; O'Brien and Wood, 1998, 335). At Chickasawba, for example, a feature with three catlinite disk pipes also contained a metal knife blade (Childs and McNutt 2009).

On the other hand, Mississippian objects also circulated north into the Oneota world. Perhaps the most important of these are face mask gorgets, ultimately derived from southern Appalachian marine shell crafting, which circulated into Oneota contexts from Tunican towns in the late 16th and early 17th century. While widespread in the Tunican world, face mask gorgets are found only sporadically at Oneota centers, such as the Utz site (Chapman 1980, fig. 6–9g) and sites at the southern end of Lake Michigan (Bluhm and Liss 1961, fig. 70a; Quimby 1966, fig. 16; Brain and Phillips 1996, 429). For example, the Anker site (11CK21) in the Chicago area had a face mask gorget, a bracket-style ear pin, which often accompany face mask gorgets and distinctive nLMV ceramic bottles (Bluhm and Liss 1961). A shell mask, associated with copper and glass beads, was also found in Allamakee County, Iowa, the same county as New Albin tablet (Bray 1963). James Collins (1995, 258) notes the close association of Calumet disk pipes and face mask gorgets, suggesting "the Allamakee County shell mask gorget was presented to an Orr phase Oneota/Ioway child as the result of participation in a Calumet ceremony that created fictive kinship between members of his group and those of an external group". Thus, the circulation of face mask gorgets and other ritual goods reflects widespread connections during the early fur trade in the early 17th century (Dye 2021b).

Oneota catlinite disk pipes being transferred southward and face mask gorgets circulating northward argues for strong ritual connections between the two areas through Calumet-like ceremonies. The presence of Oneota engraved motifs on Tunican bottles further underscores such contacts. The appearance of face mask gorgets and the presence of catlinite disk pipes on sites with early contact period trade goods, along with Oneota figural art of other-than-human beings on Tunican ceramics, underscores the proposition that interaction between Oneota and Tunican ritual practitioners was crucial to ritual negotiations during the early fur trade.

Conclusion

We have suggested that a distinct, alien engraved style found in the Tunica homeland reflects movements across Oneota and Tunican social boundaries. These boundaries were permeated through ritual sodality purchases, resulting in Oneota figural imagery and motifs on Mississippian bottles and catlinite disk pipes in Tunican ritual centers, and face mask gorgets and Tunican ceramics in the Oneota World. Oneota and Tunican artistry became entangled during the early 17th century when heightened interactions among Oneota and Tunican people were achieved through the circulation of inalienable goods crafted and transferred through ritual sodality purchases. Tunican ceramic bottles bearing Oneota motifs reflect mutually shared beliefs in cosmoscapes, which were negotiated between different sets of actors and agents who mediated their differences through the ritual requirements of culture hero, guardian spirit, and other-than-human being presence. Through the act of engraving transcendental beings on ceramic bottles, both Oneota and Tunican ritual practitioners created lines of communication and contact that evoked spirit beings, including birdmen, raptors, Thunderers, and watery realm spirits.

Oneota–Tunican interactions were sedimented in rituals resembling contact period Calumet ceremonies with the presence of Oneota motifs on Tunican ceramic bottles in the Tunican homeland of the nLMV, suggesting shared ritual protocols engendered mutually beneficial interactions between the social boundaries of often contentious and fractious neighboring polities. Although possessing their own cosmological perspectives, these interactions and negotiations during Calumet-like ritual forums resulted in an amalgam of Oneota and Tunican cosmoscapes in which both groups mutually respected and understood each other.

Acknowledgements

Numerous people and institutions over the years allowed access to their collections for analysis, photography, and study. We are appreciative of Christina Kastell (Curator of History and Anthropology) for her help at the Putnam Museum and Science Center (formerly Davenport Academy of Natural Sciences), Dan Swan (curator) at the Thomas of the Gilcrease Institute of American History and Art, Kevin Cupka (Director) and Sarah Reid (Research Specialist) at the Bernice S. Warren Center for Archaeological Research, Missouri State University (Springfield), and Candace Sall (Director) and Jessica Totsch, Museum of Anthropology and American Archaeology Division, University of Missouri. We also extend our appreciation to Jim Cherry, Dub Lyerly, and Len and Janie Weidner for their support of our research. Robert V. Sharp offered sage advice on many topics, including the engravings of other-than-human beings during research travels with David Dye. Finally, we would like to express our appreciation to the groundbreaking work of Marcia Taylor (1942–2019), who paved the way for the difficult and tedious renderings of Lower Mississippi Valley engraved bottles. We will miss her friendship and her dedication to the study of Tunican ceramics.

References

Alt, S.M. (2018) *Cahokia's Complexities: Ceremonies and politics of the first Mississippian farmers.*: University of Alabama Press, Tuscaloosa AL.

Anderson, P. and Maxwell J.M. (2019) The Tunica language. In *Language in Louisiana: Community and Culture*, eds N. Dajko and S. Wilson, 45–63. University Press of Mississippi, Jackson MI.

Baires, S.E. (2017) *Land of Water, City of the Dead: Religion and Cahokia's emergence*. University of Alabama Press Tuscaloosa AL.

Barber, S.B. and Joyce, A.A. eds (2018) *Religion and Politics in the Ancient Americas*. Routledge, New York.

Bender, H. (2020) The Thunderbird in Native American rock art. In *Anthropomorphic Images in*

Rock Art Paintings and Rock Carvings, eds T. Meaden and H. Bender, 268–78. Archaeopress, Oxford.

Benn, D.W. (1989) Hawks, serpents, and bird-men: Emergence of the Oneota mode of production. *Plains Anthropologist* 34, 233–60.

Benn, D.W. (1995) Woodland people and the roots of Oneota. In Green (ed.), 91–139.

Berlo, J.C. (2011) Navajo cosmoscapes – up, down, within. *American Art* 25.1, 10–13.

Berlo, J.C. (2014) Navajo sandpaintings in the age of cross-cultural replication. *Art History: Journal of the Association of Art Historians* 37.4, 688–707.

Berres, T.E. (2001) *Power and Gender in Oneota Culture: A study of a late prehistoric people.* Illinois University Press, DeKalb IL.

Betts, C.M. (2006) The identification of protohistoric epidemics in the Upper Mississippi Valley. *American Antiquity* 71, 233–59.

Blakeslee, D.J. (1975) The Plains interband trade system: An ethnohistoric and archaeological investigation. Unpublished PhD dissertation. Department of Anthropology, University of Wisconsin, Milwaukee WI.

Blakeslee, D.J. (1981) The origin and spread of the Calumet ceremony. *American Antiquity* 46, 759–68.

Bluhm, E.A. and Liss, A. (1961) The Anker Site. In *Chicago Area Archaeology Bulletin* 3, ed. E. Bluhm, 89–137. Archaeological Survey, University of Illinois, Urbana IL.

Bold, R. (2020) Constructing cosmoscapes: Cosmological currents in conversation and contestation in contemporary Bolivia. *HAU: Journal of Ethnographic Theory* 10, 195–208.

Bowers, A.W. (1965) *Hidatsa Social and Ceremonial Organization.* Bulletin 194, Bureau of American Ethnology, Smithsonian Institution, Washington DC.

Brain, J.P. (1988) *Tunica Archaeology*. Peabody Museum of Archaeology and Ethnology Papers 78. Harvard University, Cambridge MA.

Brain, J.P, and Phillips, P. (1996) *Shell Gorgets: Styles of the late prehistoric and protohistoric Southeast*. Peabody Museum Press, Cambridge MA.

Bray, R.T. (1963) Southern cult motifs from the Utz Site in Saline County, Missouri. *Missouri Archaeologist* 25, 1–40.

Bray, R.T. (1978) European trade goods from the Utz Site and the search for Fort Orleans. *Missouri Archaeologist* 39, 1–87.

Bray, R.T. (1991) The Utz Site: An Oneota village in central Missouri. *Missouri Archaeologist* 52, 1–146.

Brown, I.W. (1980) *Salt and the Eastern North American Indian: An archaeological study.* Lower Mississippi Survey Bulletin 6. Harvard University, Cambridge MA.

Brown, I.W. (1989) The Calumet ceremony in the Southeast and its archaeological manifestations. *American Antiquity* 54, 311–33.

Brown, I.W. (2006) The Calumet ceremony in the Southeast as observed archaeologically. In *Powhatan's Mantle: Indians in the Colonial Southeast* (rev and expanded edn), eds G.A. Waselkov, P.H. Wood and T. Hatley, 371–419. Nebraska Press, Lincoln NE

Brown, I.W. (2007) On the identity of the Birdman within Mississippian Period art and iconography. In Reilly and Garber (eds), 56–106.

Brown, J.A. and Sasso, R.F. (2001) Prelude to history on the eastern prairies. In *Societies in Eclipse: Archaeology of the Eastern Woodlands Indians, A.D. 1400-1700*, eds D.S.B.C. Wesley Cowan and R.C. Mainfort Jr., 205–28. Smithsonian Institution Press, Washington, DC.

Burnette, D.J., Dye, D.H. and Hill, A.A. (forthcoming) Migration, climate change, and ritual in the Lower Mississippi Valley. In *Following the Mississippian Spread: Using biological and archaeological evidence to measure migration and climate change*, eds R.A. Cook and A.R. Comstock. Springer, New York.

Carmody, S.B. and Barrier, C.R. eds (2020) *Shaman, Priest, Practice, Belief: Materials of ritual and religion and ritual in the Eastern North America.* University of Alabama Press, Tuscaloosa AL.

Chapman, C.H. (1980) *The Archaeology Missouri II.* University of Missouri Press, Columbia MI.

Childs, H.T. and McNutt, C.H. (2009) Chickasawba. *Arkansas Archeologist* 48, 15–56.
Cobb, C.R. and Butler, B.M. (2017) Mississippian plazas, performances, and portable histories. *Journal of Archaeological Method and Theory* 24, 676–702.
Cobb, C.R. and Stephenson, K.D. (2017) Cosmic debt and relational consumption. In *Rethinking Indigenous Consumption in American Archaeology*, ed. C.N. Cipolla, 143–61. University of Arizona Press, Tucson, AZ.
Collins, J.M. (1995) A shell mask gorget from Allamakee County, Iowa. *Plains Anthropologist* 40, 251–60.
Delâge, D. (1993) *Bitter Feast: Amerindians and Europeans in Northeastern North America, 1600-64* (trans. J. Brierley). University of British Columbia Press, Vancouver.
Diaz-Granados, C., Duncan, J.R. and Reilly, F.K. III (eds) (2015) *Picture Cave: Unravelling the mysteries of the Mississippian cosmos*. University of Texas Press, Austin TX.
Diaz-Granados, C., Simek, J., Sabo, G. III and Wagner, M. (eds) (2018) *Transforming the Landscape: Art and the Mississippian cosmos*. Oxbow Books, Oxford.
Donnellan, L. (ed.) (2020) *Archaeological Networks and Social Interaction*. Routledge, New York.
Drooker, P.B. (1997) *The View from Madisonville: Protohistoric western Fort Ancient interaction patterns*. Museum of Anthropology Memoir 11, University of Michigan, Ann Arbor MI.
Dye, D.H. (1994) The art of war in the sixteenth century Central Mississippi Valley. In *Perspectives on the Southeast: Linguistics, archaeology, and ethnohistory*, ed. P.B. Kwachka, 44–60. Southern Anthropological Society Proceedings 27. University of Georgia, Athens GA.
Dye, D.H. (2018) Ceramic wares and water spirits: Identifying religious sodalities in the Lower Mississippi Valley. In *Ceramics of Ancient America: Multidisciplinary approaches*, eds Y.P. Huntington, D.E. Arnold and J. Minich, 29–61. Florida University Press, Gainesville FL.
Dye, D.H. (2020) Mississippian symbolic weaponry at Spiro. In Singleton and Reilly (eds), 152–73.
Dye, D.H. (2021a) Fire burn and caldron bubble: Mississippian Witchcraft Agency, Animism, and Materiality. In *New Methods and Theories for Analyzing Mississippian Imagery*, edited by B. T. Giles and S. P. Lambert, Gainesville, University Press of Florida, 131–161.
Dye, D.H. (2021b) Culture Heroes, Inalienable Goods, and Religious Sodalities: Long Distance Exchange in Eastern North America at European Contact. In *Trade Before Civilization*, edited by K. Kristiansen, J. Ling, and R. Chacon. New York, Cambridge University Press, In press.
Dye, D.H. (ed.) (2021c) *Mississippian Culture Heroes, Ritual Regalia, and Sacred Bundles*. New York, Lexington Books.
Ellis, E. (2017) Petite nation with powerful networks: The Tunicas in the eighteenth century. *Louisiana History* 58, 133–78.
Fletcher, A.C. (1904) *The Hako: A Pawnee ceremony*. Bureau of American Ethnology 22nd Annual report. Smithsonian Institution, Washington DC.
Green, W. ed (1995) *Oneota Archaeology: Past, present, and future*. Office of the State Archaeologist, University of Iowa, Iowa City IO.
Griffin, J.B. (1943) *The Fort Ancient aspect: Its cultural and chronological position in Mississippi Valley archaeology*. Museum of Anthropology, University of Michigan, Ann Arbor MI.
Griffin-Pierce, T. (1992) *Earth is My Mother, Sky is My Father: Space, time and astronomy in Navajo sandpainting*. University of New Mexico Press, Albuquerque NM.
Gunderson, J.N. (1993) "Catlinite" and the spread of the Calumet ceremony. *American Antiquity* 58, 560–62.
Haas, M.M. (1940) Tunica. *Handbook of American Indian Languages* 4, 1–143.
Hall, R.L. (1997) *An Archaeology of the Soul: North American Indian belief and ritual*. University of Illinois Press, Urbana IL.
Hathcock, R. (1988) *Ancient Indian Pottery of the Mississippi River Valley* (2nd edn). Walsworth, Marceline MO.
Henning, D.R. (1970) Development and interrelationships of Oneota culture in the Lower Missouri River Valley. *Missouri Archaeologist* 32, 1–180.

Henning, D.R. (1998) Managing Oneota: A reiteration and testing of contemporary archaeological taxonomy. *Wisconsin Archaeologist* 79, 9–28.

Henning, D.R., and Hollinger, R.E. (2015) A study of red stone tablets from Oneota sites. *Northwest Chapter of the Iowa Archaeological Society* 64, 1–3.

Holland-Lulewicz, J., Conger, M.A., Birch,J., Kowalewski, S.A. and Jones, T.W. (2020) An institutional approach for archaeology. *Journal of Anthropological Archaeology* 58, 101–63.

Hollinger, E.R. (2005) Conflict and Culture Change in the Late Prehistoric and Early Historic American Midcontinent. Unpublished PhD dissertation, Department of Anthropology, University of Illinois Urbana-Champaign, IL.

Hollinger, E.R. (2018) Conflict and culture change on the Plains: The Oneota example. In *Archaeological Perspectives on Warfare on the Great Plains*, eds A.J. Clark and D.B. Bamforth, 267–74. University Press of Colorado, Louisville CO.

Hollinger, R.E. and Benn, D.W. eds (1998) Oneota taxonomy: Papers from the Oneota Symposium of the 54th Plains Anthropological Conference, 1996. *Wisconsin Archeologist* 79, 1–283.

Holmes, W.H. (1886a) Ancient pottery of the Mississippi Valley. *Bureau of American Ethnology, Annual Report* 4, 361–436.

Holmes, W.H. (1886b) Ancient pottery of the Mississippi Valley: A study of the collection of the Davenport Academy. *Proceedings of the Davenport Academy of Natural Sciences* 4, 123–96.

Holmes, W.H. (1903) *Aboriginal Pottery of the Eastern United States*. Bureau of American Ethnology Annual Report 20, Smithsonian Institution, Washington DC.

Howey, M.C.L. (2020) Other-than-human persons, Mishipishu, and danger in the Late Woodland Inland water landscape of northern Michigan. *American Antiquity* 85, 347–66.

Hudson, C. (1997) *Knights of Spain, Warriors of the Sun: Hernando de Soto and the South's ancient chiefdoms*. University of Georgia Press, Athens GA.

Jolly, F. III (1983) Late prehistoric designs from engraved Mississippian vessels: Evidence for an unrecognized iconographic tradition? *Central States Archaeological Journal* 30, 6–16.

Joyce, A.A. (2018) New directions in the archaeology of religion and politics in the Americas. In Barber and Joyce (eds), 1–26.

Kaufman, D.V. (2019) *Clues to Lower Mississippi Valley Histories: Language, archaeology, and ethnography*. University of Nebraska Press, Lincoln NE.

Kidder, T.R. (2004) Plazas as architecture: An example from the Raffman Site, northeast Louisiana. *American Antiquity* 68, 514–32.

King, A. (ed.) (2007) *Southeastern Ceremonial Complex: Chronology, content, context*. University of Alabama Press, Tuscaloosa AL.

Knight, V.J. Jr (2007) An assessment of Moundville engraved "cult" designs from potsherds. In King (ed.), 151–64.

Knight, V.J. Jr (2013) *Iconographic Method in New World Prehistory*. Cambridge University Press, New York.

Koldehoff, B.H. and Pauketat, T.R. eds (2018) *Archaeology and Ancient Religion in the American Midcontinent*. University of Alabama Press, Tuscaloosa AL.

Lankford, G.E. (2004) World on a string: Some cosmological components of the Southeastern Ceremonial complex. In Townsend and Sharp (eds), 207–17.

Lankford, G.E. (2007) The Great Serpent in eastern North America. In Reilly and Garber (eds), 107–35.

Lankford, G.E. (2008) *Looking for Lost Lore: Studies in folklore, ethnology, and iconography*. University of Alabama Press, Tuscaloosa AL.

Lankford, G.E. ed. (1987) *Native American Legends*. August House, Little Rock AR.

Lankford, G.E., Reilly, F.K. III and Garber, J.A. eds (2011) *Visualizing the Sacred: Cosmic visions, regionalism, and the art of the Mississippian world*. University of Texas Press, Austin TX.

Latour, B. (2005) *Reassembling the Social: An introduction to actor-network-theory*. Oxford University Press, New York.

McMillan, R.B. (2014) Migration legends and the origins of Missouri's Siouan-speaking tribes. *Missouri Archaeologist* 75, 5–47.

Marquette, J. (1899) Voyages du P. Jacques Marquette, 1673–1675. In *The Jesuit Relations and Allied Documents: Travels and explorations of the Jesuit missionaries in New France, 1610–1791*, ed. R.G. Thwaites. Burrows Brothers, Cleveland OH.

Mason, C.I. (2006) Iconographic (Jesuit) rings at the Utz Site. *North American Archaeologist* 27, 25–39.

Mazrim, R. and Esarey, D. (2007) Rethinking the dawn of history: The schedule, signature, and agency of European goods in protohistoric Illinois. *Midcontinental Journal of Archaeology* 32, 145–200.

Milner, G.R., Anderson, E. and Smith, V. G. (1991) Warfare in late prehistoric west-central Illinois. *American Antiquity* 56, 581–603.

Mills, B.J. (2018) Intermarriage, technological diffusion, and boundary objects in the U. S. Southwest. *Journal of Archaeological Method and Theory* 25, 1051–86.

Morphy, H. (1995) Landscape and the reproduction of the ancestral past. In *The Anthropology of Landscape*, eds E. Hirsch and M. O'Halon, 184–209. Clarendon Press, Oxford.

Morse, D.F. and Morse, P.A. (1983) *Archaeology of the Central Mississippi Valley*. Academic Press, New York.

Nordine, K.O. (2000) Building Communities: Interpreting Oneota and Mississippian interaction through paleoethnobotanical analysis at the Morton Village Site (11F2), west-central Illinois. Unpublished PhD dissertation, Department of Anthropology, Washington University, St Louis MO.

O'Brien, M.J. (1994) *Cat Monsters and Head Pots: The archaeology of Missouri's Pemiscot Bayou*. University of Missouri Press, Columbia MO.

O'Brien, M.J. and Wood, W.R. (1998) *The Prehistory of Missouri*. University of Missouri Press, Columbia, MO.

Orr, E. (1922) The New Albin inscribed tablet. *Proceedings of the Iowa Academy of Science* 29, 49–52.

Pauketat, T.R. (2013) *An Archaeology of the Cosmos: Rethinking agency and religion in ancient America*. Routledge, New York.

Pavel, T. (1981) Fiction and the Ontological landscape. *Studies in Twentieth Century Literature* 6, 149–63.

Phillips, E. (2012) Social Contexts of Production and Use of Pottery Engraved in the Hemphill Style at Moundville. Unpublished PhD dissertation, Department of Anthropology, University of Alabama Tuscaloosa AL.

Phillips, P. (1970) *Archaeological Survey in the Lower Yazoo Basin, Mississippi, 1949–1955*. Papers of the Peabody Museum of American Archaeology and Ethnology 60. Harvard University, Cambridge MA.

Phillips, P., Ford, J.A. and Griffin, J.B. (1951) *Archaeological Survey in the Lower Mississippi Alluvial Valley, 1940–1947*. Papers of the Peabody Museum of American Archaeology and Ethnology 25. Harvard University, Cambridge MA.

Pollack, D. (2004) *Caborn-Welborn: Constructing a new society after the Angel chiefdom collapse.*, University of Alabama Press, Tuscaloosa AL.

Quimby, G.I. (1966) *Indian Culture and European Trade Goods: Archaeology of the historic period in the western Great Lakes*. University of Wisconsin Press, Madison WI.

Reichel, E. (2012) The landscape in the cosmoscape, and sacred sites and species among the Tunimuka and Yukuna Amerindian tribes (northwest Amazon). In *Sacred Species and Sites: Advances in biocultural conservation*, eds G. Pungetti, G. Oviedo, and D. Hooke, 127–51. Cambridge University Press, New York.

Reilly, F.K. III (2011) The Great Serpent in the Lower Mississippi Valley. In Lankford *et al.* (eds), 118–34.

Reilly, F.K. III, and Garber, G.F. eds (2007) *Ancient Objects and Sacred Realms: Interpretations of Mississippian iconography*. University of Texas Press, Austin TX.

Roberson, J. (2020a) The new Albin tablet. *Central States Archaeological Journal* 67, 212–13.

Roberson, J. (2020b) The underwater panther tablet. *Central States Archaeological Journal* 67, 240.

Shirar, B. (2019) Honey or vinegar: Oneota interaction in the central and northeastern Plains. Unpublished Master's thesis, Department of Anthropology, St Cloud State University, St Cloud MN.

Singleton, E.D. and Reilly, F.K. III eds (2020) *Recovering Ancient Spiro: Native American art, ritual, and cosmic renewal*. National Cowboy & Western Heritage Museum, Oklahoma City OK.

Slater, D.A. (2014) Into the Heart of the Turtle: Caves, Ritual, and Power in Ancient Central Yucatan, Mexico. Unpublished PhD dissertation, Department of Anthropology, Brandeis University, Waltham MA.

Springer, J.W. and Witkowski, S.R. (1982) Siouan historical linguistics and Oneota archaeology. In *Oneota Studies*, ed. G.E. Gibbon, 69–83. Publications in Anthropology 1. University of Minnesota, Minneapolis MN.

Staller, J.E. (2008) An introduction to pre-Columbian landscapes of creation and origin. In *Pre-Columbian Landscapes of Creation and Origin*, ed. J.E. Staller, 1–9. Springer, New York.

Star, S.L. (1989) The structure of ill-structured solutions: Boundary objects and heterogeneous distributed problem solving. In *Distributed Artificial Intelligence*, eds L. Gasser and M.N. Huhns, 37–54. Morgan Kaufmann, San Mateo CA.

Star, S.L. and Griesemer, J.R. (1989) Institutional ecology, "translations" and boundary objects: Amateurs and professionals in Berkeley's Museum of Vertebrate Zoology, 1907–1939. *Social Studies of Science* 19, 387–420.

Stark, M.T. ed. (1998) *The Archaeology of Social Boundaries*. Smithsonian Institution Press, Washington DC.

Stengers, I. (2005) The Cosmopolitical proposal. In *Making Things Public*, eds B. Latour and P. Weibel, 994–1003. MIT Press, Cambridge MA.

Steponaitis, V.P. and Knight, V.J. Jr (2004) Moundville art in historical and social context. In Townsend and Sharp (eds), 167–81.

Swanton, J.R. (1929) *Myths and Tales of the Southeastern Indians*. Bureau of American Ethnology Bulletin 88. Smithsonian Institution, Washington DC.

Tolan, G., Carmody, C.C.R.S., Blair, E.H., Dye, D.H. and Russ, J. (2021) Organic residue analysis of two Mississippian Period human effigy pipes. *Journal of Archaeological Science* 35, 1–10.

Townsend, R.F. and Sharp. R.V. (eds) (2004) *Hero, Hawk, and Open Hand: American Indian art of the ancient Midwest and South*. Yale University Press, New Haven CO.

Warren, R.E. (2007) Thunderbird effigies from Plains village sites in the northern Great Plains. In *Plains Village archaeology: Bison hunting farmers in the central and northern Plains*, eds S.A. Ahler and M. Kay, 107–25.University of Utah Press, Salt Lake City UT.

Wenger, E. (1998) *Communities of Practice: Learning, meaning, and identity*. Cambridge University Press, New York.

Wenger, E. (1999) Communities of practice: The key to knowledge strategy. knowledge directions. *Journal of the Institute for Knowledge Management* 1, 48–63.

Yelton, J. K. (1998) A different view of Oneota taxonomy and origins in the Lower Missouri Valley. *Wisconsin Archaeologist* 79, 268–83.

6

Of snakes and masks: Retrospective clues to understand the meaning of Classic Maya (AD 250–900) greenstone mosaic masks

Juan C. Melendez, David A. Freidel, and Daniel E. Aquino

Introduction

Cross-culturally, the term "mask" falls within a wide spectrum of objects with facial features manufactured using diverse materials. Although several masking traditions have one thing in common – that masks are considered power objects – their meanings and the purpose for their creation are nonetheless very diverse. Masks have been considered as items of transformation (Mack 1994), magical objects (Kecskési and Vajda 2012), symbols of initiation (Cameron 2001), representations linked to the supernatural (Le Fur 2013), and even as markers of social rank (Biebuyck 1986). In this study we use "mask" as an umbrella term to include massive masks (i.e., pavements) such as the ones from La Venta (Drucker 1952; Drucker *et al.* 1959), but also portable Maya greenstone mosaic masks (GMM hereafter) (García 2004; Martínez del Campo 2010; Filloy 2014; Melendez 2019). We consider masks could have been items used by either natural and supernatural beings to characterize a particular identity while on the tessestrial plan. Levi-Strauss and Cantraine (1982) highlighted the variety of masks among people of the Longhouse culture, noting that there are maternity, beggar, counselor, tempest, and scalp masks, each with its specific use. Likewise, in terms of the size and manner of wearing them, they emphasize that the people of the Longhouse manufactured small masks (only a few centimeters long), which were used as talismans. Finally, there were also masks carved directly on living tree trunks (Levi-Strauss and Cantraine 1982).

In a nutshell, masks can be considered as vehicles through which living and supernatural beings communicate and dramatize the behaviors and temperament of identities depicted on them, no matter their size, materials that compose them, or even the manner in which they are worn or placed.

Pre-Columbian Maya portable GMM have been widely linked to high-elite power objects. Depictions of masks in the Maya artistic corpus reinforce their elite context and association with power (Coe and Kerr 1998), especially when they are made from greenstone. Portable GMM are comprised in some cases by dozens or even hundreds of carved segments called tesserae, mostly of greenstone. Each tessera was individually manufactured through sequences of reduction (e.g., abrading, polishing, and burnishing) to become part of a larger technological project resulting in a GMM. Greenish stones were considered symbolic of life, wealth, maize, water, centrality, and rulership by pre-Columbian societies in the Maya area and Mesoamerica (Taube 2005; Houston *et al.* 2009).

In this chapter, we present ideas based on contextual studies that permitted us to visualize GMM from the political angle of the Classic period (AD 250–900) in the Maya area. We propose that Late Classic (AD 550–800) portable Maya GMM were insignias of affiliation that were created, assigned, gifted, or awarded by the hegemonic regime of Kaanul, also known as the snake regime, to its fellows and allied leaders.

To explore the meaning behind GMM we tracked previous versions of stone mosaics in Mesoamerica to study the background of this technological trend. Likewise, we explore the significance of the concept of segmentation materialized in lapidary by pre-Columbian societies. In a similar way that Peter Joralemon and Kent Reilly have uncovered puzzles of the Olmec cosmos (Joralemon 1976; Reilly 1991), we carried out a series of comparisons between natural features contemplated in the past and their continued anthropogenic versions materialized in greenstones. Based on an ecological-religious model (Hultkrantz 1966), Mesoamerican scholars have utilized the natural world to explore the meaning of pre-Columbian cultural materials, such as the case of Olmec greenstone celts, which were analogies of maize cobs (Coe 1988; Joralemon 1988; Taube 2000). Both the form and the color of maize cobs were combined in greenstone celts to represent sacred and inalienable elements belonging to the Olmec cosmology in a time (ca. 900–500 BC) when maize emerged as a staple food in the Olmec heartland (Rust and Leyden 1994 cited by Taube 2004). Weiss-Krejci (2012) has unequivocally shown a conflation between elements depicted in nature (i.e., a cross design displayed on a cross-section of an allspice trunk) and their subsequent materialization in the Maya pre-Columbian artistic corpus (e.g., San Bartolo murals, see Taube *et al.* 2010), which transcend in their Maya cosmological universe as the k'an cross: a symbol that means preciousness, ripe, yellow, and seat (Matthews and Biró 2006).

An overview of portable pre-Columbian greenstone mosaic masks

To explain the purpose of GMM in pre-Columbian times, scholars have suggested that these items represent the reborn faces of deities such as the Maize god (Filloy and Martínez 2008; Martínez del Campo 2010; García Verna 2012). Other suggestions have considered GMMs as the faces of sovereigns materialized in greenstone, particularly in the case of the one found to the left side of the facial bones of K'inich Jaanab' Pakal of Palenque (hereafter Pakal) (Filloy 2014). Moreover,

GMMs have also been considered as countenances of ancestors (Hruby 2015) and even as an element that "captures the breath soul of deceased rulers" (Houston and Taube 2000, 270).

Based on contextual analyses, García (2004) proposed that GMM could have been insignias of power carried by high-elite individuals during significant events, whereas Enrique Nalda (2004), in the case of the GMM found at Dzibanche and Kinichna, emphasized that these jewels were used as insignias. However, Nalda underscored the point that GMMs do not necessarily represent symbols of authority or were conceived as elements for the afterlife, considering that GMMs were found in elite but also modest burials arranged in vaults, cists, and a cenotaph in the specific case of Dzibanche. Moreover, Nalda highlighted the location of the GMM in relation to the buried individuals at Dzibanche: they were clearly not associated with the facial bones of the deceased. Therefore, he indicates these jewels were potentially awarded to individuals of different ranks.

Most of the GMMs in the Maya area were found on the thoracic, pelvic, or upper limb areas, as well as alongside individuals buried in pre-Columbian Maya high-status sepulchres. Because of their location in the funerary arrangement, GMMs seem to have been pendants hanging from necklaces and elements attached to headdresses, collars, and belts, as well as potential portable tokens that would have been carried by hand.

Nonetheless, there are two examples of GMMs found in close association with the facial bones of high-elite individuals: the first found in the Tomb of the "Red Queen of Palenque", likely Lady Tzkab'u. At the time of its discovery the GMM seems to have not been placed directly over the face but leaning between the orbital bones and the manubrium of the sternum (González Cruz 2011, 146). The second is the GMM that partially laid, at the time of its finding, to the left of the facial bones of Pakal (Ruz Lhuillier 1973; Filloy 2014). This was probably originally placed on her face although, as a result of taphonomic processes, it slid slightly to the left side of Pakal's face (Filloy and Martínez 2008).

With the exception of Late Preclassic (400 BC–AD 150) GMMs found in Burial 28a (n=1) at La Libertad (Miller 2014), and the one recovered from Tomb II (n=1) at Kaminaljuyu (Shook and Kidder 1952), both situated in the Maya Highlands, as well as the GMM found in Burial 1 (n=1) from *Tak'alik Ab'aj* located in the Pacific Coast (Tarpy 2004; Schiebert de Lavarreda 2015), most of the GMM reported to date in the Maya area have been found in funerary contexts dated to the Classic period from sites located in the Central Maya Lowlands (CML) and the site of Oxkintok located in the Northern Maya Lowlands (NML).

A few GMM have also been recovered from caches and special deposits, such as in the case for example of El Portón (n=1; dated to AD 0–200) (Sharer and Sedat 1987), Tak'alik Ab'aj (n=6 dated to AD 150–300) (Schiebert de Lavarreda and Orrego 2011), Dzibanche (n=1 dated between AD 700 and 900) (Martínez del Campo 2010), and Lamanai (n=1 dated to AD 600–800) (Pendergast 1981). The number of GMMs found in special deposits and a cache at Tak'alik Ab'aj (n=6), contrast with the fact that only one GMM has been found in a burial of a high-elite individual at this same site.

Moreover, at Tikal, a set of miniature mosaic masks (n=7) and mosaic statuettes (n=3) comprised of tesserae of green and sometimes bluish stones, pyrite, mollusks, specular hematite, and painted stucco elements has also been recovered from caches dated to the second half of the Early Classic period (AD 400–550) (Moholy-Nagy and Coe 2008). Interestingly, six of the seven miniature mosaic masks and two of the three miniature mosaic statuettes were found in association with Structure 5D-22, which is situated at the top of the North Acropolis of Tikal. The seventh miniature mosaic mask was found in a cache aligned on the axis of Structure 5D-34, also located at the North Acropolis (Coe 1990a; 1990b; 1990c), where Burial 10 was found, perhaps the funerary precinct of ruler Yax Nuun Ahiin. The third miniature mosaic statuette was recovered in a cache associated with Structure 5D-46 (Culbert and Kosakowski 2019). Excavations at this latter structure resulted in the finding of a ceramic vessel with inscriptions that mentions a significant ruler of the 4th century AD named Chak Tok Ich'aak I (Harrison 1999).

Several GMMs have inclusions of tesserae made of obsidian and pyrite which specifically form the pupils of the eyes. Likewise, some tesserae were made of mollusks that usually form the sclerae, lips, or other decorative elements (Colour Pl. 4). Nonetheless, in most cases, greenstone tesserae comprise around 90% of the whole composition, with the exception of the GMM from Burial 28a from La Libertad (Miller 2014): in this particular case shell tesserae exceed the ones made of greenstone.

Based on observations carried out on several GMM already restored (see Martínez del Campo 2010; García 2012, 118–19; Filloy 2014, tables 31 and 33), or assembled through curative conservation processes (e.g., GMM No. 2 from El Zotz; Magee and de Alarcón 2014), and some others currently disassembled and housed at the National Museum of Archaeology and Ethnology of Guatemala (MUNAE) (see Melendez 2019), it is striking that most of them were composed by a similar set of "guide tesserae". These "guide tesserae" seem to comprise a set of key tesserae that emulate sections of a human face (e.g., dorsum nasi, alar units, lower and upper lids, chin units, as well as areas of the central forehead) following the classification of human facial sections described by Radlanski and Wesker (2012).

In some cases, at the time GMMs were found through scientific excavations, the tesserae were not assembled in their logic order as to depict a face, either due to the dissolving of their backings –composed of wood, stucco, or both– or by the collapse in pre-Columbian times of the funerary precincts (e.g., vaults) such as in the case of Burials 37 and 39 of El Perú-*Waka'* (Rich *et al.* 2007; Melendez 2014). However, in several cases the GMM found *in situ* showed a comprehensive arrangement at the time of their excavation, such as in the case of Tomb 4, Structure IIb-2nd at Calakmul (Carrasco *et al.* 1999), or that found inside Pakal's sarcophagus (Ruz Lhuillier 1973). Exceptional cases exist; however, the GMM found in association with the potential head-dress placed above the head of the female individual, likely Lady K'abel *Kaloomte'* of the Kaanul regime and ruler of *Waka'*, found in Burial 61 of El Perú-*Waka'* (Navarro *et al.* 2020) was found facing downwards. This latter example provides an unlikely scenario that exposes the meaning of placing offerings or personal items in ancient Maya funerary precincts.

As mentioned above, some GMM were assembled on surfaces made of wood or a thick layer of mortar, as reported by Martínez del Campo (2010) and García (2012). Likewise, in the case of the GMMs from Tomb 1, Structure III of Calakmul and the one found in Pakal's sarcophagus, Martínez del Campo (2010) reported the use of copal and wax extracted from the honeycomb of stingless bees (*Melipona beechii*), as a sticky additive to inlay the tesserae over a surface.

After providing a brief introduction about the context and potential meanings of pre-Columbian Maya portable GMMs, we now explore and propose a new interpretation regarding their potential role, as well as delving deeper into the meaning of these unique items, which we argue were pristinely conceived and materialized by the Olmec culture and subsequently adopted by the Maya.

Melendez (2019) considers that Late Classic GMM found at sites located in the CML and Oxkintok were portable insignias of affiliation created, carried, and gifted or awarded by the Kaanul regime to other leaders of political entities in order to establish – among other strategies such as matrilineal unions – a political and economic network in the Maya Lowlands.

The Kaanul regime was one of the most powerful and expansionist hegemonic political entities, if not the most, in the Maya area during the Late Classic period (Martin 1993; Martin and Grube 2008), and perhaps even earlier during the Early Classic period (250–550) (Martin 2017; 2020). The Kaanul regime, also known as the "Snake regime" is represented in ancient Maya texts with the head of a snake (Martin and Velásquez 2016; Martin and Beliaev 2017; Martin 2020), which alphabetically spells Kaanul and signifies "abundance of snakes" (Mathews and Bíró 2006). Melendez (2019) proposes that GMM could have been the ideal Kaanul insignia as these seem to resemble anthropomorphic countenances mixed with snake features, considering that the greenstone tesserae could represent the scales of a snake, especially when the species in question is green in color (Colour Pl. 5).

The contextual data collected to date have determined that from the Late Classic there is a high presence of GMM at Dzibanche (n=10) (Nalda 2004; Balanzario 2021) and El Perú-*Waka'* (n=7) (Eppich 2011; Rich 2011; Lee 2012; Melendez 2019; Navarro *et al.* 2020). Likewise, at Calakmul around ten GMM have been identified to date (Folan *et al.* 1995; Folan and Morales 1996; Carrasco 1999; Carrasco *et al.* 1999; Delvendahl 2008; Schneider 2008; Fitzsimmons 2009; Martínez del Campo 2010; García 2012), although three of the ten were found inside Tomb 1, Structure III dated to the 5th century AD (Folan *et al.* 1995) but not after AD 475 (Martínez 2010). Nonetheless, and based on a visual comparative study of the ceramic vessels found in this latter sepulchre with those found in burials dated to the 4th century (e.g., Tikal, El Zotz, and El Tintal) where GMM were also found, Melendez (2019) suggested that Tomb 1 in Structure III at Calakmul could be dated back to the 4th century, as the stylistic similarities and decoration depicted on the ceramics are unequivocally alike.

It has been proposed that the physical seat of power of the Snake regime was first settled around the beginning of the 6th century at the site of Dzibanche and then moved to Calakmul (Martin 2005; Velásquez Garcia 2008; Martin and Velásquez 2016) in 635 (Stuart 2012) or 636 (Martin 2020, 348). Likewise, El Perú-*Waka'* served as close vassal and ally of the Snake regime from the first half of the 6th century (Guenter 2005; Martin 2020, 247).

Fig. 6.1. (opposite) Timeline and spatial sequence of the presence of Pre-Columbian GMM in the Maya area from the 1st–9th centuries AD.

To date, around 54% (n=27) of the collection of portable GMMs found in elite pre-Columbian Maya burials in the CML and Oxkintok, currently estimated at 50 GMM, has been found at Dzibanche, Calakmul, and El Perú-*Waka'* (Colour Pl. 6). This focalized concentration of GMMs at sites with a well-established presence of the Kaanul regime, we argue, is solid contextual evidence regarding the ties that existed between the Snake regime and these portable jewels. Interestingly, if the GMM found to date at Palenque are included (n=10) in this equation, then around 75% of the GMM reported in the Maya Lowlands has been recovered from a limited number of sites, namely Dzibanche, Calakmul, El Perú-*Waka'* and Palenque (Fig. 6.1).

However, what about the greenstone mosaic masks found in burials of high-ranking individuals dated to the Early Classic, could those also be considered as Kaanul insignias? What is the evidence of the Kaanul regime in the Maya Lowlands during the Early Classic? We think that there is circumstantial evidence to believe that GMM found in elaborate burials dated to the Early Classic in the CML were also Kaanul insignias used by individuals affiliated to this hegemonic regime since the 4th century AD.

The first evidence of GMMs associated with high-ranking individuals in the CML appears around the 4th century, namely at El Tintal, Tikal, El Zotz, Holmul, Calakmul, and likely El Palmar-Petén. Following our proposal that considers GMMs as insignias linked to the Kaanul regime, this would mean that the presence of the Snake regime in the Maya Lowlands could be tracked to around the 4th century.

Coincidently, sites such as El Tintal, El Zotz, Tikal, Holmul, and Calakmul all surround the core of the "Mirador Plateau", the latter considered the ancient heartland of the Kaanul regime from the Late Middle Preclassic (500 BC) to the Terminal Preclassic (AD 150) (Hansen 2016). Several scholars have also considered the possibility that the city of El Mirador, located at the core of the Mirador Plateau, was the Preclassic seat of the Kaanul regime (Martin 1997; Hansen and Guenter 2005; Freidel 2018). Nonetheless, due to the absence of GMMs associated with burials at El Mirador, Nakbe, and other sites located at the core of the "Mirador Plateau", this assumption cannot be proved, at least from the perspective of the GMMs.

However, one possible explanation is that the core of the Mirador Plateau could have been encircled by centers under control of the Kaanul regime during the 4th century AD or even before, perhaps from a supply site where the Kaanul seat was settled at that time, probably Dzibanche or Ichkabal (Martin and Velásquez 2016), or even Calakmul.

To date, due to the shortage of ancient Maya texts with references to this regime before the 6th century, there is no clear consensus regarding the origins of Kaanul in the Maya area. The earliest accepted reference to Kaanul was identified on a carved step that forms the hieroglyphic staircase of Dzibanche, dated to around 518 (Velásquez Garcia 2005). However, based on the study of ancient Maya texts displayed on codex style dynastic ceramic vases, which seem to name a list of Kaanul rulers, Simon Martin (2017) suggested that the rise of the Kaanul dynasty could occurred around the 3rd century, closer in time to the first evidence of GMMs in the Maya Lowlands.

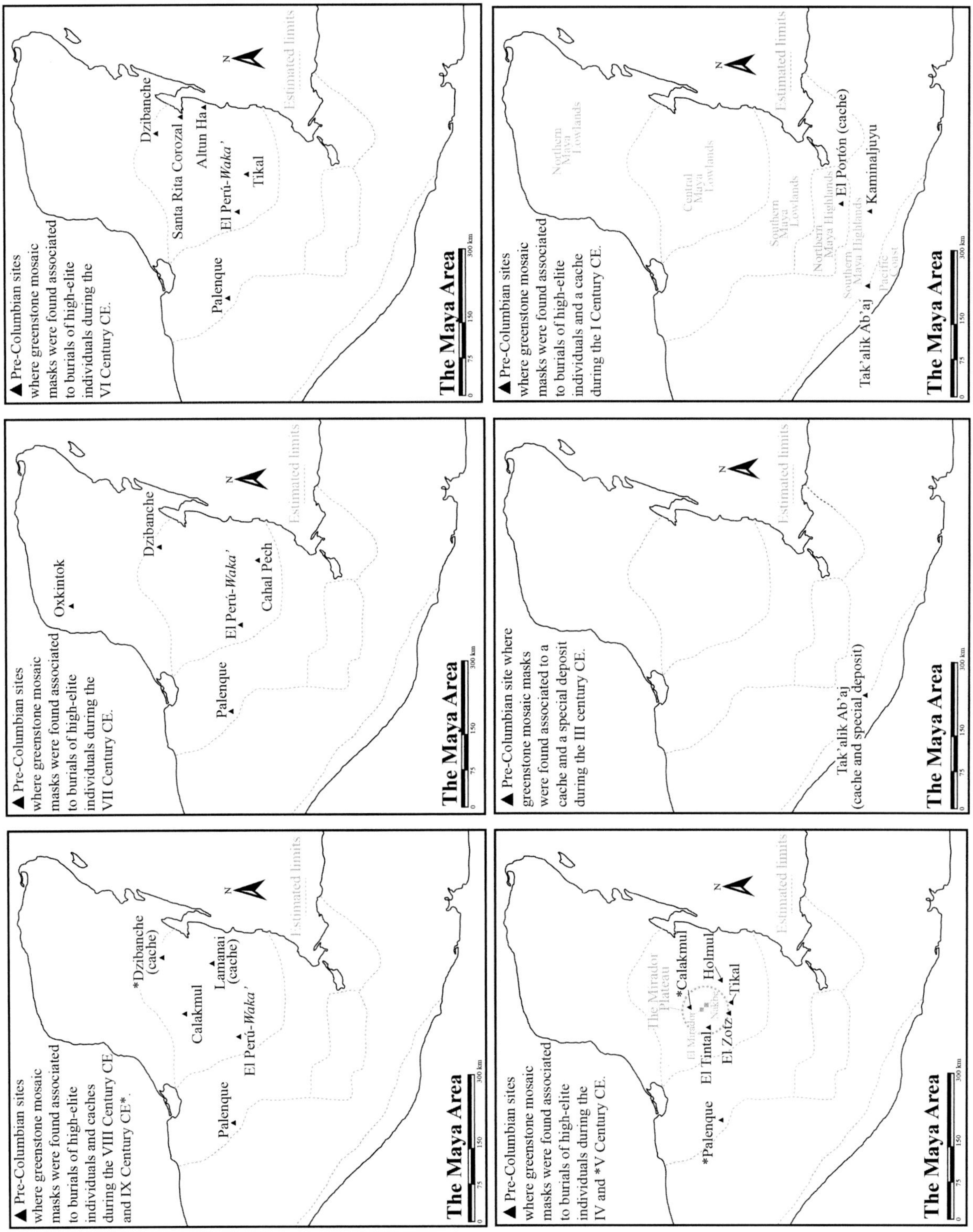
▲ Pre-Columbian sites where greenstone mosaic masks were found associated to burials of high-elite individuals and a cache during the I Century CE.
Northern Maya Lowlands
Central Maya Lowlands
Southern Maya Lowlands
Northern Maya Highlands
Southern Maya Highlands
Pacific Coast
El Portón (cache)
Kaminaljuyu
Tak'alik Ab'aj
Estimated limits
N
The Maya Area
0 75 150 300 km
▲ Pre-Columbian site where greenstone mosaic masks were found associated to a cache and a special deposit during the III century CE.
Tak'alik Ab'aj (cache and special deposit)
Estimated limits
N
The Maya Area
0 75 150 300 km
▲ Pre-Columbian sites where greenstone mosaic masks were found associated to burials of high-elite individuals during the IV and *V Century CE.
The Mirador Plateau
*Calakmul
Holmul
El Mirador
Nakbe
El Tintal
El Zotz
Tikal
*Palenque
Estimated limits
N
The Maya Area
0 75 150 300 km
▲ Pre-Columbian sites where greenstone mosaic masks were found associated to burials of high-elite individuals during the VI Century CE.
Dzibanche
Santa Rita Corozal
Altun Ha
El Perú-Waka'
Tikal
Palenque
Estimated limits
N
The Maya Area
0 75 150 300 km
▲ Pre-Columbian sites where greenstone mosaic masks were found associated to burials of high-elite individuals during the VII Century CE.
Oxkintok
Dzibanche
El Perú-Waka'
Cahal Pech
Palenque
Estimated limits
N
The Maya Area
0 75 150 300 km
▲ Pre-Columbian sites where greenstone mosaic masks were found associated to burials of high-elite individuals and caches during the VIII Century CE and IX Century CE*.
*Dzibanche (cache)
Calakmul
Lamanai (cache)
El Perú-Waka'
Palenque
Estimated limits
N
The Maya Area
0 75 150 300 km

Around the beginning of the 2nd century AD, one of the oldest and long-lasting dynasties in the Maya area was established with headquarters at the ancient Maya site of Tikal. Based on the discovery of a sumptuous and elaborate tomb identified as Burial 85, located in the North Acropolis of Tikal (Coe 1965), it was proposed that the potential founder of Tikal's dynasty was buried there around AD 100 (Martin and Grube 2008). The dynasty of Tikal, anciently named Yax-Mutal and identified in the Maya inscriptions as a topknot, was the nemesis of the Kaanul regime during the Late Classic (Martin and Grube 2008) and perhaps even earlier (Freidel 2018). The example of Tikal provides an argument to suggest the rise of dynasties in the CML around the 2nd century AD which, in the case of Tikal, was comprised of a sophisticated political organization based on a patrilineal dynasty (Freidel 2018).

At La Muerta, a site located to the south of El Mirador, an ancient Maya text carved on Monument 1 seems to represent the K'ujul Kaanul Ajaw title (Hansen 2016), which dates to around AD 300–450 (Guenter and Hansen n.d.). By this time, the largest Preclassic cities located at the core of the Mirador Plateau, such as El Mirador and Nakbe, had been abandoned (AD 150) (Hansen 2016), therefore the possible presence of the Kaanul regime at La Muerta around AD 300–450 seems to represent a sporadic or seasonal visit (i.e., pilgrimage) more than evidence of a more permanent occupation. GMM associated with high-elite individuals dated to the Late Preclassic (400 BC–AD 150) that could be linked to ancient Kaanul leaders have not been found to date in the Maya Lowlands. However, future research projects could shed light on this subject, although it is striking that after decades of research at the core of the Mirador Plateau there is no evidence of this type of jewel at Nakbe and El Mirador, which seem to have been strong candidates to be considered the cradle of the Snake regime.

Returning to the Classic Period, we are faced with various challenges in conceiving that GMMs were Kaanul insignias. One of these is related to the fact that several GMMs have been found at sites usually considered sworn enemies of the Snake regime, based on historical evidence, such as Tikal, Palenque, and even El Perú-*Waka'*, the latter before the 6th century.

Nonetheless, based on historical data, events of usurping likely carried out by external individuals seem to have occurred in the dynastic lines of Tikal at the end of both the 4th (Freidel 2018) and 5th centuries (Haviland 2015) while, at El Perú-*Waka'*, similar events seem to occur during the 6th century (Freidel 2018) and, at Palenque, during the 7th (Suart and Stuart 2008). The main individual in those episodes of usurping seems to always be the same: the Kaanul regime.

Tikal

To date, the only three GMMs reported in Tikal have been found in areas distant from the North Acropolis (Melendez 2019) which has been recognized as the royal necropolis of the long-lived Yax-Mutal dynasty or first Mutal (Harrison 1999; Martin and Grube 2008). Two of the three GMMs were recovered from Burial PNT-19 (Proyecto Nacional Tikal) dated to AD 378 and located in the central structure of the E-Group at the Lost World Complex, very likely the precinct where Chak

Tok Ich'aak I lay (Laporte 1989) after being overthrown by Sihyaj K'ahk' from Teotihuacan (Stuart 2000). Chak Tok Ich'aak I was very likely the son of K'inich Muwaan Jol, probably Kaanul's usurper in the dynastic line of Tikal during the first part of the 4th century as suggested by Freidel (2018). Coincidently, the third GMM found at Tikal was also found in the burial of a ruler, likely named Chak Tok Ich'aak II, as suggested by Fitzsimmons (2009, 192), identified as Burial 160, located far from the royal necropolis of Tikal. Nonetheless, Haviland (2015) suggests the individual in Burial 160 could also be Kaloomte' Bahlam, who was denied the right of being buried at the royal necropolis at the North Acropolis as result of an usurping event that occurred at Tikal after his passing. His interment was found to the southeast of the city, namely below Structure 7F-30 (Haviland 2015). We propose that the individual in Burial 160, either Kaloomte' Bahlam or Chak Tok Ich'aak II, was not allowed or, requested not to, be buried in the Necropolis of Tikal due to his lineage being tied to different ancestors, very likely Kaanul ones, which seem to have maintained a persistent presence at Tikal from the Early Classic (Freidel 2018).

Moholy-Nagy and Coe (2008, 50) has also reported two other "masks of composite assembled of finely worked elements of stone and shell laid down upon a support of entirely disintegrated material", which could have been considered as GMM. These two GMMs are composed of tiny pieces, and according to Moholy-Nagy and Coe these could not be reconstructed. These two GMM were found in Burial 10 (Structure 5D-34) and Burial 48 (Structure 5D-33), both located at the North Acropolis of Tikal (Coe 1990c). Burial 10 is the funerary precinct where Yax Nuun Ahiin I likely lay, while the main individual in Burial 48 could have been Sihyaj Chan K'awiil II. Both rulers were likely installed, blessed, and aligned to the interests of the ancient Metropolis of Teotihuacan after the violent event of AD 378 (Stuart 2000; Martin and Grube 2008).

However, after close observation of the components that form these GMMs, as well as studying the archaeological context from which these artifacts were recovered, it seems they were intentionally disassembled, perhaps destroyed, and subsequently included as incomplete (Burial 48), or fragmented (Burial 10) funerary offerings.

The potential GMM from Burial 10 was composed of more than 3000 tiny greenstone tesserae with varying dimensions ranging between ~3 mm and 5 mm, with one polished side and amorphous edges (Moholy-Nagy and Coe 2008). The tiny tesserae were agglomerated in three specific areas within the burial: a) two were located to the northwest and northeast sides of the main individual's head (i.e., Skeleton A) buried in this sepulchre; b) the third area of tiny greenstone tesserae were placed to the south of its feet (Coe 1990c). Pale greenstone tesserae form the sclerae of this GMM, while dark greenstone segments could form the pupils of the eyes (Moholy-Nagy and Coe 2008), which all seem to be associated with the agglomerations of the tiny greenstone tesserae associated with the head of the ruler (Coe 1990c). According to Coe (1990c) this potential GMM could have been originally attached to the head-dress of this ruler. There is only one GMM with similar technological features (i.e., formed by tiny, polished greenstone tesserae of irregular edges) that could resemble the one from Burial 10 of Tikal: it was found in Burial 3, Structure XV of Calakmul and dated around AD 700 (Delvendahl 2008). Nonetheless, this GMM from Calakmul is comprised of sclerae, teeth, and lips carved from mollusks and pupils carved from obsidian, showing a clear association with the facial elements.

In the case of the incomplete mosaic assemblage recovered from Burial 48, this is comprised of only ten tesserae that could form sections of the two lower lids, two pupils, four sclerae, and two sections of the upper lids (see Moholy-Nagy and Coe 2008, fig. 89a) which together basically form the orbital region of a face. Coe (1990c) stated that the sclerae and upper lids are made of shell and green stucco while the pupils were carved in hematite. Whereas Moholy-Nagy and Coe (2008) on the other hand indicates that the upper lids and sclerae are made of pale green jade and the pupils manufactured from pyrite with shale backing. Coe (1990a, 121) also indicated that these orbital regions were found in association with almost 700 jade elements in "scatter fashion" that very likely form a circular pattern, which remind us of the one found in Burial 10. Coe (1990c) suggested that this incomplete mask could have been attached to the potential head-ress of the main individual buried in this sepulchre although he does not discard the possibility that it was included in the burial within a bundle.

The presence of potential GMMs in Burials 10 and 48 of Tikal is confusing. Certainly, the style and form of their tesserae contrast with the ones recovered from Early Classic high-elite burials at Tikal (i.e., Burial PNT-19 and Burial 160) as well as at other sites at the CML (e.g., Burial 9 at El Zotz; Burial 1 at El Tintal; Burial 1, Structure III of Calakmul, and the one from Structure B, Group 2 at Holmul). In our opinion, the inclusion and location of these "potential" GMMs as tiny fragments that do not follow a logic facial order could also be the result of a desecrating event. Probably, these concentrations of scattered amorphous segments deliberately represent trophies more than personal items, as in the particular case of the GMM in Burial 10. If these tesserae had been part of the head-dress' decoration, then what would have been the point of placing a portion of these fragments in association with the ruler's feet?

The contextual similarities between the two "potential" GMMs in Burials 10 and 48 – namely because of their almost fragmented segmentation – as well the fact that both rulers associated with them seem to have been linked to the ancestral and medullar kinship of Tikal, very likely aligned to Teotihuacan during the 5th century, could represent a symbolic desecration. Perhaps these fragmented segmentations were intentional symbolic actions against the Kaanul regime, a faction that very likely cohabited with the Yax-Mutal dynasty at Tikal. The co-existence of political antagonist factions at Tikal it is not a novel hypothesis, it was previously proposed by Laporte (1989) after conducting an impeccable research project at the "Lost World" Group, located to the southeast of the core of this city.

El Perú-*Waka'*

The incursion of Teotihuacan into the Maya area during the 4th century led to the establishment of a new order at several sites including Bejucal, El Zotz,

Uaxactun, Tikal, and El Perú-*Waka'* under the supervision of Teotihuacan (Freidel 2018). For almost two centuries, El Perú-*Waka'* seems to have been a loyal ally of Tikal, the latter the main seat of the new order (Freidel 2015; Martin and Believ 2017). Nonetheless, during the middle of the 6th century, El Perú-*Waka'* drastically changed its alliance in favor of the Kaanul regime (Guenter pers. comm. 2013 and cited by Martin and Believ 2017; Freidel pers. comm. 2014). The ruler, Chak Tok Ich'aak, who is mentioned on Stela 44 of El Perú-*Waka'*, dedicated in AD 564 (Pérez and Navarro-Farr 2013), seems potentially to be responsible for this change of alliance blessed by the Kaanul regime. Stuart *et al.* (2018) suggest this same individual is also mentioned on Altar 5 of La Corona, a site located 30 km north of El Perú-*Waka'*. Based on the decipherment of the hieroglyphs depicted on Altar 5, Stuart *et al.* (2018) describe how, in AD 544 Chak Tok Ich'aak, ruler of La Corona, traveled to a place called Baaktuunil to celebrate a period ending. On the other hand, Stela 44 is a commemorative monument dedicated by the ruler of El Perú-*Waka'*, named Wa'oom Uch'ab Ahk, to his father, Chak Tok Ich'aak, who also ruled El Perú-*Waka'*, very likely under the auspice of the Kaanul ruler named Tuun K'ab Hix (Martin and Believ 2017). For Stuart *et al.* (2018), Chak Tok Ich'aak was a ruler at both La Corona and El Perú-*Waka'*. We consider that Chak Tok Ich'aak could have been a close collaborator of Tuun K'ab Hix from Kaanul who, besides being proclaimed ruler at La Corona, instituted a new dynastic branch at El Perú-*Waka'*, likely as an usurper of the local reigning royal branch with ties to Tikal.

The references that accompany Chak Tok Ich'aak on Altar 5 of La Corona as a fellow of the *sak wahyis* house connect him to several leaders of La Corona that also carried this title. Likewise, the *sak wahyis* title has ties to potential seats where this dynasty seems to have been installed during the Late Classic, very likely in the northern part of the Central Maya Lowlands (Stuart *et al.* 2018).

The fact that Lady Ikoom, very likely Chak Tok Ich'aak's wife, is mentioned on Stela 44 of El Perú-*Waka'* and linked to the title *sak wahyis* as well as the one known as *k'uhul chatahn winik*, is another indication that allows us to speculate on the close ties between El Perú-*Waka'* with the Kaanul regime. References to the house of *chatahn winik* have been identified at Calakmul during the 6th century (Valencia and Esparza 2014).

Coincidently, at El Perú-*Waka'*, Burial 37 could have been the funerary precinct where the ruler Chak Tok Ich'aak lay. The sepulture was placed at the center of the city within the highest pyramid located at the core of the site (Melendez 2014). Based on contextual analyses of the funerary arrangement and the typological study of the ceramic vessels found in this burial, Melendez (2014) and David Freidel (2008) suggested that the ruler Chak Tok Ich'aak, mentioned on Stela 44 of El Perú-*Waka'*, was the individual placed in Burial 37 around AD 550–600. Undoubtedly, the GMM found next to the occipital region of the individual's cranium in Burial 37 stands out for purposes of this study.

Stuart *et al.* (2018) stated a striking point regarding the way the ruler's name Chak Tok Ich'aak appears on Altar 5 of La Corona and Stela 44 at El Perú-*Waka'*, noting these were written in the same extended form that those identified at Tikal and attributed to the rulers Chak Tok Ich'aak I and II of Tikal. As we proposed above, these same rulers could have been related to events of usurping and, coincidently, GMM have been found in their potential burials. Martin and Beliaev (2017) have also highlighted the likely lineage connection between the ruler Chak Tok Ich'aak of both El Perú-*Waka'* and La Corona (~AD 550) with those from Tikal (e.g., Chak Tok Ich'aak I, AD 378, and Chak Tok Ich'aak II, AD 508). There is a clear link between the Chak Tok Ich'aak's rulers from Tikal, El Perú-*Waka'*, and La Corona not only because they are homonymous and their names were written using a specific set of hieroglyphs during a span of 200 years. Surprisingly, it seems these rulers were also implicated in events of usurping and, coincidently, GMM have been found associated with the burials where very likely they were buried. If GMM were certainly Kaanul regime's insignias, then these rulers seem to have been united by their Kaanul ancestors.

Palenque

According to the decipherment of ancient Maya texts, Palenque was defeated twice in AD 599 and 611 by the forces of the Snake regime (Martin and Grube 2008). Following these two defeats, Palenque emerged as one of the most important economic and political centers in the Maya Lowlands led by the local ruler Pakal who ruled between 615 and 683 (Stuart and Stuart 2008). Curiously, Palenque's defeats and its subsequent apogee both occurred during the rulership of two of the most expansionist and powerful rulers known in Maya history: Scroll Serpent and Yuknoom Ch'een II who led the Snake regime between 579 and 686 (Martin and Grube 2008). It seems that Palenque's rise could have occurred under the supervision of the Kaanul regime, perhaps through a political maneuver consisting in the installation of a leader that corresponded to the interest of the Snake regime.

David Freidel (2018) underscores the two hypotheses proposed by George and David Stuart (2008) regarding the ascension of the young ruler Pakal to the throne of Palenque. These scholars suggest that Pakal could have been the inheritor of an "auxiliary branch" of Palenque's ancestral dynasty. The second hypothesis considers that the Kaanul regime could have installed the child Pakal in 615 as a puppet ruler, after its recent victory in 611 over Palenque (Stuart and Stuart 2008). This maneuver would permit the Kaanul regime to extend its control and campaign of expansion (Martin and Grube 2008) over strategic cities to the west of the Lowlands. Stuart and Stuart (2008) also highlight the intriguing sudden presence of K'an Hix Mo' – father of *Pakal* – in the history of Palenque, arriving to this city likely as a noble from a foreign center, although never acceding to the throne of Palenque.

In summary, rulers and high-ranking individuals that have been linked to these latter episodes of usurping, likely persuaded by the Kaanul regime, such as in the case of Chak Tok Ich'aak at El Perú-*Waka'*, Chak Tok Ich'aak I and II at Tikal, and K'an Hix Mo' and his son Pakal in Palenque, all were buried with GMMs as part of their regalia (Ruz Lhuillier 1973; Moholy-Nagy and Coe 2008; Melgar *et al.* 2013; Haviland 2015; Melendez and Melgar 2018; Melendez 2019).

The political scenarios that took place during the 6th and 8th centuries in the Maya Lowlands show the complexity of the strategies and virtuosity of the negotiations undertaken by the Kaanul regime that sought to consolidate a solid sophisticated political and economic network. Based on the number of GMMs reported from ruler and elite burials during the Late Classic (n=40), we consider that between the 6th and 8th centuries, GMMs were essential elements of affiliation used by the Snake regime to link through time and across space a web of key players – either rulers, courtiers, or emissaries who may have played the role of ambassadors – hatched by the Kaanul regime in the CML and beyond. Fragments of historical evidence collected to date (Hansen 2016; Martin 2017) portend the existence of the Kaanul's presence in the Central Maya Lowlands since the 3rd or 4th centuries AD.

If GMM were in fact representative insignias of the Kannul regime, very likely since its emergence, then it would be possible to track its potential extension across the CML from the 4th century, a time when the first GMMs were associated with sepulchres of high-elite individuals.

Interestingly, the ten GMM reported to date from the CML recovered from funerary contexts dated to the 4th century, were recovered from sites that surround the core of the Mirador Plateau (i.e., Calakmul, El Tintal, El Zotz, Tikal, Holmul, and likely El Palmar-Petén). Here we emphasize again that, to date, there is no evidence of GMM associated with pre-Columbian high-elite burials at sites located at the core of the Mirador Plateau such as El Mirador or Nakbe.

Because the Mirador Plateau was severely depopulated around AD 150, and modestly re-occupied between 550 and 900, mainly at sites located at the south of the plateau (Hansen 2016), we discard the idea that sites such as El Mirador and Nakbe were potential seats of the Kaanul regime around the 3rd century.

Which was the potential location of a Kaanul's seat(s) during the 3rd or 4th century? Could any of the sites that surround the core of the Mirador Plateau, where GMM were reported, be a seat of the Kaanul regime at that time? Was there a unique Kaanul seat during this period, or was this regime composed of a political structure comprised by parallel seats? What are the chances that other monumental sites with an occupation between the 2nd and 4th centuries in the CML could rival the ones located at the core of the Mirador Plateau as a potential seat of the Kaanul regime? Martin and Velásquez (2016) have suggested that Ichkabal, a monumental Preclassic site located 11 miles/3.35 km away from Dzibanche, could be a striking contender.

In any case, we propose that the presence of GMMs as part of the grave goods included in burials of individuals, as well as the ones found in potential cenotaphs (e.g., Dzibanche: Chamber 2, Cormorant Temple; Nalda 2004) are indicative of the presence of the Kaanul regime across the Maya Lowlands.

Beyond the Maya Lowlands, only three GMMs have been reported found in high-elite burials in the Maya area before the 3rd century: the GMM found in Tomb II, Mound E-III-3 at Kaminaljuyu (Shook and Kidder 1952) and the one associated with the hip of the earliest ruler found in Tak'alik Ab'aj (Tarpy 2004; Schiebert de Lavarreda 2015), both dated to the end of the Late Preclassic (AD 100). The earliest archaeological context where a mosaic mask has been reported was found in Burial 28a at the site of La Libertad, dated to the beginning of the Late Preclassic (500–300 BC) (Miller 2014) which, according to the image published by

Miller, is comprised of a larger number of tesserae made of mollusks compared to those made of greenstone.

The main idea behind GMMs

Prior to the Late Preclassic (500/400 BC–AD 100) GMMs identified at sites located on the Pacific Coast and the Maya Highlands, the only known mosaic masks in Mesoamerica, were the three pavements made of carved serpentine blocks that form the massive GMM at the Olmec site of La Venta (Drucker 1952, 57, 74; Drucker *et al.* 1959, 94). Pavements 1 and 3 were dated to the Phase II (860–750 BC), whereas Pavement 2 was dated to Phase IV (600–400 BC) (Tate 2012, 143). Originally, Drucker (1952, 56) suggested that these pavements were conventional jaguar masks, an idea that would be perpetuated for decades.

Four decades later, Kent Reilly (1994) suggested that the pavements were the fusion of three elements: a double step, which symbolizes the entrance to the Underworld; the four dots; and a bar that is narrowly related to the Olmec GI deity, also known as the Olmec dragon, who floats on the primordial pool. Additionally, the diamond-shape fringes at the bottom of the mosaic mask pavements could represent waterlily plants.

Nonetheless, we propose a new explanation for the scenes depicted on the Olmec pavements which is linked to our interpretation regarding the mosaic techniques and technological style materialized on Classic period portable greenstone mosaic masks. An extract written in *The Maya Cosmos* book published by Freidel *et al.* (1993), piqued the curiosity of the first author of this chapter: the ethnographer Johannes Wilbert advises Linda Schele "to look to nature for the source of mythological symbolism" (Freidel *et al.* 1993, 76). This phrase was key, as it led Melendez (2019) to turn to nature to seek for a potential explanation regarding the meaning behind the GMM and the signification of segmentation (i.e., tesserae) and subsequent aggregation (i.e., mosaics) of elements which, when assembled in a logic order, conveyed the countenances (i.e., masks) of living beings. Melendez's (2019) ideas seem to harmoniously weave together with those of Kent Reilly, who had conceived a new interpretation of the Olmec pavements as a result of his meticulous contextual analyses. Following different lines of evidence, Melendez and Reilly arrived at the conclusion that the massive GMM of La Venta could represent faces of snakes. Collectively, the authors of this chapter developed this latter argument as summarized below.

We believe that the pavements that constitute the massive GMM in La Venta, which seem to be the first mosaic expressions in Mesoamerica, are lifelike representation of a snake's face, where each carved block used to recreate the massive mosaic mask represents a scale on a snake. Kent Reilly (pers. comm. 2019) also believes this interpretation. Nonetheless, he emphasizes the presence of yellowish clay reported by Drucker *et al.* (1959, 95) which was found inside the four diamond-shaped patterns attached to the bottom of the massive GMM No. 3 (i.e., Pavement No. 3), highlighting that those could be associated with the colored segments found on the body of certain poisonous snake species in the Olmec area. David Freidel (2008) pointed out that the pattern of carved *spondylus* shells included in the forehead of the face that forms one of the three portable Maya GMMs discovered in Tomb 1, Structure III from Calakmul, could be related to the reddish brown spots found on the green body of the eyelash palm-pit viper (*Bothriechis schlegelii*), a venomous species of snake (Köhler 2008) belonging to the viperidae family, found from the north of Chiapas to the north of the Maya area (Campbell 1998).

Some specimens of the eyelash palm-pit viper are greenish with rust-colored and reddish brown spots on their body and head (Campbell 1998). However, it is another feature that drew our attention, namely the pronounced scales that stick out from the supraciliary region above the eyes. The two upper corners that diverge from the cleft located at the top of the massive GMM remind us of these supraciliary scales found on the eyelash palm-pit viper.

Likewise, we noted that snakes belonging to the viperidae family have two nostrils and two pits on each side of the face. These features are, in our opinion, represented on the massive GMM by the two blank areas which were originally interpreted as the four eyes of a jaguar (Druker 1952). Whereas the central blank section between the two so-called four eyes would form the nose and below these features, the larger blank space inside the mask would represent the mouth (Colour Pl. 7).The three pavements that likely represent snake faces in the same manner as the portable GMMs are outstanding in that they present the idea of segmentation, and subsequently the aggregation of elements, in order to materialize animal faces using precious stones.

In the case of an oval mirror formed by 59 polygonal pyrite tesserae discovered in association with a ruler buried in a tomb at Bonampak, Mary Miller and Simon Martin (2004, 44) suggest this "form[s] an idealized turtle carapace." Clearly, Miller and Martin (2004) recognized that ancient Maya artisans conceived of the idea of segmentation in order to materialize patterns that resembled animal skins or exoskeletons which, in the specific example of the mosaic pyrite mirror, resembles the carapace of a turtle that, in turn, represents the mother earth to the ancient Maya.

The fact that the massive GMMs (i.e., Pavements 1 and 3) from La Venta could represent snake faces does not take away from the original multi-leveled Olmec cosmos proposed by Reilly (1994), as these lay on massive offerings composed of layers of serpentine amorphous blocks that could represent pools of water. When we consider the adaptability of snakes to climb trees, creep on the ground, and swim, their placement is comprehensible within the Olmec cultural landscape (Sauer 1925).

Concluding thoughts

We suggest that the idea of segmentation and its subsequent materialization in stones through lapidary practices to then aggregate them to compose mosaics which, assembled in a logic manner, represent masks, seems to be pristinely materialized as a monumental project at La Venta (i.e., Monumental GMM – Pavements 1 and 3) around the 8th century BC. The idea of segmentation, as we have proposed in this paper, seems to have been emulated from features manifested on animals with scales or scutta, very likely snakes, turtles, or crocodiles. However, not all the GMMs represent faces of reptiles. Few GMM seem to represent the countenances of bats, such as in the case of the GMM found in the offering associated with Structure 6 of Tak'alik Ab'aj (~AD 300) (Schiebert de Lavarreda 2015), or the one that formed the pendant of an individual buried at Monte Albán (~AD 250) (Acosta 1949). Additionally, the GMM found in Tomb II at Kaminaljuyu seems to represent a bird (Guernsey 2006). Nonetheless, we do not discard the possibility that representations or features of two or more animals or beings were conflated and materialized in a GMM. The best example is the feathered serpent deity that appears in several Mesoamerican pantheons and which could have had its origins among the Olmec culture around the Middle Preclassic (Taube 2004). Features of two animals included into a single GMM, as a dual scene, are also visible on the GMM found in Burial 160 of Tikal. Coggins (1975) noted that a beak carved of greenstone that emerges from the forehead of this latter GMM could represent the one belonging to a quetzal (*Pharomachrus mocinno*), which, conflated to the potential features of a snake's face, could be linked to Quetzalcoatl, the feathered serpent, also known as the War Serpent and which is associated with contexts of rulership (Taube 2018).

Mosaic as a lapidary technique seems to be adopted by the ancient Maya to produce portable GMM at sites located in the Maya Highlands during the transition between the Middle and Late Preclassic (300 BC), such as in the case of the site of La Libertad, and then this technological and stylistic tradition appears at El Portón, Kaminaljuyu and Tak'alik Ab'aj. Scholars have also noted the adoption of cultural manifestations from the Olmec cosmos and rulership by the ancient populations from Izapa and the Maya area (Fields 1989; Reilly 1991; Freidel *et al.* 1993; Taube 2004; Fields and Reents-Budet 2005; Freidel 2008; Guernsey 2006). Subsequently, during the Early and Late Classic, the link between mosaic masks representing the face of snakes persisted, although embedded in the political sphere of that time, very likely as idealized symbols representative of a political regime.

Because of the large number of GMMs, which we consider are idealized countenances of snakes, found associated with Late Classic sites politically affiliated to the hegemonic regime of Kaanul – the Mayan word that means "abundance of snakes" – we consider that GMM were used as symbols and insignias of their leaders, allies, and close collaborators. Even though the presence and expansion of the Kaanul regime in the Maya Lowlands has been tracked based on the appearance of its emblem glyph represented by the face of a snake, we propose that GMM found in the Maya Lowlands could also be an indication of the presence and expansion of this regime. The way in that we see GMMs could provide a new path to explore the reach of the Kaanul regime's expansion not only spatially (e.g., presence of GMMs at Oxkintok) but through time, namely at the moment of its probable arising as a political entity around the 2nd or 3rd century AD (Martin 2017).

Based on the data collected in this study and in combination with our own intuition, we have tried to provide a scenario regarding the political dynamics in the Central Maya Lowlands during pre-Columbian times, through the lens of GMM, which situate the Kaanul regime, either as a sodality, dynasty, or any other political manifestation, as an active key player during the 4th century AD. Following a *hiatus* noted by the near absence of GMM during the 5th century, the emergence of these insignias since the middle of the 6th century is indeed striking; a trend that persisted until the 9th century, namely at sites such as Palenque, El Perú-*Waka'*, Dzibanche, and Calakmul. The idea of segmentation linked to the vivid representations of a snake's scales to subsequently form masks seems to have been a straightforward idealization of natural perceptions among the Olmecs during the Middle Preclassic period. For the ancient Maya of the Classic period, however, even though the main idea of segmentation associated to serpent scales and in turn snake countenances remains, this seems to be monopolized by the political discourse of that time.

References

Acosta, J. (1949) El pectoral de jade de Monte Albán. *Anales del Instituto Nacional de Antropología e Historia* 3, 17–25.

Balanzario, S. (2021) Exploraciones arqueológicas en Dzibanché, Quintana Roo. Unpublished paper presented at the 2021 Virtual Mesoamerica Meetings "News From The Field: Archaeological Perspectives from Mesoamerica", University of Texas at Austin, January 2021.

Biebuyck, D. (1986) *Eastern Zaire.* The Arts of Zaire 2. University of California Press, Berkeley CA.

Cameron, E. (2001) *Art of the Lega.* UCLA Fowler Museum of Cultural History, Los Angeles CA.

Campbell, J. (1998) *Amphibians and Reptiles of Northern Guatemala, the Yucatán, and Belize.* University of Oklahoma Press, Norman OK.

Carrasco, R. (1999) Tumbas Reales de Calakmul: Ritos Funerarios y Estructura de Poder. *Arqueología Mexicana* 7, 28–31.

Carrasco, R., Boucher, S., Alvarez, P., Tiesler, V., García, V., García, R. and Vázquez, J. (1999) A dynastic tomb from Campeche, Mexico: New evidence on Jaguar Paw, a ruler of Calakmul. *Latin American Antiquity* 10, 47–58.

Coe, M. (1988) Ideology of the Maya tomb. In *Maya Iconography*, eds E. Benson and G. Griffin, 222–35. Princeton University Press, Princeton NJ.

Coe, M. and Kerr, J. (1997) *The Art of the Maya Scribe.* Harry N. Abrams, New York.

Coe, W. (1965) T ikal: Ten years of study of a Maya ruin in the lowlands of Guatemala. *Expedition* 8, 1–56.

Coe, W. (1990a) *Excavations in the Great Plaza, North Terrace and North Acropolis of Tikal.* Tikal Report 14.I, University Museum Monograph 61, University of Pennsylvania, Philadelphia PA.

Coe, W. (1990b) *Excavations in the Great Plaza, North Terrace and North Acropolis of Tikal.* Tikal Report 14.II, University Museum Monograph 61, University of Pennsylvania, Philadelphia PA.

Coe, W. (1990c) Excavations in the Great Plaza, North Terrace and North Acropolis of Tikal. Tikal Report 14. IV, University Museum Monograph 61, University of Pennsylvania, Philadelphia.

Coe, W. (1990d) Excavations in the Great Plaza, North Terrace and North Acropolis of Tikal. *Tikal Report 14,* Volume V, University Museum Monograph 61, University of Pennsylvania, Philadelphia.

Coggins, C. (1975) Painting and Drawing Styles at Tikal: An historical and iconographic reconstruction. Unpublished Ph.D.Dissertation, Department of Fine Arts, Harvard University, Cambridge MA.

Delvendahl, K. (2008) *Calakmul in Sight. History and Archaeology of an Ancient Maya City.* Unas letras industria editorial, Yucatán.

Drucker, P. (1952) *La Venta, Tabasco: A study of Olmec ceramics and Art.* Bureau of American Ethnology Bulletin 153, Smithsonian Institution, Washington DC.

Drucker, P., Heizer, R.F. and Squier, R.J. (1959) *Excavations at La Venta, Tabasco, 1955.* Bureau of American Ethnology Bulletin 170, Smithsonian Institution, Washington DC.

Eppich, K. (2011) Lineage and State at El Perú-Waka': Ceramic and architectural perspectives on the Classic Maya social dynamic. Unpublished Ph.D. dissertation, Department of Anthropology, Southern Methodist University, Dallas TX.

Fields, V. (1989) The Origins of Divine Kingship among the Lowland Classic Maya. Unpublished Ph.D. dissertation, Department of Anthropology, University of Texas at Austin, Austin TX.

Fields, V. and Reents-Budet, D. (2005) *Lords of Creation: The origins of sacred Maya kingship.* Los Angeles County Museum of Artand Scala Publishers, Los Angeles CA.

Filloy, L. (2014) *Costume et Insignes d'un Gouvernant Maya, K'inich Janaab' Pakal de Palenque.* British Archaeological Report S2590, Oxford.

Filloy, L. and Martínez, S. (2008) La restauración de la máscara funeraria de Pakal: esencia e imagen del soberano. In *Culto funerario en la sociedad maya. Memoria de la Cuarta Mesa Redonda de Palenque,* ed. R. Cobos, 609–26. Instituto Nacional de Antropología e Historia, México City.

Fitzsimmons, J. (2009) *Death and the Classic Maya Kings.* University of Texas Press, Austin TX.

Folan, W. and Morales, A. (1996) C alakmul, Campeche, México: La Estructura II-H, sus entierros y otras funciones ceremonialesy habitacionales. *Revista Española de Antropología Americana* 26, 9–28.

Folan, W., Marcus, J., Pincemin, S., Domínguez, M.R., Fletcher, L. and López, A.M. (1995) Calakmul: New data from an ancient Maya capital in Campeche, Mexico. *Latin AmericanAntiquity* 6, 310–34.

Freidel, D. (2008) Maya divine kingship. in *Religion and Power: Divine kingship in the ancient world and beyond,* eds N. Brisch and E. Brothers, 191–206. Ann Arbor MI.

Freidel, D. (2018) Maya and the idea of empire. In *Pathways to Complexity, A View from the Maya Lowlands,* eds M.K. Brown and G.J. Bey III, 363–86. University Press of Florida, Gainesville FL.

Freidel, D., Schele, L. and Parker, J. eds (1993) *Maya Cosmos. Three Thousand Years on the Shaman's Path.* William Morrow and Co, New York.

García, V.A. (2004) Máscaras para la vida o para la muerte? Una reflexión sobre la función de las máscaras de mosaico de jadeíta en el área Maya. In *Culto funerario en la sociedad maya. Memoria de la CuartaMesa Redonda de Palenque,* coord. Rafael Cobos, 609–26. Instituto Nacional de Antropología e Historia, México City.

García, V.A. (2012) Función de las máscaras de jade entre las elites Mayas del Clásico. Implicaciones en el procesode manufactura. In *El Jade y Otras Piedra Verdes. Perspectivas Interdisciplinarias e Interculturales,* eds W. Wiesheu and G. Guzzy, 115–43. Instituto Nacional de Antropología e Historia, México City.

González Cruz, A. (2011) *La Reina Roja: Una Tumba Real de Palenque.* Consejo Nacional para las Artes, InstitutoNacional de Antropología e Historia, México City.

Guenter, S. (2005) Informe preliminar de la epigrafía de El Perú. In *Proyecto Arqueológico*

El Perú-Waka': Informe No. 2, Temporada 2004, eds H. Escobedo and D. Freidel, 363–99. Unpublished report submittedto the Instituto de Antropología e Historia, Guatemala City.

Guenter, S. and Hansen, R. (n.d.) *El Reino Serpiente en el Preclásico y Clásico Temprano.* FARES/University of Utah, Salt Lake City.

Guernsey, J. (2006) *Ritual and Power in Stone: The performance of rulership in Mesoamerican Izapan Style Art.* University of Texas Press, Austin TX.

Hansen, R. (2016) Cultural and environmental components of the First Maya states: A perspective from the Central and Southern Maya Lowlands. In *The Origins of Maya States*, eds L. Traxler and R. Sharer, 329–416. University Pennsylvania Museum of Archaeology and Anthropology, Philadelphia PA.

Hansen, R. and Guenter, S. (2005) Early social complexity and kingship in the Mirador Basin. In *Lords of Creation: The origins of sacred Maya kingship*, eds V. Fields and D. Reents-Budet, 60–1. Los Angeles County Museum and Scala, Los Angeles CA.

Harrison, P. (1999) *The Lords of Tikal. Rulers of an Ancient Maya City*, Thames and Hudson, New York.

Haviland, W. (2015) *Excavations in Residential Areas of Tikal, Group 7F-1.* Tikal Report 22, University Museum Monograph 141. University of Pennsylvania, Philadelphia PA.

Houston, S. and Taube, K. (2000) A n a rchaeology of the senses: Perception and cultural expression in ancient Mesoamerica. *Cambridge Archaeological Journal* 10, 261–94.

Houston, S., Brittenham, C., Mesick, C., Tokovinine, A. and Warinner, C. eds (2009) *Veiled Brightness. A History of Ancient Maya Color.* University of Texas Press, Austin TX.

Hultkrantz, A. (1966) An ecological approach to religion. *Ethnos* 31, 131–50.

Hruby, Z. (2015) Lithics and minerals. In *Temple of the Night Sun. A Royal Tomb at El Diablo, Guatemala*, eds S. Houston, S. Newman, E. Román and T. Garrison, 234–40. Precolumbian Mesoweb Press, San Francisco CA.

Joralemon, P.D. (1976) The Olmec dragon: A study in pre-Columbian iconography. In *Origins of Religious Art and Iconography in Preclassic Mesoamerica*, eds H. Nicholson, 27–71. UCLA Latin American Center Publications, Los Angeles CA.

Jaralemon, P.D. (1988) The Olmec. In *The Face of Ancient America. The Wally and Branda Zollman Collection of Pre-Columbian Art*, by L. Parsons, J. Carlson, and P. Joralemon, 9–51. Indiana University Press, Bloomington IN.

Kecskési, M. and Vajda, L. (2012) I am not myself. In *African Masks: The Barbier-Mueller Collection*, eds M. Kecskési and L. Vajda, 11–36. Prestel, Munich.

Köhler, G. (2008) *Reptiles of Central America.* Herpeton, Offenbach.

Laporte, J.P. (1989) Alternativas del Clásico Temprano en la Relación Tikal-Teotihuacán: Grupo 6C-XVI, Tikal, Petén, Guatemala. Unpublished Ph.D. dissertation, Department of Anthropology, Universidad Nacional Autónoma de México, Mexico City.

Lee, D. (2012) Approaching the End: Maya Royal Ritual in the Palace Group at El Peru-Waka', Petén, Guatemala. Unpublished Ph.D. dissertation, Department of Anthropology, Southern Methodist University, Dallas TX.

Le Fur, Y. (2013) Masks: Beauty of the spirits. In *Masks, Masterpieces from the Musée du Quai Branly*, 6–11. Musée du Quai Branly, Paris.

Levi-Strauss, C. and Cantraine, Y. (1982) North American masks. *Drama Review* 26, 4–8.

Mack, J. (1994) Introduction. In *Masks and the Art of Expression*, eds J. Mack and Harry N.Abrams, 8–31. Harry N. Abrams Inc., New York.

Magee, C. and de Alarcón, T. (2015) Artifact conservation. In *Temple of the Night Sun. A Royal Tomb at El Diablo, Guatemala*, eds S. Houston, S. Newman, E. Román and T. Garrison, , 242–8. Precolumbian Mesoweb Press, San Francisco CA.

Martin, S. (1993) ' Site Q': The Case for a Classic Maya Super-Polity [https://www.mesoweb.com/articles/martin/SiteQ-OCR.pdf], accessed April 4th 2020.

Martin, S. (1997) The Painted King List: A commentary on codex-style dynastic vases. *Maya Vase Book* 5, 846–67.

Martin, S. (2005) Of snakes and bats: Shifting identities at Calakmul. *The PARI Journal* 6, 5–15.

Martin, S. (2017) Secrets of the Painted King List: Recovering the early history of the Snake Dynasty. *Maya Decipherment. Ideas on Ancient Maya Writing and Iconography* [https://decipherment.wordpress.com/2017/05/05/secrets-of-the-painted-king-list-recovering-the-early-history-of-the-snake-dynasty/], accessed April 4th 2020.

Martin, S. (2020) *Ancient Maya Politics. A Political Anthropology of the Classic Period 150–900 CE.* CambridgeUniversity Press, Cambridge.

Martin, S. and Beliaev, D. (2017) *K'ahk' Ti' Ch'ich'*: A New Snake King from the Early Classic Period. *The PARI Journal* 17, 1–7.

Martin, S. and Grube, N. eds (2008) *Chronicle of the Maya Kings and Queens: Deciphering the dynasties of the ancient Maya.* Thames & Hudson, London.

Martin, S. and Velásquez, E. (2016) P olities and places: Tracing the toponyms of the Snake Dynasty. *The PARI Journal* 17, 23–33.

Martínez del Campo, S. (2010) *Rostros de la Divinidad. Los Mosaicos Mayas de Piedra Verde*, Instituto Nacional deAntropología e Historia, México City.

Mathews, P. and Bíró, P. (2006) *Maya Hieroglyph Dictionary*. Foundation for the Advancement of Mesoamerican Studies. [http://research.famsi.org/mdp/mdp_list.php?rowstart=15&mayaSearch=&englishWordSearch=&spanishWordSearch=&TSearch=&TranSearch=&dateSearch=&letterSearch=K&englishSearch=& spanishSearch=&display=15], accessed April 4th 2020.

Melendez, J.C. (2014) Contextualizing Burial 37 from El Perú-Waka', Petén, Guatemala. Unpublished Master thesis, Department of Anthropology, Washington University, St Louis MI.

Melendez, J.C. (2019) A Contextual and Technological Study of Ancient Maya Greenstone Mosaic Masks. Unpublished Ph.D. Dissertation, Department of Anthropology, Washington University St Louis MI.

Melendez, J.C. and Melgar, E. (2018) Explorando las Órbitas Tecnológicas de Dos Rostros de Mosaico de Piedra Verde de Tikal, Petén, Guatemala. *Revista Española de Antropología Americana* 48, 191–210.

Melgar, E., Solís, R. and Filloy, L. (2013) Análisis tecnológico de las piezas de jadeíta y pedernal del cinturón de poder de la banda frontalde *K'inich Janaab' Pakal* de Palenque. In *Técnicas analíticas aplicadas a la caracterización y producción de materiales arqueológicos en el area Maya*, eds A. Velázquez and L. Lowe, 135–78. Universidad Nacional Autónoma de México. Mexico City.

Miller, D. (2014) *Excavations at La Libertad, a Middle Formative Ceremonial Center in Chiapas, Mexico.* Papers of the New World Archaeological Foundation 64. Brigham Young University, Provo UT.

Miller, M. and Martin, S. (2004) *Courtly Art of the Ancient Maya.* Thames and Hudson, New York.

Moholy-Nagy, H. (ed.) (2019) *The Ceramic Sequence of Tikal: Tikal Report 25B.* University of Museum Monograph 152, University of Pennsylvania, Philadelphia, PA.

Moholy-Nagy, H. and Coe, W. (2008) *The Artifacts of Tikal: Ornamental and Ceremonial Artifacts and Unworked Material.* Tikal Report 27, A. University Museum Monograph 127, University of Pennsylvania, Philadelphia PA.

Nalda, E. (2004) Las Máscaras de Jade de Dzibanché, Quintana Roo. *Arqueología Mexicana* Edición Especial 16, 26–9.

Navarro-Farr, O., Kelly, M.K., Rich, M. and Pérez, G. (2020) Expanding the canon: Lady K'abel the Ix Kaloomte' and the political narratives of ClassicMaya queens. *Feminist Anthropology* 1–18.

Pendergast, D. (1981) Lamanai, Belize: Summary of excavations results, 1974–1980. *Journal of Field Archaeology* 8, 29–53.

Pérez R.G. and Navarro-Farr, O. (2013) WK-01: Excavaciones en M13-1 y el Descubrimiento de La Estela 44. In Proyecto Regional Arqueológico El Perú-Waka': Informe No. 11, Temporada 2013, eds J.C. Pérez and D. Freidel, 3–26. Unpublished report submitted to the Instituto de Antropología e Historia, Guatemala.

Radlanski, R. and Wesker, K. (2012) *The Face: Pictorial atlas of clinical anatomy.* Quintessence Publishing, Chicago IL.

Reilly, F.K. III (1991) Olmec iconographic influences on the symbols of Maya rulership: An examination of possible symbols. In *Sixth Palenque Round Table*, 1986, eds M.G. Robertson and V. Fields, 151–66. University of Oklahoma Press, Norman OK.

Reilly, F.K. III (1994) Enclosed ritual spaces and the watery Underworld in formative period architecture: New observations on the function of La Venta Complex A. In *Seventh Palenque Round Table*, ed. M.G. Robertson, 125–35. The Pre-Columbian Art Research Institute, San Francisco CA.

Rich, M. (2011) Ritual, Royalty and Classic Period Politics: The archaeology of the Mirador Group at El Perú-Waka', Petén, Guatemala. Unpublished Ph.D. dissertation, Department of Anthropology, Southern Methodist University, Dallas TX.

Rich, M., Matute, V. and Piehl, J. (2007) WK-11: Excavaciones en la Estructura 014-04. In Proyecto Arqueológico El Perú-Waka': Informe No. 4, Temporada 2006, eds H. Escobedo and D. Freidel, 217–58. Unpublished report submitted to the Dirección General del Patrimonio Cultural y Natural de Guatemala, Guatemala City.

Rust, W. and Leyden, B.F. (1994) Evidence of maize use at Early and Middle Preclassic La Venta Olmec sites. In *Corn and Culture in the Prehistoric New World*, eds S. Johannessen and C. Hastorf, 181–201. Westview Press, Boulder CO.

Ruz Lhuillier, A. (1973) *El Templo de las Inscripciones, Palenque.* Fondo de Cultura Económica, México City.

Sauer, C. (1925) The morphology of landscape. *University of California Publications in Geography* 2, 19–53.

Schieber de Lavarreda, C. (2015) Cabezas Ceremoniales de Mosaicos de Jadeíta de Tak'alik Ab'aj, Guatemala. *Arqueología Mexicana* 133, 62–7.

Schieber de Lavarreda, C. and Orrego, M. (2011) La pasión del 'Señor de la Greca'. In *XXIV Simposio de Investigaciones Arqueológicas en Guatemala*, eds B. Arroyo, L. Paiz, A. Linares and A. Arroyave, 644–62. Museo Nacional de Arqueología y Etnología, Guatemala City.

Schneider, R. (2008) *El Fardo Funerario de la Tumba 1 de Calakmul. Conservación, Restauración y Montaje*. Instituto Nacional de Antropología e Historia, Mexico City.

Sharer, R.J. and Sedat, D.W. (1987) *Archaeological Investigations in the Northern Maya Highlands, Guatemala. Interaction and the development of Maya civilization,* University Museum Monograph 59, University Museum, University of Pennsylvania, Philadelphia PA.

Shook, E. and Kidder, A. (1952) *Mound E-III-3, Kaminaljuyu, Guatemala.* Contributions to American Anthropology and History 53. Carnegie Institution of Washington, Washington DC.

Stuart, D. (2000) "The Arrival of Strangers": Teotihuacan and Tollan in Classic Maya history. In *Mesoamerica's Classic Heritage: From Teotihuacan to the Aztecs*, eds D. Carrasco, L. Jones and S. Sessions, 465–513. University of Colorado Press, Boulder CO.

Stuart, D. (2012) Notes on a new text from La Corona. *Maya Decipherment. Ideas on Ancient Maya Writing and Iconography.* [www.decipherment.wordpress.com/2012/06/30/notes-on-a-new-text-from-la-corona/], accessed February 22nd 2015.

Stuart, D. and Stuart, G. (2008) *Palenque: Eternal City of the Maya.* Thames and Hudson, New York.

Stuart, D., Canuto, M., Barrientos, T. and González, A. (2018) A preliminary analysis of Altar 5 from La Corona. *The PARI Journal* 19, 1–20.

Tarpy, C. (2004) Maya royal grave. Unearthing a king from the dawn of the Maya. *National Geographic* 205, 66–79.

Tate, C. (2012) *Reconsidering Olmec Visual Culture. The Unborn, Women, and Creation.* University of Texas Press, Austin TX.

Taube, K.A. (2000) Lightning celts and corn fetishes: The Formative Olmec and the development of maize symbolism in Mesoamerica and the American Southwest. In *Olmec Art and Archaeology in Mesoamerica*, eds J. Clark and M. Pye, 297–338. Yale University Press, New Heaven CO.

Taube, K.A. (2004) Olmec art at Dumbarton Oaks. *Pre-Columbian Art at Dumbarton Oaks* 2, Dumbarton Oaks Research Library and Collection, Washington DC.

Taube, K.A. (2005) The symbolism of jade in Classic Maya religion. *Ancient Mesoamerica* 16, 23–50.

Taube, K.A. (2018) *Studies in Ancient Mesoamerican Art and Architecture. Selected Works by Karl Andreas Taube* 1. Precolumbia Mesoweb Press, San Francisco CA.

Taube, K.A., Saturno, W.A., Stuart, D. and Hurst, H. (2010) *Los Murales de San Bartolo, El Petén, Guatemala, parte 2: El Mural Poniente*, Ancient America 10, Precolumbian Mesoweb Press. [http://www.mesoweb.com/bearc/caa/AA10-es.pdf], accessed July 17th, 2019.

Valencia, R. and Esparza, O.Q. (2014) La conformación política de Calakmul durante el Clásico Temprano. *Arqueología Mexicana* 22, 36–40.

Velásquez Garcia, E. (2005) The captives of Dzibanche. *The PARI Journal* 6, 1–4. [http://www.mesoweb.com/pari/publications/journal/602/Captives_e.pdf], accessed March 9th 2015.

Velásquez Garcia, E. (2008) Los posibles alcances territoriales de la influencia política de Dzibanché durante el Clásico temprano: nuevas alternativas para interpretar las menciones históricas sobre la entidad política de Kan. In *El territorio Maya: memoria de la Quinta Mesa Redonda de Palenque*, ed. R.L. Stuardo, 323–352. Instituto Nacional de Antropología e Historia, México City.

Weiss-Krejci, E. (2012) Allspice as template for the Classic Maya K'an Sign. *The PARI Journal* 12, 1–6.

7

Sacrifice and the Sun: The Aztec Calendar Stone, its origins, and the symbolism of autosacrifice

Annabeth Headrick

The term "masterpiece" gets bantered about far too often without firm reins on its precise definition nor a thoughtful consideration of just how restrictive this category should be. While a reasonable criticism of the word's use might be that it is all too often applied to objects from the European tradition, in my own consideration of its use, the object must intrinsically embody as Merriam-Webster suggests "a supreme intellectual or artistic achievement" (2022) or, better yet, art that is a supreme intellectual achievement. In the extant world of Mesoamerican art, the Calendar Stone, dating to the early part of the 16th century, effortlessly meets such criteria, for it is not solely the vision of one artist or patron but it attempts to coalesce centuries of Mesoamerican religious, scientific, and political thought into one single object.[1] It is an artwork that simultaneously attempts to depict a cosmological model of the world, humanity's relationship to that cosmology, and, specifically, the political role of the ruler within the cosmological model. That it does so on a monument that is laden with numerous visual components yet still materializes as one cohesive object is is a mark of extraordinary ingenuity. It is this dense complexity married with a powerful graphic presence that has kept scholars returning time and time again to puzzle over its varied meaning since Fray Diego Durán saw it in the Zócalo 30 years after the conquest, but the object surely spawned scholarly debate during Aztec times (Durán 1994, 264; Villela *et al.* 2010, 4). Masterpieces such as the Calendar Stone remarkably encompass, or at least attempt to encompass, the philosophical expanse of an entire culture; as such, they elicit intellectual deliberation even as they are instantaneously perceived as a cultural icon.

Overview of the Calendar Stone's Iconography

As an icon, the predominant image on the Calendar Stone is that of the Sun (Fig. 7.1).[2] The circular format includes eight triangular projections that that easily read as the rays of a resplendent sun. Each of these rays is symmetrical but their origins

Fig. 7.1. The Calendar Stone: A) solar rays/stingray spines; B) bone awls; C) paper ties (photograph by author).

can be traced to earlier central Mexican solar images at Teotihuacan. As Jesper Nielsen and Christophe Helmke (2018, 77) cogently demonstrated, at Teotihuacan there was an "inherent relationship between fire and the sun – the hot, burning, and powerful celestial body par excellence". In a detail from a Teotihuacan tripod vessel, a sun with a celestial star at its center has a ring of fiery projections around its entire circumference (Fig. 7.2a). Artists at this Early Classic period city (A.D. 50-600) depicted these flames with an asymmetrical curled base that terminated in a point.[3] Although there are differences, the visual similarity makes it easy to see the Teotihuacan flaming sun as an ideological precedent for Postclassic (AD 1000–1521) solar images like the Calendar Stone. The circular format and the flaming rays are simplified in the Teotihuacan imag, but the Calendar Stone still maintains the essential form despite the many iconographic additions.

Outside the rays are a pair of *xiuhcocoaha*, or turquoise fire serpents, whose fiery

Fig. 7.2. Images of solar and lunar rays: A) solar image, detail of a Teotihuacan tripod vase (after Nielsen and Helmke 2018, fig. 4.3); B) gilded copper disk from the Sacred Cenote, Chichen Itza (after Lothrop 1952, fig. 59); C) tin disk from the Sacred Cenote, Chichen Itza (after Lothrop 1952, fig. 62).

presence emphasizes the flaming identity of the Sun (Townsend 1979, 66; Seler 1990, III, 130). To reinforce the theme of heat and fire, these serpents have flames on their backs (Taube 2000, 319–23). Looking to *xiuhcocoaha* in Mexican codices, Hermann Beyer (2010, 136–9) persuasively asserted that these creatures convey the Sun on their backs and their circular arrangement on the outside of the solar image suggests the rotational movement that the *xiuhcocoaha* provide to the Sun.

The dominant aspect of the Sun itself is the face at its center which has generated many a heated debate about its identity. Beyer (2010, 125–9) compared the face to images from post-conquest codices and offered the strongest argument that the face was the Sun god, Tonatiuh, an identification accepted by many scholars. On the other hand, Navarrete and Heyden (1974) as well as Townsend (1979) identified the face as that of Tlaltecuhtli. One of the compelling attributes to support this assertion are the clawed hands positioned to either side of the face which frequently appear on images of earth deities like Tlaltecuhtli. Cecelia Klein's (1976) identification fell somewhat in the middle with her proposal that the face was Yohualteuctli, an earthly aspect of the Sun at night. More recently, David Stuart (2016) reasoned that the clawed hands and knife-like tongue were not solely attributes of earth deities, but elements shared by all deities who demanded and received sacrificial offerings, including blood and human hearts.

The 16th century accounts of Sahagún and his collaborators make it clear that the Aztec gave sacrifice and blood offerings to the Sun as a form of nourishment. As they relate:

> *The first movable feast was celebrated in honor of the sun ... On this feast they offered, to the image of the sun, quail, and they offered incense. And at noon they slew captives before it in honor of the sun. On this same day, all drew blood from their ears—children and those who were grown—in honor of the sun, and they offered it that blood.* (Sahagún 1950–1982, II, 35).

Later, this same text makes clear the intrinsic connection between the Sun, fire, and sacrifice, explaining:

> *This nourishing was thus done. When the ear [lobes] were cut, they spattered the blood upward or they sprinkled it into the fire. Thus, it was said they nourished the fire and the sun* (Sahagún 1950–1982, II, 204)

Such accounts from the colonial period reinforce that the Sun had a fiery nature, and they also reveal that the Sun required blood sacrifice from both captives and, in the form of autosacrifice, the resident population.

Stuart (2016) has offered a nuanced identification of the central face on the Calendar Stone by underlining Umberger's (1981, 205; 1988) assertion that the hieroglyphs above the face, on either side of another triangular point, are that of Moteuczoma II and 1 Flint.[4] The former is the name glyph of the Mexica ruler who commissioned the sculpture and the latter is the birth date of Tenochtitlan's patron, Huitzilopochtli, a deity associated with the Sun. Stressing the presence of the ruler's name glyph, Stuart identifies the face as none other than Moteuczoma II himself, yet he proceeds to offer more layers to this identification. In that Huitzilopochtli's glyph also rests above the face, he acknowledges that this hieroglyph similarly refers to the visage at the center of the monument. As he states, the "face is directly labeled by these hieroglyphs as a portrait of the deified ruler who embodies and exemplifies the Mexica patron god." Not uncharacteristically within Mesoamerican traditions, the sculpture presents the ruler as both man and deity, a concept that Alfredo López Austin (1973; 2015) referred to as the "man-god." Because the image depicts the indivisible entity of Moteuczoma II–Huitzilopochtli, it projects this ruler's official dual identity and proclaims his inalienable right to power through his proclaimed deification. Considering the solar symbolism of the Calendar Stone and Huitzilopochtli's identification with the Sun, it is important to note that the ruler is deified by intrinsically linking him to the most prominent element in the cosmos, the Sun.

The solar theme continues around the face with four hieroglyphs, framed by rectangular enclosures, representing the four previous solar eras which each ended and subsequently resulted in the creation of a new, fifth Sun.[5] The arrangement of the four solar eras combined with the point directly over the face create the shape of the glyph *ollin*, or movement, which refers to the earthquake which would someday destroy the final Sun.[6] This fifth Sun represents the era of the Aztecs themselves, thus Moteuczoma II presented himself as the Sun of the present era.

Just outside the glyphs for the five solar eras is a circular band that contains the 20 day signs which combined with 13 numbers to create the sacred *tonalpohualli,* a divinatory calendar of 260 days. While the presence of the day signs of the sacred calendar has led to the popular name of the monument, they do not form a functioning calendar but convey more generally the passage of solar time (Beyer 2010; Seler 1990, III, 129). Just as the five solar eras at the heart of the monument place the Sun within epic constructs of deep, mythical and cyclical time, the day signs speak of the constant march of the *tonalpohualli* and its similar repetitious nature. A final band surrounds the day signs which consists of turquoise symbols that signify water, sacredness, and preciousness (Townsend 1979, 66).

Taken as a whole, the monument presents the viewer with the striking image of the Sun portrayed as a radiant entity with its flaming presence on full display. However, the complete cosmological vision of this Sun is more nuanced through the iconographic details. The *xiuhcocoaha* communicate the circular motion of the Sun just as the encircling calendrical symbols express the endless march of time. The signs of the five solar eras convey the concept of epic periods that rise and fall, transmitting to the Calendar Stone's original audience that their cosmological era was threatened with destruction. The turquoise symbols offer a tone of sacredness and preciousness to this cosmological model of time and space and, at the heart of it all, is the deified ruler in the guise of the Sun ready to receive sacrificial offerings with his greedy, clawed hands and sharp-bladed tongue.

The iconic image of the Sun surely dominates the monument and the intricate details afford a rich complexity. Ultimately, the whole resplendent image dazzles the eye. In all truth, this extraordinarily brief summation of a densely iconographic monument omits some elements and does little justice to the particulars of each component, let alone the multifarious meanings generated from the interaction of these components. Yet for the purposes at hand, it serves to offer a setting for the discussion of a few iconographic elements that merit further exploration, the aim of which is to expand upon the sacrificial symbolism of the Calendar Stone as well as to suggest a perspectival shift in how we view the monument.

The function of the Calendar Stone

The function of the Calendar Stone is marginally contested but is central to the following discussion. The source of any debate about the original use of the monument likely stems from the vertical display of the Calendar Stone from the Spanish colonial period into the present at the Museo Nacional de Antropología.[7] While this makes for spectacular exhibition design, the sculptors more likely created the composition for, and positioned the stone in, a horizontal position. This is important because most scholars agree that the Calendar Stone fits into the category of *cuauhxicalli,* or "eagle vessels", which were used as the receptacle for sacrificial hearts and blood offerings (Seler 1990, III, 128; Beyer 2010, 119–20; Chavero 2010, 91–6; Viella *et al.* 2010, 3). Furthermore, the stone was part of another category of objects called *temalacatl,* or so-called gladiator stones.[8] The firmest support for these identifications come from the writings of the 16th century friar, Diego Durán (1994, 188–93). He devotes a chapter to a large monument carved with the likeness of the Sun and in vivid detail describes how prisoners were stretched upon such monuments and subsequently had their hearts removed as the blood pooled on the solar image. The textual account and the accompanying image of a sacrificial victim upon a solar stone demonstrate its purpose as a receptacle for the blood from human sacrifice (Colour Pl. 8).

In another chapter, Durán (1994, 169–72) describes the rituals of the *temalacatl* where prisoners were outfitted with wooden swords that lacked one indispensable element, their obsidian blades. Holding these ineffective weapons, the prisoners had one leg tied via a rope to the center of the *temalacatl* and then they were forced into a futile battle with a fully armed Aztec warrior. With such unbalanced weaponry, the Aztec warrior inevitably won and proceeded to sacrifice the prisoner on the monument after the sham battle. The Calendar Stone was but one of many in the category of *temalacatl* and, while some smaller extant examples have a bar at their center to secure a rope, larger ones like the Calendar Stone apparently could forgo the rope attachment, leaving the captive to scamper helplessly upon the surface as Aztec warriors surrounded him.[9] All of these *temalacatl* are circular and have an image of the Sun carved upon their surface, whether it be elaborate like the Calendar Stone, or simplified as on several others.[10] On the Tizoc Stone, another grand vison of these sacrificial stones, sculptors added a channel from a depression at the center to the edge of the large stone to heighten the effect of the blood spilling over the side (Townsend 1979, figs 19 and 20).[11] Such observations have been made before, but they are critical here to establish that the Aztec used such monuments for sacrificial purposes. Where I want to add to the discussion of the Calendar Stone is that its imagery and overall symbolism did not only refer to the practice of human sacrifice, specifically the sacrifice of others but, like the textual accounts from Sahagún and his collaborators, I want to establish that autosacrifice was an intrinsic aspect of its imagery. In short, the iconography of the Calendar Stone explicitly proclaims the importance of royal autosacrifice, an assertion demonstrated through two key iconographic elements.

The solar rays as stingray spines

The first of these emerges from an analysis of the solar rays projecting out from the central image of the monument. The eight rays reinforce the dominant solar icon as they convey the Sun's luminosity. Evenly arranged on the surface, the rays point toward the four cardinal directions as well as the four intercardinals, particularly when the Calendar Stone was displayed horizontally. In this way, the imagery communicates not only the Sun's rise in the east, its setting in the west, and the directions of north and south but, through the intercardinals, the monument conveys the importance of the solstice points, the positions on the horizon which had a long history of observance in Mesoamerica. The rays of the Sun, therefore, conceptualize the nature of horizontal space for the Aztec and the movement of the Sun on a daily and annual basis. They express a world organized into four quadrants and simultaneously acknowledge the horizontal movement of the Sun on the horizon throughout the year. With elegant simplicity, the rays layout the nature of cosmic space and the regular, temporal movement of time.

A closer inspection reveals, however, that the cardinal and intercardinal rays have slight variations in their design. While the intercardinals are abbreviated and seem to emerge from underneath the concentric band with turquoise symbols, the cardinal directions appear in full form and include triangular points with distinctive curled volutes at their base. This small flourish at the bottom of the ray has received scant attention, yet it is essential to understanding a central tenant of the monument; that is, sacrifice is critical to the functioning of the cosmos. By tracing this shape iconographically, I would assert that the point with curled volutes at the base has an association with an important subset of blood sacrifice, royal autosacrifice (Headrick 2007). To demonstrate this, it is necessary to trace the origins of the iconography on the Calendar Stone, a process that reveals the autosacrificial intent of the monument and elucidates the extensive ideological and visual traditions that preceded this monument and informed its imagery.

In Classic Maya (AD 300–950) imagery, a common iconographic element is a sacrificial bowl and a set of accompanying accouterments placed inside the bowl, an assemblage referred to as the quadripartite badge. One of the most elaborate portrayals of this motif appears at Palenque on the Tablet of the Cross (*c.* AD 690), positioned within a shrine room inside the Temple of the Cross (Fig. 7.3). In between the two human figures, the artist depicted the bowl in profile with a distinct rim projecting above the bowl's basin. The vessel has the hieroglyph of the Sun emblazoned on its exterior, recognizable by the sign's four-petaled flower. The floral motif reads as *k'in* or Sun in Mayan. Epigraphically, the bowl reads as *lak* in Mayan and, when combined with the Sun or *k'in* reading, the result is *lak'in*, or east. This directional label serves as a reference to the rising Sun emerging from the earth (Stuart 1998, 392; Stuart and Stuart 2008, 198). Resting inside this eastern-marked bowl are objects associated with sacrifice and ritual offering. On the left is a bundle marked with the crossed bands of the sky and on the right is a shell from the watery underworld, jointly referencing the vertical organization of the cosmos itself, from the Underworld to the Celestial realm. The object resting between the bundle and the shell represents the human component that contributes to the well-being of that cosmos. The object is a stingray spine which was arguably the preferred bloodletter for elite and royal sacrifice as early as the Middle Formative period (1000–300 BC).[12] Effigy stingray spines fashioned in greenstone appear within the material record of the Olmec and they are frequently found in cache offerings and tombs, the residue of bloodletting events. Obtained from an animal that swims in the Underworld-associated ocean, the danger of obtaining such an object was echoed by the barbs on the spine which encourage a continued forward motion after the initial penetration of the skin; the barbs would cause increased pain by ripping the flesh if the spine were extracted in a reverse direction.[13]

In the quadripartite badge of the Palenque image, the social contract between humans and their cosmos is unequivocal. Remembering that the *k'in* glyph denotes

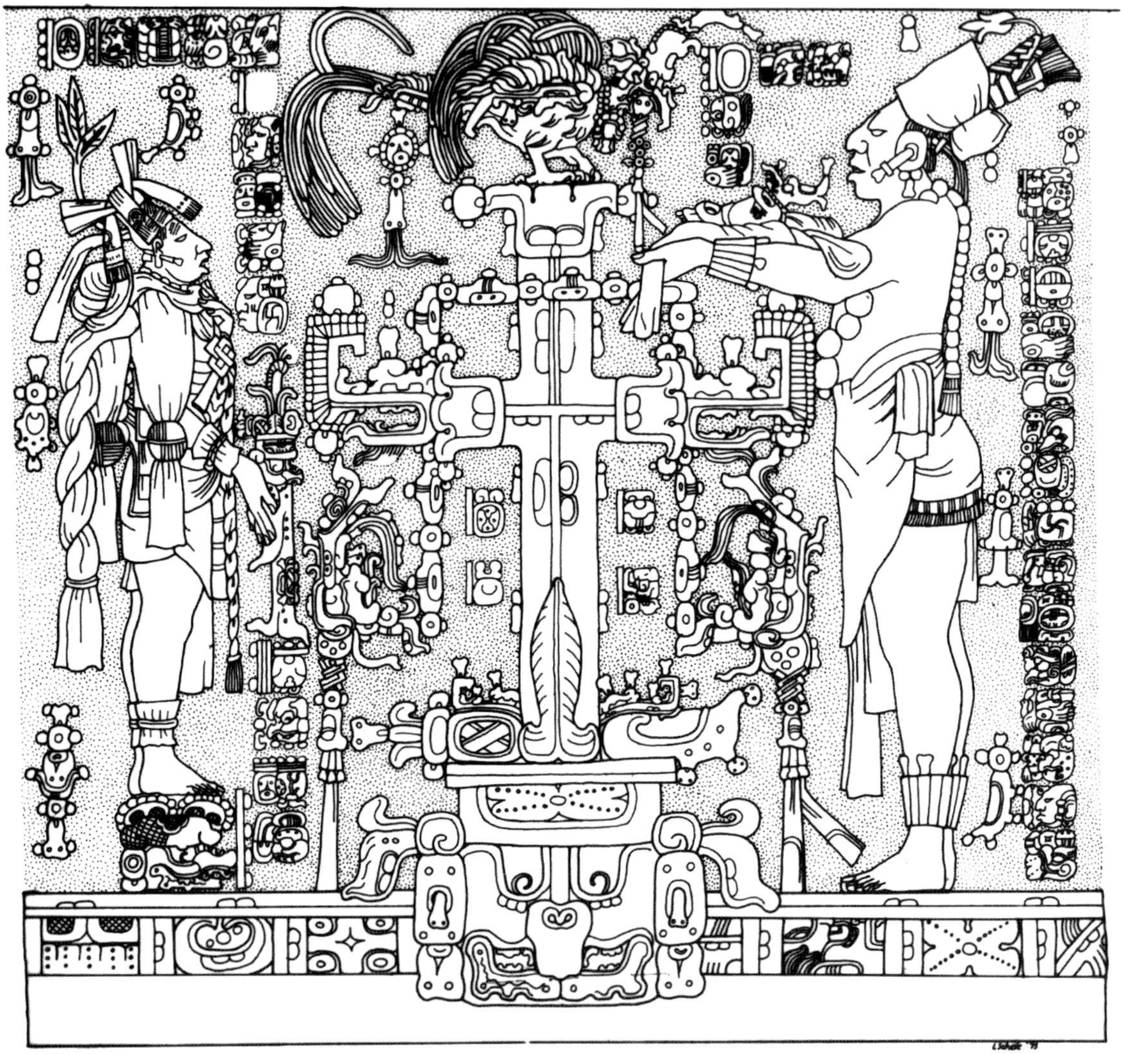

Fig. 7.3. Interior panel from the Temple of the Cross, Palenque (drawing by Linda Schele).

the Sun and that the glyphic reading of the bowl and Sun read as *lak'in* the textual references are to both the Sun itself and its daily emergence on the eastern horizon. As such, the continued cosmic organization and motion of the Sun was dependent on human blood sacrifice, as symbolized by the stingray spine. K'inich Kan Bahlam, the king and patron of the image, appears on either side, as a youth and a grown man, and his presence explicitly declares that it is royal autosacrificial blood that the cosmos requires. His younger self holds a personified bloodletter to underscore the message that Kan Bahlam has fed the Sun with his blood throughout his entire life. John Monaghan (1990) characterized the Mesoamerican relationship between sacrifice and the supernatural as a covenant between humans and their gods. In his model, the divine resources of the world, whether they be the earthly gifts of agriculture or the celestial gifts of rain, required a form of payment or feeding.

Writing about the Mixtec from the state of Oaxaca, he explained that the burial of a human body in the ground was a form of payback for the sustenance that the earth had provided during the individual's life. He cites a common saying in the Nuyoo language that eloquently articulates this covenant: "we eat the Earth, and the Earth eats us" (Monaghan 1990, 562–3). On the Tablet of the Cross, the quadripartite badge is an equally beautiful expression of this covenant. The ruler deposited his blood into the sun-marked offering bowl and a luscious tree grows forth from this offering. Agricultural growth (the tree), solar movement (the eastern, rising Sun), and even the vertical organization of water and sky (the shell and the bundle) were dependent on royal autosacrifice.

An understanding of this blood-fueled covenant is pertinent to the discussion of the Calendar Stone because it is but one example of a long history of solar-associated sacrifice from the centuries that preceded the Postclassic period. The stingray spine used for royal autosacrifice that rests within a sun-emblazoned bowl at Palenque aligns with the later Aztec practice of sacrificing individuals on a stone carved with a solar image. Just as the Maya ruler of Palenque placed his blood within a sun-marked bowl, so too Aztec rulers oversaw the spillage of blood on their solar monument (Colour Pl. 8 and Fig. 7.3). However, the shape of the stingray spine in the Palenque image is also a telling factor, for although depicted with a curvaceous swelling at its middle, the form is, nevertheless, reminiscent of the solar rays on the Calendar Stone (Figs 7.1 and 7.3). Both consist of a pointed end with curled volutes though, arguably, the Maya object appears with the characteristic naturalism exhibited in that culture's artistic tradition, while the Aztec highly stylized their spines and their art in general (Headrick 2007).

Curiously, while Maya images of stingray spines commonly have these curled volutes at their base, actual stingray spines, when extracted from the animal, do not have these, raising the question of why Maya artists chose to include this element. In an article exploring the ritual use of stingray spines, Haines *et al.* (2008, 84–6) argue that stingrays from the family Daasyatidae are the most common in Maya waters and, therefore, the most likely source of stingray spines. Intriguingly, the image they provide of this category of stingrays have paired pelvic fins at the base of the tail that are rounded and approximate the curled volutes seen on the Palenque spines. It is possible that these rounded pelvic fins positioned on the fleshy animal just above the stingray spine inspired the artists to include the volute shapes on the extracted spines.[14] Nevertheless, in images like that of the Tablet of the Cross, the Maya did indeed depict stingray spines with curled volutes at the base and a point on the other end. Furthermore, the similarity of the form to four of the rays on the Calendar Stone suggest that the Aztec inherited a solar-associated practice of autosacrifice and incorporated highly stylized stingray spines into their image of the Sun.

If this assertion is accurate, that the rays with volutes reference stingray spines, then the Calendar Stone incorporates the blood sacrifice of captives through the events Durán recorded, by stretching the captives atop the stone and removing their hearts to feed the solar image with the blood spilt upon its surface. However, recognizing that the Calendar Stone iconography includes stylized stingray spines, imagery that doubles as solar rays mapping the cardinal directions, indicates that royal autosacrifice was an implicit part of the Aztec covenant. The presence of stingray spines/solar rays on the monument conveys that captive sacrifice and autosacrifice mutually sustained cosmic organization and solar motion.

Visual perspectives and sacrificial solar monuments

The Palenque image offers another parallel to the Calendar Stone when contemplating the latter's identity as a *cuauhxicalli*, an "eagle vessel", a repository for sacrificial offering. It might be perplexing to consider a flat surface of the Calendar Stone as a vessel without a comparison to the Maya quadripartite badge. At Palenque, the viewer sees the solar-marked vessel in profile with its contents rising above its rim (Fig. 7.3). In actuality, these objects would have been deposited within the interior of the bowl and invisible from this perspective, so the Maya artist elevates the objects and positions them above the bowl's rim, thereby allowing the viewer to see the bowl's contents. The sun depicted on the exterior of the bowl might arguably have been conceived of as inside the bowl to facilitate the sun receiving the blood offering. The Calendar Stone, however, changes this perspective and, instead of a profile view, the viewer looks down into the bowl's interior from a bird's-eye view to see a vision of a rapacious sun with its clawed hands and a sacrificial knife for a tongue. The viewer sees a sun ready to receive the blood offering it demanded. At a diameter of 11ft 5 in (ca. 3.48 m), the circular form of the Calendar Stone has more than enough space to contain much of the blood spilt upon its surface; it is a receptacle (Villela *et al.* 2010, 1) Both objects, the bowl depicted at Palenque and the Calendar Stone, are essentially the same in their core meaning and each managed their essential function of holding the blood offered to that solar entity, whether that be within the depression of a bowl or a large, flat surface. It is important to note that Mesoamerican artists had many perspectives at their disposal when depicting a sacrificial vessel, including profile and bird's-eye views.

A gilded copper disk retrieved from the Sacred Cenote at Chichen Itza (Fig. 7.2B) illustrates how the concepts embodied by the quadripartite badge evolved in the Late Postclassic (1450–1539).[15] On this object there are four equally spaced elements on the outer ring of the disk. Each has a bifurcated stem that terminates in the distinct curled volutes seen on the stingray spine from Palenque and the rays/ spines on the Calendar Stone. The points on the Chichen example are abbreviated by the edge of the disk, but the form is altogether recognizable.[16] It is as though the artist of the metal disk has reduced the rays on the Calendar Stone to four and chopped off their pointy ends. As delineated on the Classic period Palenque spine, the Chichen spines have a line down their centers but the artist has highly stylized these spines and replicated them toward each of the cardinal directions on a horizontal plane, echoing the Aztec image. The gilded copper disk transforms the sacrificial vessel from a profile bowl to a viewpoint that looks down into the vessel even as it simultaneously offers an image of shining celestial entity.

In the case of the metal disk, Clemency Coggins (1984, 120–1) identified the central figure as the god, Ek Chuah, a patron of exchange and exotic goods. This fits well with the increased importance of trade in the Postclassic which led to the introduction of metals into much of Mesoamerica, particularly sites with coastal connections like Chichen Itza. Ek Chuah also had a celestial connotation because *ek* translates as both "star" and "black," thus the abstracted stingray spines also read as rays of a celestial body, and the gold surface accentuates this by approximating the shiny, yellow color of the Sun.[17] Another metal disk from the Sacred Cenote has the same four rays with curled volutes, although this one depicts the Moon, indicating that several radiant celestial bodies used this iconography (Fig. 7.2C).[18]

Ultimately, the Chichen image may be read in multiple ways. The stingray spines, though abstracted, suggest a vessel for autosacrifice even if this is more symbolic than functional as the disk is rather small. At 13.9 cm the imagery on the metal disk portrays the idea of a sacrificial offering vessel instead of operating as one. On the other hand, when reading the points as the rays of a celestial body, the embossed decoration projects a brilliant image in a manner similar to the Early Classic Teotihuacan Sun (Fig. 7.2A). When reading the projections as rays the gilding is central because the shiny gold material reinforces the imagery to make the celestial symbolism unmistakable.

Considering this triad of images (Figs 7.1, 7.2A, and 7.3) in concert, the transformation of stingray spine imagery and the sacrificial offering vessel of which it was a part becomes transparent and recognizable. Whether an actual receptacle or only a symbolic depiction of one, each conveys the idea that autosacrifice was a critical element for the vitality of the Sun and other celestial entities. In the Palenque image, the stingray spine is quite literal and naturalistic but, over time, it transformed into a stylized element that signaled not only autosacrificial blood but also the entity to which that blood was spilt – a shining celestial body, most commonly the Sun. These three images demonstrate that the imagery on the Calendar Stone emerged from a long, deep tradition and in that tradition the stingray spines became highly abstracted and only the curled volutes at the base of the element reveal the original referent.

Surprisingly, ethnographic research offers intriguing evidence that the symbolism and transformation of sacrificial vessels survived long after the Spanish conquest; that is, vessels with stingray spine symbolism continued to have a lasting legacy. In Robert Redfield and Alfonso Villa Rojas' well-known book *Chan Kom: A Maya village* (1934), they describe a wedding in a 1930s Maya village. As part of the festivities, the groom's father provided a lavish gift of food to the bride's father. Acting as a master of ceremonies on behalf of the bridegroom's father, an individual known as a *kuleb*, brought in from the kitchen a turkey. About the presentation of the turkey they write: "until recently, it was customary to put this turkey (prepared as *escabeche*) in a large clay vessel with an edge ornamented with small points, or fluting, known as *kix-lak*" (Redfield and Villa Rojas 1934, 197). The ceremonial nature of this turkey was emphasized by arches of two intersecting flowered vines over the bird, an arrangement still used today above a ritual Ch'a-Chak altar. On the altar, these are called "the cords of the sky" and in their assembled, crossed arrangement, they create a "sky-platform" (Freidel *et al.* 1993, 56–7). Furthermore, the father-of-the-bride received two piles of tortillas, each with 13 tortillas, the sacred number used in the Maya calendar.

Because the vessel referred to as a *kix-lak* was no longer in use when Redfield and Villa Rojas conducted their research, there is no image or further description of the container, so the exact appearance of the points remains a mystery. However, the name of the large dish is enticing. In Mayan *kix* translates as stingray spine and *lak* as plate or bowl. Even if the decoration on the bowl resembled the fluting of a pie-crust, the name "stingray spine bowl" is intriguingly similar to the concepts discussed above. Obviously human sacrifice was no longer a practice in 1930s Chan Kom so the turkey itself may have served as the offering but the ceremonial function of the vessel at a wedding feast alone demonstrates the ritual association of the container. The arched floral vines and the paired stacks of 13 tortillas suggest that the vessel and its offering embodied meanings well beyond a simple gift of food. The name may indicate that this ceremonial vessel was a vestige of a belief and tradition stemming back thousands of years, a tradition that survived long after Maya kings ceased piercing themselves with a stingray spine for bloodletting (Headrick 2007). Quite simply, by calling their vessel a *kix-lak* the Maya of this Yucatecan village may have preserved a concept of ceremonial, sacrificial vessels associated with stingray spines.

Bone awls: a Postclassic autosacrifical implement

The stingray spine as an instrument for elite, if not royal, autosacrifice is securely established for the Classic Maya, but as Cecelia Klein (pers. comm. 2021) pointed out, there is no archaeological or visual evidence that the Aztecs used stingray spines for perforation. Instead, as Klein (1987) makes clear in her seminal essay on Aztec autosacrifice, the most prominent royal perforator in Postclassic central Mexico were sharpened bones. This assuredly problematizes the identification of the solar rays on the Calendar Stone as stingray spines; however, I would suggest that their highly stylized nature is key to this dilemma.

It is possible that over time the motif of the stingray spine became so stylized that not only was its original form distorted in the transformation, but the very meaning of the motif may have been lost or even altered over the centuries, to the point that the visual language of the motif was somewhat misunderstood or lost some of its cultural relevance. The stingray spines on the Calendar Stone may be a product of archaism where in language or visual art an obsolete element persists, and in that persistence the original function or meaning of the element changes, sometimes to humorous effect. One such example appears in a rose window of St Thomas More Catholic Church in St Paul, Minnesota. Circling around the center point of the window is a series of radiating classical columns. Like many columns in American architectural vernacular, those here refer to a concept of antiquity but, to those versed in that antiquity, the fact that these "columns" do not have even a nominal appearance of structurally holding something up is maddening. They simply circle around the center point of the window and confoundingly connect with the remaining latticework of the window devoid of any understanding of a column's original context. If my identifications of stingray spine imagery on the Chichen gold disk and the Calendar Stone are accurate, it is possible that

Fig. 7.4. Bone awls on Aztec monuments: A. Dedication Stone (after Seler 1960–1961, 2, 766, fig. 47); B. bench relief from the southwest corner of the Templo Mayor (after Beyer 1955, fig. e); C. drawing of the top of the Teocalli (drawing by Emily Umberger); D. backrest of the Teocalli (drawing by Emily Umberger).

the Aztec similarly used this motif as an archaism and lost the original meaning of their function as bloodletters, replaced by their identity as solar rays. That acknowledged, I suspect that the original autosacrificial meaning did survive and continued to express the covenant of blood offerings between humans and their solar deity. However, during the Postclassic, the Aztec may have considered the stingray spine archaic and old fashioned, as they replaced it with their own modern bone awls.

To support this position, a second motif on the Calendar Stone deserves attention, because the stingray spine is not the only bloodletter that appears on it. In Klein's (1987) article she carefully details the imagery of royal autosacrifice and helps the modern viewer distinguish its visual elements. As seen on the Dedication Stone (AD 1487) two Aztec rulers pierce themselves with bone awls and shed blood (Fig. 7.4A). The rulers here are Ahuitzotl on the right and the previous ruler, Tizoc, on the left (Klein 1987, 318). In this sculptural portrayal, the awls are rather naturalistic. The twin rounded ends of the femur clearly appear at the base of the awls as the men perforate their ears and blood flows over their heads in an arch. Subsequently, after performing autosacrifice Aztec rulers inserted the bloody perforators into a woven grass ball called a *zacatapayolli* (Klein 1987, 296). Jeanette Peterson (1983, 117–21) argued that the grass balls were made of *malinalli* grass which represented the hair and skin of the earth deity who would receive the sacred offering. On the Dedication Stone two such perforators, now more stylized and perhaps decorated, pierce the grass ball in a V-shape.

As Klein demonstrates, royal autosacrifice was endemic in Aztec state art and similar scenes appear on public monuments, like a bench relief found at the southwest corner of the Templo Mayor and the Teocalli, a lavishly decorated throne commissioned by Moteuczoma II that takes the shape of a miniature temple (Umberger 1984). On the bench relief, dated to the reign of Itzcoatl (AD 1427–1440), the sacrificial act has already occurred and the two men stand on either side of the *zacatapayolli* with three perforators inserted into its surface (Fig. 7.4B).[19] In this example the perforators are even more stylized and consist of a rectangular base topped by a circular end, presumably a nod to the rounded end of a femur. Each circular end of the perforator has a second circular decoration at its center, perhaps to indicate that they are pierced and also a secondary nod to the *chalchihuitl* symbol designating turquoise and preciousness. On the Teocalli, the *zacatapayolli* appears on the very top of the miniature temple (Fig. 7.4C) and would been just behind Moteuczoma II's head when he sat on the throne. The grass ball depicted on the Teocalli has just two perforators, yet they appear quite similar to those of the bench relief consisting of rectangles capped by circles. On both examples, flames and smoke rise up from the ball, as the practice was to light them, thereby giving the blood offering to the earth symbolized by the grass, and the sky via the smoke. In all three of these Aztec images the artists depicted the grass balls with their bloodletters in profile, but on the Teocalli there is evidence that this concept of the grass ball, the receptacle or "vessel" for Aztec blood offerings, could also materialize in a flat, bird's-eye view.

Adjacent to the Teocalli grass ball is an archetypal image of the Sun which would have served as the backrest of this throne (Fig. 7.4D).[20] Two Aztec rulers, Moteuczoma II on the right and the deceased and apotheosized Ahuitzotl on the left, stand on either side letting blood; their bloodletters appear in their extended hands (Klein 1987, 339–44). Solar images like the one on the Teocalli and the Calendar Stone are generally associated with the blood sacrifice of prisoners, yet contextually, these two rulers flank the Sun with their bloodletters, clearly indicating that it is royal, autosacrifical blood that is being offered to the Sun in efforts to sustain it. Furthermore, when Moteuczoma II sat on the Teocalli, he sat directly in front of the solar image and blocked it; thus, in a bit of political theater, he replaced the solar image and essentially became the Sun. Such a strategy equates with Stuart's (2016) assertion that the face on the Calendar Stone is Moteuczoma II doubling as the Sun-associated deity of Huitzilopochtli. In other words, on the Calendar Stone and the Teocalli, Moteuczoma II takes on the persona of the defied Sun. By extension, when sitting on the throne, Moteuczoma II would have been the recipient of his own blood offering and that of his predecessor, a tactic that further cemented the ruler's divine identity because gods, not humans, were the recipients of sacrificial blood.[21]

The positioning of the rulers facing the Sun with their bloodletters is convincing evidence that solar images like that on the Teocalli and the Calendar Stone had royal autosacrificial symbolism. Furthermore, an iconographic element not yet discussed on the Calendar Stone or the Teocalli's Sun offers concrete evidence that these solar images explicitly incorporate the imagery of autosacrifice. Specifically, the imagery includes the autosacrificial bone bloodletters favored by the Aztec and, furthermore, the whole image may additionally be interpreted as a *zacatapayolli* but seen from above not in the more recognizable profile view.

The perimeter of the Teocalli's solar image consists of a series of circles with smaller circles at their centers, and not surprisingly, these circles attach to rectangular forms (Fig. 7.4D). This assemblage precisely matches the rectangles with circles previously identified as the ends of bloodletters jammed into grass balls (Fig. 7.4B, C). As such, on the Teocalli's solar image the eight elements alternating with the solar rays/stingray spines materialize as bloodletters inserted into a *malinalli* grass ball meaning that, in essence, the solar image on the Teocalli has an additional identity as a *zacatapayolli* seen from above. Understanding the image from this perspective, the circular element is really a rounded three-dimensional ball with perforators spreading out over its surface like a pin-cushion. The image on the backrest of the Teocalli thus conveys that the two rulers have let their own blood and inserted the bone awls into the *zacatapayolli* before them. Of course, the central image on the Teocalli backrest is not only a *zacatapayolli* but it is also the Sun. In a bit of a *double entendre*, the earth, symbolized by the *malinalli* grass ball, and the celestial Sun, the flaming central image, are both sustained by the blood of the rulers, a re-enactment of the covenant between rulers and the cosmos.

Returning to the Calendar Stone itself (Fig. 7.1), the Postclassic bone awl bloodletters also appear on this larger, more elaborate image of the Sun. In between each of the solar rays/stingray spines is a circular element attached to a rectangular shape, although on the Calendar Stone the rectangular form tapers to more of a trapezoid shape.[22] Like the solar image on the Teocalli, these bloodletters penetrate the circular form around the entire circumference, leading to the conclusion that the Calendar Stone not only is a solar image but also a grass ball with its earthly association (Headrick 2007).

Just as with the Teocalli, the Calendar Stone thereby encapsulates the whole universe in a grand, cosmological form. As a *zacatapayolli* the *malinalli* grass, implied but not depicted, is the hair and skin of the earth deity and the blood offering would therefore symbolically seep into the inner reaches of the earth. The image of the Sun with its rayed presence and the glyphic portrayal of the five solar eras bespeaks of the ultimate divine celestial entity who likewise receives the precious sacred offering. In a beautiful expression of totality, the Aztec offered the blood to the whole of the universe from the nether regions to the sky above through an image that captures a complete vertical cosmogram. Recalling that the solar rays point to the cardinal and intercardinal directions, the image extends in all directions, demonstrating that the blood offering was made to the totality of horizonal space as well. The blood spilt upon this surface, then, was not solely intended for the Sun but for the entirety of the cosmos.

While Durán's (1994, 188–93) account made it clear that sacrificial victims were the source of the blood that sustained the Sun and cosmos, Sahagún's (1950–1982, II, 35) account indicates that the Aztec populace contributed to that sustenance through their own autosacrifice. The recognition that the Calendar Stone and other Postclassic solar images included autosacrificial imagery validates Sahagún's description of ritual. The autosacrificial iconography expresses that the sacrifice of one's own blood, but particularly the blood of rulers, was additionally critical to the functioning of the universe. One of the most profound contributions of Klein's (1987) work on autosacrifice was that while the killing of another human has received so much attention, the penitential act of autosacrifice was far more common. It occurred on a daily basis in personal acts of devotion and publicly, often with the populace simultaneously piercing themselves in the same rituals where humans were killed. In this manner every Aztec acknowledged the covenant between themselves and their gods through the painful precious gift of blood as a repayment for the sustenance those gods provided. Humanity fed the deities, and the deities fed the humans.

The imagery on the Teocalli backrest is vital for understanding this reciprocal relationship, however, because it records that the Aztec rulers directed autosacrificial bloodletting towards solar imagery like that on the Calendar Stone. While the massive Calendar Stone stands alone in its majesty, the human actors who engaged with the monument are lost, save for accounts like Durán's. Captivated by the bloody scene of human sacrifice on its surface, he did not directly record the accompanying royal autosacrifice that was surely involved in the event. Yet the Teocalli does capture this aspect with its two rulers, one alive and one deceased, bloodletting before the solar image as role models to their people and deified beings giving their sacred blood. The Teocalli fleshes out Durán's textual account of the Calendar Stone's use with a visual account that chronicles the royal bloodletting also involved with the monument.

Concluding thoughts

The iconography of the Calendar Stone and solar monuments like it include archaic stingray spines transformed into and doubling as solar rays; therefore, these Postclassic monuments retain some vestige of the exemplary bloodletter of the Formative and Classic periods. The highly stylized stingray spines recall an ancient tradition of royal persons offering their blood to the Sun. Likewise, the stylized bone awls decorating the perimeter of the Postclassic solar images update the tradition with the bloodletting implements of Aztec royalty. The presence of the awls within the imagery makes a clear statement that royal autosacrifice was a constant within the ritual functions of the Calendar Stone. Piercing the Sun on every side, the awls communicate that Aztec rulers let their own blood and inserted the bloody awls into an object that was at once the earth and the sky. Yes, the gods demanded the blood of others but it was the blood of the rulers that ultimately sustained the cosmos. It must be remembered that these are monuments commissioned by Aztec rulers and their purpose was not just to express religious ideals but also to justify political rule. By including imagery of autosacrifice within these monuments the royal patrons conveyed the centrality and importance of royal bloodletting to the continued existence of the universe and the people.

Nielsen and Helmke (2018) asserted that the rays of the Sun in earlier Teotihuacan imagery were flames and, in their discussion, this is critical because fire was the ultimate "transformative agent" in Mesoamerican religion and ideology. They explain that virgin fires in New Fire rituals symbolized transitions in temporal and political eras, and that the burning of elite ancestral bundles converted these humans through a fiery rebirth. A flaming Sun, therefore, was an agent of change and transition. This same concept survived for hundreds of years, for fire was involved in the final step in Aztec solar rituals.

In Durán's account of a sacrificial ceremony in honor of an image of the Sun he describes the sacrifice and heart extraction of eight victims upon its surface. After each sacrifice the ruler raised the heart to the Sun in a gesture of offering and then threw it into a depression of this solar image.[23] After this, he continues,

> *When the sacrifice had ended, the priests took from the shrine of Huitzilopochtli a serpent made of paper coiled about a pole, all made of [red arara] feathers ... He then set it on fire and walked around the stone, incensing it with smoke. While it was still burning, he climbed to the top of the monolith and threw the still smoldering serpent upon all the blood that bathed the stone. At this moment a great paper mantel was brought and was cast upon the stone. It burned together with the serpent until there was nothing left of it and the blood was consumed or had dried.* (Durán 1994, 190–1)

The illustration that Durán included of this event (Colour Pl. 8) vividly displays the victim stretched upon a sun stone, the five priests opening his chest, and the blood which spilled upon the solar image. In the upper middle of the image, the priest with the flaming paper serpent emerges from the Sun-associated temple of Huitzilopochtli. This paper serpent is none other than one of the *xiuhcocoaha*, or fire serpents seen circling the edge of the Calendar Stone (Fig. 7.1), as demonstrated by the four paper ties on the tail of each serpent (Durán 1994, 191, n.4). As Durán explained, the priest in this illustration would descend the temple steps and perambulate the monument, in essence duplicating the action of the *xiuhcocoaha* on the Calendar Stone. In this way, the imagery of the Calendar Stone preserved the ephemeral ritual events because even when the priest with his paper fire serpent was not physically present and circling the Sun, the carved *xiuhcocoaha* were.

When the priest threw the burning paper serpent and additional paper fuel on the solar image, the Sun literally embodied its fiery nature and became a flaming entity of transformation. Celebrants could view the climax of the event in multiple ways. The burning and smoldering monument could be read as a burning *zacatapayolli* wherein the blood on the solar image fed the earth deity for the agricultural bounty it provided. As mentioned above, Durán does not acknowledge that royal autosacrifice occurred at this ritual even though Sahagún recognizes that it was a vital part of the events. The recognition that bone awls pierce the circumference of the Calendar Stone reinforces Sahagún's account and projects to the populace that royal blood was always implied. Even without an explicit depiction of the *malinalli* grass, conceptually, the Calendar Stone was a *zacatapayolli* pierced with bloody awls that honored the earth and conveyed blood offerings to it. The now archaic stingray spines on the Calendar Stone linked the Aztec ritual back to ancestral times and earlier forms of bloodletters even as the simultaneously created the rays of a brilliant Sun. Likewise, the encirclement of the *ollin* glyph with the four previous eras similarly reveals that the creators of the Calendar Stone wanted to connect the Mexica era with that of earlier civilizations. In essence, the monument acknowledges that traditions and events of the past carried forward into their own era, even as they revised and reframed these traditions to fit their own realities and political agendas.

The flames were also essential in this ritual because they revealed the fiery nature of the central icon, the Sun. They facilitated the transformation of the blood offering into smoke which had the ability to reach the heavenly realm of the Sun. The Sun on the Calendar Stone is a greedy presence with is clawed hands and knifed tongue poised to seize the blood which spread upon its surface. In that the visage was also Moteuczoma II, the ruler himself receives the offering, even as the imagery of bloodletting implements signals that he provides and consumes his own blood. The symbolism of the monument emerges like a house of mirrors, where the ruler graphically feeds earth and sky with his blood and that of others, but he also feeds himself, and through this act of offering and receiving Moteuczoma II transforms into the divine provider and receiver of life.

Notes

1 Umberger (1988) effectively tied the glyphic and stylistic aspects of the Calendar Stone to the reign of Moteuczoma II and Stuart (2016) emphasizes the late date of the monument. The Calendar Stone is located in the National Museum of Anthropology, Mexico City. Encyclopedia Britannica states it is "12 feet (3.7 metres) in diameter and weighing some 25 tons"(https://www.britannica.com/topic/calendar-stone).

2 Often, and perhaps more accurately, this monument is also called the Sun Stone; however, I will refer to it as the Calendar Stone throughout this essay because, however flawed, it is the more common name.

3 These dates best approximate the period of monumental building and habitation at Teotihuacan; although, the earlier period, 50 BC to AD 200, falls within the period commonly described as the Late Formative period.

4 The spellings for this ruler's name are varied, and I follow Stuart's (2016) suggestion that this spelling is more accurate. In addition, Peñafiel (1890) also identified the hieroglyph to the left above the face as Moteuczoma.

5 Seler (1990, V, 28) explains this early identification, but it has been further documented and elaborated upon by a host of previous scholars. I offer only a summation of the dense iconography and meanings of the Calendar Stone, and for a more in-depth, collective resource, see Villela and Miller (2010).

6 Combined with the four dots on either side of the clawed hands on the Calendar Stone, the central glyph reads, 4-Ollin, the day the fifth sun is prophesized to end.

7 For a concise description of the monument's history, including its rediscovery and installation on the southwest tower of the cathedral, see Villela *et al.* (2010, 4).

8 For a comprehensive discussion of monuments in the category of *temalacatl* and *cuauhxicalli* see Solís and Velasco Alonso (2004).

9 The absence of a bar to secure the captive and the pristine nature of the Calendar Stone may suggest that it was not actually used as a *temalacatl*; however, even if it did not function as a *temalacatl*, the iconography of the Calendar Stone is so consistent with other monuments in this category that, at the very least, it represents a *temalacatl*. Any member of the city of Tenochtitlan who had seen a sacrifice upon a *temalacatl* would undoubtedly associate the Calendar Stone with such monuments.
10 Beyer (2010, 119–25) explored these classifications and offers images of some of the other monuments with similar iconography and function.
11 It is important to note, however, that this channel could be a later modification from the colonial period (Townsend 1979, 46).
12 See Joyce *et al.* (1991) for a discussion of Olmec bloodletting, and for an in-depth exploration of Maya bloodletting, see Schele and Miller (1986).
13 The well-known death of the television personality Steve Irwin from repeated stabbings of a stingray are a lesson in how a normally docile animal can also be life-threatening (Lynch 2014).
14 This explanation that the stingray's pelvic fins inspired the curled volutes on Maya images of stingray spines was inspired by a suggestion from William Barnes (pers. comm. 2022).
15 Coggins (1984, 121) and Lothrop (1952, 7 4–77) place this disk within the Santa Rita style through comparisons to murals at Santa Rita Corozal.
16 Solís and Velasco Alonso (2004) offer a useful and extensive comparative discussion of images, including those at Chichen Itza, that served as precursors to the Aztec Calendar Stone.
17 Taube (1992, 90) cites evidence that rituals to this merchant deity included burning incense at night, therefore associating him with night and fire. Such associations might indicate that this image of Ek Chuah and the disk as a whole refers to a nighttime celestial body.
18 See Coggins (1984, 118–19) for metal disks from Chichen Itza depicting the Sun and the Moon. In addition, the many images of the Sun and in the Postclassic and early post-conquest codices provide ample evidence that the Moon shared the rayed iconography.
19 The dating of this monument was first proposed by Hermann Beyer (1955) and confirmed by Klein (1987, 298–300).
20 For full views of the Teocalli which outline the various positions of its carvings, see Townsend (1979, 50–1).
21 The throne room of the Neo-Assyrian king, Assurnasirpal II, at Nimrud portrays a similar strategy. As Irene Winter (1981) demonstrates, the king's throne sat right in front of a sacred tree being tended by the king and winged genii. When Assurnasirpal II sat upon the throne, he, in turn, became the sacred tree which was the *axis mundi*. Likewise, both the genii and king himself tended to the king.
22 Matos (2004, 70) notes that these elements remind him of "barbs used in sacrifice" and that this is fitting given that the Sun only moved after the gods sacrificed themselves in Aztec mythology. Likewise, in the same text, Solís and Velasco Alonso (2004) repeatedly refer to the objects between the solar rays as "sacred thorns."
23 Heyden (Durán 1994, 188, n.1) suggests that the mention of a depression may indicate that this account refers to the Stone of Tizoc or the Arzobispado Stone.

References

Beyer, H. (1955) La procession de los señores, decoración del primer teocallo de piedra en Mexico-Tenochtitlan, *El México Antiguo* 8, 1–42.

Beyer, H. (2010) The so-called "Calendario Azteca": Description and interpretation of the Cuauhxicalli of the "House of the Eagles" (1921). In Villela and Miller (eds), 118–50.

Chavero, A. (2010) The "Aztec Calendar Stone" (1876). In Villela and Miller (eds), 90–100.

Coggins, C. (1984) *Cenote of Sacrifice: Maya treasures from the sacred well at Chichén Itzá.* University of Texas Press, Austin TX.

Durán, Fr. D. (1994) *The History of the Indies of New Spain* (trans. and annot. D. Heyden). University of Oklahoma Press, Norman OK and London.

Freidel, D., Schele, L. and Parker, J. (1993) *Maya Cosmos: Three thousand years on the shaman's path.* William Morrow and Co., New York.

Haines, H., Willink, P. and Maxwell, D. (2008) Stingray spine use and Maya bloodletting rituals. A cautionary tale. *Latin American Antiquity* 19, 83–98.

Headrick, A. (2007) Canonical Complexity and the Aztec Calendar Stone. Unpublished paper presented at 95th Annual Conference of the College Art Association in New York, 15 February, 2007.

Joyce, R.A., Edging, R., Lorenz, K. and Gillespie, S.D. (1991) Olmec bloodletting: An iconographic study. In *Sixth Palenque Round Table, 1986*, ed. V.M. Fields, 143–50. University of Oklahoma Press, Norman OK.

Klein, C. (1976) The identity of the central face on the Aztec Calendar Stone. *Art Bulletin* 58, 1–12.

Klein, C. (1987) The ideology of autosacrifice at the Templo Mayor. In *The Aztec Templo Mayor*, ed. E.H. Boone, 293–370. Dumbarton Oaks Research Library and Collection, Washington DC.

López Austin, A. (1973) *Hombre-dios: Religión en el mundo Náhuatl.* Universidad Nacional Autónoma de México, Instituto de Investigaciones Históricas, Mexico City.

López Austin, A. (2015) *The Myth of Quetzalcoatl: Religion rulership, and history in the Nahua world* (trans. R. Davidson and G. Oliver), University of Colorado Press, Boulder CO.

Lothrop, S.K. (1952) *Metals from the Cenote of Sacrifice, Chichen Itza, Yucatan.* Memoirs of the Peabody Museum of Archaeology and Ethnology 10.2. Harvard University, Cambridge MA.

Lynch, R. (2014) 'Crocodile hunter' cameraman: Footage of Steve Irwin death is private, *Los Angeles Times*, 10 March 2014. [https://www.latimes.com/nation/la-sh-crocodile-hunter-steve-irwins-last-words-im-dying-20140310-story.html], accessed December 13th 2021.

Matos, E. (2004) The Aztec Calendar. In *The Aztec Calendar and Other Solar Monuments*, E. Matos and F. Solis, 12–75. Conaculta-Instituto Nacional de Antropología e Historia, Mexico City.

Mirriam-Webster (2021) Masterpiece. [https://www.merriam-webster.com/dictionary/masterpiece], accessed December 9th 2021.

Monaghan, J. (1990) Sacrifice, death, and the origins of agriculture in the Codex Vienna. *American Antiquity*, 55, 559–69.

Navarrete, C. and Heyden, D. (1974) La cara central de la Piedra del sol: una hipótesis. *Estudios de de Cultura Nahuatl* 11, 355–76.

Nielsen, J. and Helmke. C. (2018) "Where the Sun Came into Being": Rite of pyrolatry, transition, and transformation in Early Classic Teotihuacan. In *Smoke, Flames, and the Human Body in Mesoamerican Ritual Practice*, eds V. Tiesler and A.K. Scherer, 77–107. Dumbarton Oaks Research Library and Collection, Washington DC.

Peñafiel, A. (1890) *Monumentos del arte mexicano antiguo: Ornamentación, mitología, tributos y monumentos.* A. Asher, Berlin.

Peterson, J. (1983) Sacrificial earth: The iconography and function of malinalli grass in Aztec culture. In *Flora and Fauna Imagery in Precolumbian Culture. Proceedings of the 44th International Congress of Americanists, Manchester*, ed. J. Peterson, 113–48. British Archaeological Report S171, Oxford.

Redfield, R. and Villa Rojas, A. (1934) *Chan Kom: A Maya village.* Carnegie Institution of Washington, Washington DC.

Sahagún, Fr. B. de (1950–1982) *Florentine Codex: General history of the things of New Spain* (trans. C.E. Dibble and A.J.O. Anderson). Monographs of the School of American Research and the Museum of New Mexico Books 1–13, School of American Research and University of Utah, Santa Fe NM.

Schele, L. and Miller, M.E. (1986) *The Blood of Kings: Dynasty and ritual in Maya art.* George Braziller and Kimbell Art Museum, New York and Fort Worth TX.

Seler, E. (1960–1961). *Gesammelte Abhandlungen zur amerikanischen Sprach- und Altertumskunde.* Akademische Druk- u. Verlagsanstalt, Graz.

Seler, E. (1990) *Collected Works in Mesoamerican Linguistics and Archaeology* (English trans. German papers from *Gesammelte Abhandlungen zur Amerikanischen Sprach- und Alterthumskunde* vols I, III, and V. Labyrinthos, Lancaster, England.

Solís, F. and Velasco Alonso, R. (2004) Archaeological monuments of sun worship in pre-Hispanic Mexico. In *The Aztec Calendar and Other Solar Monuments*, E. Matos and F. Solis, 76–147. Conaculta-Instituto Nacional de Antropología e Historia, Mexico City.

Stuart, D. (1998) "The fire enters his house": Architecture and ritual in Classic Maya texts. In *Function and Meaning in Classic Maya Architecture*, ed. S.D. Houston, 373–425. Dumbarton Oaks Research Library and Collection, Washington DC.

Stuart, D. (2016) The face of the Calendar Stone: A new interpretation, 13 June 2016. [https://mayadecipherment.com/2016/06/13/the-face-of-the-calendar-stone-a-new-interpretation/], accessed December 15th 2021.

Stuart, D. and Stuart, G. (2008) *Palenque: Eternal city of the Maya.* Thames and Hudson, London.

Taube, K.A. (1992) *The Major Gods of Yucatan.* Dumbarton Oaks Research Library and Collection, Washington DC.

Taube, K.A. (2000) The turquoise hearth: Fire, self sacrifice and the central Mexican cult of sacred war. In *Mesoamerica's Classic Heritage: From Teotihuacan to the Aztecs*, eds D. Carrasco, L. Jones, and S. Sessions, 269–340. University Press of Colorado, Boulder CO.

Townsend, R. (1979) State and cosmos in the art of Tenochtitlan. *Studies in Pre-Columbian Art and Archaeology* 20. Dumbarton Oaks Research Library and Collection, Washington DC.

Umberger, E. (1981) Aztec Sculptures, Hieroglyphs, and History. Unpublished Ph.D. dissertation, Graduate School of Arts and Sciences, Columbia University, New York.

Umberger, E. (1984) El trono de Moctezuma. *Estudios de Cultura Náhuatl* 17, 63–87.

Umberger, E. (1988) A reconsideration of some hieroglyphs on the Mexica Calendar Stone. In *Smoke and Mist: Mesoamerican studies in memory of Thelma D. Sullivan*, eds J.K. Josserand and K. Dakin, 345–88. British Archaeological Report S402, Oxford.

Villela, K.D. and Miller, M. eds (2010) *The Aztec Calendar.* The Getty Research Institute, Los Angeles CA.

Villela, K.D., Robb, M.H. and Miller M. (2010) Introduction. In Villela and Miller (eds), 1–41.

Winter, I. (1981) Royal rhetoric and the development of historical narrative in Neo-Assyrian reliefs. *Studies in Visual Communication* 7, 2–38.

Plate 1. Nepcetaq Mask, Yup'ik culture (*c.* 1900), Alaska. (St Louis Art Museum, Object 99:2013).

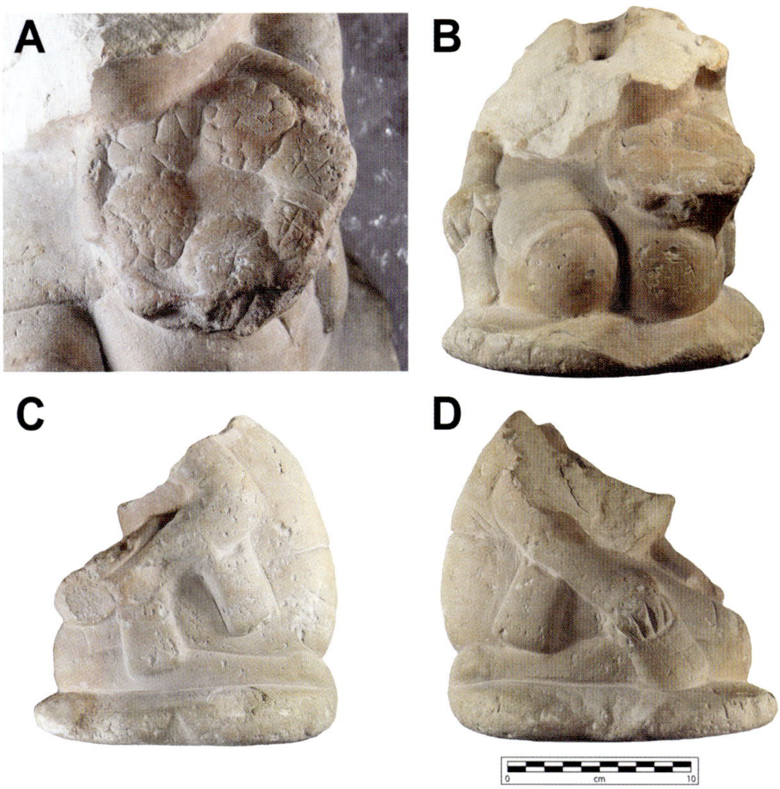

Plate 2. McBeth figurine, Pickaway County, Ohio (limestone).

Sample #21

Sample #22

a

b

Plate 3. Polychrome painted bottles (Gilcrease Museum, Tulsa OK).

Plate 4. Preliminary reconstruction of the greenstone mosaic masks (GMM) found in burials of elite individuals at ancient settlements of the Central Maya Lowlands of Guatemala: a) El Perú-*Waka'*, Burial 61; b) El Perú-*Waka'*, Burial 38; c) El Perú-*Waka'*, Burial 39; d) El Perú-*Waka'*, Burial 37; e) Tikal, Burial 160; f–h) El Perú-*Waka'*, Burial 8; i–j) El Zotz, Burial 9; k–l) Tikal, Burial 19; m) El Tinatl, Burial 1 (courtesy of the Ministerio de Cultural y Deportes, the Dirección General del Patrimonio Cultural y Natural, the Museo Nacional de Arqueología y Etnología de Guatemala, and the Proyecto Arqueológico *Waka'*).

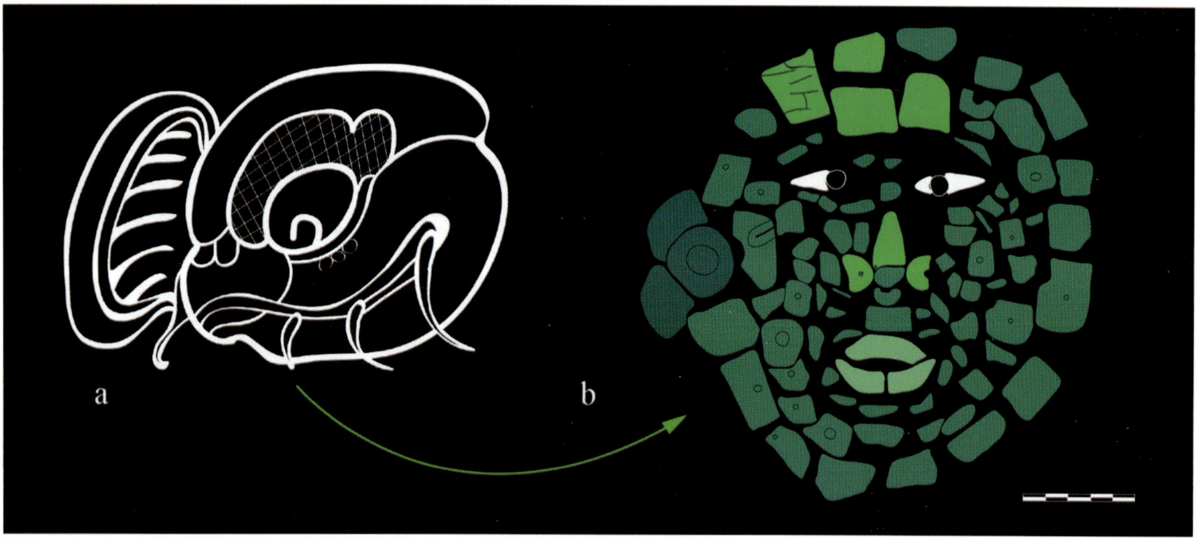

Plate 5. a) Emblem glyph of the Kaanul regime represented by the head of a snake (redrawn from Martin and Grube 2008); b) GMM found in Burial 61 of El Perú-*Waka'*.

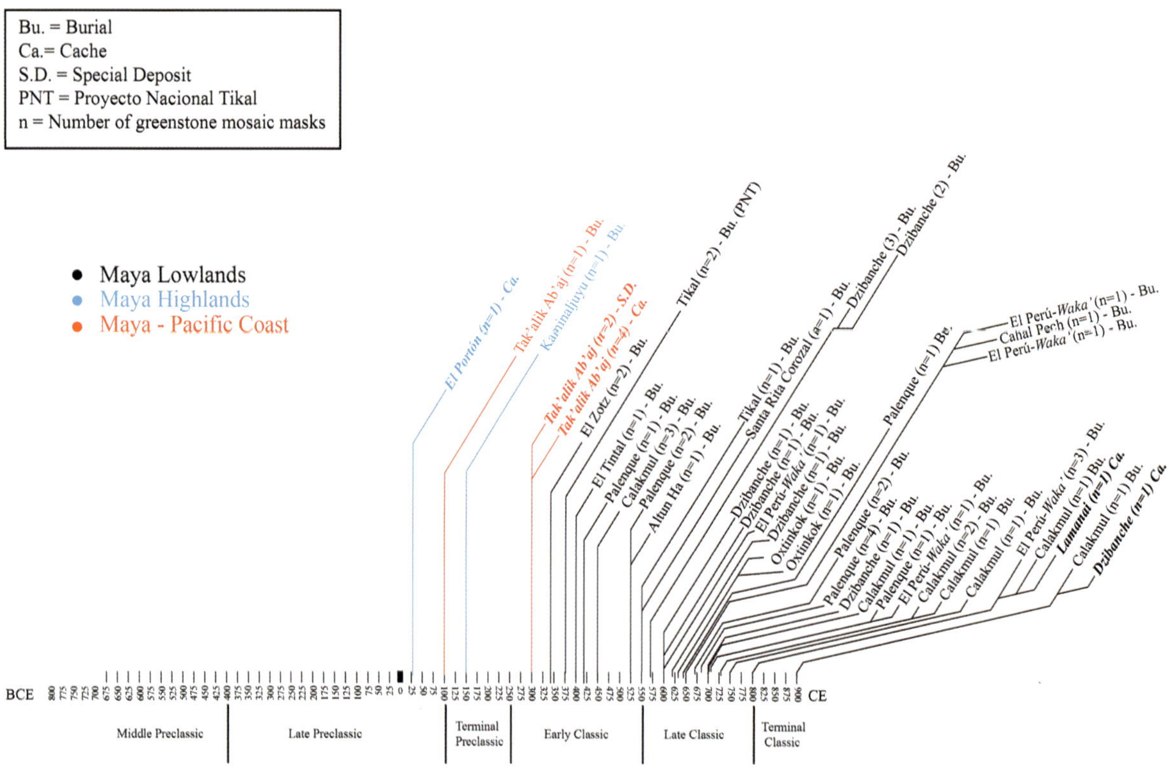

Plate 6. Timeline showing a list of pre-Columbian sites where portable Maya GMM (AD1–900) have been reported. The data were obtained from academic publications and presentations. The dates assigned to each archaeological context (e.g., burial, cache, or special deposit) were estimated based on *terminus post quo*.

Plate 7. Drawings of the massive GMM pavements from the Olmec site of La Venta: a) Pavement 3; b) Pavement 1, ca. 750 BC; which show a simulated version of the colored clay and sand reported by Drucker (1952) and Drucker *et al.* (1959) (drawings after Drucker (1952) and (Drucker *et al.* 1959).

Plate 8. Prisoner executed on a sun stone (modified from Durán 1994, pl. 17).

Plate 9. Results of viewshed analysis with results indicated for the landscape before and after the beginning of the Stirling phase (post-AD 1100).

Plate 10. A seminal example of Braden from Picture Cave. Morning star figure, often referred to in the ethnographic literature as "He Who Wears Human Heads as Ear Ornaments"

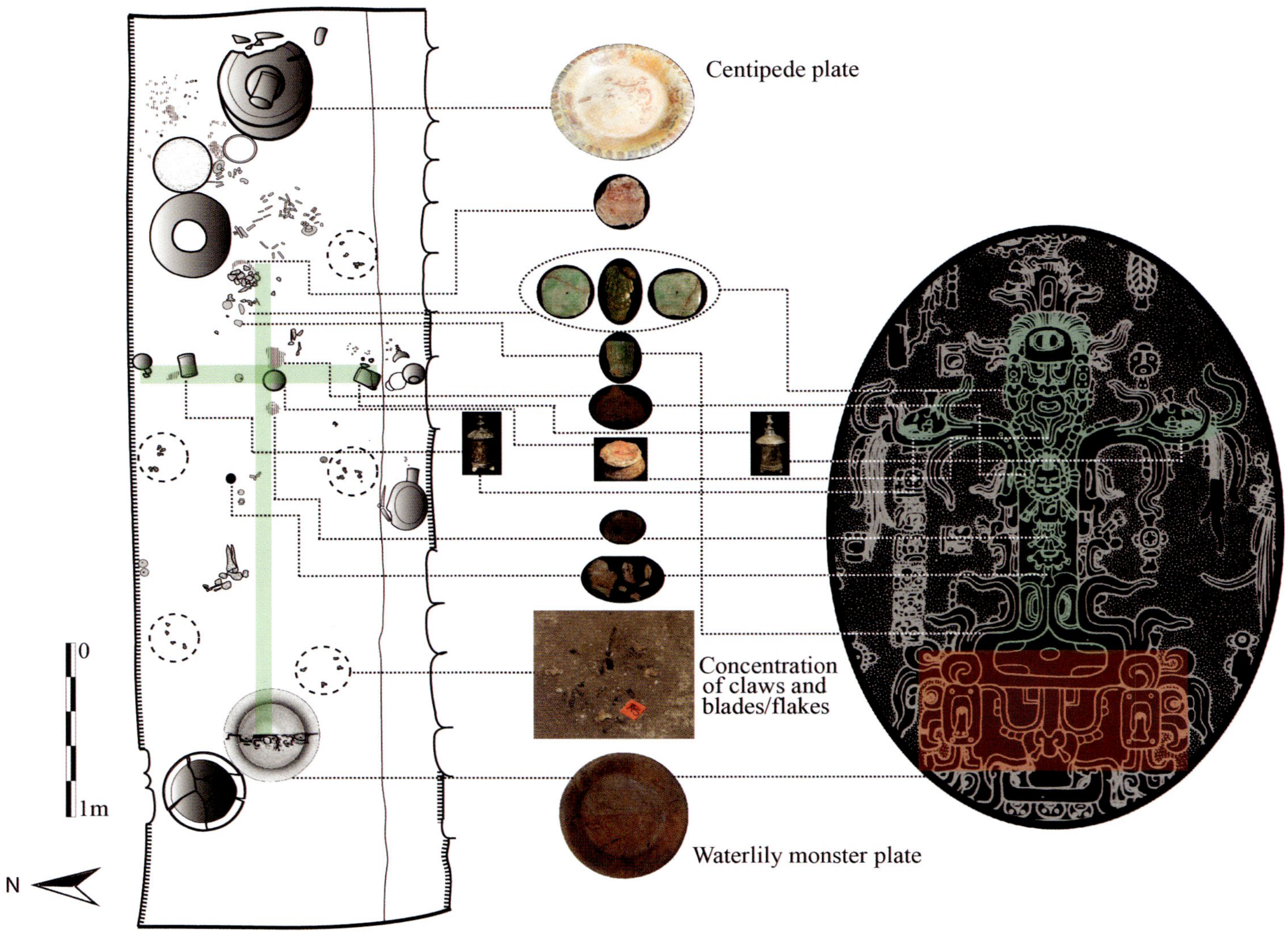

Plate 11. Preliminary reconstruction of the greenstone mosaic masks (GMM) found in burials of elite individuals at ancient settlements of the Central Maya Lowlands of Guatemala. a) El Perú-Waka', Burial 61; b) El Perú-Waka', Burial 38; c) El Perú-Waka', Burial 39; d) El Perú-Waka', Burial 37; e) Tikal, Burial 160; f,g,h) El Perú-Waka', Burial 8; i,j) El Zotz, Burial 9; k,l) Tikal, Burial 19; m) El Tintal, Burial 1. Courtesy of the Ministerio de Cultura y Deportes, the Dirección General del Patrimonio Cultural y Natural, the Museo Nacional de Arqueología y Etnología de Guatemala, and the Proyecto Arqueológico Waka', with the support of the musée du quai Branly – Jacques Chirac.

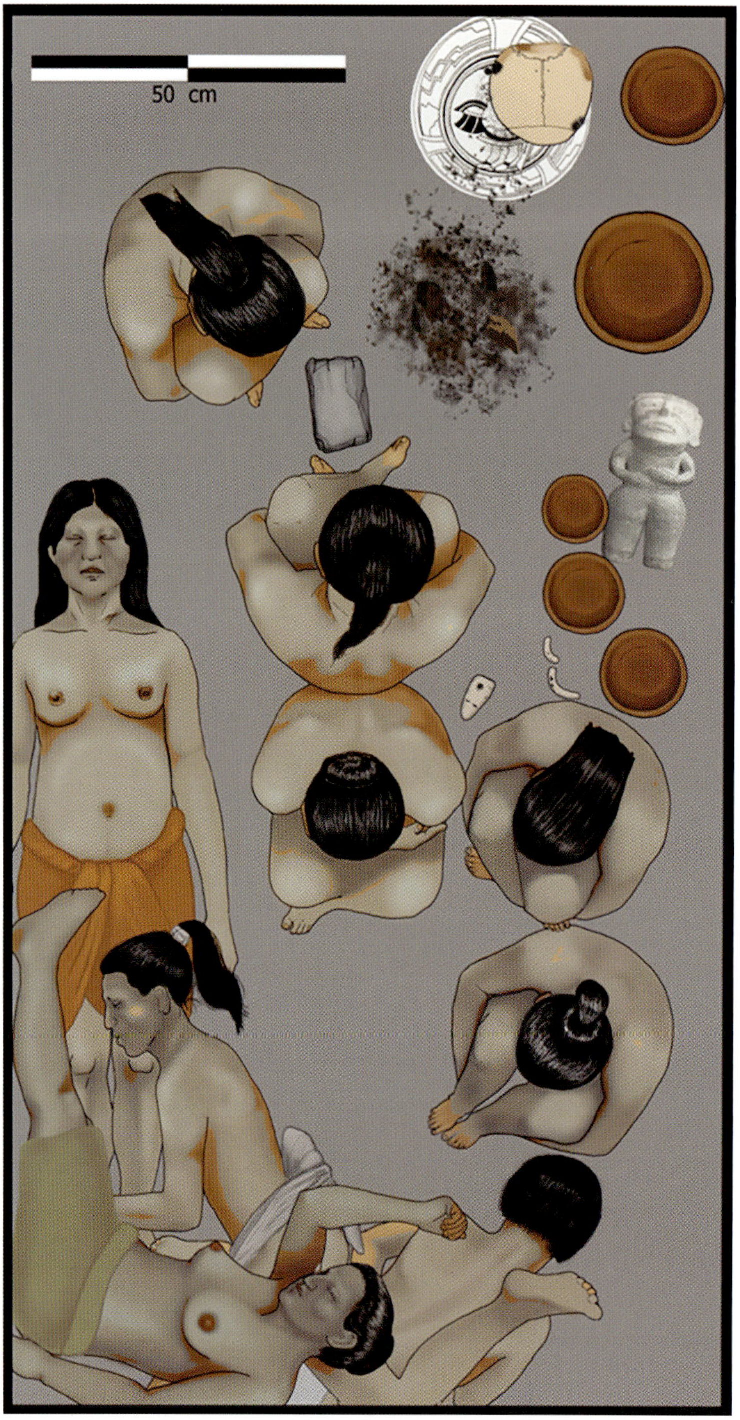

Plate 12. Early Classic Maya Burial 24 in the north acropolis of Yaxuna.

Part 2

Place-making and cultivating cosmoscapes

8

Center posts, thunder symbolism, and community organization at Cahokia Mounds, Illinois

Joy Mersmann and J. Grant Stauffer

Introduction

As a fundamental aspect of cultural practice, human beings must reconcile what they know about the world with what they experience in it; as social animals this process happens in the context of one's community and culture. Collectively, ancient cultural groups iteratively reconciled their shared knowledge about the world with prescribed ritual experiences, which often employed complex symbol systems and transformed occupied landscapes (Ellen 1986; Hall 1997; Dalan *et al.* 2003; Reilly 2004). Long Kantian dialogues in philosophical texts consider how the interaction between experience and abstract knowledge is a necessary part of knowledge acquisition (Kant 1950; Waldmann 1996, 51–2). From a simplified version of this perspective, knowledge is only possible when sensory input is interpreted with "*a priori* categories of knowledge" (Waldman 1996, 51). In this way, existing knowledge is continuously being reinvented by new experiences people have and being translated into written and unwritten records of the past.

Although many cultures did not record their oral histories or philosophies (in the Americas especially), it is clear that all cultures have *cosmologies*, belief-based understandings of how the cosmos was created and the nature of its organization (Aveni 2002, 122–7). They also created *cosmoscapes*, "overarching model[s] and template[s] for the shape and scope of the cosmos" (Reichel 2012, 136–7). Across the pre-Columbian Americas both cosmologies and cosmoscapes exhibit a tripartite organization of the cosmos that was codified iconographically (Wheatley 1971; Eliade 1959; Ellen 1986; Reilly 2004). By changing the nature of their immediate environments, humans made cosmoscapes out of pre-existing landscapes and we contend that Cahokia's Mississippian period (AD 1050–1400) organization is one prominent example. Inspired by Reilly's (1994; 2004) seminal works on the cosmology of the Olmec La Venta site and the iconography of Native North Americans, our chapter investigates how Native Americans at Cahokia altered the pre-existing landscape into a cosmoscape; one that articulated with forces in nature like thunder, rain, movements of the Sun, and the sacred winds (*sensu*

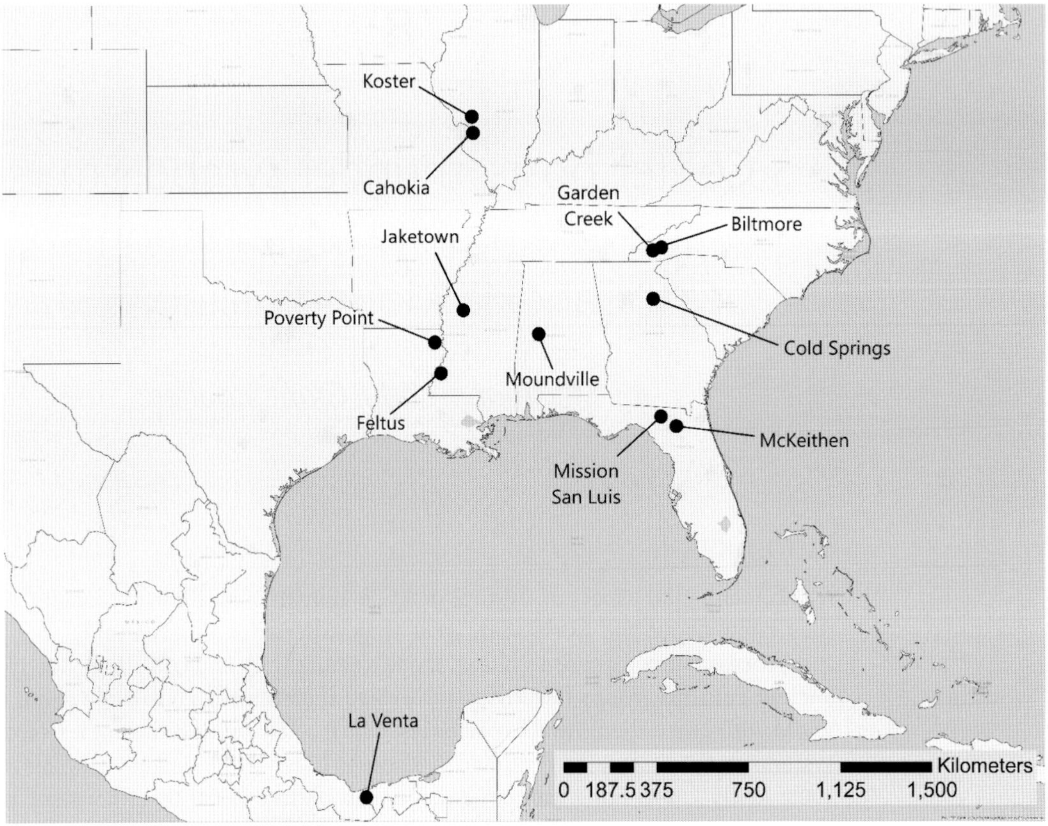

Fig. 8.1. Map of sites mentioned in the text.

Hall 1997; see also Hultkrantz 1979, 27–83). Consequently, our chapter examines how related architectures are organized in manners that display the knowledge shared by community and structure the actions of that community to maintain a commonly perceived state of order in reality.

To do this, we employ a geographic information system (GIS) of ground-truthed (isolated and central) post features from the Cahokia site to examine patterned changes in the site's architectural layout over time. We approach post features as components of the Cahokia cosmoscape that were highlighted by lightning and other Above World forces and whose layouts shifted according to Native American perceptions of cosmic order. We conceive of center post features – posts which stand alone in the center of plazas or building clusters, independent of other structures – as active agents who facilitated connections between Above, Middle, and Beneath World cosmic realms, as well as prominent architectural features (*sensu* Reilly 2004). Based on the results of our viewshed analysis we propose that the patterning of center pole placements across the Cahokia site indicate an important shift from alignments oriented north–south to east–west alignments that highlight views of the eastern horizon from the Woodhenge circles west of Monks Mound, beginning in the early 12th century. The distribution of sites discussed in the text is shown in Figure 8.1.

Cross-cultural perspectives of ancient urban cosmoscapes

Cosmology is a linchpin connecting man-made landscapes, the natural environment, and social order, codified in creation and hero myths that identify the domains of natural features, animals, plants, people, and other-than-human persons in reality (Eliade 1958; Ellen 1986; Reilly 2004; Reichel 2012; Wade 2018). Geographers, philosophers, and archaeologists alike recognize that people created and structured their pre-conceived notions of cosmic order architecturally, when the advent of urbanism occurred in disparate pockets of the ancient world (Wheatley 1971; Barry and Dahmann 2001). Although focused on Shang and Zhou dynasty urban sites within modern China, geographer Paul Wheatley (1971) proposed that, universally, cultures that built large ceremonial spaces tend to quarter architectural spaces around an *axis mundi* (center of the world), drawing from Eliade (1958). Arguably North America's first city, Cahokia's layout after the mid-11th century reflects efforts to organize the site according to a widely known set of cosmological principles and establish it as a cosmoscape (Kelly and Brown 2014). As an ancient city, Cahokia bears many similarities to other ancient cities globally, reinforcing ideas initially proposed by Wheatley (1971) and expanded upon in more recent examinations of cosmoscapes (Pavel 1981; Ellen 1986; Berlo 2010; Reichel 2012; Bold 2020).

In a synthesizing paper, Barry and Dahmann (2001) define the following key concepts that capture Wheatley's perspective on urban site organization: centripetality, cardinality, and inductance. Centripetality captures how urban site layouts often mirror *a priori* understandings of the cosmos's structure and with attention to transitions between cosmic planes, often referencing the cardinal directions and an *axis mundi* (center of the world). Cardinality describes the nesting of architectural features within an urban site-space around a "sacred enclave" that acts as the city's *axis mundi*. Inductance refers to the structuring of architectural space around a central point and with parallels to an *a priori* understanding of celestial space, in order to direct the movement of people within the site in a prescribed fashion (Barry and Dahmann 2001, 741–2). Within this theoretical scheme Cahokia's cardinally oriented plazas around Monks Mound and encapsulation by a massive palisade wall can be examined as a cosmoscape that was actively occupied and changed according to the cultural values of its residents, in order to articulate their existence with an idealized order of the cosmos itself.

Native North American cosmoscapes consist of dynamically animated realms that are typically divided into tripartite Above, Middle, and Beneath Worlds. Particularly in the Muskogean cosmos, an Above World or "sky vault" rotates about a Middle World plane of earth that floats upon the watery Beneath World realm, functioning as the respective day-time and night-time skies (see Azar and Steponaitis, this volume; Lankford 2007a; Swanton 2000, 477–8). Community spaces like historic square grounds are organized around an idealized *axis mundi* that penetrates through the Middle World and is actualized through the arrangement of lit central fires, iconographically represented by center cross motifs (Reilly 2004; Lankford 2007a). In addition to central fires, isolated posts could also serve as materialized *axes mundi* that were personified as lineage founders like the

"First Man" personage of Siouan origin (Fletcher 1895). Among the Omaha, the personified "First Man" sacred pole was not always a fixed monument but an actor that was transported to and involved in important ceremonial events (Fletcher 1895). Consequently, ceremonial spaces host behaviors that illustrate the concepts highlighted by Barry and Dahmann (2001) and even material components of them exhibit agency.

Architectural features like historic Muskogean arbors are arranged in quadripartite fashion to honor the sacred directions, quartering an idealized Middle World space (Lankford 2007a, 14–20, fig. 2.4). Cross-culturally, such quarters anchor the floating Middle World and are referred to with iconographic and metaphorical tropes, such as the sacred winds (Kansas and Santee), crested birds or "Grandfathers of the Winds" (Shawnee), boys (Caddo and Cherokee), Thunderbirds or Thunderers (Ojibwa and Sauk) (Dorsey 1885, 676; Fletcher 1884, 289; Fletcher and La Flesche 1911, 63; Skinner 1923, 35; Smith 1995, 77; Lankford 2007a, 25–6). Ceremonial dances among Muskogean, Siouan, and Algonquian communities are often interpreted as a means of channeling the dynamic motions of natural forces and migrations of animals observed in nature, in fashions not unlike the looped square motifs that don Cox Mound style shell gorgets and illustrate the "Four Quarters ... upholding the earth ... connected with thunder or lightning as well as the wind" (Fletcher 1884, 289; see also Swanton 2000, 534–614; Lankford 2007a, 21). Moreover, ceremonial actions like striking central poles to mourn the passage of deceased souls emulate the sounds of thunder and associate them with forces that anchor and transcend the Middle World as portals channeling the forces that propel spirits into the night-time sky (Beneath World) and day-time sky (Above World). Consequently, the organization of ceremonial spaces within communities properly directs the forces that animate cosmoscapes in prescribed ways.

As another example of how pre-Columbian Native Americans transformed their host landscapes into cosmoscapes, Reilly (1994) has shown that the central mound (Complex C) at the site of La Venta was a symbol for the sacred mountain of origin, beyond which an embanked sunken court (Complex A) commemorated a sanctified space for divine Olmec rulers at the apex of the site's central axis; a site-wide alignment intended to convey an image of the World Tree at the center of the cosmos. From his perspective, processions of people from Complex C into the sunken court of Complex A was akin to descending from a sky realm into a watery Beneath World (Reilly 1994). Perhaps the efforts of Cahokia's residents attempted to model the site-space in a similar way.

As an illustration of the way center poles facilitated experiences with forces in nature that Native Americans respected and admired at the Cahokia site, we highlight Reed's (2009) descriptions of frequent lightning strikes that destroyed reconstructed center poles atop Monks Mound, the highest occupation surface within the site, largest earthen mound north of Mexico, and center point of Cahokia's mound-and-plaza compounds. According to him, an 11 m tall center post reconstructed by Jim Porter was struct by lightning 3 days after it was raised and several other replacement posts met the same fate in highly visible spectacles atop the highest surface within a 3 mile (4.8 km) radius. The largest Mississippian period structure ever documented was also excavated atop this same terrace of Monks Mound, along with dog burials at the entrance of a screen that surrounded it (Reed 2009, 61, 66). These strikingly visible features atop Monks Mound have led some to claim that Cahokia was arranged as a panopticon that facilitated social surveillance and reinforced the authority of those permitted to occupy these potent spaces (Pierce and Matisziw 2018).

Located immediately south of Monks Mound's third terrace center pole and arguably in purposeful alignment with it, another center post of similar size preceded the earliest stages of Mound 72's elaborate mortuary constructions that involved 252 documented burials (Fowler *et al.* 1999, 193–7, appx b). This correlation inspired Reed (2009) to propose that the large central post on Monks Mound played a role in its mortuary symbolism, noting that the transect created by that post, the entrance to the Monks Mound charnel house, and Mounds 56, 60, 66, and 72 define a 5° east-of-north alignment. He references Lankford's (2007b, 200) study of "Path of Souls" rituals and related iconography that highlighted ways to process the dead to an afterlife, specifically identifying Cahokia's Woodhenges as analogues for historic Sun Dance lodges. This same 5° offset was first identified by Fowler (1997; Fowler *et al.* 1999, 5, fig. 1.3) and has been incorporated in Kelly's (1996) and Kelly and Brown's (2014) quadripartite model of Cahokia's architectural organization at the beginning of the 12th century. This proposed central axis for the Cahokia site is further reinforced by examinations of the Rattlesnake Causeway by Baires (2014, 147, fig. 1; 2017), who links the practice of building causeways to preceding Middle Woodland (ca. 150 BC–AD 400) Hopewell sites in Ohio and compares them to the *sacbeob* that facilitated travel between extensive Maya settlements. The two dates Baires (2014, 153) sampled from her excavation unit into the Rattlesnake Causeway fall between the late 11th and early 13th centuries, indicating its likely creation during the Stirling phase (1100–1200). Altogether, the placement of center poles, mounds, and the Rattlesnake Causeway reinforce the alignment that Reed (2009) interprets to be a mirrored reflection of the "Path of Souls" on Cahokia's monumental landscape, resembling the Milky Way across the night sky above the site and lying east of the known Woodhenge circles in Tract 15A between them and the eastern horizon.

If Reed (2009), Fowler (1997; Fowler *et al.* 1999), and Kelly and Brown's (2014) claims for a purposeful organization of the Cahokia site are true, then the possibility that center poles were placed in specifically chosen places for important events can be examined further. Consequently, we hypothesize that, like the organization of mounds and plazas, the locations of center poles were also part of the site's architectural plan and organized the occurrence of historically important event-sites within a coherent cosmoscape. More specifically, we emphasize how the general alignments evidenced by the placement of central poles at the Cahokia site highlight the cruciform arrangement of shared plaza spaces circumscribed by earthen mounds and centered by the largest example, Monks Mound, as has been suggested by authors like Kelly (1997, 145). Testing this hypothesis also permits interpretations about the nature of community and authority at the site and examines how politico-religious events were managed by its occupants (Table 8.1).

Language:		*Muskogee*	
Tribe:	*Creek*	*Choctaw*	*Apalachee**
Migration	x	x	
Warfare	x		x
Creation			x
Gaming	x		x
Death	x	x	

Language:		*Dhegiha Sioux*		
Tribe:	*Winnebago*	*Omaha**	*Osage*	*Ponca**
Migration				
Warfare		x	x	
Creation		x	x	
Gaming	x		x	
Death	x			x

Language:	*Timucua*	*Iroquois*	*Algonquian*	*Caddo*
Tribe:	*Timucua*	*Cherokee*	*Shawnee*	*Pawnee*
Migration		x		x
Warfare			x	x
Creation			x	x
Gaming	x			
Death			x	

** denotes tribes with explicit associations of raptors or thunderbirds with center posts*

Table 8.1. Thematic associations of center posts in Native American folklore (see Kelly 2003).

Cultural background

Native North Americans in the Midwest and Southeast held important ceremonial events that included raising and arranging tall "center poles" that were used to establish sightlines for architectural and astronomical phenomena (Wittry 1973; 1980; Hann 1988; Fowler 1996; Hall 1997; Emerson 2003; Kelly 2003; Pauketat and Alt 2005). Center poles appear in the oral accounts and iconographic art of many Eastern Woodland tribes. Among the historic Apalachee of modern Florida, center poles with bird effigies at their tops also functioned as goal posts in ball games held in a central plaza at Mission San Luis, near the modern capital city of Tallahassee (Hann 1988; DeBoer 1993; Stauffer and Reilly 2017). The oldest recorded myth from Native North America, documented by Father Juan Paiva in 1676, details the origins of the ball game and how a culture hero, named *Nicoguadca*, earned a political rank or office through his supernaturally gifted athletic performances (Hann 1988, 328–53). Similar ball posts and elaborately decorated center poles were illustrated by Jacques le Moyne in 1564 and block-printed by Theodore de Bry in 1591, portraying them among the Timucua people (Fundaburk 1958, 8, 16, 35, 36). The Omaha also possessed a sacred pole who was considered "First Man" personified and made ceremonious appearances (Fletcher 1895; Kelly 2003). Relating general categories of Archaic period material evidence to historic accounts, Claasen (2015, 40) suggests that mimicking thunderclaps was an important practice, bringing to mind the Shawnee "War Dance" that involved striking scalp-adorned center poles in plazas (Howard 1968; Kelly 2003, 111). The rich details offered by these historical contexts provide a useful template for generating analogies about archaeological cultures that had similar center pole ceremonials in deep antiquity. Conversely, examining many center post contexts at a larger scale can reveal their broader functions at large sites like Cahokia. In sum, a multi-scalar examination of archaeological contexts from a cosmoscape perspective can permit broader understandings of center pole ceremonialism.

Contextual evidence from the Poverty Point site, Louisiana, reveals that center poles were created in conjunction with large open plaza spaces, concentric earthen ridges opening to the east, and mounds from the Late Archaic, sometimes even in circular arrangements called "Woodhenges" that were generally oriented toward auspicious solar events (Haag 1990; 1993, 103). Additional features discovered among Middle Archaic (ca. 6400 BC) contexts at the Koster site, Illinois, have been highlighted as potential center poles, in association with the remains of dogs and humans (James 2006; Classen 2015, 90). Recent excavations at the Middle and Late Archaic Jaketown site in western Mississippi have unearthed a large center post feature that may have been placed atop the summit of the long buried Mound X feature at the site but radiocarbon dates for the feature have not yet been processed (Seth Grooms pers. comm. 2021). Although existing evidence of center poles from Archaic period contexts is sparse, existing studies that highlight the contexts of feasting deposits in association with shell and earthen monuments opening toward prominent landscape features and solstitial points along the eastern horizon lead us to suspect that center pole ceremonialism may have roots in these ancient times (Anderson 2004; Sassaman *et al.* 2019).

Center poles also fulfilled prominent roles during many Middle (200 BC–AD 500) and Late (AD 700–1000) Woodland period situations (*sensu* Henry *et al.* 2020, 206–7; see also Widlock 2016, 135). Early in this period, Adena groups in central Kentucky built enclosures that often included wooden post enclosures (Henry *et al.* 2020, 207). At Garden Creek and Biltmore, North Carolina, center poles were associated with "ritual paraphernalia" crafted from meaningful animal parts and minerals that were useful for shamanic practices (Knight 1990; 2001; Warshauer 2015; Kassabaum and Nelson 2016, 9–11). Later, Coles Creek inhabitants of the Feltus site, Mississippi, set large posts in the south plaza area between the late 8th and late 11th centuries (Ballina Phase), in conjunction with feasting events that preceded Mound D's construction (Kassabaum and Nelson 2016). Center posts were used during complex mortuary rituals at McKeithen, Florida, and Cold Springs sites, Georgia, also (Milanich *et al.* 1984; Jeffries 1994). Needless to say, center post ceremonialism was a widespread Woodland period phenomenon.

From the Late Woodland (AD 600–850) to Emergent Mississippian (AD 850–1050) and Mississippian periods (AD 1050–1400) in the American Bottom and the Central Mississippi River Valley (Morse and Morse 2000), center poles appeared in increasingly diverse contexts that were associated with both isolated architectural features and plazas, sometimes in conjunction with hearths, occupation surfaces, house structures, and mortuary contexts (Kelly 2003; Skousen 2012, 60–3, tables 1–2). At the Range site in the American Bottom region, Kelly (1990a) identified a palimpsest of community spaces, consisting of several house structures surrounding open courtyards with large posts in their center, occasionally flanked in quadripartite fashion by limestone-lined pit features. Recognizing these courtyard groups as distinct occupation areas that contained the fundamental elements of Native American communities on site, he traced the chronological sequence of these stratigraphically superimposed courtyard groups from the Patrick (AD 600–700) to Stirling (1100–1200) phases (Kelly 1990a). Importantly, courtyard groups with shared center post features of the Late Woodland and Mississippian periods "were built together, reconstructed together, and even abandoned as a group", whether they existed at large mound sites or rural settlements (Pauketat 1994, 31; Alt 2001; Pauketat and Alt 2005, 220). At Cahokia, the placement of center poles in the middle of late Emergent Mississippian and Mississippian communities have likewise been ground-truthed through ambitious excavations in the ICT-II, 15A, 15B, and Dunham tracts (Collins 1990; Pauketat 1998; 2013; Betzenhauser and Pauketat 2019). In sum, the creation, reconstruction, and removal of center posts across American Bottom sites from the Late Woodland through Mississippian periods corresponded with the lifespans of whole communities.

In addition to their placement in the center of courtyard groups that were collectively occupied, rebuilt, and abandoned, center posts are also placed beneath and atop mound construction stages (Morse and Morse 1983, 309; Pauketat and Alt 2005, 216). Timing the region-wide advent of building earthen mounds in these courtyard groups and their incorporation into the organization of community space is an ongoing process but current evidence from the Morrison Site immediately northwest of Cahokia's monumental core and the Washausen Site farther south indicates that mounds became another fundamental element of community spaces during the 11th century (Kelly 1990b, 135; Barrier and Horsley 2014; Betzenhauser *et al.* 2015). Preston Holder's excavations into the Kunnemann Mounds and the structures distributed throughout their construction sequence, Melvin Fowler's excavations of the Mound 72 mortuary complex, and Harriet Smith's excavations into the construction stages of Murdock Mound that included a cruciform shaped structure, reveal that the placement of center posts was of critical importance in the mound building process (Smith 1969; Pauketat 1993; Fowler *et al.* 1999). Moreover, the overall placement of mounds atop the locations of large and architecturally unusual house structures –the Murdock Mound's placement atop the cruciform shaped building, for example – emphasizes the importance of ritual spaces and suggests important symbolic metaphors connected houses, mounds, and center posts (see Giles *et al.* in this volume). Consistent with the theme of this volume, we view all three architectural forms (center poles, houses, and mounds) as fundamental elements of the Cahokian cosmoscape that were symbolically linked by nesting their architectural forms.

At Cahokia, large Woodhenge circles unearthed at Tract 15A were raised in multiple events during the 12th and 13th centuries, but center poles also dot several occupation areas on site that include the locations of plazas and mounds (Haag 1993; Pauketat 1998; Fowler *et al.* 1999; Betzenhauser and Pauketat 2019). Additionally, Fowler (1996) exposed large posts beneath and around Mound 72 that he proposes could be associated with one or more additional Woodhenge circles in this southern portion of the Cahokia site. Initial research into the Woodhenge circles at Tract 15A proposed that they had astronomical and calendrical functions (Norrish 1978a; 1978b), while Fowler's (1996, 36–7, 41, table 4.1, figure 4.3; Fowler *et al.* 1999) additional findings provided the additional consideration that they practically functioned as backsights for aligning Cahokia's monumental architectures to site-wide alignments. The large central posts at Cahokia's Woodhenge were, therefore, "complete monuments codifying a world view of Mississippian peoples and even became cognitive maps of the community and its values" (Fowler 1996, 40). Whether they were erected in the center of community spaces or collectively arranged in large Woodhenge circles, central posts carry meaningful insights into the ways communities were organized within the cosmos as perceived by occupants of the Cahokia site and American Bottom region in general.

Iconographically, center posts appear prominently on Mississippian period shell gorgets and cups in several recognized styles, as well as the famous Moundville Palette and other stone media (Fig. 8.2). Cahokia's Ramey Tablet, in particular, offers a prominent example of a center pole motif associated with decapitated heads and crested birds that are likely portrayals of woodpeckers, similar in many respects to Hixton style shell gorgets from Tennessee and Alabama (Peet 1891; Emerson 1982; Kelly 2003, 111–12). They appear in compositions that illustrate multiple themes, such as depictions of transcendental beings, culture heroes, and scenes from otherworldly realms (see Azar and Steponaitis, this volume). For example, Braden and Craig style engraved shell cup fragments from the Spiro Site in Oklahoma depict hero twins holding center poles in whole and broken form, as well as dancing scenes around center pole motifs that can be three-dimensionalized using the cut-out-and-fold-up technique (*sensu* Reilly 2004, fig. 11). On Eddyville style engraved shell gorgets, center pole motifs are shown as objects being pulled from pots by human-like beings. These iconographic depictions not only highlight the function of center poles in ritual spaces like the archaeologically excavated courtyard and plaza compounds across the American Bottom region, but also suggest the importance of pots in Native American cosmoscapes (see Lambert, this volume).

In addition to center pole motifs observed across several styles, center cross motifs also appear across styles and media that bear affiliations with center poles (Fig. 8.2). Pickett and Oktibbeha style shell gorgets (*sensu* Brain and Phillips 1996, 26–7) provide interesting examples of center pole and center cross motifs being combined to the point where they are almost indistinguishable from each other. Both motifs appear across several Mississippian iconographic styles, often on the same composition. Center cross motifs also appear on elaborately crafted beakers collected from Tract 15A in compositions likened to the winter solstitice alignments of Woodhenge circle centerpoints to the eastern horizon, in the direction of Mound

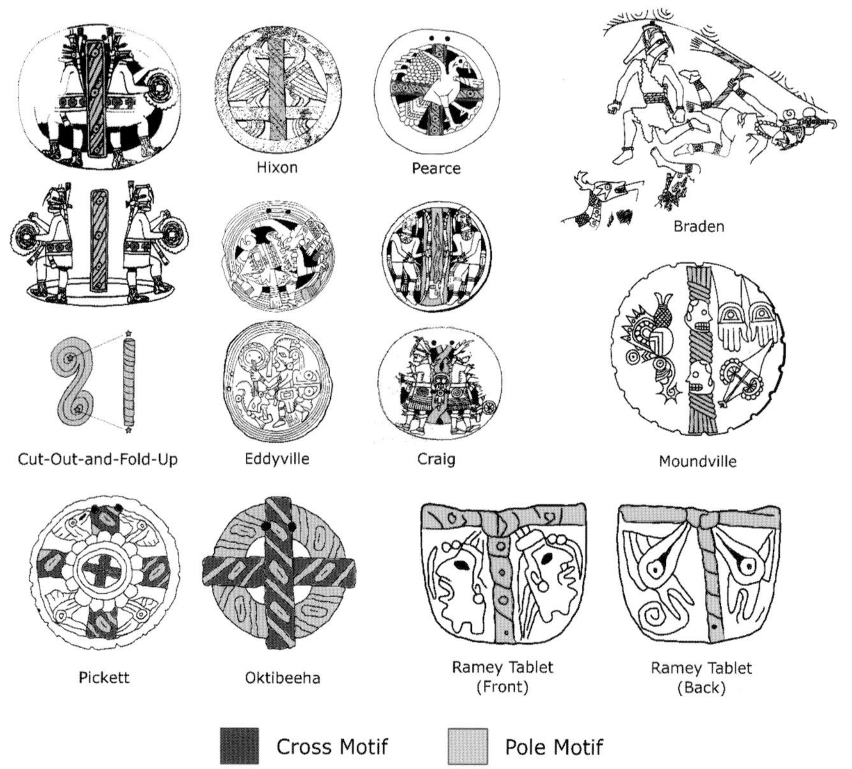

Fig. 8.2. Compositions featuring center pole motifs on shell gorgets, cups, and stone pallets. Pickett and Oktibeeha styles include combinations of these motifs.

72 (Fowler 1996, 39, fig. 4.2). This association of center posts and crosses is also illustrated ethnographically, described in Hoffman's (1891, 155) work on the "Grand Medicine Society of the Ojibway" (the *Midē'wiwin* society), where he reports the following account of Marquett's visit with the Miamis, Maskoutens, and Kikabeaux:

> *When I arriv'd (sic) there, I was very glad to see a great Cross set up in the middle of the Village, adorn'd (sic) with several White Skins, Red Girdles, Bows, and Arrows, which that good People had offer'd to the* Great Manitou ... Manitou, *is the name they give in general to all Spirits whom they think to be above the Nature of Man.*

These cross-examinations of iconographic and ethnohistoric analogues reinforces existing interpretations of the center cross motif as a representation of a Native American *axis mundi* (*sensu* Eliade 1959; Reilly 2004, 127). The conflation of center cross and center pole motifs consequently illustrate a symbolic connection to the Middle World realm of the Native American cosmoscape, perhaps symbolizing the linkages that center poles establish between the rotating celestial sphere (the Above and Beneath Worlds in motion) and the shared courtyard groups that were inhabited and abandoned collectively during episodes of occupation.

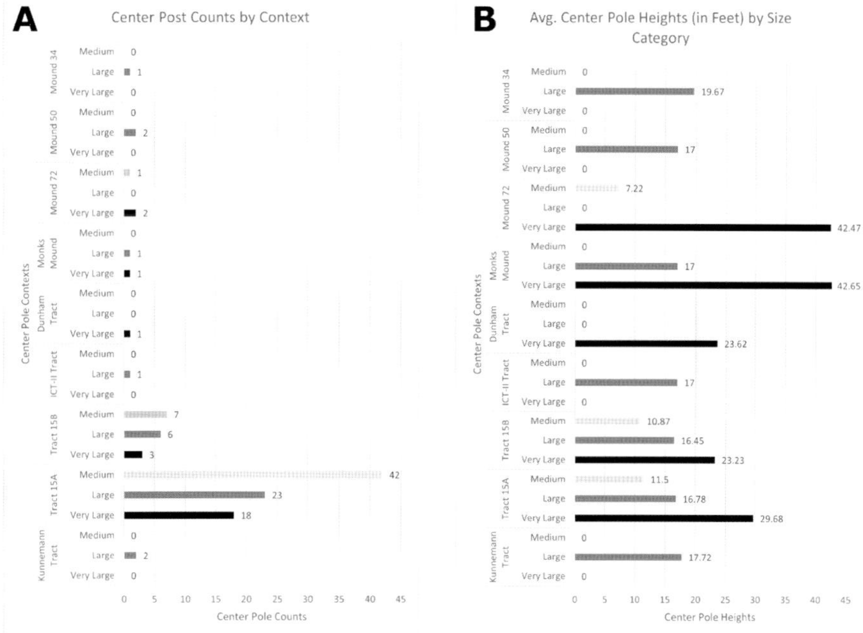

Fig. 8.3. Metrics of isolated and center pole features: A) average estimated pole heights by category and tract; B) center pole counts by category and tract.

Methods

To understand the relationship between pole-raising event locations, their visibility across the site, and the overall layout of the site during these events, we documented the locations and sizes of large post features that were excavated at Cahokia. These included 235 examples of isolated and center post features. Isolated posts included post remains that did not exhibit any associations with nearby features. Center posts were larger posts located near the center of larger architectural features, such as houses and plazas. After logging these data into a geographic information system (GIS) with the aid of ArcGIS, we estimated the heights of each pole feature, using a formula for modern telephone poles that was reported by Reed (2009, 42). This formula essentially multiplies the post-hole depth by four and adds it to the surface elevation of the post-hole feature to get its height above the ground surface. This formula does not automatically take into account the impact of modern cultivation, which would undoubtedly reduce the apparent depth of the post-hole and therefore the projected height. Excavation across multiple areas of Cahokia has shown, however, that plow zone depth at Cahokia rarely exceeds 40 cm below surface and ends 20–30 cm below surface on average (Iseminger *et al.* 1990, 22–4; Pauketat 1993; 1998; 2013). Given the post heights reported in this project (Fig. 8.3), the observed impact of modern cultivation evidenced by various plow zone depths and a consequent reduction of the predicted post heights bears no consequences for our interpretations.

Once post height values were determined, the collected post features were grouped into size categories, where very small posts were less than 5 ft (ca. 1.5 m) tall, small ones were 5–10 ft (ca. 1.5–3 m), medium ones were 10–15 ft (ca. 4.6 m), large ones 15–20 ft (ca. 4.6–6.1 m), and very large ones over 20 ft (ca. 6.1 m+) tall. Within our size categories, 66 posts were very small, 65 small, 49 medium, large, and 25 very large. Across all categories, the average pole height was 10.64 ft (3.24 m); 111 pole features less than 10 ft tall were excluded from viewshed and alignment analysis after documentation, due to the ambiguity of their function in their broader excavation contexts. The tallest examples of center posts included the post atop Monks Mound (43 ft/13.1 m), beneath Mound 72 (44 ft/13.4 m), and in Tract 15A (46 ft/14 m).

Fig. 8.4. (opposite) The orientations of posts with each other before and after the beginning of the Stirling phase (post-AD 1100).

With their locations oriented to the Cahokia Grid (Reed 2009, 8), all isolated and center pole features were plotted in ArcMap, where their general alignments and visibilities were examined to estimate quantifiable measures of each quality. Those which had been identified to a time period (n=225) were grouped into two broad categories: posts which were placed before the Stirling phase (n=43) and posts which were placed during or after the Stirling phase (n=182). Visibility analyses were run on the 16 largest posts of each group and the results were evaluated for the percentage of the central precinct and adjacent areas which were within visible range of at least one central post, as well as for the degree of overlap between visibilities of different posts.

Results

The post features found in the course of our literature review are displayed in Figure 8.4. Pre-Stirling phase posts are found across Cahokia's central precinct, as well northward towards the Kunnemann Mound group. The 16 largest of these pre-Stirling posts form a distinct axis running approximately north–south from the Kunnemann Mound group to Mound 72. A distinct cluster of pre-Stirling posts (n=31) is found immediately north of the center point of that axis, associated with Tract 15B. The remaining pre-Stirling posts are similarly arranged either on this axis or associated with the north-central cluster. A single outlier (Feature 53 from Tract 15B) is found to the west of this axis in the area later associated with Woodhenge circles. The north–south axis associated with the pre-Stirling posts falls between the places where Monks Mound and Woodhenge were later built.

In contrast, the Stirling or later posts are clustered primarily on an east–west axis, with the 16 largest posts of this phase, found either at Monks Mound on the east side of the axis or the Woodhenge on the west. The remaining posts fall along this alignment, or else fall into one of two large clusters. As with the pre-Stirling posts, there is a distinct cluster of posts (n=30) found just to the north of the central point of this axis, associated with Tract 15B. This cluster overlaps with the matching cluster of pre-Stirling posts. While seven of the 16 largest pre-Stirling posts are found associated with this combined cluster, none of the 16 largest Stirling or later posts is found in this group. A significantly larger cluster of Stirling or later posts is found at and around the Woodhenge, with 147 of the Stirling or later posts being associated with the Woodhenge cluster.

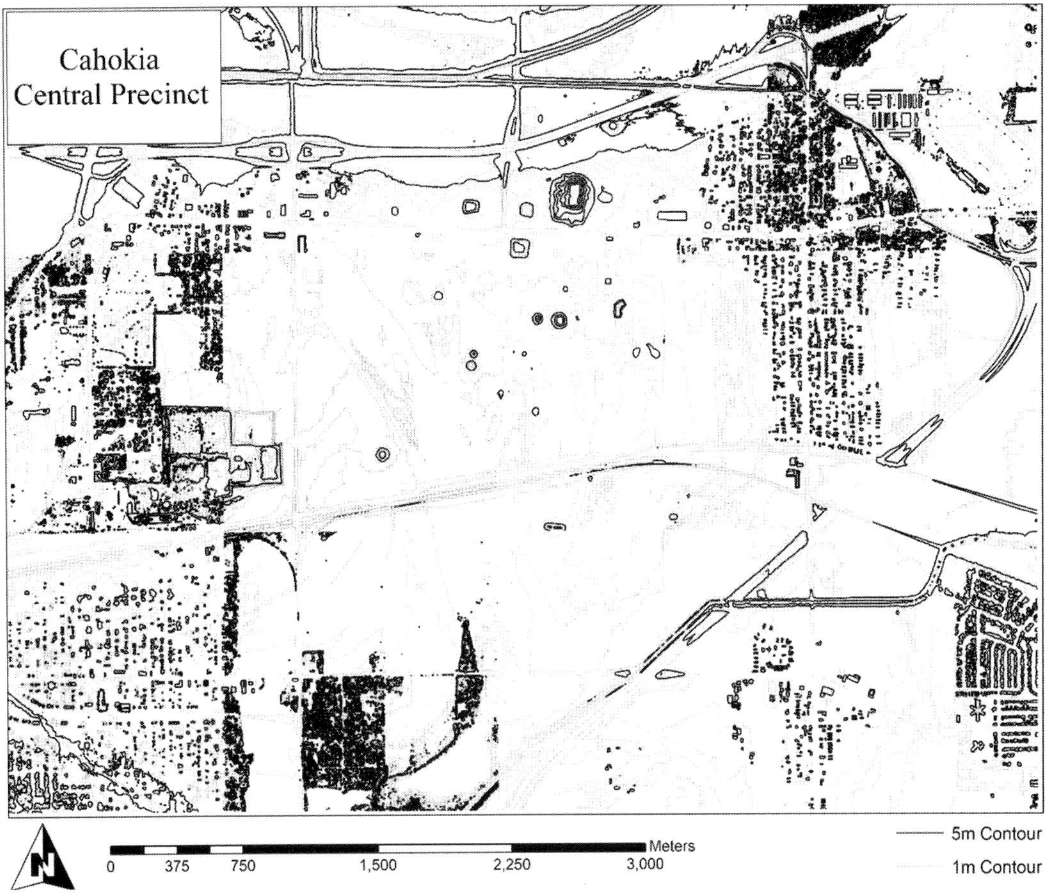
Cahokia
Central Precinct
Meters
0
375
750
1,500
2,250
3,000
5m Contour
1m Contour

North-South (pre-Stirling)
East-West
(Stirling or Later)
Legend
Posts: 16 largest, pre-Stirling
Posts: 16 largest, Stirling or later
Posts: pre-Stirling
Posts: Stirling or later
Digital elevation model (DEM)
Value
High : 158.237 mamsl
Low : 121.281 mamsl

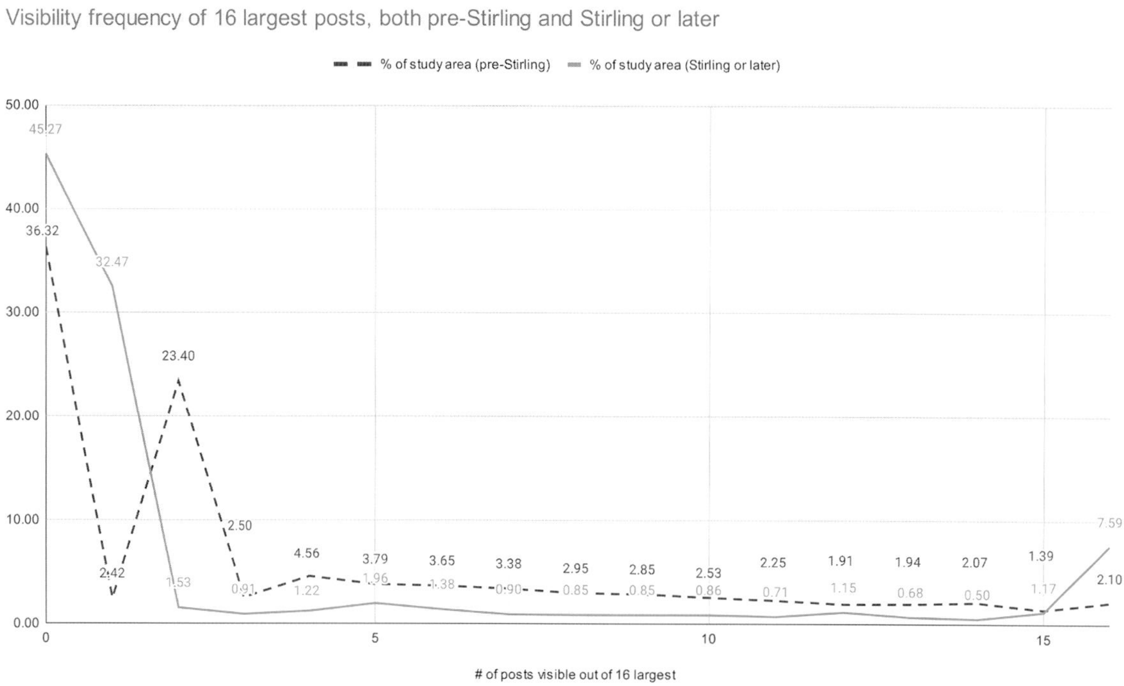

Fig. 8.5. Results of viewshed analysis with results indicated for the landscape before and after the beginning of the Stirling phase (post-AD 1100).

The two axes created by the 16 largest posts in each era match existing thoughts about the alignment of Cahokia with cardinal directions (Kelly and Brown 2014). These axes are typically seen as matching in dimensions, or with a broader east–west axis than the north–south axis, forming a diamond shape. However, the axes of large central posts found in our work indicate a trend over time of spatial consolidation, with the long, extended north–south alignment of the pre-Stirling era consolidating into the short, condensed east–west alignment of the Stirling and later era. During the twilight of Cahokia's occupation after the 13th century, these north–south and east–west alignments together exhibited the major axes along which Cahokia's monuments and community spaces were laid out. This lends credence to the axes Fowler (1996, 41, fig. 4.3) recognized as purposeful sightlines for organizing the site as a whole. Thus, our recognition of the shift in these major sight lines during the 12th century evoke considerations of how site-organization was negotiated and considers how they might reflect significant sociopolitical changes took place while respecting deeply embedded perspectives of cosmos.

The results of the visibility analysis followed similar trends of consolidation over time (Fig. 8.5 and Colour Pl. 9). In the pre-Stirling landscape, 63.68% of the study area can see at least one of the 16 largest posts. However, only 2.42% of the study area can see only a single largest post. The majority of "visible space" (i.e., space that can see at least one of the 16 largest posts) can see between two and ten of the total 16 largest central posts (49.61% of total study area, 77.91% of total visible space). The overall trend is a landscape of considerable overlap between the visibilities of different central posts, but very few areas in which either only a single post or a strong majority of posts are visible.

In the Stirling and later landscape, 54.73% of the study area can see at least one of the 16 largest posts and therefore falls within "visible space." In a dramatic shift from the pre-Stirling landscape, 32.47% of the study area can only see a single central post. Feature 78 on Monks Mound accounts for the majority of this area, as 32.28% of the total study area (58.97% of total visible space) can see only this post feature in the Stirling and later landscape. Areas which can see all sixteen of the largest posts also see a significant increase compared to the pre-Stirling landscape, rising from 2.10% of the pre-Stirling landscape to 7.59% of the Stirling and later landscape.

Discussion and interpretations

Center post alignments and arrangements tied together important architectural contexts across the Cahokia site, resulting in an arrangement of microcosms embodied by individual mounds, plazas, and special use structures (see Giles *et al.*, this volume). Within the geographical space of the site, poles connected potent spaces to Cahokia's architectural layout and facilitated the organization of physical space into a visually striking cosmoscape.

Consistent with Dhegiha Siouan stories about "First Man" and historical examples of sacred poles, center poles are persons whose souls were "available to their living descendants for counsel and power" that could be brought into the world of the living (Lankford 2007b, 179; Skousen 2012, 64). If sacrificial victims were indeed associated with pole raising ceremonies as contextual evidence from East St Louis and Cahokia's Mound 72 suggests (Hall 2000; Hargrave 2007, 785; Bukowski 2010, 24; Skousen 2012, 60), perhaps this is an important aspect of Native American "reciprocity" (Hall 1997; Geertz *et al.* 2011). To access another person beyond death perhaps you had to provide another living person who would come into contact with the raptor described in Path of Souls folklore (Lankford 2007b). In this way, the use of human bodies in conjunction with poles was more than a mere display of economic surplus (*sensu* Dalton 1977; Porubcan 2000, 208–10), but a means of responsibly accessing special places and people in distant parts of their cosmoscape without causing disruption.

Relevant to Cahokia's landscape of social authority, center poles as persons were critical members of historical Dhegiha Siouan communities because of their role in tying together the community as mutual descendants of a representative First Man who served as a source of council. Like the center of ball courts or other performance spaces in historical ethnography, central posts tied together communities through mutual participation in or mutual witnessing of community events. More than just being markers of a central space, central posts were themselves the axis of community life around which social-spiritual forces moved. When the Cahokian landscape shifted from a system of organized but spatially separated central posts to a system of centralized and consolidated posts, it represents not just a shift in architectural design but in the nature of social organization. Rather than seeing the reproduction of many distinct communities with their own central posts and overlapping and co-existing spheres of influence, we see the emergence of a singular community, oriented around a singular (or at least centralizing) set of center posts into and after the 12th century.

This centralization of community space may have taken many forms from an emic perspective. In the Stirling phase landscape and later the Woodhenge posts are significantly less visible than the Monks Mound post, with the eastern half of the site unable to see any of the 16 largest posts associated with the Woodhenge. When any Woodhenge post is visible, one or more other Woodhenge posts are also visible. The posts of Woodhenge do not stand on their own as independently visible objects and are only visible within the context of the rest of the circle. This means that, visually, the single central post of the Stirling and later Cahokian landscape would have been the post on Monks Mound, as the largest and most visible post which stood alone on the landscape. In a Dhegiha Siouan lens, the pre-Stirling Cahokian community seen in our analysis may have been the home of many First Men and their associated descendant communities, all of whom co-existed in a mosaic of overlapping spheres of influence and kinship. The transition into a Stirling and later landscape brings a consolidation of these descendant communities under what appears to be the banner of a single First Man, one who was literally raised above the rest by their position on Monks Mound, and a circle of First Men standing together as equals at Woodhenge. Through the lens of other communities, such as the Apalachee, where central posts served as the goalpost of ball games, the shifting arrangement of large central posts at Cahokia may indicate a centralization of community ritual and authority affirming performances. Any of these forms of cultural and spiritual centralization would also have been accompanied by a centralization of existing hierarchies, leading to a consolidation of political and ritual authority.

A significant literature exists on the consolidation of authority at Cahokia during the Stirling phase, particularly with regards to the demarcation of space through the construction of the palisade wall (Iseminger 2010) and the manifestation of a panopticon through the construction of Monks Mound (Pierce and Matisziw 2018). If, as posited here, large central post features at Cahokia are connected to the rich, ethnographically described traditions of central poles that served a variety of spiritual and metaphysical roles in uniting the community around them, then the shifting placement of large central posts at Cahokia over time may stand as another marker of this Stirling phase shift in Cahokian organization of political authority. Rather than a series of central pole features – which may have indicated distinct kinship or cultural groupings and therefore distinct hierarchies – aligned into a north–south axis through cooperative settlement design, the Stirling phase brings a single central post literally elevated above the rest on Monks Mound. The Woodhenge posts, though standing taller than the majority of the pre-Stirling central posts, remain positioned at ground level and are therefore overshadowed, both metaphorically and literally, by the Monks Mound Feature 78 post. Through this single large central post, and through the consolidation of large posts into a central area, Cahokia is brought into a singular cultural and spiritual community and therefore brought under a singular locus of authority.

Conclusion

Central posts hold a wide range of cosmological roles and meanings across the American Southeast, but universally these features act as highly visible *axes mundi* which unite the community around them through cosmological and ritual significance. Pole raising and other highly visible public performances which occurred in central plazas formed the spiritual relationship between a community and the surrounding world, playing a critical role in community cohesion (Kelly and Brown 2014). Natural forces may have been included among these highly visible performances, as both anecdotally and ethnographically thunder iconography and the high potential for lightning strikes on free-standing poles served to highlight these performance spaces. Based on existing research on the cosmological underpinnings of Cahokia's urban design, the placement of central posts within Cahokia was likely tied directly to the cosmological nature of Cahokia's community and to Cahokia's standing as a cosmoscape. Through this, these central posts would also have been tied to the changing nature of politico-religious authority at Cahokia.

The large central posts identified in our analysis would have served the Cahokian community as both the site of community unifying performances and highly visible centralizing features in their own right. Over the course of the Stirling phase, the long north–south axis created by a series of large central posts in the site's initial layout condensed into a short east–west axis created by the combination of the Monks Mound Feature 78 post and the Woodhenge. Together, these two axes create a cruciform shape, echoing iconographic representations of center-cross motifs that are often strongly associated with central posts. The Stirling phase was also marked not only by extensive construction of both mounds and plazas, but also by a shift in the nature of central post visibility across the site. Where before the visibilities of the largest posts overlapped frequently but rarely in great numbers, the Stirling and later landscape saw a sharp increase in the percentage of site area which could see all the largest posts and a corresponding decrease in the area which could see only a partial set. The landscape was therefore sharply divided between areas that could see none of the central posts, areas which could see only the Monks Mound central post, and areas which could see all the largest central posts. This trend of consolidation, centralization and the strict delineation of "visible space" from "non-visible space" would have brought the Cahokian community under a single cultural aegis and therefore a single hierarchy, as opposed to the overlapping but distinct communities and hierarchies indicated by the protracted spacing of central posts found pre-Stirling. The centralization of the ritual and spiritual meanings of central posts would have meant a centralization of the politico-religious authority generated by them during public performances, whether those performances were man-made ones such as ballgames or natural performances such as lightning strikes.

Questions of community organization and political authority at Cahokia have long been connected with discussions of its architectural design. The scale of its earthworks, its large population, and clear evidence of an architectural design spanning significant space and time all serve to mark Cahokia as unique in its sphere of influence. Given the size of this sphere of influence, which suggests extention across much of the Southeast and Midwest and was carried by Moorehead phase emigrants (Parish and McNutt 2020), Cahokia stands out all the more. With this new evidence concerning the changing use of ritually charged central post features during the Stirling phase, backed by ethnographic and iconographic knowledge of Cahokia as a likely cosmoscape, we have new context for thoughts about the social structures and hierarchies that are imbedded in Cahokia's unique architectural design and also made Cahokia's unique design and scale possible. As future excavation continues to uncover new areas of the site it is likely that as-yet-uncovered central post features will add further dimensions to our understanding of central post placement and visibility at Cahokia. Connecting ritual and domestic material assemblages to areas of central post visibility may also serve to shed new light on the practices and identities associated with a central post's sphere of ritual influence. The connection between central post features and thunder iconography is strongly suggested by ethnographic data, yet still requires ground-truthing through examination of material culture. With these additional lines of evidence, the connection between central post features, political and ritual authority, community identity, and cosmology at Cahokia may continue to grow, shaping our understanding of Cahokia as both an urban center and as a Mississippian cosmoscape.

References

Alt, S. (2001) Cahokian change and the authority of tradition. In *The Archaeology of Traditions: Agency and history before and after Columbus*, ed. T. Pauketat, 141–56. University Press of Florida Press, Gainesville FL.

Anderson, D. (2004) Archaic mounds and the archaeology of Southeastern tribal societies. In *Signs of Power: The rise of cultural complexity in the Southeast*, eds J. Gibson and P. Carr, 270–364. University of Alabama Press, Tuscaloosa AL.

Aveni, A. (2002) *Behind the Crystal Ball: Magic, science, and the occult from antiquity through the new age* (rev. edn). University Press of Colorado, Boulder CO.

Baires, S. (2014) Cahokia's Rattlesnake Causeway, *Midcontinental Journal of Archaeology* 39, 145–62.

Barrier, C.R., and Horsley, T. (2014) Shifting communities: Demographic profiles of early village population growth and decline in the central American Bottom. *American Antiquity* 79, 295–313.

Barry, B.J.L. and Dahmann, D.C. (2001) In memoriam: Paul Wheatley, 1921–1999. *Annals of the Association of American Geographers* 9, 734–47.

Berlo, J.C. (2014) Navajo sandpainting in the age of cross-cultural replication. *Art History: Journal of the Association of Art Historians* 37, 688–707.

Betzenhauser, A. and Pauketat, T. (2019) Elements of Cahokia neighborhoods. *Archaeological Papers of the American Anthropological Association* 30, 133–47.

Betzenhauser, A., Pauketat, T., Malouchose, E., Lopinot, N. and Marovitch, D. (2015) The

Morrison Site: Evidence for terminal Late Woodland mound construction in the American Bottom. *Illinois Archaeology* 27, 6–32.

Bold, R. (2020) Constructing cosmoscapes: Cosmological currents in conversation and contestation in contemporary Bolivia. *HAU: Journal of Ethnographic Theory* 10, 195–208.

Brain, J. and Phillips, P. (1996) *Shell Gorgets: Styles of the late prehistoric and protohistoric Southeast*. Peabody Museum Press, Cambridge MA.

Bukowski, J. (2010) Human remains from the Dickison South Mound Group (11P787). *Illinois Archaeology* 22, 726–46.

Claasen, C. (2015) *Beliefs and Rituals in Archaic Eastern North America: An interpretive guide.* University of Alabama Press, Tuscaloosa AL.

Collins, J. (1990) *The Archaeology of the Cahokia Mounds ICT-II: Site structure.* Illinois Cultural Resources Study 10, Illinois Historic Preservation Agency, Springfield IL.

Dalan, R.A., Holley, G.R., Woods, W.I., Watters, H.W. and Koepke, J.A. (2003) *Envisioning Cahokia: A landscape perspective.* Northern Illinois University Press, Dekalb IL.

Dalton, G. (1977) Aboriginal economics in stateless societies. In *Exchange Systems in Prehistory*, eds T.K. Earle and J.E. Ericson, 191–212. Academic Press, New York.

DeBoer, W.R. (1993) Like a rolling stone: The chunkey game and political organization in eastern North America. *Southeastern Archaeology* 12, 83–92.

Dorsey, J.O. (1885) Mourning and war customs of the Kansas. *American Naturalist* 20, 211–22.

Ellen, R. (1986) Microcosm, macrocosm and the Nuaulu house: Concerning the reductionist fallacy as applied to metaphorical levels. *Bijdragen tot de Taal-, Land- en Volkenkunde* 177, 1–30.

Eliade, M. (1959) *The Sacred and the Profane: The nature of religion* (trans. W.R. Trask). Harcourt, New York.

Emerson, T. (1982) *Mississippian Stone Images in Illinois.* Illinois Archaeological Survey Circular 6, University of Illinois Press, Urbana IL.

Emerson, T. (2003) Crossing boundaries between worlds: Changing beliefs and mortuary practices at Cahokia. *Wisconsin Archaeologist* 84, 73–80.

Fletcher, A. (1884) *Religious Ceremony of the Four Winds or Quarters, as Observed by the Santee Sioux.* Annual Report of the Peabody Museum 3, Harvard University, Cambridge MA.

Fletcher, A. (1895) The Sacred Pole of the Omaha tribe. *American Antiquarian* 17, 257–68.

Fletcher, A. and La Flesche, F. (1911) *The Omaha Tribe.* Bureau of American Ethnology Annual Report 27, Washington, DC.

Fowler, M. ed. (1996) The ancient skies and Skywatchers of Cahokia: Woodhenges, eclipses, and Cahokian cosmology. *The Wisconsin Archaeologist* 77, 3–11.

Fowler, M. (1997) *The Cahokia Atlas: A historical atlas of Cahokia archaeology* (rev. edn). Illinois Archaeological Research Program, University of Illinois, Urbana-Champaign IL.

Fowler, M., Rose, J., Vander Leest, B. and Ahler, S. (1999) *The Mound 72 Area: Dedicated and sacred space in early Cahokia.* Illinois State Museum Reports of Investigations 54, Illinois State Museum Society, Springfield IL.

Fundaburk, E. ed. (1958) *Southeastern Indians Life Portraits: A catalogue of pictures, 1564–1935.* University of Alabama Press, Tuscaloosa AL.

Geertz, A., O'Connor, J., Morrison, K., Fulbright, J. and Irwin, L. (2011) On reciprocity and mutual reflection in the study of Native American religions. *Religion* 24, 1–22.

Haag, W. (1990) Excavations at the Poverty Point Site: 1972–1975. *Louisiana Archaeology* 13, 1–36.

Haag, W. (1993) Archaeoastronomy in the Southeast. in *Archaeology of Eastern North America: Papers in Honor of Stephen Williams*, ed. J. Stoltman, 103–10. Archaeological Report 25, Mississippi Department of Archives and History, Jackson MI.

Hall, R. (1997) *An Archaeology of the Soul: Native American Indian belief and ritual.* University of Illinois Press, Urbana IL.

Hall, R. (2000) Sacrificed foursomes and green corn ceremonialism. In *Mounds, Modoc, and*

Mesoamerica: Papers in honor of Melvin Fowler, ed. S. Ahler, 245–54. Illinois State Museum Scientific Papers 28, Illinois State Museum, Springfield IL.

Hann, J. (1988) *Apalachee: Land between the rivers.* Ripley P. Bullen Monographs in Anthropology and History 7, University of Florida Press, Gainesville FL.

Hargrave, E. (2007) Human remains. In *The Archaeology of the East St. Louis Mound Center, Part II: The northside excavations*, ed. A.C. Fortier, 77–83. Illinois Transportation Archaeological Research Program Report 22, University of Illinois Press, Urbana-Champaign IL.

Henry, E., Mickelson, A. and Mickelson, M. (2020) Documenting ceremonial situations and institutional change at Middle Woodland geometric enclosures in central Kentucky. *Midcontinental Journal of Archaeology* 45, 203–25.

Hoffman, W.J. (1891) *The Midē'wiwin or "Grand Medicine Society" of the Ojibway.* Seventh Annual Report of the Bureau of American Ethnology, Smithsonian Institution, Washington DC.

Holley, G., Dalan, R., Lopinot, N. and Smith, P. (1990) *Investigations in the Grand Plaza, Cahokia Mounds State Historic Site, St. Clair County, Illinois.* Contract Archaeology Program at Southern Illinois University at Edwardsville, Illinois Historic Preservation Agency, Springfield IL.

Howard, J. (1968) *The Southeastern Ceremonial Complex and Its Interpretation.* Memoirs of the Missouri Archaeological Society 6, Oklahoma State University, Stillwater OK.

Hultkrantz, Å. (1979) *Religions of the American Indians.* University of California Press, Berkeley CA.

Iseminger, W. (2010) *Cahokia Mounds: America's first city.* The History Press, Charleston SC.

Iseminger, W., Pauketat, T., Koldehoff, B., Kelly, L. and Blake, L. (1990) *Archaeology of the Cahokia Palisade: East Palisade investigations*, Illinois Cultural Resource Study 14, Illinois Historic Preservation Agency, Springfield IL.

James, J. (2006) The Dog Tribe. *Southern Anthropologist* 32, 17–46.

Jeffries, R. (1994) The Swift Creek Site and Woodland platform mounds in the Southeastern United States. In *Ocmulgee Archaeology 1936–1986*, ed. D. Hally, 71–83. University of Georgia Press, Athens GA.

Kant, I. (1950) *Critique of Pure Reason* (trans. N.K. Smith, Original published in 1781). Macmillan, London.

Kassabaum, M. and Nelson, E. (2016) Standing posts and special substances: Gathering and ritual deposition at Feltus (22JE500), Jefferson County, Mississippi. *Southeastern Archaeology* 35, 134–54.

Kelly, J. (1990a) Range Site community patterns and the Mississippian emergence. In *The Mississippian Emergence*, ed. B.D. Smith, 67–112. University of Alabama Press, Tuscaloosa AL.

Kelly, J. (1990b) The emergence of Mississippian culture in the American Bottom Region. In *The Mississippian Emergence*, ed. B.D. Smith, 113–52. University of Alabama Press, Tuscaloosa AL.

Kelly, J. (1996) Redefining Cahokia: Principles and elements of community organization. *Wisconsin Archaeologist* 6, 97–119.

Kelly, J. (1997) Stirling Phase socio-political activity at East St. Louis and Cahokia in *Cahokia: Domination and ideology in the Mississippian world*, eds T. Pauketat and T. Emerson, 141–66. University of Nebraska Press, Lincoln NE.

Kelly, J. (2003) The context of the post pit and meaning of the sacred pole at the East St. Louis mound group. *Wisconsin Archaeologist* 84, 107–25.

Kelly, J. and Brown, J. (2014) Cahokia: The processes and principles of the creation of an early Mississippian City. In *Making Ancient Cities*, eds A.T. Creekmore III and K.D. Fisher, 292–336. Cambridge University Press, Cambridge.

Kelly, J., Brown, J., Hamlin, J., Kelly, L., Kozuch, L., Parker, K. and Van Nest, J. (2007) Mound 34: The context for the early evidence of the Southeastern ceremonial complex. In

Southeastern Ceremonial Complex: Chronology, content, context, ed. A. King, 57–87. University of Alabama Press, Tuscaloosa AL.

Knight, V.J. (1990) *Excavation of the Truncated Mound at the Walling Site: Middle Woodland Culture and Copena in the Tennessee Valley.* Report of Investigations 56, Alabama Museum of Natural History, Division of Archaeology, University of Alabama, Tuscaloosa AL.

Knight, V.J. (2001) Feasting and the emergence of platform mound ceremonialism in eastern North America. In *Feasts: Archaeological and ethnographic perspectives on food, politics, and power*, eds M. Dietler and B. Hayden, 311–33. Smithsonian Institution Press, Washington DC.

Lankford, G. (2007a) Some cosmological motifs in the Southeastern ceremonial complex. In *Ancient Objects and Sacred Realms: Interpretations of Mississippian iconography*, eds F.K. Reilly and J.F. Garber, 8–38. University of Texas Press, Austin TX.

Lankford, G. (2007b) The "Path of Souls": Some death imagery in the Southeastern ceremonial complex. In *Ancient Objects and Sacred Realms: Interpretations of Mississippian iconography*, eds F.K. Reilly III and J.F. Garber, 174–212. University of Texas Press, Austin TX.

Milanich, J., Kohler, T., Cordell, A., Knight, V. and Sigler-Lavelle, B. (1984) *Archaeology of Northern Florida, A.D. 200–900: The McKeithen Weeden Island Culture.* Academic Press, New York.

Morse, D. and Morse, P. (1983) *Archaeology of the Central Mississippi Valley.* Academic Press, New York.

Morse, D. and Morse, P. (2000) Social interaction between the American Bottom of Cahokia and the Crowley's Ridge Lowlands Division of the Lower Mississippi River AD 800–1200. In *Mounds, Modoc, and Mesoamerica: Papers in honor of Melvin Fowler*, ed. S. Ahler, 347–60. Illinois State Museum Scientific Papers 28, Illinois State Museum, Springfield IL.

Norrish, R. (1978a) Woodhenge: Red cedar found. *Cahokian* 3, 10–11.

Norrish, R. (1978b) Woodhenge – work of a Genius. *Cahokian* 3, 17–27.

Parish, R. and McNutt, C. (2020) Introduction. In *Cahokia in Context: Hegemony and diaspora*, eds C. McNutt and R. Parish, 1–10. University Press of Florida, Gainesville FL.

Pauketat, T. (1993) *Temples for Cahokia Lords: Preston Holder's 1955–1956 excavations of Kunnemann Mound.* Memoires of the Museum of Anthropology 26, University of Michigan Press, Ann Arbor MI.

Pauketat, T. (1994) *The Ascent of Chiefs: Cahokia and Mississippian politics in Native North America.* University of Alabama Press, Tuscaloosa AL.

Pauketat, T. (1998) *The Archaeology of Downtown Cahokia: The Tract 15A and Dunham Tract excavations.* Studies in Archaeology 1, Illinois Transportation Archaeological Research Program, University of Illinois, Urbana-Champaign IL.

Pauketat, T. (2013) *The Archaeology of Downtown Cahokia II: The 1960 excavation of Tract 15B.* Studies in Archaeology 8, Illinois State Archaeological Survey, University of Illinois Press, Urbana IL.

Pauketat, T. and Alt, S. (1998) *The Archaeology of Downtown Cahokia: The Tract 15A and Dunham Tract excavations.* Studies in Archaeology 1, Illinois Transportation Archaeological Research Program, University of Illinois, Urbana-Champaign IL.

Pauketat, T. and Alt, S. (2005) Agency in a postmold? Physicality and the archaeology of culture-making. *Journal of Archaeological Method and Theory* 12, 213–35.

Pavel, T.G. (1981) Fiction and the ontological landscape. *Studies in 20th Century Literature* 6, 149–63.

Peet, S.D. (1891) Archaeological notes. *American Antiquarian* 8, 57–170.

Pierce, D. and Matisziw, T. (2018) Prehistoric panopticon: Settlement visibility at ancient Cahokia mounds. *Space and Culture* 24, 1–24. [https://journals.sagepub.com/doi/full/10.1177/1206331218805388], accessed February 18th 2020.

Porubcan, P. (2000) Human and nonhuman surplus display at Mound 72, Cahokia. In *Mounds,*

Modoc, and Mesoamerica: Papers in honor of Melvin Fowler, ed. S. Ahler, 207–19. Illinois State Museum Scientific Papers 28, Illinois State Museum, Springfield IL.

Reed, N. (2009) Excavations on the third terrace of Monks Mound: A personal narrative by Nelson Reed. *Illinois Archaeology* 21, 1–89.

Reichel, E. (2012) The landscape in the cosmoscape, and sacred sites and species among the Tanimuka and Yukuna Amerindian tribes (north-west Amazon). In *Sacred Species and Sites: Advances in biocultural conservation*, eds G. Pungetti, G. Oviedo and D. Hooke, 127–51. Cambridge University Press, Cambridge.

Reilly, F.K. III (1994) Enclosed ritual spaces and the Watery Underworld in Formative Period architecture: New observations on the function of La Venta Complex A. In *Seventh Palenque Table, 1989*, eds M.G. Robertson and V.M. Fields, 1–14. Pre-Columbian Art Research Institute, San Francisco CA Electronic document. [http://www.mesoweb.com/pari/publications/RT09/EnclosedSpaces.pdf], accessed February 20th 2020.

Reilly, F.K. III (2004) People of earth, people of sky: Visualizing the sacred in Native American art of the Mississippian Period. In *Hero, Hawk, and Open Hand: American Indian art of the ancient Midwest and South*, eds R.F. Townsend and R.V. Sharp, 125–38. Art Institute of Chicago in association with Yale University Press, New Haven CO.

Sassaman, K., Blessing, M., Goodwin, J., Jenkins, J., Mahar, G., Boucher, A., Barbour, T. and Donop, M. (2019) Maritime ritual economies of cosmic synchronicity: Summer solstice events at a civic-ceremonial center on the northern Gulf Coast of Florida. *American Antiquity* 85, 22–50.

Skinner, A. (1923) *Observations on the Ethnology of the Sauk Indians.* Public Museum of the City of Milwaukee Bulletin 5, Milwaukee WI.

Skousen, J. (2012) Posts, places, ancestors, and worlds: Dividual personhood in the American Bottom region. *Southeastern Archaeology* 31, 57–69.

Smith, H. (1969) The Murdock Mound, Cahokia Site. In *Explorations into Cahokia Archaeology*, ed. M. Fowler, 49–88. Illinois Archaeology Bulletin 7, University of Illinois Press, Urbana IL.

Smith, T.S. (1995) *The Island of the Anishnaabeg*, University of Idaho Press, Moscow ID.

Stauffer, J.G. and Reilly, F.K. III (2017) Playing the Apalachee Ballgame in the Fields of the Thunder God. In *Prehistoric Games of North America: Subarctic to Mesoamerica*, ed. B. Voorhies, 34–47. University of Utah Press, Salt Lake City UT.

Swanton, J. (2000) *Creek Religion and Medicine* (reprint, originally published 1928). University of Nebraska Press, Lincoln NE.

Wade, L. (2018) The City at the beginning of the World. *Archaeology* 71, 26–31.

Waldmann, M. (1996) Knowledge-based causal induction. *The Psychology of Learning and Motivation* 34, 47–88.

Warshauer, I. (2015) Seeking Clarity in Postholes: An examination of Coles Creek earthfast architecture. Senior honors thesis, Department of Anthropology, University of North Carolina, Chapel Hill.

Wheatley, P. (1971) *Pivot of the Four Quarters: A preliminary enquiry into the origins and character of the ancient Chinese city.* Aldine, London.

Widlock, T. (2016) Hunter-gatherer situations: Keynote speech at the 11th conference on hunting and gathering societies (CHAGS XI), Vienna, Austria, 7 September 2015. *Hunter Gatherer Research* 2, 127–43 [DOI:10.3828/HGR.2016.7].

Wittry, W. (1973) The American Woodhenge. In *Explorations into Cahokia Archaeology* (rev. edn), ed. M. Fowler, 43–8. Bulletin of the Illinois Archaeological Survey 7, University of Illinois Press, Urbana IL.

Wittry, W. (1980) Cahokia Woodhenge update. *Archeoastronomy* 3, 12.

9

Picture Cave and the birth of the Braden Art Style

James R. Duncan and Carol Diaz-Granados

This chapter is a discussion concerning the beginnings of an important art style. The art style includes images of spirit beings, important to the traditions of the ancestors of the people who built the large Western Mississippian mound groups, Cahokia, East Saint Louis and the Mound City of St Louis near the confluence of the Missouri and Mississippi Rivers. We believe this style evolved into what Philip Phillips and James Brown (1978, 33–8) labeled as the Braden Art Style in their study of the engraved shell cups found in the Craig Mound near Spiro, Oklahoma. For almost 150 years this art has been subjected to a great deal of study beginning with William H. Holmes (1883). There are still a few who insist that it was not wholly the work of local indigenous people. The difficulty in assigning it to the ancestors of present-day societies is complicated. These groups, who have been tucked away on reservations with a long history of introduced pandemic disease, population decimation, cultural eradication, and attempted assimilation, merit intense study. The birthplace of this spectacular seminal art style, so inseparably linked to the Cahokia area, was produced in the Lower Missouri and Middle Mississippi Valleys.

This area has long been adversely impacted by agriculture and industry that damaged key archaeological sites (Phillips and Brown 1978, 4–5; Morse and Morse 1983, 20). This seminal or early formative art style was the work of a southern Siouan speaking people, most likely the ancestors of the modern Dhegiha, especially the Osage and their kin, who began to rapidly evolve socially and culturally, coalescing into the large population centers at the confluence of the Missouri and Mississippi Rivers (Morse and Morse 1983, 233; Diaz-Granados 1993, 384; 2011, 93–5; Diaz-Granados and Duncan 2000, 215–17; Brown 2007, 56; 2011, 39–41; Kehoe 2007). The Dhegiha have preserved elements of their unique heritage, allowing several ethnographers to record and describe important vestiges of their complex hierarchical society (Ponziglione 1897, 21–4; Tixier 1940; Hall 1997, 53; La Flesche in Bailey 1995, 19–49). Using work, principally by Francis LaFlesche, we have been engaged in a long-term study of the Dhegiha, including collecting oral traditions. Combining past findings with present traditions is crucial to a holistic understanding of the symbolism and iconographic signatures of the Braden Art Style.

Seeking the beginnings of the Braden Art Style

Several years ago, while helping the RedCorn family prepare for the In-Lon-shka summer solstice dances on the Osage Reservation in Oklahoma, we experienced something that we thought was special. One of the preparatory projects was the building of a low wooden platform, roughly 3 m square, and 0.5 m tall. During the construction of the platform we had a lot of questions. Patiently, lead carpenter Charles RedCorn answered every query. It seems that the "Old People" liked to sit around in warm weather and eat communally on platforms. They also liked to sit on these platforms and play "Chinese Checkers" with big, colorful glass marbles on the star patterned boards. But most of all, they liked to just sit on a platform and quietly visit, telling stories, all the while watching the stars, often all night long.

Human beings have long been fascinated by stars; ancient American Indians knew the stars and the Osage or Dhegiha were no exception. They and their ancestors have long been watching and studying, not just the stars but everything in both the night sky and the day-time sky. To the Osage and their kin the stars, Moon, rainbows, sun dogs, and other heavenly phenomena represented spirit beings, ancient ancestors dwelling in a complex layered cosmos. The movement of these stellar objects was especially important to the Dhegiha; they still carefully emulate this dignified movement during their dances, often moving counterclockwise in harmony with the cosmic order.

Before AD 800, the ancestors of the Dhegiha made few depictions of these spirit beings associated with both the night and day-time sky. Before this date, the rock art imagery was limited to small silhouettes in red or black pigment of animals, objects, and occasional human figures. Add to this inventory, a few tiny, fired clay figurines with incised facial markings (tattoos?), several fragmentary avian shell pendants, and an occasional miniscule profile of a humanized bird on ceramic containers round out the collection. We can be sure that complex oral traditions did exist, reinforced by clan symbolism, expressed in apparel, especially ritual regalia, and possibly on textiles and portable woven containers. Also, a tiny corpus of curated objects made after AD 200 and before AD 450 seem to have been present, especially among elite families.

Then, in AD 941, something major happened in the sky, possibly a spectacular dawn where the rising sun was in full eclipse mode (Weisman, pers. comm.). This celestial event may have been commemorated by the reconsecration of an unusual, layered sandstone and limestone cave on the north side of the Missouri River. This sacred site was within an easy two day journey by dugout canoe from the confluence of the Missouri and Mississippi rivers. This layered cave, possessing all the supernatural requirements, had been the focus of visits going back in time to the Late Archaic. A large double chevron design in red ocher decorates one of its sandstone walls in isolated splendor, possibly dating to this period.

The iconography of this design, found engraved on occasional atlatl weights, is associated with water, the Beneath Worlds, and the ancient imagery of powerful and gigantic water dwelling spirit beings (Colour Pl. 10).

The cave itself is an embodiment of the feminine world. In the complex Dhegihan layered cosmos, the earth is the creation of the principal feminine spirit, First Woman, *Wa-ko' Pa-hon'-gthe xtsi*. She, in the guise of a spider, creates the middle layer of the cosmos. She weaves the fleeting trap or web of life, the *Ho'-e-ga*, with her gift of life. This cave has been defined by the Osage philosopher and holy man, Charles Pratt, as the "Womb of the Universe." Also, by being the Womb of the Universe, Charles stated that the cave "contains all of her children" (Duncan 2015, 186–7; Diaz-Granados *et al.* 2015).

The most intriguing discovery about this cave, other than the unique and defining imagery that covers its sandstone walls, is a narration recorded in the 19th century of a quest involving such a cave by spiritual ancestors of the modern Osage. This description was collected by a Jesuit priest, Father Paul Marie Ponziglione (1897, 11–16), who ministered the Osage people then on their reservation in "Kansas Indian Territory". This oral tradition tells of the youngest daughter, Evening Star, born to the principal spirit beings, First Woman and First Man. Evening Star sets out on a vision quest. After 7 days of wandering, strict fasting, crying, and weeping, she enters a large cave to rest. In this marvelous cave she is given a vision, the cave becomes enveloped in brightness, in a rainbow of colors where the cyclical movement of the heavenly bodies defines the unlimited productive power of the earth. She now understands the cycle of life, death, and rebirth. The writings of Father Ponziglione (1897, 19–20) are revealing because he acknowledges that the Osage have many origin or genesis traditions, but he labels the cave narration as the most remarkable and attributes it to one of their most "intelligent priests." It is most remarkable in that Ponziglione was able to hear the story in its original format, in the Dhegihan Sioux dialect, probably during the winter when such traditions could be narrated. Incidently, this treasured narration by the "intelligent priest" was a reciprocal gift to Ponziglione for the gospel stories that he was able to tell his Osage audience in their own language.

In February 1997, while talking to Osage Yvonne Lookout, the subject of the marvelous cave came up and Ms Lookout remembered hearing about such a place as a young child. All that she could remember was that the cave was somewhere near their old home territory. Ponziglione's translation of the cave vision story contains several references to plants, flowers, and fruit. Pretty Hair's great-grand daughter, Mary Carter related information about elite Osage men not being allowed to dig holes, drive posts. or light fires on the earth, which seems to compliment the cave vision. It was the young woman who was given the knowledge and role of propagation, of both agricultural production and the Osage population. This oral tradition incorporates an important theme, the dichotomous division of labor, the result of a powerful incest taboo, where elite Osage men were not allowed to penetrate or desecrate the body of their grandmother, the earth.

The second part of the vision quest narration involves the youngest brother of the young woman who also goes to seek a vision. On following his sister's tracks, he comes to the place where she received her vision; there he claps his hands, stomps his feet and shouts in a loud voice, asking for a vision ... he is answered by immense peals of thunder, lightning, and a terrible storm. Running to find shelter under a tree, he is engulfed by the storm and is thrown into a deep crevice along with the sheltering tree. He then sees an immense being standing amidst the storm. This being lifts him up and places him between two large rocks that are covered by the hilltop torn loose during the storm. This makes a spacious lodge for the young man. The giant figure builds a fire from the tree limbs and throws a hand full of gravel from the uprooted soil into the fire – tools and weapons are formed. Thus, the youngest male, the last to come, gains the power to make tools and weapons along with the knowledge of how to use them (Ponziglione 1897, 17–19). This dichotomous separation of labor is found in all sedentary Siouan societies along the Middle and Lower Missouri River Valley (Bowers 1992, 105; 2004, 46; Duncan 2021, 39–40). It is evident from the preceding accounts, that this unique cave has long been considered the sole site of the genesis of the Dhegiha people, especially the Osage. Picture Cave in Missouri, with its unique content and detailed drawings, is indeed, the "Womb of the Universe."

The reconsecration of Picture Cave during the Terminal Late Woodland or Emergent Mississippian Period sparked a renewed interest in rendering additional imagery on its sandstone walls that resulted in multiple vignettes being added. These new figures were rendered in at least three distinct styles separated by technique. All the styles seem to express the same principles: realistic proportions are used in depicting anthropomorphs, only profile depictions are used for human faces, frequently the figures are in motion and, finally, there is the strict and careful rendering of details in depicting tattoos and regalia (see Fig. 9.3, below). As in all art, a seminal genesis set might contain experimental variations, an invented set of rules that over time become canonical.

The figures uniformly represent powerful spirit beings, emerging into this world from behind the sandstone walls. Natural features were used by the artist to heighten this effect. Also, several of the figures utilize naturally oxidized sandstone surfaces as a part their coloration. Certain figures are depicted as emerging from fissures and cracks in the cave wall. Stylistically there were several artists working and some of the figures have been modified by abrading away or covering old images with new ones. In some instances, parts of an image are redrawn. All of this indicates that the creators considered the images to be animate, living spirit beings.

These three germinal styles are described beginning with the earliest, based on location, possible superimposition and later modifications or additions to a vignette.

Style 1

The most complex of the styles, and probably the earliest, uses finely engraved lines on the sandstone wall. The outlined human figures are then selectively abraded to expose the brilliant white, unpatinated sandstone matrix. This technique leaves portions of the figures with a reddish orange oxidized cortex, for instance the upper body and face. Final application of black pigment with a fine brush, or possibly a "charred twig", completes the composition. Surprisingly, this earliest style portrays foreshortening, a three-quarter facial rendering, and attention to perspective. The regalia, tattooing, facial and body painting are precise.

The two principal images in this style were rendered to appear to be emerging from a prominent, eroded, and colorful horizontal fissure. This intentional placement just above a natural fissure may have been used by the artist or artists to represent the horizon at dawn. The natural iron oxide coloration of the sandstone imitates the rosy coloration of the eastern sky at sunrise. Water once percolated through the porous sandstone during times of abundant rainfall creating bands of naturally pigmented color. These bands anchor many of the figures, especially when they form a horizon; many of the images seem to be floating. This is a bit disconcerting when seen by a headlamp or flashlight in the dark zone they inhabit. During the last major study session, with the use of a generator, many feet of heavy-duty electrical cords, and double halogen work lights, the floating groups of figures could finally be seen as complex vignettes.

This complex style is found only at Picture Cave and in a simpler format at the related Gottschall site in southern Wisconsin. The images are not of worldly beings, they are supernatural beings. Style 1 has an interesting signature. The format involves emphasizing the head and torso, drawn a little larger than life size and always in profile. The noses are depicted as being quite prominent. Unlike Gotschall, this style at Picture Cave includes complete appendages with simplified hands and feet. The arrows are drawn in a sophisticated manner and a well rendered recurved bow is also present. These images, while done on a small scale (30 cm), are drawn with a remarkable amount of details. This is a very sophisticated style and appears monumental in "unscaled" photographs.

Style 2

Well-proportioned human, animal, and therianthropic figures, in a kinetic format, are outlined and then filled with solid black or red pigment resulting in a silhouette, a shadow technique. These shadow figures are often small, rarely more than 15–20 cm in height. Arranged in vignettes, these are some of the most animated figures at Picture Cave. From a content standpoint, these kinetic vignettes often seem to portray rituals (Fig. 9.1a), warfare (Fig. 9.1b), and especially dancing (Fig. 9.1c). Some of these shadow figures are precisely rendered, a female figure (rare) has prominent labia, while a running male figure with muscular calves has a penis of gigantic proportion. All images seem to be of supernatural beings. The small active figures are often painted, using a delicate brush technique. Because several drawn lines and fine splattering overlay these images, they are probably older than the larger, charred stick rendered drawings. Because of their small size we were unable to obtain a pigment sample large enough to date without damaging the images.

This silhouette style, in red pigment, is also seen in the monumental, 1 m tall, Classic Braden dancing warrior on the wall of a shallow sandstone shelter at Rattlesnake Bluff in Franklin County, Missouri (Fig. 9.2).

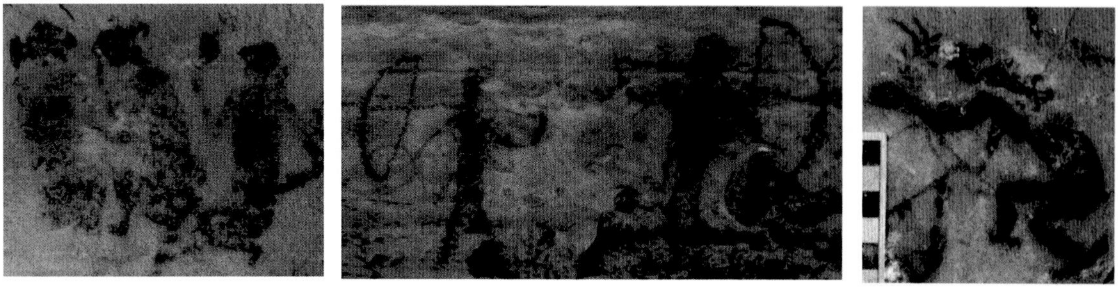

A B C

Fig. 9.1. A. Group of three seated figures engaged in ritual activities; B. armed figures with bows and arrows; C. small figure in dancing posture with probable willow frond; silhouette style (Style 2) (photo: Alan Cressler).

Style 3

Human, animal and therianthropic figures, are realistically rendered with drawn or painted lines. The drawings are made primarily with "charred sticks," but red hematite paint is also used, especially for red accents that overlay the foundational black, carbon-based imagery. These pigments have complex formulas, the paints contain Aluminum phosphate, a compound that has been found only at Picture Cave (Blankenship 2015). Details such as clothing, painting, and tattooing are carefully depicted (Fig. 9.3). The facial renderings of this style are among the most skillfully done, several being exceptional, unique renderings expressing great sensitivity reminiscent of Daumier's 19th century drawings. An Underwater Spirit, an eyeless figure that probably represents Death, and the "toothy mouth" are among the very few rendered full face.

Portions of the figures have been abraded and additions made. Accents consisting of red pigment made from either heated or natural hematite or ochre in addition to complex binders are added to the figures in the form of apparel, sashes, or even blood. Broad, overlaying charred stick strokes and splattering indicate that images using Style 3 are the most recent additions to the compositions. The details such as tattooing are often precise and male genitalia are present. All human and therianthropic images are obviously supernatural beings, characters not of this world.

The Braden imagery has an adherence to a set of rules governing its composition. This was first explored by Phillips and Brown (1978, 40–68) and subjected to a careful analysis. Two powerful themes are mentioned, motion and dancing. We agree with this premise. Dancing and an overall animated nature of the seminal Braden figures at Picture Cave support Phillips and Brown's description. One figure at Picture Cave is so well executed, we can actually name the ritual dance by the posture and the object in hand, the *He' dewachi* rite. We noticed that even if the figures seem to be floating, they are balanced in that usually an equal number move counter-directionally, that is if two figures dance toward the left (west), two figures often dance toward the right (east).

Fig. 9.2. (opposite) Dancing Warrior at Rattlesnake Bluff in Missouri. Image is rendered in Classic Braden Style (2) with in red pigment, although very worn (drawing: Jim Duncan from slide).

Another governing feature is a center or axial focal point for the movement of the characters, usually achieving a compositional balance. This compositional mode is likely driven by complex cosmological ideology (Bailey 2004, 27–38). Exceptions to an orderly composition exist both in the seminal Braden narration

at Picture Cave and on Classic Braden shell cups, especially when portraying the decapitated heads of Hawk and his companions as in cup No. 17 (Phillips and Brown 1978, 43). Another constraint is found in portraying spirit beings in their human format, they are always rendered as profiles. This rule does not apply to depictions of the chief of the Water Spirits. He is drawn full-face at Picture Cave and much later as repoussé copper maskettes and engraved on ceramic bottles, especially from the Berry Site 23PM59 in extreme southeast Missouri. The Braden Style persisted for many hundreds of years. An elk antler quirt displaying a skillfully engraved figure of an Osage warrior, the Symbolic Man, exists in the collections of the Linden-Museum, Stuttgart, Germany. The quirt was made in the first quarter of the 19th century (Bailey and Swan 2004, 16). This figure follows all the canons of the Braden Style.

Among the many vignettes, the Style 3 figures are distinctive enough that they can be separated by the abilities of the artist(s). Some of the figures are expertly drawn and rendered in an extremely realistic format, while others are very amateurish and not realistically depicted. The figures in the first group seem to have been the work of a single artist, quite an accomplished one. Even more interesting, all his figures seem to be Beneath World inhabitants. In contrast, the smaller group seems to have been done by someone with little skill. This group's subject matter is most likely Above World characters; characters with spectacular attributes that are rendered in a haphazard manner by someone with only a mediocre talent for drawing. It is very apparent that talent and skill are not always required in rendering this foundational imagery. What seems to drive these germinal efforts, the earliest Braden expression, is the artists' lineage. We see this where the major battle scene gives us an overlap of the two styles. It seems that the same artist who gave us the spectacular figures with their fantastic head-dresses and expressive facial features also had a hand in drawing some of the silhouettes of Beneath World warriors. Clan membership seems to be the principal requirement for rendering specific characters of a complex narration in all three styles. Since the imagery was considered to be charged with spiritual essence, only artists with established relationships and the esoteric knowledge were capable of bringing the spirit's likeness into existence.

Probably only bundle keepers or clan priests would have been able to depict specific attributes of a clan's spiritual ancestor. It is well known from work done by LaFlesche and Bowers with the sedentary Siouan farming societies, especially the Dhegiha, Mandan, and Hidatsa, that clan bundles were in the care of specific individuals who were responsible for teaching others about the lore of the bundles' attendant spirit beings (Bowers 2004, 93). In all cases, this is an owned right, sanctioned by their expenditure in time and wealth in acquiring a bundle or priestly office.

In the case of the Osage and probably most of their Dhegihan relations, another level of organization existed within their society – complex priesthoods without clan affiliation, with multiple levels of attained knowledge. These priests were keepers of major bundles not belonging to specific clans. All the priests practiced a form of esoteric, restricted knowledge, the true meanings of their songs and

Fig. 9.3. (opposite) A: Stoval Cup detail. Classic Braden Style, note concentric shoulder tattoos, military hat, forked eye, and open mouth (redrawn from photograph by Jim Duncan); B. The Black Warrior (Dark Wolf) at Picture Cave, with military hat, forked eye and open mouth); C. detail of face and shoulder of "The Giant" at Picture Cave with concentric shoulder tattoos, forked eye and open mouth (Redrawn from photography by Jim Duncan); D. Snake Hide figure with forked eye, open mouth, and elaborate headdress (Redrawn from photography by Jim Duncan).

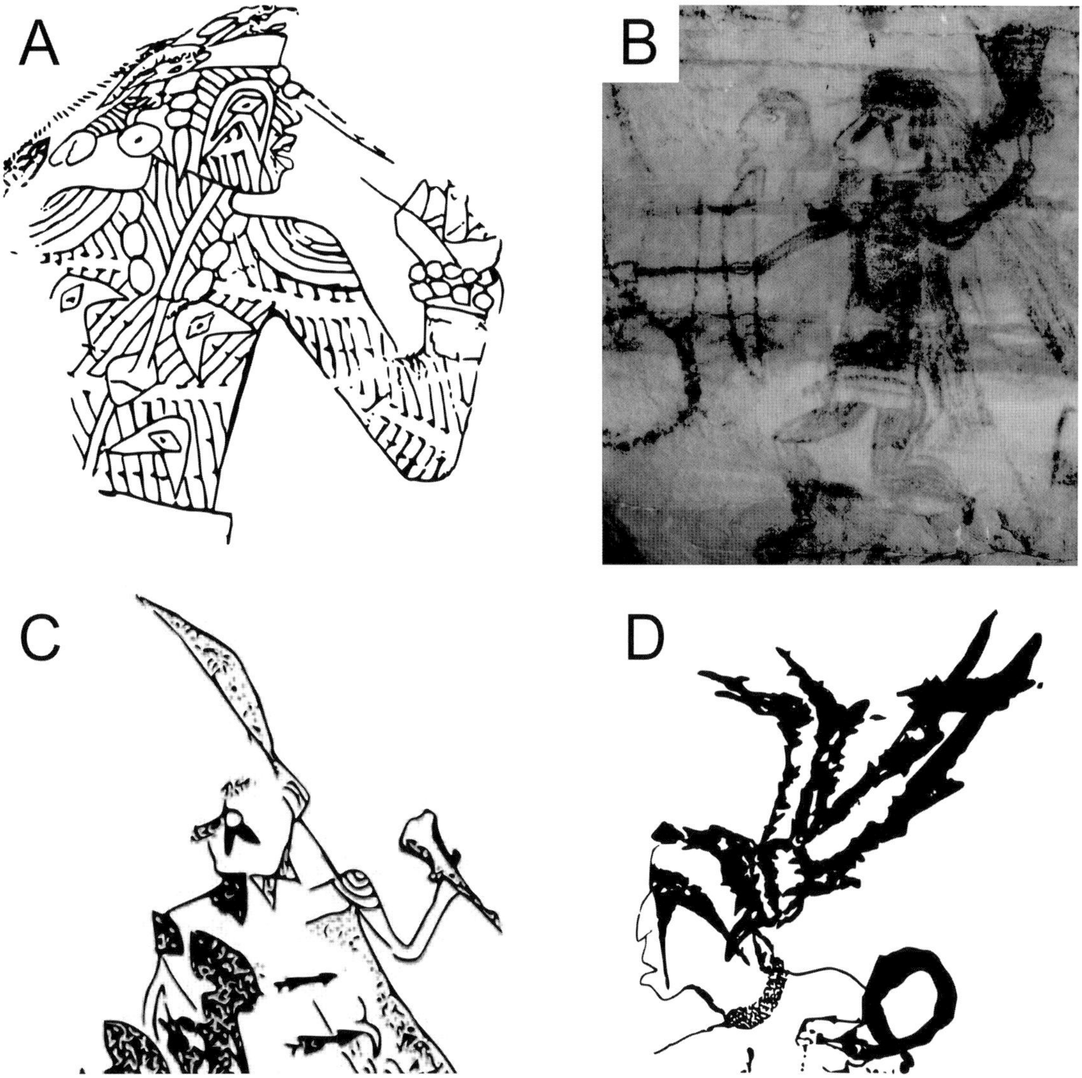

narrations were often hidden, known only to those who had made the investment in time and wealth (Bailey 1995, 82).

The foundation of the Braden Art movement is not just tied to supernatural images representing natural forces in both human and therianthropic format but also to their place in the cosmic structure, a complex layered universe with portals. Sacred bundles and bundling have a long, well-established history in Siouan societies (Dye 2021, 183–4). Arrays of objects, many non-utilitarian, are common in funeral deposits going back several thousand years. The prevalent human format of the sacred natural powers is likely a reflection of impersonation by bundle owners. Bundle owners impersonated the bundle's personified natural force using tattoos, body painting, and specific regalia during rituals, often involving gifting and feasting (Bowers 1992; 2004; Howard 1995). Standardized imagery became an important link in elite recognition. However, among the Dhegiha, the clans contained persons of distinction who were linear descendants of the ancestral spirit beings. Thus, among the Dhegiha these persons of distinction assumed the role of their spiritual ancestors with age and attainment of honors; hence an adherence to a realistic human aspect in the Braden Style imagery.

Style is driven by sanctions in the society

Gaining access to this sacred knowledge was largely done by fasting and seeking a vision. Mutual reciprocity was universal and all the advisers were compensated. Accessing the sacred information was determined by an initiate's family and clan, their ability to provide the necessary food and gifts, hosting ritual meetings. The system was wealth driven (Duncan and Diaz-Granados 2016, 94–7). The fasting penitents were instructed by clan and bundle priests who possessed the right to guide the seekers to a place most advantageous for the contact with the prospective spirit helpers. These helpers would ensure success in hunting, warfare, and social enterprise. At the end of the fasting ritual, the penitent recalled any events during their experience that allowed the attending priest to define the recipient's obligations to the supernatural helper. Herein lies the foundation of Braden imagery, the reason for its creation. As previously mentioned, regalia, including painting and tattooing, chartered clan membership and accomplishments and enhanced positions of leadership. In the sedentary Plains/Prairie societies, Bowers (2004, 93–4) found that aspiring leaders, who were the best informed about clan lore and the oral traditions connected to sacred bundles, enjoyed the most political success. The need for a mnemonic system that would be an aid in recounting this information led to the development of a uniform canonical manner of preserving this lore, the Braden Art Style.

As the result of a favorable climate shift, which enhanced agricultural production, Late Woodland populations increased between AD 600 and 900 in the Middle and Lower Missouri River Valley. The populations adjacent to the confluence of the Missouri and Mississippi rivers began interacting with greater frequency. Archaeological evidence indicates that some of the interactions may not have been peaceful (Perino 1973, 66–97). The value of women as the principal farmers and entrepreneurs made them a target for acquisition through raiding and warfare. With increasing populations, territorial acquisition through warfare also became more prevalent. Thus, for the abrogation of conflict, diplomacy involving complex sanctions becomes a more pressing need. Diplomacy increases the frequency of gifting and feasting which, in turn, leads to more complex alliances with rigidly sanctioned behaviors (Provinse 1970). The combination of the need for increased knowledge of oral traditions and the increasing complexity of diplomacy also empowered a new renaissance in visual communication technology involving the newly created imagery.

Archaeologically, this rapid expansion of mnemonic aids and the rapidly developing technology are accompanied by increased ceramic forms and decoration, larger population centers (some fortified), larger more complex burial mounds, chunkey rollers made of exotic material, tobacco pipes, and an increase in marine shell artifacts, to name a few. With increased diplomacy there still existed a pre-occupation with warfare. This militarism is evidenced by new forms of weapons such as flared bit celts and elaborate arrow points. However, this was balanced by an increase in peaceful interaction. Seeking stability and unity, the rapidly evolving populations began to focus on a geological formation, a cave that had long been known and was identified as the "cosmic birthplace."

Oral traditions supporting the genesis of elite clans in a shrine as important as Picture Cave are just what one would expect and thankfully, a Jesuit recorded the importance of Picture Cave and its connection to the oral traditions of the First Man and First Woman and their descendants. Further expectations are met by the mix of ceramic types, all of them roughly contemporaneous, from looters' pits near the lower panels. Finally, close examination of the complex array of talent in the artistry also supports the assumption that there was a rapid effort, by a modest group, a few people with a formidable array of esoteric knowledge, who created most of the art, the earliest expression of the germinal and ensuing formative Braden Style.

During the Terminal Late Woodland Period, towns and hamlets developed along the lower Missouri River, its tributaries and its confluence with the Mississippi River. This increased their interactions and these people began to merge and converge on the confluence region (Pauketat 1994, 3–7; Duncan 2015, 105). These Late Woodland societies had been closely interacting, through the ritual exchange of goods, especially garden seeds; this rite being an essential part of the women's agricultural ceremonies (Bowers 1992, 338–47; 2004, 156–63; Colvin 2012). Thus, populations that had been rapidly growing in size and complexity began to merge for mutual protection, alliances led to unification (Bareis and Porter 1984, 128–30; Hall 1991, 10; Pauketat and Emerson 1997, 7; Iseminger 2010, 21). Large, unified populations meant more mouths to feed and more efficient agricultural practices, including a need for better seed stocks. Other exchange rituals involving both men and women intensified, to reduce conflict and to further promote unity.

The presence of the shell Long-Nosed Maskette on a principal figure at Picture Cave is a key to the all-important, principal amelioration ritual, the adoption rite (see Colour pl. 10) (Hall 1997, 145–54; Duncan and Diaz-Granados 2000, 8–12; Duncan 2013, 195–203; Mueller and Fritz 2016, 208–13). Adoption rites and the seed exchanges helped to reinforced peaceful societal intercourse along with an amazing inventory of sanctions (Provinse 1970). These commonly held sanctions, along with a need to protect themselves from competitive neighbors and possibly a common language, were among the principal reasons for unity among these merging populations. It is likely that another hierarchical layer was created to promote and perpetuate the stability and unity of this steadily growing population. Promoting a common genesis tradition also aided immensely in establishing unity, especially one promoting a common ancestor, First Man who was the father of all human beings. This First Man figure was coupled with another character, First

Woman. These common ancestors were enshrined in a generalized genesis tradition and expressed by Braden, a new, realistic, and distinctive art style.

The cosmic connections

Prior to AD 1630, all of the Siouan speaking agricultural, semi-sedentary populations, along the Middle and Lower Missouri River Valley, shared a common model of the cosmos, were matrilocal and generally had a system of bicameral leadership. Knowledge of this cosmology sanctions the Braden Style in its depiction of supernatural beings. Added regalia, painting, and tattooing are skillfully rendered to assist the viewer in determining the image's identity and place in the cosmos.

The Dhegiha and their kindred neighbors believed that the multi-layered cosmos was created by an animistic spiritual force, all powerful but invisible. The two parental spirit beings who were created, First Man and First Woman, both possessed great spiritual powers (Ponziglione 1897). These two cohabited and First Woman bore six children, three boys and three girls. This core genesis tradition was shared by the Hidatsa, Mandan, and Dhegiha and many of their neighbors (Bowers 1992, 333–8; 2004, 263–4). The two eldest children of First Man and First Woman were Morning Star or Hawk and Evening Star. They were the focus of much of the genesis oral traditions (Hall 1997, 48–58). Morning Star or Hawk is the paramount warrior figure in Prairie/Plains oral traditions. Hawk bundles represent the courage and combativeness of all the warriors. Being born of both day, First Man and night, First Woman both major divisions – all of the clans were represented (Bailey 1995, 50–1). In today's Osage Big Moon Peyote Church, Hawk is represented by an arrow-shaped staff, made of fruit wood and dressed as a warrior with an additional opossum hide dressed as a woman.

Evening Star's importance was also, in part, due to her two sons, Stone and the Dark Wolf, the powerful Thunderers who are foundational to the genesis traditions. A review of the catalogue of Picture Cave art was undertaken over a period of several weeks. Besides accumulating a vast pile of scrap paper in an effort to quantify the number of images of Beneath World "snakes" and Upper World hero twins – there was a surprise. The ratio appeared to be almost 1:1 – that is, half and half! While no qualitative design was used, simply "a hunch" for choosing the character's identity, the general feeling is that a numerical balance exists between the imagery of snakes versus that of the hero twins.

The ancient Dhegiha used their cosmic model to arrange their ceremonial centers, towns, gatherings, even their iconography – everything was tied to its cosmic placement. Beginning in the Terminal Late Woodland and continuing through the Emergent Mississippian Period, excavated village sites in the American Bottom have single, central posts in plaza areas, surrounded by house structures (Kelly *et al.* 1984, 128–49). The central post, often with four offering pits, a shrine, becomes the focus of ritual activity. These same village sites have numbers of limestone and sandstone chunkey stones, as well as comparatively larger amounts of agricultural tools than earlier Late Woodland sites. The single posts and their plaza areas closely resemble the "Lone" or "First Man" posts of the Mandan and their Dhegihan neighbors (Bowers 2004, 109–12; Duncan 2021, 29–49).

With the advent of the full blown Western Mississippian Sterling and Moorehead phases, the poles become much larger, the chunkey rollers more exotic and a famous classic Braden repoussé copper plaque shows two figures tethered to thongs or cords attached to their chests probably with wooden or bone skewers. This Braden plaque shows the twins, Stone and Dark Wolf, being tortured by Long Arm, chief of the sky people (Bowers 1992, 312–20). Long Arm iconography exists at the seminal Braden Style Picture Cave and at the post-diaspora Maddin Creek Petroglyph site in eastern Missouri. The Dhegihan Ponca and probably the Omaha were still practicing the tethering of skewered warriors to dance around a single pole during a rite similar to the famous Mandan Okipa rite (Bowers 2004, 347–65; Howard 2010, 104–5; Duncan 2021, 48–9). Rather than being a ritual adopted from their northwestern neighbors, the Dhegiha's principal sanction did not connect the ritual to a "vow," the participants were selected by priests adding that distinctive Dhegihan layer of authorization.

Linking the Early Formative art to the classic Braden

There exists a close relationship between several of the anthropomorphic figures at Picture Cave and the shell cup art depicted in Phillips and Brown's (1978) monumental work on the engraved shell art found in the Craig Mound at Spiro, Oklahoma. We are particularly interested in the cup drawn on plate 6 of Phillips and Brown (1978, 6), called the "Stoval Cup" (Fig. 9.3A). A photograph of the boldly engraved cup fragment shows a skillfully rendered figure with exceptional hands, as asymmetrical fists and a bandeau style military hat made of an animal pelt (possibly otter). If one excuses the thin arms and ball like hands of the Dark Wolf warrior figure at Picture Cave (Fig. 9.3B), Cat. No. 123, we can see the entire Stoval figure. Picture Cave No. 123 has well drawn legs with their muscular calves and the beautifully rendered head and face with what look to be prominent chin whiskers – an exceptional rendering. It is the Dark Wolf's profiled left eye that is so impressive. It is carefully drawn and the iris is partially covered by the upper eye lid. Like the Stovall Cup figure, the figure has the Falconid eye markings of a warrior.

We believe that the oculi on the body of the Stovall Cup figure are intentional archaic features reminiscent of the oculi on the body of figure 104, one of the most important images at Picture Cave. Additionally, the shoulder markings of the Stovall Cup figure have the Osprey wing markings found on figure 130 at Picture Cave. Both the Stovall Cup figure and the Dark Wolf have sashes with the Dark Wolf's one having horizontal bands, and both figures also have hair buns. While the Stovall Cup figure has nothing in either hand, the Dark Wolf at Picture Cave has an elaborate crowned mace or war club in the right hand and bow and cruciform arrow in the left hand. This bow is an almost "primitive" rendering that may have been added at some later time by someone with less talent than the original artist.

The Stovall Cup artist embellished his figures with individually rendered globular shell beads, a bi-lobed arrow and a "breath of life" line connected to the tip of the columella shell pendant. He or she did not place any objects within the hands, sadly for us. However, the Dark Wolf's animated dancing or running stance and open mouth match the pose of the figure on the Stovall Cup well . Not surprisingly the Picture Cave figure is just above a prominent horizontal fissure, heavily stained by iron oxides. Unlike any later art, the Dark Wolf figure has a line drawing of a head including a hair bun, similar to his, in front of his face. This detached head does not have a military bandeau nor is it painted black with the red bud charcoal as the Dark Wolf wears, the paint that denotes a successful warrior. Might this head be a reminder that the Dark Wolf has a twin, Stone? The Dark Wolf has an analog, the Man of Mystery, who is associated with the "red metal," (copper), and judges warriors engaged in battle in the day-time. He is also the principal priest who consecrates the clan Hawk Bundles that represent the bravery of the Dhegihan (Osage) warriors (La Flesche 1975, 362; Bailey 1995, 68).

Conclusion: Turning art into words

As on the shell cups, some of the figures at Picture Cave seem to be floating in the night sky, the uppermost level of the Beneath Worlds (Phillips and Brown 1978, 42–4; Duncan 2011, 28–9; 2015, 214–16). It seems that the principal theme of the Picture Cave panels follows the most important Dhegihan oral tradition, the Mon Thin Kagaxe, the contention between man and monsters and the making of the Earth (Fletcher and La Flesche 1992, 171). The all-powerful ancestral spirits, the twins "Stone" and "Dark Wolf," sons of Evening Star, are the champions of humanity. They defeat the monsters and enable their Grandmother to gain the mysterious power to resurrect all her children. The Dark Wolf can be felt and heard as Thunder – but never seen. He exchanges his power with his brother when the Earth inverts herself at sunset, Stone who becomes the judge in the night sky, the star Deneb, sits in judgment of the souls traveling along the Milky Way, the Great Serpent, the "Way of Souls." Once an Osage dies they begin their journey along the Milky Way. Ghosts were spirits that, for some reason, had not begun their journey but remained, for one reason or another, with the living (Bailey 1995, 280).

Now arises a pertinent question: Why did the early Western Mississippians so carefully and deliberately depict images of humanized natural forces that they could not see? The learned priests interviewed by La Flesche were emphatic in denying that their powerful ancestral spirits had humanized form (Bailey 1995, 282). Our only clue is the Jesuit relation written in 1897 that clearly records a description of "Thunder" as having the shape and size of "a man of gigantic proportions" (Ponziglione 1897, 18). Can we assume that in a short span of time, the Terminal Late Woodland imagery grew to reflect the grandeur of size and shape of the seminal Braden Style imagery at Picture Cave? Elaborating on the animated

Braden shell cup figures, do they belong to that long ago period, an asynchronous period, when only gigantic spirit ancestors existed, a period before time began? We argue these figures are still alive in oral traditions that are of such importance to the American Indian people that they are carefully passed down from generation to generation, often with many sanctions. Just as Bowers and Parks have shown, these traditions are living in the memories of many whose ancestors were not constrained by European bias (Parks 1996, 23–31; Bowers 2004, 1–7).

There is always an exception, and it becomes quickly apparent at Picture Cave! The Great Serpent chief of the Beneath Worlds and his offspring are not always humanized, just some of the time. This supernatural character has whitetail deer antlers and the humanized forms have elaborate antler-like feathers attached to their occipital hair buns. When initially trying to interpret the various groups or vignettes of figures at Picture Cave, a suggestion was made by F. Kent Reilly: make "story board" sketches using 35 mm slides of the figures and employing the logic method of arranging them in sequences that follow the oral traditions. Using the regalia of the figures, and with a lot of sorting and matching, something began to appear in the arrangements resembling the Siouan Great Medicine rite. The greatest amount of congruency was with the Ho-Chunk traditions involving a cultural hero and his "sons" and the parallel Iowa traditions describing another example of the same general Genesis story. Taking both these sources as peripheral survivors of a larger, more complex tradition not well known, the next step was to involve an Osage well versed in ancient lore. The material was taken to Pawhuska on the Osage Reservation, and several quiet evenings were spent in Cora Jean Big Elk Jech's living room in deep discussion with a selection of Osages in attendance. The most favored guest invited by Cora Jean and feted for our benefit was Charles Pratt, Shunkahmolah's (*Shon'-ge-mon-in*) grandson. With Charles and his heritage, a good part of the Picture Cave inventory was interpreted with a corroborated synthesis. The ancient artists had recorded for posterity their all-important Genesis traditions, the Making of the Earth rite. However, there is much that we could not connect and interpret. What we recorded in 2015 was a core outline of what still appears to be a complex narrative.

Lately, several prominent members of the archaeological community have expressed disdain for the application of oral traditions of heirs in reconstructing and explaining ancestral imagery. This attitude sadly echoes Robert Lowie (1993, 3) who referred to his collection of Crow Indian stories as "tales" and "fiction". Opposing the followers of Lowie there are people yet living among the many American Indian Nations, both men and women, who carefully relate ancient lore, allowing recording methods as long as their sanctions are followed, especially a deep respect for the fountainheads of oral traditions (Keats 2021). Outsiders are treated to such revelations in Osage Society in the presence of "rememberers," persons carefully selected to carry important cultural information and assimilate it to interested parties inside and outside of their society. We were introduced to this treasure trove of information by William Samuel Fletcher, one of a tiny number of full-blood Osage still living. Mr Fletcher carefully described and enumerated the necessity for such individuals within the complex society of the Dhegihan/

Osage. These "rememberers" are rewarded with gifts, especially during naming rites, just to name one of many functions.

One of the greatest of many wonderful days that we experienced was when William Samuel Fletcher identified a key image in Picture Cave. While carefully studying the black painted image of a warrior with a military hat and sash, carrying a large, black painted crowned mace, Fletcher said: "My Grandfather, who the white people called Black Dog (*Shon-ton-ca-be*), his name really meant the 'Black or Dark Wolf'". The Dark Wolf is the Dhegihan homologue for one of the Celestial Twins or Thunderers – the two most important characters in the Osage Genesis story, The Making of the Earth. His place in the night sky is the leading star in the handle of the Big Dipper, leading the four Sun Bearers as they carry the dead Sun's soul on a litter to be resurrected at dawn. This interpretation became the focal point for reconstructing the major portion of the vignettes that cover the walls of Picture Cave.

References

Bailey, G. ed. (1995) *The Osage and the Invisible World: From the works of Francis LaFlesche*. University of Oklahoma Press, Norman OK.

Bailey, G.A. (2004) Osage daily life: Living as a prayer. In Bailey and Swan, (eds), 49–67.

Bailey, G. (2010) *Traditions of the Osage*. University of New Mexico Press, Albuquerque NM.

Bailey, G. and Swan, D. (2004) *Art of the Osage*. St Louis Art Museum in association with University of Washington Press, Seattle WA and London.

Bareis, C. and Porter, J. (1984) *American Bottom Archaeology: A summary of the FAI-270 Project contribution to the culture history of the Mississippi River Valley*. Illinois Department of Transportation. University of Illinois Press, Urbana and Chicago IL.

Blankenship, S.A. (2015) Geochemical analyses of prehistoric pigment materials from Picture Cave. In Diaz-Granados *et al.* (eds), 37–46.

Bowers, A. (1992) *Hidatsa Social and Ceremonial Organization*. University of Nebraska Press, Lincoln NE.

Bowers, A. (2004) *Mandan Social and Ceremonial Organization* (reprint of 1950 edn). University of Chicago Press, Chicago IL.

Brown, J. (2007) Sequencing the Braden Art Style within Mississippian Period art and iconography. In *Ancient Objects and Sacred Realms: Interpretations of Mississippian iconography*, eds F.K. Reilly, III and J. Garber, 213–45. University of Texas Press, Austin TX.

Brown, J. (2011) The regional culture signature of the Braden Art Style/ In *Visualizing the Sacred: Cosmic visions, regionalism, and the art of the Mississippian world*, eds G. Lankford, F.K. Reilly III and J. Garber, 37–63. University of Texas Press, Austin TX.

Colvin, M. (2012) Old-Woman-Who-Never-Dies: A Mississippian survival in the Hidatsa world. Unpublished M.A. Thesis, Anthropology Department, Texas State University, San Marcos TX.

Diaz-Granados, C. (1993) Petroglyphs and Pictographs of Missouri: A distributional, stylistic, contextual, functional, and temporal analysis of the state's rock graphics. Unpublished Ph.D. Dissertation, Department of Anthropology, Washington University, St Louis, (UMI #94-17574), MO.

Diaz-Granados, C. (2011) Early manifestations of Mississippian iconography in Middle Mississippi Valley rock art. In *Visualizing the Sacred: Cosmic visions, regionalism, and the art of the Mississippian world*, eds G. Lankford, F.K. Reilly, III and J. Garber, 64–98. University of Texas Press, Austin TX.

Diaz-Granados, C. and Duncan, J. (2000) *The Petroglyphs and Pictographs of Missouri.* University of Alabama Press, Tuscaloosa AL.

Diaz-Granados, C., Duncan, J., and Reilly, F.K. III, eds (2015) *Picture Cave: Unraveling the mysteries of the Mississippian cosmos*, University of Texas Press, Austin TX.

Duncan, J. (2011) The Cosmology of the Osage. In *Visualizing the Sacred: Cosmic visions, regionalism, and the art of the Mississippian world*, eds G. Lankford, F.K. Reilly III and J. Garber, 18–33. University of Texas Press, Austin TX.

Duncan, J. (2013) Dhegihan Tattoos. In *Drawing with Great Needles: Ancient tattoo traditions of North America*, eds A. Deter-Wolf and C. Diaz-Granados, 195–213. University of Texas Press, Austin TX

Duncan, J. (2015) Identifying the characters on the walls of Picture Cave. In Diaz-Granados *et al.* (eds), 209–37.

Duncan, J. (2021) Dressing and caring for the spirits: The role of sacred bundles in Siouan society. In *Mississippian Culture Heroes, Ritual Regalia, and Sacred Bundles*, ed D. Dye, 29–56. Lexington Books Washington DC and London.

Duncan, J. and Diaz-Granados, C. (2000) Of masks and myths. *Midcontinetal Journal of Archaeology* 25, 1–26.

Duncan, J. and Diaz-Granados, C. (2016) Rock art, gender, and the Dhegihan landscape. In *Native American Landscapes*, ed. C. Claassen, 85–108. University of Tennessee Press, Knoxville TN.

Dye, D. (2021) The Link Farm Cache: Invoking the ancestors and supplicating the Hero Twins. In *Mississippian Culture Heroes, Ritual Regalia, and Sacred Bundles*, ed. D. Dye, 161–210. Lexington Books, Lanham MD.

Fletcher, A. and La Flesche, F. (1992) *The Osage Tribe.* University of Nebraska Press, Lincoln NE.

Hall, R. (1997) *An Archaeology of the Soul.* University of Illinois Press, Urbana and Chicago IL.

Hall, R. (1991) The Cahokia identity and interaction models of Cahokia Mississippian. In *Cahokia and the Hinterlands*, eds T. Emerson. and R.B. Lewis, 3–34. University of Illinois Press, Urbana and Chicago IL.

Holmes, W. (1883) *Art in Shell of the Ancient Americans.* Smithsonian Institution, Bureau of American Ethnology, 2nd Annual Report, 1880–1881, Smithsonian Institute, Washington, D.C.

Howard, J.H. (1995) *The Ponca Tribe.* University of Nebraska Press, Lincoln NE.

Howard, J. (2010) *The Ponca Tribe.* University of Nebraska Press, Lincoln NE and London.

Iseminger, W. (2010) *Cahokia Mounds.* History Press, Charleston SC.

Keats, J. (2021) Speaking the past. *Discover Magazine* March/April, 30–7

Kehoe, A. (2007) Osage texts and Cahokia data. In *Ancient Objects and Sacred Realms: Interpretations of Mississippian iconography*, eds F.K. Reilly III and J. Garber, 246–63. University of Texas Press, Austin TX.

Kelly, J., Finney, F., McElrath, D. and Ozuk, S. (1984) Late Woodland Period. In *American Bottom Archaeology: A summary of the FAI-270 Project contribution to the culture history of the Mississippi River Valley*, eds C. Bareis and J. Porter, 128–57. University of Illinois Press, Chicago IL.

LaFlesche, F. (1975) *A Dictionary of the Osage Language.* Smithsonian Institution Bulletin 109, Bureau of American Ethnology, 43rd Annual Report 1925–1926, Smithsonian Institute, Washington DC.

Lowie, R. (1993) *Myths and Traditions of the Crow Indians.* University of Nebraska Press, Lincoln NE and London.

Morse, D. and Morse P. (1983) *Archaeology of the Central Mississippi Valley.* Academic Press/ Harcourt Brace Janovich, New York and London.

Mueller, N. and Fritz G. (2016) Women as symbols and actors in the Mississippi Valley. In *Native American Landscapes*, ed. C. Cheryl, 108–48. University of Tennessee Press, Knoxville TN.

Parks, D. (1996) *Myths and Traditions of the Arikara Indians*. University of Nebraska Press, Lincoln NE and London.

Pauketat, T. (1994) *The Ascent of Chiefs*. University of Alabama Press, Tuscaloosa AL and London.

Pauketat, T. and Emerson, T. eds (1997) *Cahokia Domination and Ideology in the Mississippian World*. University of Nebraska Press, Lincoln NE and London.

Perino, G. (1973) The Late Woodland component at the Pete Klunk Site, Calhoun County, IL. In *Late Woodland Site Archaeology in Illinois*, ed. P. Munson, 58–141. Illinois Archaeological Survey Bulletin 9, University of Illinois, Urbana IL.

Phillips, P. and Brown J. (1978) *Pre-Columbian Shell Engravings from the Craig Mound at Spiro, OK*. Peabody Museum of Archaeology and Ethnology, Harvard University, Cambridge MA.

Ponziglione, P.S.J. (1897) *The Osages and Father John Schoenmakers. Interesting Memoirs Collected from Legends, Traditions and Historical Documents*. Handwritten manuscript, on file at Midwest Jesuit Archives, St Louis, Missouri.

Provinse, J. (1970) The underlying sanctions of Plains Indian culture. In *Social Anthropology of North American Tribes*, ed R. Eggan, 341–74. University of Chicago Press, Chicago IL and London

Tixier, M.C. (1940) *Tixier's Travels on the Osage Prairies*, ed. J.F. McDermott. University of Oklahoma Press, Norman OK.

10

A whirlwind of a woman: An iconographic interpretation of the Mississippian Earth Mother

Melinda A. Martin

Mississippian cosmoscapes provide a perceived, yet concealed, existence of spiritual realms inhabited by other-than-human beings who interact, influence, and interfere with the tangible landscape through natural and material contexts. To conceptualize the world around them, various cultures during the Mississippian Period focused on a tripartite organization: the Above World, Middle World, and Beneath World (i.e., the Underworld) (Diaz-Granados 2004; Lankford 2004; Reilly 2004; Duncan 2011; Duncan and Diaz-Granados 2018a). Regions exist within each of these three realms, including the Path of Souls and the Realm of the Dead (Lankford 2004; 2011; Reilly 2004; Martin 2019). According to George Lankford (2007) the Realm of the Dead can only be accessed by walking the Milky Way (i.e., Path of Souls), across its expanse in the night sky. Throughout these realms, including the Path of Souls and the Realm of the Dead, reside multiple other-than-human beings possessing powers allowing them to influence the Middle World. In this chapter, I focus on the duality between Earth Mother, who commands vortexes or tornadoes from the Above World, and the Great Serpent who has power over vortexes or whirlpools in the Beneath World. I also investigate how vortexes may be presented in the Middle World. An iconographic interpretation, of vortex motifs (recurring elements with symbolic significance) present on ceramic effigies, reveals the centrality of death and rebirth as a component of the Mississippian cultural period cosmoscapes.

Iconographic symbols and motifs

Through iconographic analyses, accompanied by the archaeological record, and ethnohistoric and ethnographic narratives, archaeologists have examined various other-than-human beings who reside in the tripartite Mississippian cosmoscapes. These non-human persons are recognized through dominant symbols and motifs which are distinct and can be independent (Mueller and Fritz 2016, 112), and recreate the Mississippian cosmoscapes on a smaller scale, (i.e., a microcosm)

(Lankford 2004). Iconographers utilize such key motifs to create linkages between ethnohistorical accounts and the archaeological record to better appreciate and understand the Mississippian cosmoscapes and to evaluate how the tripartite cosmology is illustrated through objects that serve to connect humans to other-than-human beings. These distinct symbol patternings may also become polysemous and involve complex concepts, in which their intent may vary depending on the context and other symbols and motifs included within that context (Turner 1967; Mueller and Fritz 2016).

The iconographic interpretation, in this chapter, will focus on key terminology such as symbols, motifs, and elements. For clarification a *symbol* is used to identify a set of individual elements, which may not stand independently though compiled together form a symbolic meaning for the viewer. Such examples may be a tri-fork eye surround, a swirl, and lines in a specific context such as emitting from the mouth of effigies or anthropomorphs. A *motif*, as used here, will be referenced as a dominant repeated idea with associated referents such as a cross-in-circle, *axis mundi*, swirl-cross, or other quadripartite designs. These symbols and motifs will be categorized through terms such as a command symbol/motif in which a specific function or power is being addressed; locatives which identify the cosmoscape the symbol and or motif is portraying; positional symbols/motifs or the way in which symbols and motifs react to one another based on their associated location in imagery; and polysemous symbols/motifs which suggests symbolic sets may have many differing referents based on the context the motif is portraying (Turner 1967; Lankford 2004; Mueller and Fritz 2016).

Vernon Knight (2013) provides guidelines to assist the iconographer in understanding and appreciating pre-Columbian imagery, as has George Lankford (2004) in his discussions on centering devices and the ability to dismantle a motif into elements. Mueller and Fritz (2016) build on Victor Turner's (1967) seminal work concerning dominant symbols and the three aspects of symbolic meaning in the form of exegetical, operational, and positional, which focus on how meanings were obtained by ethnographers. Deflem (1991, 6) expands on Turner's work with dominant symbols by defining them as meanings that, "possess a high degree of autonomy and consistency throughout the total symbolic system". Mueller and Fritz (2016, 113) employ Turner's (1967, 31–2) approach to analyze Mississippian women as symbols in Mississippian art. They examine polysemous symbols and elements and how they have many differing referents based on the context in which the motif is portrayed. Mueller and Fritz also pose the question: "Is it possible to recover the nuances of representation intended by Mississippian people from their symbols" (Mueller and Fritz 2016, 113). This question is answered by understanding how our interpretation of symbols are based on the interaction between them and, "how and by whom a symbol is deployed" (Mueller and Fritz 2016, 113). This consideration of how and by whom is crucial to understanding varying referents and why multiple symbols, creating a motif, can result in differing interpretations not only by iconographers but also through Native American ethnographies.

In this chapter, I use the concepts of dominant symbols and motifs to suggest polysemous symbols and motifs and their meanings may alter and take on new roles within Mississippian iconography. Dominant symbols, motifs, and their internal elements, along with external contextual symbols. may identity the realm for which the imagery or the other-than-human being is being portrayed (as a locative symbol); a specific other-than-human being such as the Great Serpent; a Piasa, or underwater spirit; the power being commanded by that other-than-human being at the time the imagery was created (as a command symbol/motif); and any creation mythology being expressed (positional symbol/motifs) for the imager's overall narrative.

The dominant symbols and motifs I examine are not a new contribution to the appreciation of Mississippian cosmoscapes. Iconographers have analyzed pre-Columbian representational imagery for decades and have identified patterning associated with them on various media (Lankford 2004; 2011; Reilly 2004; King and Sawyer 2017). However, I suggest motifs and elements associated with portals, *axes mundi*, and incised or engraved lines on effigies, in particular female effigies and cat serpents, may illustrate components of the Mississippian cosmoscapes and the powers of certain other-than-human beings not yet recognized in the iconographic literature.

Iconographic analyses consider several kinds of relationships between symbols that have been offered specific categories. These include positional symbols or the way in which symbols interact with one another (Turner 1967, 31, 32; Mueller and Fritz 2016, 113); certain symbols served as locatives or shorthands that focus the viewer's attention on the specific realm being depicted by the imagery (Lankford 2004, 214; Reilly 2004, 129). What I have termed command symbols and motifs, identify the specific power being commanded in the imagery. I examine a possible connection between wind and Earth Mother, especially those involving winds demonstrated in strong vortexes such as tornadoes. I also expand on previous literature which references the Great Serpent and his command of the watery realm through vortexes (Reilly 2011; Dye 2018).

These powers that control tornadoes and whirlpools are immaterial or intangible, being obscured in the archaeological record. Unlike flooding, fires, droughts, or earthquakes, vortexes in the form of tornadoes leave no material remains or scars in the soil to observe. Thus, recognizing these weather powers in objects associated with the cosmoscapes is vital to understanding how cosmoscapes were conceptualized by varying Mississippian cultures and how they employed such objects to understand the world around them.

Identifying the cosmos

In discussions of microcosms (Ellen 1886, 2), a depiction of the cosmoscapes in a smaller form, Lankford (2004, 208) suggests elements in complex designs each have "meaning[s] of [their] own" and since the designs frequently seem to be cosmological "the individual elements probably represent particular parts of the cosmic structure" (also see Stauffer *et al.* in this volume). Lankford (2004) examines this further by addressing variability in the way in which the Great Serpent is represented. The Great Serpent inhabits and rules the Beneath World, in direct opposition, or in a duality, to the beings in the Above World. Iconographic studies suggesting the Great Serpent could also be depicted in the sky, as the dominant symbol of the serpent itself, seems to change its referred meaning as portraying an inhabitant of the Beneath World.

Lankford suggests that when the Great Serpent is associated with the Above World the locative of wings is provided and when the Great Serpent is in the Beneath World then a swastika or swirled cross-in-circle motif may be used as an identifier (Lankford 2004; 2011). These locatives assist the viewer in apprehending the world the motif or symbol represents, which may coincide with command motifs and symbols when the power being displayed is also illustrated through a motif, symbol, or element that can also be utilized as a locative. The Great Serpent's powers are different when the swastika motif is presented than when wings are in context with this other-than-human being. Dominant motifs have the ability to become polysemous when the context changes, such as the addition of locatives or shorthands. Not only can their location in the cosmoscape change but the power they possess may also differ.

Earth Mother's command of the wind

Microcosms (also see Ellen 1986) are "images of total cosmic structure made very small" (Lankford 2004, 208) and tend to include dominant motifs with a repeated referent that assist the viewer in understanding not only which realm is being viewed, but also the other-than-human beings that are portrayed. When these dominant motifs are independent it is assumed they maintain the same meaning even though there is no context or positional symbols or other motifs associated with them. For example, Duncan and Diaz-Granados investigate Old Woman or Earth Mother dominant motifs in rock art. One such feminine dominant motif is a vulva motif identified as a portal (Duncan and Diaz-Granados 2018b). Other dominant motifs, which become polysemous based on other positional symbols and motifs, include a swirling parallel line motif and spinning crosses which Duncan and Diaz-Granados (2018b, 67) state "are all linked to the First or Old Woman". An example of a dominant motif that is polysemous with reference to other positional motifs that I examine is the broad quadripartite characteristic of many symbols which identify patterning and theme identified through motifs. Iconographic symbol systems usually contain a quadripartite aspect whether that be in the form of four creatures, loops, nested circles, or a scene on media such as shell, ceramic, or cave walls, divided into four sections. The overall dominant motif associated with a quadripartite division is the cross-in-circle motif (see Mersmann and Stauffer, this volume). This motif has been identified on numerous media and interpreted in various ways differing temporally and spatially. The cross-in-circle motif has been suggested to represent the cardinal directions (Reilly 2004, 128), the sacred fire (Howard 1968; King and Sawyer 2017), a sun symbol (Waring 1968), and the four winds (Pybus 2009). I suggest the motif is a locative, which requires a broader context to assign it as a particular referent due to the various positions and regions in which the motif and its elements have been identified. King and Sawyer (2017, 4) refer to the-cross-in circle motif as a sacred fire that "connects This Earthly World to the Above World". The location of the cross-in-circle motif, according to King and Sawyer (2017), in the cosmoscapes is the Middle World and Above World. King and Sawyer arrive at this conclusion by stating the central element of the motif represents the sacred fire. They also examine the square which surrounds the motif, and suggest it is associated with the earth, since the Middle World is recognized as an island floating on a sea (King and Sawyer 2017; Sawyer 2009). I argue that the square identified by King and Sawyer identifies and associates with the cross-in-circle motif as an added positional motif, changing the dominant motif to polysemous (having different meanings based on context) brought about by a change in the context of the cross-in-circle motif, possibly varying its meaning to fit a regional variant or a different realm or power being displayed.

In my iconographic interpretation of Earth Mother and the Great Serpent ceramic assemblages, I suggest quadripartite symbols associated with specific Earth Mother hooded effigy bottles and Cat Serpent effigies function as command symbols that may also act as locatives. The quadripartite motifs in the form of a cross-in-circle, swirled four wind patterns, or swirled cross-in-circle is not to necessarily define where in the cosmoscapes they are being associated, though it may assist the viewer in acting as a locative. Instead, the motif is utilized to display the power being identified at that moment and by which other-than-human being. The motifs and sometimes the individual elements are exhibiting what the other-than-human being is capable of doing in specific settings. In this way the motif is acting as a dual referent: as a locative to notate which cosmoscape is being identified and as a command symbol illustrating the power or magic the imagery is portraying. One of these quadripartite command symbols, which occurs on Earth Mother hooded effigy bottles in a variety of examples, is what I interpret as vortex imagery, which appears as a four sectioned swirl motif as seen in Figure 10.1A, or a large counter-clockwise swirl with four lines radiating out from the center. This command motif suggests the command of winds, possibly the four winds.

Earth Mother has many names such as First Woman, Grandmother, Old-Woman-Who-Never- Dies, and I suggest Whirlwind Woman (Diaz-Granados 2004; Reilly 2004; Sharp *et al.* 2011; Mueller and Fritz 2016; Duncan and Diaz-Granados 2018b; Sharp 2021). In Siouan Plains village mythic narratives, Grandmother had influence over the return of waterbirds in the spring and she may have arrived with these birds during this time (Mueller and Fritz 2016, 111). She also had the power to bring rains in the summer (Bowers 1992). Her association with spring and summer storms is interesting considering it is at this time that 60% of the annual rain fall occurs in the central Mississippi River Valley, where many of the ceramics representing her have been found (Pybus 2009; Aguade and Burt 2015). I suggest the occurrence of these ceramics is due to severe thunderstorms producing tornadic storms and the association with Earth Mother. Earth Mother is also linked with two mythical grandsons termed Thunder Boy and Stone for the Osage and Lightning and Thunder Boy for the Cherokee (Duncan and Diaz Granados 2018a; Dye forthcoming).

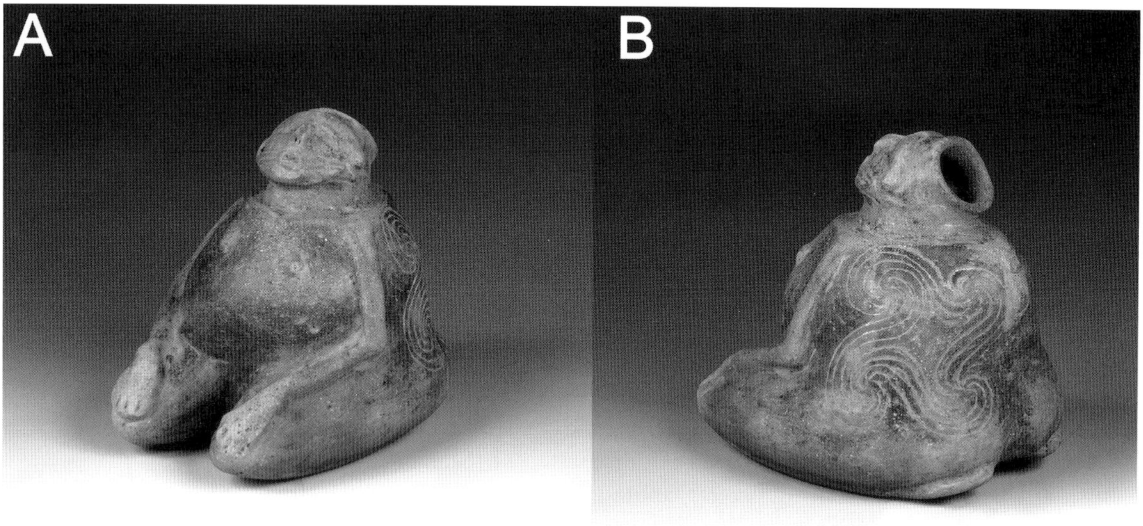

These mythical grandsons are noted in ethnographies as having command of lightning and thunder which frequently accompany tornadic storms. In her study of tornado related myths of Native American Traditions, Nani Pybus (2009, 2), describes "a primal deity that helps create the world or a season deity that returns each year". Could Earth Mother return each spring as mentioned in the Siouan Plains Village mythic narratives in which Grandmother returns in the spring with the winds and brings back the waterfowl through her command of the winds? Arapaho mythic narratives associate Whirlwind Woman as the first woman on earth and have memorialized her in a lodge ornament design known as the Track of the Whirlwind (Kroeber 1902, 60–1). Mandan mythology, collected by Alfred Bowers, frequently associates strong winds, "to their agricultural deity, Old Woman Who Never Dies" (Pybus 2009, 50). Shawnee descriptions of Grandmother or Old-Woman-Who-Never-Dies "have stated that her personal name is revealed as Cloud" (Reilly 2004, 134), possibly suggesting an association with rain and storms.

A female figure, frequently referred to as Old-Woman-Who-Never-Dies is presented in the form of a hooded effigy bottle with her face lifted towards the sky (Fig. 10.1A). On her back is a quadripartite motif containing four swirled patterns all connected to make one large counterclockwise vortex, with a void in the center where the lines flow around (Fig. 10.1B). I suggest this motif is a locative identifying the Above World, as well as a command motif identifying a tornado, whirlwind, or a sky vortex. Together, they communicate the Earth Mother's ability to create and control them. In North America, the majority of tornadoes and low-pressure systems rotate in a counter-clockwise motion, similar to the rotation of the vortex command motif located on Earth Mother ceramics (Fig. 10.1; Aguade and Burt 2015). The duality of the Beneath World and Above Worlds may suggest she is occupying the Above World in her creation of this vortex, whereas the Great Serpent has been noted to control vortexes in the Beneath World (Reilly 2004; 2011; Dye 2018).

Fig. 10.1. A. Female effigy hooded bottle (frontal view) illustrating lines flanking the mouth possibly portraying wind; B. Female Effigy Hooded Bottle (rear view) illustrating a quadripartite symbol, possibly a vortex or tornado (photos courtesy of David H. Dye).

Fig. 10.2. Cat Serpent vessel from the Campbell Site (23PM5) illustrating a swirled vortex symbol on the side of the vessel (photo courtesy of David H. Dye).

The duality of Above and Beneath World vortexes

The Great Serpent is identified as "lord of this watery domain" meaning the Underworld or the Beneath World in the tripartite cosmoscape of the Mississippians (Reilly 2004, 128). As mentioned above, he can also occupy the Above World, which may be indicated by wing locatives (Lankford 2004). Figure 10.2 illustrates the Great Serpent as an Underwater Panther with a curved nose, pointed teeth, a curved tail, a triforked-eye surround motif, possible horns on its head, and lines emitting from the nose or upper mouth area connecting to a counterclockwise swirl on its body.

Reilly (2004, 128) notes that the Underwater Panther could thrash its tail and "stir the surface of lakes and rivers into dangerous whirlpools". Lankford (2011) in discussing the interlocking scroll design on an engraved Cat Serpent vessel, suggests the motif may represent a portal or a vortex. Dye (2018, 42, 43) also references the swirl cross motif stating it may define a vortex and that "such rotations are often identified with tornadoes or whirlpools-natural referents for axes mundi". I suggest the motif on the body of the vessel in Figure 10.2 is a command motif denoting the Great Serpent's ability to create and control a vortex or whirlpool in the Beneath World. I further suggest that in the absence of a locative such as the swirled cross-in-circle or the swastika, this command motif may also be a locative that references the Beneath World, based on its context association with the Great Serpent as an Underwater Panther effigy. While Figure 10.2 does not have an easily identifiable locative such as the swirled cross-in-circle, an incised beaker from the Kersey site in Pemiscot, Co. Missouri, depicts two intertwined serpents seemingly wrapped around a counterclockwise swirled cross-in-circle motif suggesting the serpents may have created this vortex; according to Lankford (2004) this vortex is being created in the Beneath World (Reilly 2011, 125, fig 6.2a). A similar set of motifs has been identified in the form of a sub-globular vessel with entwined rattlesnakes surrounding an ogee motif from the Richardson Landing Site in Tipton, Co. Tennessee (Reilly 2011, 125, fig 6.2d).

Portals to other realms

Lankford (2004) describes the swastika or the swirled cross-in-circle motif as a locative indicating the Beneath World. Reilly (2011) references a four-armed swirl motif as a possible portal. In defining the swastika motif Lankford states that the motifs "differ from crosses only in the slight curving bend at the end of the arms of an equal-armed cross" (Lankford 2011, 251). The two motifs vary enough to suggest possible regional differences but I argue that they present the same referent associated with the Beneath World and a portal in the form of a vortex, created by the Great Serpent.

Lankford (2011) examines what he calls the swirl-cross in which he discusses the ability of the motif to stand alone and its connections with other motifs and elements sometimes presented with it. He suggests the swirl-cross may represent two motifs that may form a complex symbol set, or two differing symbols sets in the form of the Sun and fire. He notes these two elements may be the ends of a column or an *axis mundi* (center of the world; see Mersmann and Stauffer in this volume). From this view he argues the swirled cross motif is a two-dimensional representation of what would be viewed as a three-dimensional object. He goes on to state that "the cross still seems to be identifiable as a symbol of the Center" (Lankford 2011, 255).

Lankford has described the *axis mundi* as "the center of the world" with the ability to be presented as "an actual vertical column" (Lankford 2004, 210). He compares the *axis mundi* to an elevator shaft which allows for access to each level of the cosmos (Lankford 2004). In a visual description he states "the columnar axis penetrates through the earth-disk into the Beneath World" (Lankford 2004, 215). In his reference to the column as a "sun-fire column" (Lankford 2004, 215) he mentions this might not be an appropriate description because it must also act as "a central axis for the water world" (Lankford 2004, 215). I argue that this vertical column, sometimes depicted as a striped pole, possibly suggesting rotation to the viewer, is a referent for a tornado. The tornado as a funnel cloud in the sky has the ability to reach from the Above World and make contact with the surface of the Middle World. It can then also connect to water in the form of a waterspout. An *axis mundi* has the ability to appear individually in the sky as a funnel, the water as a whirlpool, or as a direct connection to all three realms.

The interpretation of the swirled-cross motif as a portal and its association with the Great Serpent and the Beneath World (Lankford 2004) may portray the opening portal to the Beneath World in the form of a whirlpool. The Great Serpent would have commanded the power to create and open this portal for access to the realm he ruled over. With the Great Serpent's association with death and the Realm of the Dead, whirlpools may have been seen as an entrance along the Path of Souls for the deceased and for ritual specialists wishing to contact ancestors or other-than-human beings.

Lankford (2004) suggests, the two motifs may represent the Sun and fire with each possessing the end of a column on an *axis mundi*. I would agree that they represent each end of an *axis mundi* and are the portals in which to access it. One of these access points, the bottom one, is in the form of a vortex occurring in bodies of water, known as whirlpools, and commanded by the Great Serpent as indicated by the swirled cross-in-circle sometimes associated with him, and the swirled elements illustrated on Cat Serpent effigies (see Azar and Steponaitis, this volume). The second access point may illustrate the top of this column and may be represented by a cross-in-circle in the form of the four winds seen on certain Earth Mother effigies. The column itself, with its two dual openings from the Above and Beneath World, is a naturally occurring column of air, with its natural prototype being a tornado.

The tornado is a crucial component of the Mississippian cosmoscapes, as an *axis mundi* which connects the three realms and is portrayed in varying iconographic imagery. The *axis mundi* has been identified as a central pole, a sacred tree, a pole with spiral stripes and dotted circles, a sacred mountain, and, as I would argue, as a tornado (Lankford 2004; Reilly 2004; 2011). The variations of the *axis mundi* as a tree, a pole, or a vortex may vary depending on its context and the symbols and elements associated with it. As with the discussion of the quadripartite symbols and their referents as the four winds, a vortex, the sun, or a sacred central fire, these seemingly contrasting interpretations may infer different referents regarding the context of the symbols and motifs accompanying it.

The keeper and the extinguisher of the animating winds

The final symbolic elements I examine are the lines illustrated on Earth Mother and the Great Serpent which seem to emerge from the nose or mouth and spread outwards. Figure 10.1A illustrates a female hooded effigy bottle, in a kneeling position, with her legs tucked under her body and her hands residing on her knees. Her eyes seem to be closed, her head is elevated towards the sky, and two horizontal lines flank her mouth, which is slightly open. Incised and engraved lines occurring on the facial region of human and anthropomorphic beings are commonly referred to as tattoos (Walker 2004; Cherry 2009). These markings frequently occur on Mississippian head pots and range from detailed iconographic imagery to lines occurring around the mouth. While the lines may suggest tattooing in specific contexts, I argue that the lines on the Earth Mother figurine, accompanied with the four winds or vortex motif on her back and her mouth agape, act as a command symbol illustrating her ability to produce wind. The idea of a wind can take on multiple meanings. One interpretation is the wind associated with natural phenomena such as storms and tornadoes. A second interpretation is the wind of life, or the Breath of the Earth, sometimes referred to as Wa-kon-da by the Osage and (Pauketat 2013, 61; Duncan and Diaz-Granados 2018a, 54) which animates all living beings. In Native American ethnologies, from the southwest region, a Keeper of the Breath was responsible for "the whirlwind and the air which men breathe" (Patterson 1992, 186). This breath originated "from this keeper's mouth" and was represented by a double spiral design symbol and a line emitting from a figures mouth. The Jicarilla Apache have a form of a Keeper of the Breath which is related in a creation myth concerning an other-than-human being who wanted to create a human. In this creation story the being drew a figure onto the ground and then "sent Whirlwind into the figure he had traced on the ground and rendered it animate" (Opler 1960, 133). Evidence of this animation by the whirlwind may be seen in the swirled pattern on the fingertips of humans.

Robert Sharp (2021, 2) examines multiple female figurines and concludes they "were ultimately part of ritual mortuary practices devoted to the death of children, for it is in their graves that these figures were interred". Yuchi mythology relates the story of an Old Woman who controls souls in the spirit world and has the ability to re-animate some of them to being alive again (Grantham 2002). Voegelin (1936) recorded prayers and items such as tobacco being offered at children's graves "with the request that the deceased child be returned as one of the future children of the parents" (Voegelin 1936, 15). The Earth Mother in her ability to command wind or the wind of animating breath may be viewed as having the power to re-animate souls, especially those of children.

Great Serpent imagery also possesses symbolic elements in the form of incised or engraved lines in the mouth or nose region. The Cat Serpent effigy bowl depicted in Figure 10.2 has lines radiating from the mouth or nose region and extending down its neck and to a swirl symbol dominating the body of the vessel. These lines have been described as plumes or hair on globular bottles containing Cat Serpent imagery and/or possibly representing the four cardinal directions (Dye 2018). I suggest these lines emitting from the nose or mouth area of these other-than-human beings are similar to those illustrated on Figure 10.1a of the Earth Mother hooded effigy vessel.

These lines act as command symbols to illustrate the ability of the Great Serpent to create the vortex noted on the side of the vessel. It may also act in a similar manner to the Earth Mother's ability to renew or animate life through the breath of wind. However, I suggest this breath issued by the Great Serpent may have been the opposite of animation, instead demonstrating his ability to remove that animation and send the deceased to the Realm of the Dead through the vortex he commands. According to the Jicarilla Apache mythology associated with the animation of life being recorded as a swirl on the fingertips, they also believe that death leaves a material mark on the human body caused by the spirit leaving the body "as a whirlwind from the bottoms of the feet" (Ophler 1960, 133).

The whirlwind and its command symbol of the swirl plays a role not only in the creation of life but the extinguisher of it as well. This duality of life and death can be viewed in Earth Mother's vortex or column of winds associated with life giving storms in the spring and summer, her ability to animate and re-animate life through a master breath, along with a possible link to the re-incarnation of children's souls. In opposition of this is the Great Serpent with his power to form a whirlpool with the ability to drown unsuspecting humans, to send souls to his Realm of the Dead through his vortex and extract the master breath back out of those that Earth Mother animated.

Discussion and interpretations

Earth Mother and the Great Serpent both have iconographic imagery that suggests a connection with the environmental phenomena associated with vortexes. While the Great Serpent's ability to command vortexes in the Beneath World waters have been noted (Reilly 2011; Dye 2018), the Earth Mother's association with winds, a master of breath, and the ability to form funnels and tornadoes from the Above World have not been addressed. Through an iconographic analysis of dominant symbols, motifs, and elements, and their combinations as polysemous symbols and motifs with differing locatives that reference various places in the cosmos, imagery which has been referred to with varying meanings can assume new roles.

Lankford (2004, 214) identifies the use of locatives to determine which cosmoscape the imagery being viewed is associated. He has also examined

Fig. 10.3. Ceramic bottle from the Murphy Site (23PM43) illustrating headless anthropomorphic other-than-human beings with serpents coiled in a swirl motif above the heads (photo: courtesy of David H. Dye).

dominant symbols and motifs and their ability to function independently and in connection with other dominant symbols to inform the viewer of a larger picture not able to be presented by one symbol, motif, or element. I suggest command symbols may add an additional layer to tools available to iconographers in assigning referents to the corpus of symbols and motifs associated with Mississippian cosmoscapes. These command symbols enable the creator of the imagery to demonstrate the power associated with individual imagery and its ability to play differing roles based on the contexts of symbols associated with it. These positional, locative, and command symbols may also be combined to strengthen the argument associated with what these symbols, mean in certain contexts. For example, Figure 10.3 illustrates the duality of the Earth Mother and the Great Serpent within regard to their command of vortexes.

Figure 10.3 also depicts four headless anthropomorphs with serpents in the form of counterclockwise swirls just above and sometimes seemingly attached to the headless figures. The anthropomorphic figures are in a presumed birthing position suggesting this imagery may portray Earth Mother and her ability to renew life (Duncan and Diaz Granados 2018a; 2018b). The asterisms in between the figures may represent the Above World or the night sky. While the serpents do not contain a locative, such as wings, their contextual association with stars may imply that they are found in the night sky or, possibly, their ability to flip the day-time, into a night-time status similar to how severe storms block out the Sun and turn the day dark. This image demonstrates a possible connection between Earth Mother and the Great Serpent with vortexes, whether Earth Mother is commanding them from the Above World, the Great Serpent is controlling them from the Beneath World, or some form of joint control occurs during severe thunderstorm activity. Dominant symbols, motifs, and elements are viewed in imagery such as serpents, female figures, swirled elements, and stars. However, these dominant symbols may not refer to the same referent in the mentioned imagery, as they do in other imagery with differing positional symbols presenting a different context.

Conclusion

The Mississippian cosmoscape is portrayed in various aspects of the Mississippian world and recreated as microcosms, or the cosmos on a smaller scale (Lankford 2004), to create linkages between humans and other-than-human beings who inhabit these sacred spaces. While Mississippians left behind no written language to help guide archaeologists into a better understanding of the relationships between Mississippian period cultures' ontologies and these other-than-human beings, they did leave behind imagery containing symbols that may independently or in association with other symbols and motifs provide clues as to their possible referents.

Building upon previous iconographic work (Turner 1967; Lankford 2004; Reilly 2004; Knight 2013; Mueller and Fritz 2016) I suggest some symbols and motifs display not only the location of the imagery in relation to the cosmos (*sensu* Lankford 2004) but the particular command of power the imagery is demonstrating. Through iconographic interpretation of the Great Serpent and Earth Mother imagery in the form of Cat Serpent effigy vessels and female hooded effigy bottles respectively, I suggest certain command symbols demonstrate an association between these two other-than-human beings and environmental and weather phenomena in the form of vortexes. These same symbols and motifs may possess varying roles and also have the ability to suggest an association with the Above World through the four-wind vortex symbol on the back of Figure 10.1, and a swirl-cross in circle locative and command motif which sometimes occur on the back of Cat Serpent heads similar to the Cat Serpent effigy in Figure 10.2. Figure 10.3 may show a locative in its use of stars and the appearance of a Beneath World and Above World deity in the form of Earth Mother and Serpents. It may further emphasize the dualism of opposing powers, or their consolidation communicated with the use of a vortex motif in the command of the Great Serpent and Earth Mother.

Through iconographic interpretation of ceramic assemblages containing vortex motifs, I suggest assigning these symbols static meanings would be a disservice to the role they were meant to possess in illustrating the cosmoscape on a smaller scale, along with the other-than-human beings who inhabited them and the powers they commanded. The use of polysemous symbols and the understanding that the referents vary based on positional and locative symbols in the imagery, archaeological contexts, and ethnohistoric accounts may help archaeologists better conceptualize the cosmoscapes envisioned by Mississippian cultures over time.

References

Aguado, E. and Burt, J.E. (2015) *Understanding Weather and Climate* (7th edn). Pearson, London.

Bowers, A.W. (1992) *Hidatsa Social and Ceremonial Organization* (original publication 1963), University of Nebraska Press, Lincoln NE and London.

Cherry, J.F. (2009) *The Headpots of Northeast Arkansas and Southern Pemiscot County Missouri.* University of Arkansas Press, Fayetteville AR.

Deflem, M. (1991) Ritual, anti-structure, and religion: A discussion of Victor Turner's processual symbolic analysis. *Journal for the Scientific Study of Religion* 30, 1–25.

Diaz-Granados, C. (2004) Marking stone, land, body, and spirit: Rock art and Mississippian iconography. in *Hero, Hawk, and Open Hand: American Indian art of the ancient Midwest and South*, eds R.F. Townsend and R.V. Sharp, 139–50. Yale University Press, New Haven CO.

Duncan, J.R. (2011) The cosmology of the Osage: The Star People and their universe. In *Visualizing the Sacred: Cosmic visions, regionalism, and the art of the Mississippian world*, eds G.E. Lankford, F.K. Reilly III and J.F. Garber, 18–36. University of Texas Press, Austin TX

Duncan, J.R. and Diaz-Granados, C. (2018a) The Big Five petroglyph sites: Their place on the landscape and relation to their creators. In *Transforming the Landscape: Rock art and the Mississippian cosmos*, eds C. Diaz-Granados, J. Simek, G. Sabo III and M. Wagner, 30–56. Oxbow Books, Oxford.

Duncan, J.R. and Diaz-Granados, C. (2018b) Landscape, cosmology, and the Old Woman: A strong feminine presence. In *Transforming the Landscape: Rock art and the Mississippian cosmos*, eds C. Diaz-Granados, J. Simek, G. Sabo III and M. Wagner. 57–75. Oxbow Books, Oxford.

Dye, D.H. (2018) Ceramic wares and Water Spirits identifying religious sodalities in the lower Mississippi Valley. In *Ceramics of Ancient America Multidisciplinary Approaches*, eds Y.P. Huntington, D.E. Arnold and J. Minich, 30–61. University Press of Florida, Gainesville FL.

Dye, D.H. (forthcoming) The Hero Twins in the Lower Mississippi Valley. In *Explaining the Mississippians: American Indian Ancestors, their cosmos and iconography*, ed. C. Diaz-Granados. University of Alabama Press, Tuscaloosa AL.

Ellen, R. (1986) Microcosm, Macrocosm and the Nuaulu house: Concerning the reductionist fallacy as applied to metaphorical levels. *Bijdragen tot de Taal-, Land- en Volkenkunde* 177, 1–30.

Grantham, B. (2002) *Creation Myths and Legends of the Creek Indians*. University Press of Florida, Gainesville FL.

Howard, J.H. (1968) *The Southeastern Ceremonial Complex and Its Interpretation.* Memoir 6, Missouri Archaeological Society, Columbia MI.

King, A. and Sawyer, J.A. (2017) Shell gorgets, hybridity, and identity creation in the High Tower region. In *Forging Southeastern Identities: Social archaeology, ethnohistory, and folklore of the Mississippian to Early Historic South*, eds G.A. Waselkov and M.T. Smith, 1–15. University of Alabama Press, Tuscaloosa, AL.

Knight, V.J. (2013) *Iconographic Method in New World Prehistory.* Cambridge University Press, New York.

Kroeber, A.L. (1902) Preliminary sketch of the Mohave Indians. *American Anthropologist* 4, 276–85.

Lankford, G.E. (2004) World on a String: Some cosmological components of the Southeastern ceremonial complex. In *Hero, Hawk, and Open Hand: American Indian art of the ancient Midwest and South*, eds R.F. Townsend and R.V. Sharp, 207–17. Yale University Press, New Haven CO.

Lankford, G.E. (2007) The Great Serpent in Eastern North America. In *Ancient Objects and Sacred Realms*, eds K.F. Reilly III and J.F. Garber, 107–35. University of Texas Press, Austin TX.

Lankford, G.E. (2011) The swirl-cross and the center. In *Visualizing the Sacred: Cosmic visions, regionalism, and the art of the Mississippian world*, eds G.E. Lankford, F.K. Reilly III, and J.F. Garber, 251–75. University of Texas Press, Austin TX.

Martin, M.A. (2019) Paths of Power: Assessing the role of Cahokia-style beakers. Unpublished M.A. thesis, Department of Earth Sciences, University of Memphis, Memphis TN.

Mueller, N. and Fritz, G.J. (2016) Women as symbols and actors in the Mississippi Valley: Evidence from female flint clay statues and effigy vessels. In *Native American Landscapes: An engendered perspective*, ed. C. Claasen, 109–48. University of Tennessee Press, Knoxville TN.

Opler, M.E. (1941) *An Apache Life-way: The economic, social, and religious institutions of the Chiricahua Indians.* University of Chicago Press, Chicago IL.

Opler, M.E. (1960) Myth and practice in Jicarilla Apache eschatology. *Journal of American Folklore* 73, 133–53.

Patterson, A. (1992) *A Field Guide to Rock Art Symbols of the Greater Southwest.* Johnson Books, Boulder CO.

Pauketat, T. (2013) *An Archaeology of the Cosmos: Rethinking agency and religion in ancient America*. Routledge, New York.

Pybus, N.S. (2009) Whirlwind Woman: Native American tornado mythology and global parallels. Unpublished Ph.D. dissertation, Department of Anthropology, Oklahoma State University, Stillwater OK.

Reilly, K.F. III (2004) Visualizing the sacred in Native American art of the Mississippian period. In *Hero, Hawk, and Open Hand American Indian art of the ancient Midwest and South.* eds R.F. Townsend and R.V. Sharp, 194–213. Yale University Press, New Haven CO.

Reilly, K.F. III (2011) The Great Serpent in the Lower Mississippi Valley. In *Visualizing the Sacred: Cosmic visions, regionalism, and the art of the Mississippian world*, eds G.E. Lankford, F.K. Reilly III and J.F. Garber, 118–34. University of Texas Press, Austin TX.

Sawyer, J.A. (2009) The Mississippian Period Crib Theme: Context, chronology, and iconography. Unpublished M.A. thesis, Department of Anthropology, Texas State University-San Marcos, San Marcos TX.

Sharp, R.V. (2021) Earth Mother in the Middle Cumberland, Beneath World powers, and a portal to the Otherworld. In *Mississippian Culture Heroes, Ritual Regalia, and Sacred Bundles*, ed. D.H. Dye, 211–70. Lexington Books, New York.

Sharp, R.V. Knight, V.J. Jr. and Lankford, G.E. (2011) Woman in the patterned shawl: Female effigy vessels and figurines from the Middle Cumberland River basin. In *Visualizing the Sacred: Cosmic visions, regionalism, and the art of the Mississippian world*, eds G.E. Lankford, F.K. Reilly III and J.F. Garber, 177–98. University of Texas Press, Austin TX.

Turner, V. (1967) *The Forest of Symbols: Aspects of Ndembu ritual.* Cornell University Press, Ithaca, New York.

Voegelin, C.F. (1936) *The Shawnee Female Deity.* Yale University Publications in Anthropology 10, Yale University Press, New Haven CO.

Walker, C.P. (2004) Prehistoric art of the Central Mississippi Valley. In *Hero, Hawk, and Open Hand: American Indian art of the ancient Midwest and South*, eds R.F. Townsend and R.V. Sharp, 219–30. Yale University Press, New Haven CO.

Waring, A.J. (1968) *The Waring Papers: The Collected Works of Antonio J. Waring Jr.* (ed. S. Williams) Peabody Museum, Harvard University, Cambridge MA.

11

Mound 2 at the Hopewell Site as cosmoscape

Bretton T. Giles, Brian M. Rowe, and Ryan M. Parish

Introduction

The mounds at the Hopewell typesite reflect the ephemerality and cyclicality of Middle Woodland ritual regimes, ca. 50 BC–AD 400 (Clay 2002; Giles 2010a; 2010b; Giles *et al.* 2020; Everhart 2020; Henry and Miller 2020; Henry *et al.* 2020). Their ephemerality relates to the way Middle Woodland peoples constructed ritual precincts to house elaborate (sometimes mortuary focused) ceremonies only to cyclically dismantle and mound over these precincts. Their transitory characteristics emphasize "motion rather than a captured moment of stasis" emblematic of Native American linguistic, conceptual, and artistic systems (Giles 2010a; 2010b; Berlo 2011, 10).

Parallels exist between the ceremonial regimes that resulted in Mound 2 at the Hopewell site and how other Native American imagery and ceremonies provide partial, perspectival glimpses of cosmoscapes (cf. Hallowell 1960; Morrison 2000; Berlo 2011; 2014; Reichel 2012; Bold 2020). Since cosmoscapes are perspectival, we therefore tack between different analytical perspectives on the ritual deposits and burials found on the lower floor below Mound 2 at the Hopewell typesite. An iconographic analysis serves as our entry point and we explore how an anthropomorphic statuette (Cat No. S278) from Mound City is portrayed wearing several pieces of ceremonial regalia prominently interred with these burials, namely – quadriconcave plates, sagittal headplates, and earspools. We also examine how this statuette is portrayed with falconoid imagery on its visage, while some Middle Woodland falconoid avimorphic representations seem to portray "lost" and/or "decapitated" heads, paralleling the Late Woodland and Mississippian Birdman theme (Brown 2007a; Brown and Dye 2007). Accordingly, we assess whether the burials and features on the lower floor under Mound 2 illustrate representations of important archetypical characters and activities that were probably associated with mythopoetic times. We conclude that the deposits and burials found beneath Mound 2 were arranged into a Middle Woodland cosmoscape or, in other words, a "momentary glimpse into a complex epistemological landscape" (Berlo 2011, 10).

Native American cosmoscapes

A cosmoscape, as discussed in earlier chapters of this volume, is "an overarching model and template for the shape and scope of the cosmos" (Reichel 2012, 136–7) or, in other words, an ontological landscape (cf. Pavel 1981, 154; Berlo 2011; Bold 2020). Yet societies do not typically have homogenous perspectives of the cosmoscapes they inhabit and minor differences often exist. Moreover, societies with "religious" ontologies frequently make distinctions between the sacred and the profane, which signal multi-level ontologies that assign different ontological weights to specific persons/beings, places, objects, and times (Pavel 1981, 153). These distinctions can serve to restrict the sacred to specific objects, events on a ceremonial calendar, or spaces such as temples, churches, charnel houses, and places of sacrifice. These sacred times, places, and objects constitute connections, articulation points, or *axis mundi* (centers) between ontological levels, while non-holy objects, activities, and times are elements of the profane world (Pavel 1981, 153–4).

Profound differences also exist between modern western and non-modern ontologies (Latour 1993; Serres and Latour 1995). For instance, modern western sciences have historically focused on the mechanics of solids (Serres and Latour 1995) while non-western ontologies are more apt to emphasize processes, the interchange of substances, and the importance of ephemeralities, like smells, sounds (including speech/song), smoke, and clouds that presence the invisible/intangible (cf. Morrison 2000; Berlo 2011; 2014). In this vein, Native American cosmoscapes emphasize dynamic motion and how proper interpersonal relations emerge from fulfilling reciprocal obligations (Giles 2010; 2010b; Morrison 2000; Berlo 2011; 2014). Similarly, these non-western cosmoscapes are typically envisioned as containing multiple *axis mundi* sometimes at different scales (micro-macrocosms) that can shift, based on perspective and context (Ellen 1986; Giles 2010a).

Navajo sandpainting (*'iikááh*) ceremonies are a useful example because their transitory designs offer "momentary glimpses" into the *Dine'é* (Navajo) cosmoscape (Berlo 2011, 10). Navajo sandpaintings consist of a "multi-night ritual involving singing, praying and the use of herbal medicine, in which a person who seeks physical and/or psychological healing sits within this image" (Berlo 2014, 690). These ceremonies are performed in a medicine lodge or hogan, the traditional polygonal Navajo domicile, whose structure constitutes a model of the cosmos (Berlo 2011, 11). In turn, the sandpaintings portray narratives featuring the actions of the *Diyin Dine'é* (Gods or "holy" [non-human] persons) in specific locales at a mythopoetic time, especially how they created images from the ephemeral material of the universe, such as "unrolling a sheet of clouds and making images with rainbows and lightning" (Berlo 2014, 690–1). All these elements are intended to invite the *Diyin Dine'é* to the ceremony and induce their aid in healing (Berlo 2014, 690). It is fitting that the Navajo word for these sandpainting ceremonies is *'iikááh*, which literally means the "place where the gods (i.e., *Diyin Dine'é*) come and go" (Parezo 1983, 1). After the *'iikááh* is complete, the Navajo let the wind ritually disperse the sandpainting, while the ceremonies' accoutrements are carefully disposed of and returned to the desert (Berlo 2014, 691).

Northwest Coast potlatches incorporate several analogous principles although they are part of broader ritual regimes that serve to "finish the dead" (Seguin 1984; Kan 1989; Masco 1995). These funerary regimes highlight how material release through the consumption (i.e., transformation/transference/destruction) of various things facilitates the re-incarnation of 'intangibles' temporarily contained within material vessels. This belief partially explains why the Tlingit describe the human body as a house for the spirit and allude to how the flesh was deemed "a container or cover for some other components of the person" (Kan 1989, 49–50). It also relates to how the human body and house operated as intertwined microcosms in Northwest Coast cosmoscapes (Kan 1989). Conversely, potlatches are the culmination of Northwest Coast funerary regimes and an event where the wealth of the matrilineage is consumed by its guests to empty it of the influence of the dead (Seguin 1984). During potlatches, the hosts fed, entertained, and presented their guests with gifts at the same time they memorialized and satiated the ancestral dead/spirits. Alternately, the masks, ceremonial regalia, crests, and other accoutrements displayed during potlatches materialize individuals'/families' connections to their found ancestral (animal) spirits and "symbolize the essential consanguinity of all living beings" (Masco 1995, 67). Moreover, the completion of a potlatch allows the deceased person's heir to claim their titles, crests, prerogatives, and other possessions; an act also tied to the wellbeing of the community (cf. Seguin 1984; Kan 1989; Masco 1995).

Hopewell ritual regimes parallel these principles because they emphasize continual motion by covering burials and transitory ceremonial spaces with mounds (Giles 2010a, 2010b; Clay 2002; Henry and Miller 2020). These spaces were probably covered by mounds because they were perceived as powerful, dangerous (liminal) places, whose significance was likely influenced by their connection to funerary regimes and how they incorporated cosmological models, templates, and beliefs (cf. Brown 2004; Giles 2010a; 2010b; Carr 2022). Moreover, the ceremonial caches found in Ohio Hopewell sub-mound contexts suggest the importance Middle Woodland peoples placed on attracting the attention of significant non-human persons through ritual oblations (Morrison 2000; Giles 2010a; Giles *et al.* 2020). We interpret these ritual regimes as designed to capture the attention and sympathy of important non-human persons, in order to heal the community's grief and loss, and placate the dead/ancestors (*sensu* Bloch and Parry 1982; Metcalf and Huntington 1991; Parker Pearson 1999).

Mound 2 at the Hopewell typesite

The Hopewell typesite is located along the North Fork of Paint Creek, which is part of the Scioto River watershed in Ohio. It is one of the largest earthwork sites in Eastern North America, covering 45 ha (cf. Greber and Ruhl 1989; Pederson Weinberger 2006; Lynott 2015; Ruby 2019; Giles *et al.* 2020, 244). The site consists of four earthen enclosures, a woodhenge, and 40 documented mounds positioned on terraces above the creek, which generally date ca. 50 BC–AD 400.[1] The number of

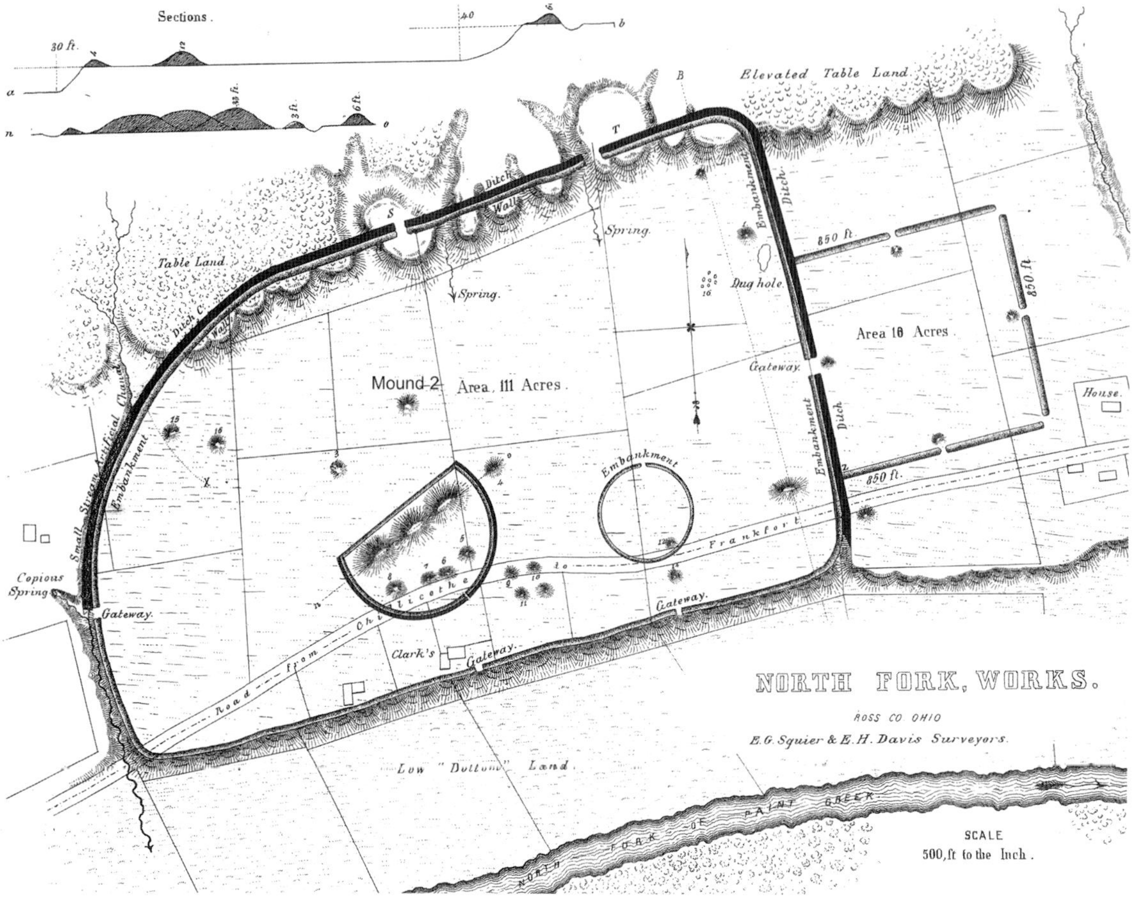

Fig. 11.1. Mound 2 on Squier and Davis's 1848 map (pl. x) of the Hopewell typesite, originally titled the "North Fork Works".

mounds, quantity and diversity of artifacts, and its sheer size make the Hopewell typesite remarkable (Seeman 1979; 2004; Greber and Ruhl 1989; Lloyd 2002; Ruby 2019; Giles *et al.* 2020, 244).

Mound 2 was positioned in the center of the large enclosure at the Hopewell site (Fig. 11.1). Henry Shetrone's excavations in the early 1920s identified two surfaces or floors under Mound 2 on which were placed large caches of blue-gray chert bifaces. The upper floor was probably extensively disturbed prior to the 1920s, so that the only feature definitively associated with it was the upper biface cache (Giles *et al.* 2020, 245). In contrast, Shetrone's excavations provided more information about the lower surface. For example, he identified post-molds on it that probably represented one or more timber structures, as well as a puddled clay basin-shaped hearth (e.g., altar/crematory), five burials, the lower cache of bifaces, and several other archaeological features (Shetrone 1926; Greber and Ruhl 1989; Giles *et al.* 2020). Spatially, the basin-shaped hearth was located on the eastern edge of the (lower) biface cache and constructed from the "typical" bright yellow puddled clay (Shetrone 1926, 22–3). Burials 1 and 2 were interred on a raised earthen platform in the southeastern corner, while Burial 3 was placed in

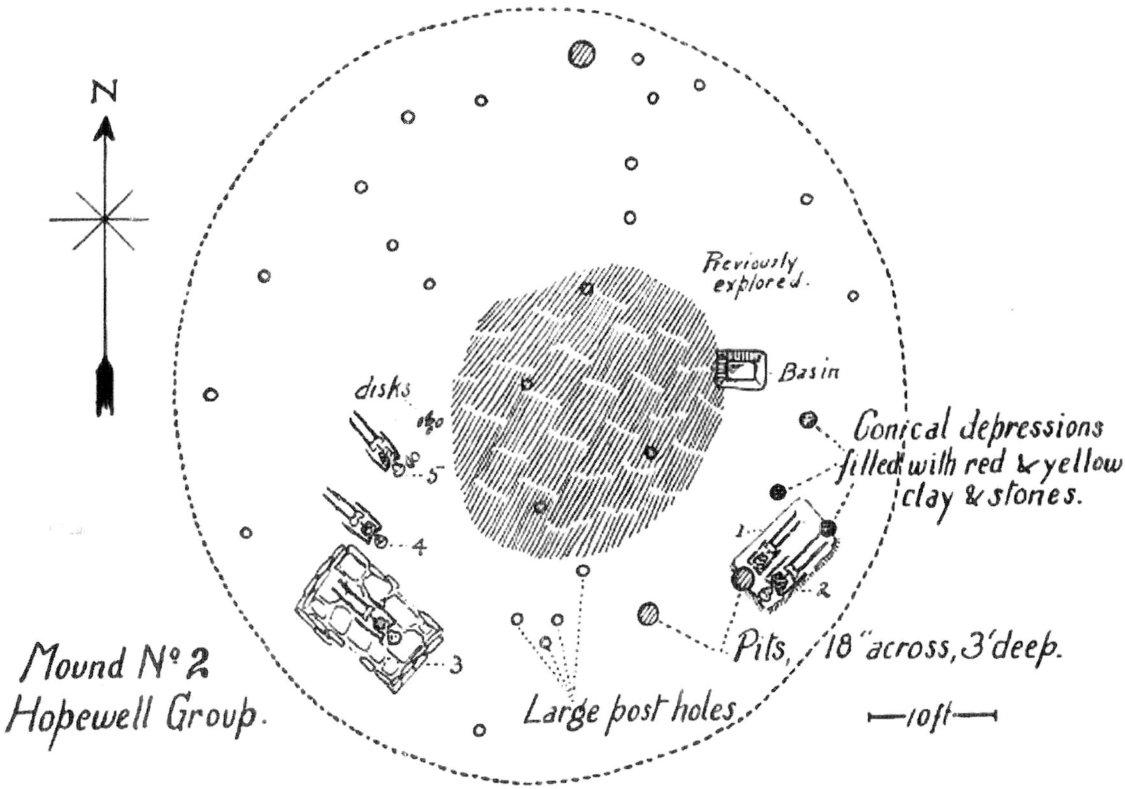

Fig. 11.2. Henry Shetrone's (1926) map of the burials and features identified under Hopewell Mound 2.

a stone-lined recessed crypt in the southwest corner. Burials 4 and 5 were placed directly on this lower floor, immediately northeast of Burial 3 (Fig. 11.2; Table 11.1). An isolated skull, wearing a copper coronal plate, was also placed next to Burial 5. Several pits and three inverted cone-shaped features filled with stones and brightly colored burned red and yellow [clay] hearth fragments were also identified on this floor (Shetrone 1926, 22).

Shetrone's (1926) plan of the lower floor below Mound 2 suggests a prepared surface with around a 17 m (57 ft) diameter (Lloyd 2002, 127). Yet it is difficult to infer the shape of the timber structure or structures it contained, as well as their relationship to the five burials, basin-shaped hearth, and other features (Giles *et al.* 2020). For instance, the building or buildings could have been either roofed or unroofed, while the unusually large and deep post-molds documented by Shetrone (1926, 27) that ranged from 15 cm to 25 cm (6–10 in) in diameter and 0.9–1.07 m (3–3½ ft) deep, might have been principally central support posts. Accordingly, some of the peripheral posts, associated with the structure/structures, might remain undocumented, based on comparable excavations of sub-mound buildings at Mound City (*sensu* Brown 2004; 2017). One way or another, the timber structure

Burial no.	*Sex est.*	*Age est.*	*Artifacts*	*Depositional context*	*Notes*
1	M	30–40	2 copper earspools (hands); copper sagittal headplate (above head)	Earthen platform (152 mm (6 in) in height) with Burial 2	Pit (0.762 m) dug above shoulders of Burial 1. pit contained Burial 1's cranium & several vertebrae
2	I/M	14–19	100 copper beads (left hand); copper celt (left foot)	Earthen platform (152 mm (6 in) in height) with Burial 1	
3	F	20–25	Conch shell (right side of head); several thousand shell beads (head, face, neck, & shoulders); copper quadriconcave plate (under left shoulder); copper quadriconcave plate (under hips); 2 copper earspools (hands); small copper celt (between feet)	Recessed stone-lined crypt (3.35 × 2.43 m) dug 0.61 m (2 ft)	
4	F	20–25	Conch shell (right side of head); shell & pearl beads (head & neck); quadriconcave plate (under base of head); 2 copper earspools (hands)	Floor NW of Burial 3 SW of Burial 5	
5	I	24–49	Conch Shell (head); shell beads (neck); quadriconcave plate (under head); 2 copper earspools (hands); mussel shell spoon (right foot); mica plate (right shoulder)	Floor NE of Burial 4	Isolated cranium with copper sagittal headplate placed 25 cm (10 in) to right of Burial 5
IC	M	35–45	Copper sagittal headplate (on isolated cranium)	10 in (25 cm) to right of Burial 5's cranium	Near SW edge of cache of blue-gray chert bifaces

Table 11.1. Burials found by Henry Shetrone (1926) on the lower floor under Hopewell Mound 2

(or structures) appears to have been dismantled before this ceremonial precinct or, at least portions of it, were covered with a "very hard black muck or gumbo soil" (Shetrone 1926). The upper floor was constructed on these soils and associated with a thin layer of coarse, whiteish limestone gravel on which the upper cache of blue-gray bifaces was placed. As noted above, this upper surface appears to have been extensively disturbed by historic agriculture and prior excavations, but it might have been covered with another layer of "very hard black muck or gumbo soil" (mound fill) and capped with two sand layers (Shetrone 1926, 20).

The blue-gray chert biface caches constitute one of Mound 2's noteworthy aspects. Unfortunately, the number of bifaces from each deposit is unknown because the upper and lower caches are not curated separately, but their combined total of over 8200 make them some of the largest Middle Woodland caches of their kind (see Giles *et al.* 2020, 256–257). The caches found on these two surfaces under Mound 2 were grouped into piles of a half dozen, creating a herringbone-like organization that could have originally resulted from stacked bags filled with bifaces (Dorsey 1898; Moorehead 1922; Shetrone 1926). Jennifer Pederson Weinberger (2006, 147) indicates that "evidence for large-scale biface production is not present at the Hopewell site" so carrying these bifaces in containers might have facilitated their movement to the Hopewell earthworks (see also Greber 1996, 162). Their non-local production is also supported by a recent reflectance spectrographic analysis of a sample of 172 bifaces which indicated that they were primarily produced from a range of St Genevieve and Upper St Louis cherts, while a minority were made from Vanport and Zaleski cherts that outcrop in Ohio (Giles *et al.* 2020, 259). As documented cross-culturally in other sacrificial regimes, these caches probably served as ritual oblations to important non-human persons intended to capture their attention and sympathy, as well as to elicit return gifts and mutual remembrance (Giles 2010a; 2010b; Giles *et al.* 2020).

The precinct under Mound 2 was therefore a sacred place, rather than profane space (*sensu* Pavel 1981, 153–4), given its ceremonial linkages and use in liminal funerary rites (Metcalf and Huntington 1991; Parker Pearson 1999). In particular, we contend that the caches of blue-gray chert bifaces were sacrificial offerings intended to invite and induce the aid of important non-human persons in ways that they could not fail to notice. Moreover, the senior author has suggested that the ceremonial structures found under Ohio Hopewell mounds were elements of a microcosmic repertoire (*sensu* Ellen 1986) that served as models of the cosmos (Giles 2010a) in a manner roughly analogous to the Navajo hogan (Berlo 2011). This lower ceremonial surface can thus be interpreted as a place that connects ontological levels. Accordingly, the spatial organization of the burials and other features on this floor were likely cosmologically charged, while the burials might have served as proxies for important non-human persons associated with mythopoetic narratives.[2]

Contextual and iconographic entry points to the Mound 2 cosmoscape

Other reasons also exist to believe that the Mound 2 burials from the Hopewell site are connected to important Middle Woodland figures/heroes and narratives, as has been argued by Knight *et al.* (2001) for later Mississippian imagery. One entry point to these associations is that the pieces of ceremonial regalia – quadriconcave plates, sagittal headplates, and earspools – interred with the Mound 2 burials (Table 11.1) are depicted on a small anthropomorphic statuette (S278) found in the famous cache of effigy platform pipes and other ritual paraphernalia in Mound City, Mound 8. The symbolic associations of the Mound 2 burials therefore appear intertwined with this anthropomorphic statuette's (S278) referent and how this character/person was perceived by Middle Woodland peoples.

This statuette (S278) portrays an older man elaborately bedecked in ceremonial regalia, whose face appears tattooed, painted, or adorned with falconoid imagery

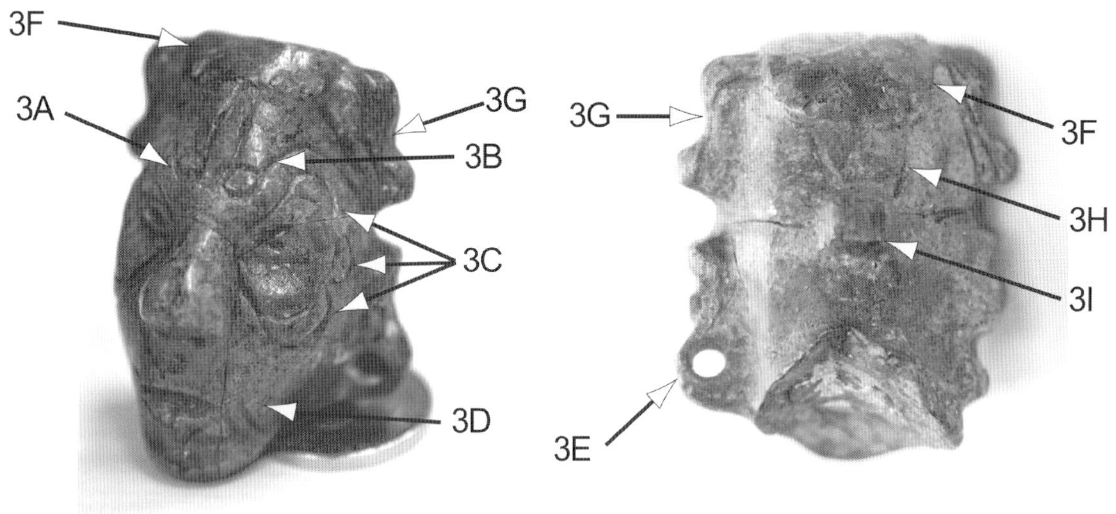

Fig. 11.3. Anthropomorphic statuette (S278), from the cache under Mound City, Mound 8, portrayed with avian (falconoid) motifs and wearing various pieces of ceremonial regalia: A) roundels (bird's secondary eyes); B) linear eyebrows (prominent falconoid supercilium); C) rounded trifurcated avian eye surrounds (wings); D) fan-shaped motif (tail feathers); E) perforation for earspools; F) sagittal headplate; G) quadriconcave plate; H) hair pulled back; I) occipital hair bun.

that parallels aspects of the Late Woodland and Mississippian Birdman theme (Giles 2010b; 2019). For instance, there are two small roundels on its forehead that probably represent the eyes of the bird (Fig. 11.3, A), while the attached linear parallel motifs likely depict the prominent supercilia commonly portrayed on the heads of Hopewellian representations of falcons (compare Fig. 11.3, B to Fig. 11.4A; Giles 2010b; 2020). It also has rounded trifurcated eye-surrounds that likely represent stylized wings (Fig. 11.3, C) and a fan-shaped design on his chin that could portray the bird's tail feathers (Fig. 11.3, D; Giles 2010b; 2019; 2020). Consequently, S278 has falcon imagery emblazoned *pars pro toto* on its visage that notably includes stylized wings depicted as rounded trifurcated eye-surrounds, which anticipate the later Late Woodland and Mississippian Birdman theme – specifically its forked eye motifs (Giles 2019).

The falconoid imagery emblazed on the visage of statuette (S278) also links certain ceremonial regalia to Middle Woodland avian iconographic themes (Giles 2010b; 2019). Accordingly, its perforated ears suggest that this man was likely portrayed wearing earspools (Fig. 11.3, E), while the rectangular cameo motif on the top of its head seems to represent a sagittal headplate (compare Fig. 11.3, F to Fig. 11.4B) and a motif towards the posterior of its head appears to portray a quadriconcave plate (compare Fig. 11., 3G to Fig. 11.4C). It also has a differentiated inverted trapezoidal area on the back of its head that connects to a raised rounded motif. This trapezoidal area appears to depict how the man's hair was pulled and secured into a hair bun or knot, as represented by a raised rounded motif (Fig. 11.3, H and I). Similar coiffures are portrayed on other Hopewellian anthropomorphs (cf. Keller and Carr 2005), but it is analogous to certain (later) Mississippian hair buns, knots, or plaits, as well (Brown 2007a; 2007b; Smith and Miller 2009).

Statuette S278 is also an example of a broader Middle Woodland corpus that

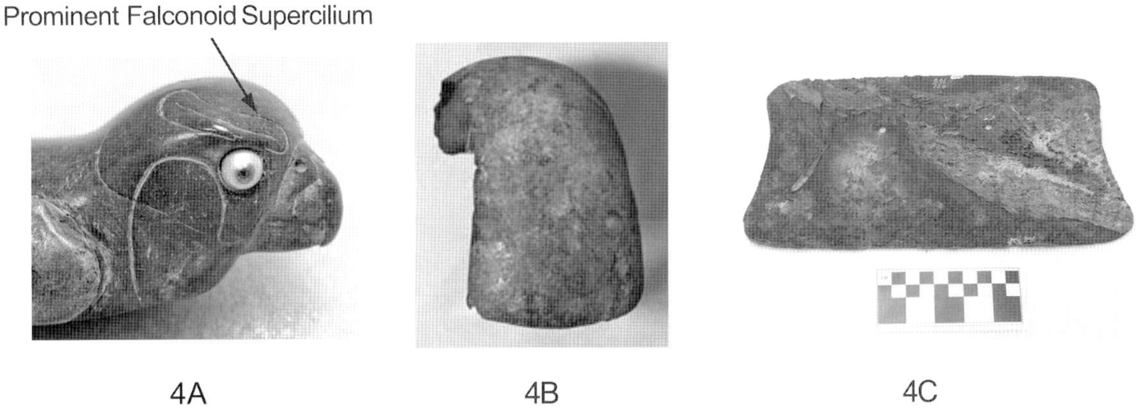

Fig. 11.4. Middle Woodland ritual objects from the Hopewell Site connected to the imagery on the anthropomorphic statuette (S278), from Mound City: A) falcon effigy boatstone (OHS 283/113) with prominent supercilium from Shetrone's Mound 17; B) Hopewell copper sagittal headplate; C) copper quadriconcave plate.

depicts certain anthropomorphic figures with avian features and motifs (Giles 2010b; 2013; 2019; 2020). For instance, this corpus includes three mica cutouts from Turner that portray an anthropomorph with a bird overlain on the face, through a visual pun (Fig. 11.5A; cf. Carr and Case 2005; Giles 2010b; 2019). This avimorph has a three-tiered head-dress and a long nose and lip that create the beak of the raptorial bird, while its prominent "eyebrows" could correspond to falconoid supercilia (cf. Carr and Case 2005; Giles 2010b; 2019). Additionally, this anthropomorphic head has a squared-off neck that could portray that it was severed or decapitated. Alternately, the Lankin A tablet seems to depict an isolated, decapitated head next to an avimorph (i.e., an avian-anthropomorph) with five fingers and five toes, as well as falconoid supercilia on its head (Fig. 11.5B; cf. Webb and Baby 1957; Giles 2020;).[3] Other artifacts might express comparable imagery, since the Vance tubular pipe seems to portray the torso and upper pelvic region of an anthropomorph with a prominent navel holding a bird over their [absent] head (Smith 1964).

Accordingly, this Middle Woodland avian-anthropomorphic imagery resonates and intersects with multiple aspects of the subsequent (Late Woodland and Mississippian) Birdman theme (Giles 2019). In this vein, James Brown's (2007a) iconographic analysis has linked certain mythic narratives to the Mississippian Birdman theme, which typically features an anthropomorph – with avian, falconoid characteristics including forked eye- (or mouth-) surrounds – who carries a decapitated head in one hand and a weapon in the other (Fig. 11.5C). Brown (2007a) links this iconographic theme to how an important archetypical hero – implicitly the Sun – loses his life and his head as the result of a game of chunkey. His sons then need to reclaim his head often from the Beneath World; a process that allows one of them (often "Morning Star") to be reborn as the Sun and take on his mantle (i.e., become the reborn Sun). The narrative therefore chronicles the cyclical death and rebirth of the Sun (Dye 2004; Brown 2007a; Brown and Dye 2007; King 2011; 2020; King and Reilly 2011). We therefore note that there are specific morphological motifs (i.e., avian eye-surrounds) that appear generally analogous to features from the subsequent (Late Woodland and Mississippian) Birdman theme, as well as specific referential

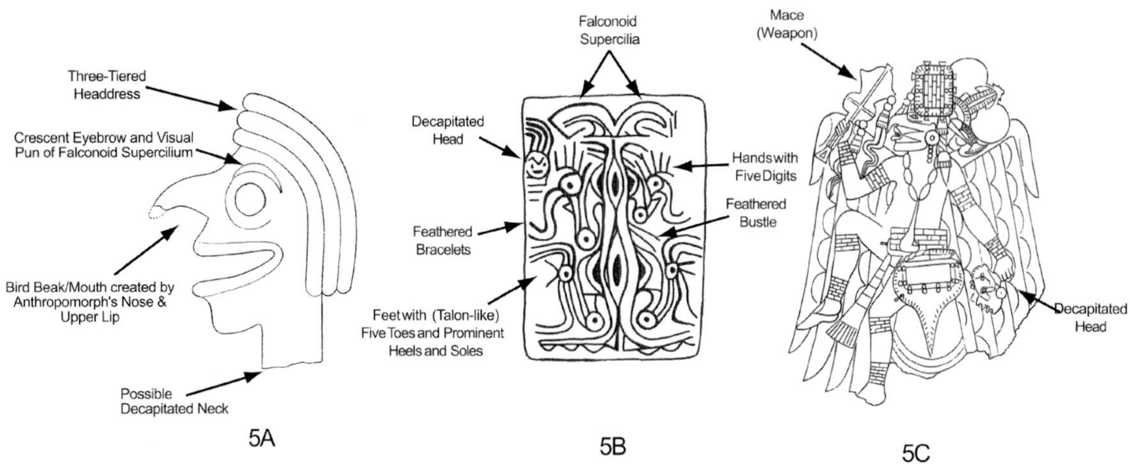

Fig. 11.5. Middle Woodland and Mississippian anthropomorphic imagery with avian characteristics and motifs; A) Drawing of the mica anthropomorphic face from cache under Turner Mound 4 from Willoughby (1916, 499, pl. 9k); B) sketch of the sandstone, Lankin A tablet (by Bretton Giles after Penney 1980, 34, fig. 12); C) Rogan copper plate from Etowah Mound C illustrating a Braden-Style Birdman with a bifurcated avian mouth surround carrying a decapitated head and a mace (drawing from Thomas 1888, 102, fig. 43, pl. 1).

content (i.e., decapitated heads). Moreover, Statuette S278 appears particularly pertinent in how it juxtaposes avian, falconoid motifs depicted *pars pro toto* on an anthropomorphic visage with the ceremonial regalia found with the burials from Mound 2 (Table 11.1).

Burials on lower floor under Mound 2

In the following sections, we provide a brief overview of the five burials interred on the lower floor under Mound 2 that discusses their age/sex estimations, depositional contexts, grave goods, mortuary furniture, and relative spatial position (Fig. 11.2).

Burials 1 and 2

Burials 1 and 2 were placed on a 6-inch (15.3 cm) high, earthen platform, located under the southeastern portion of Mound 2 (Fig. 11.2). Burial 1 was interred on the platform immediately northeast of Burial 2 and there was a pit dug just above the shoulders of this burial that contained its cranium, mandible, and several vertebrae (Table 11.1). In contrast, a curved copper sagittal headplate was found at the top of the pit (Shetrone 1926, 20–1). A copper earspool was placed in each of Burial 1's hands, like Burials 3, 4, and 5 (Table 11.1). The presence of these skeletal elements in the pit [immediately above its shoulders to the southwest] suggests extensive postmortem manipulation and symbolism. In this sense, the pit above this individual's shoulders, which extended through the earthen platform, does not have parallels to other Middle Woodland Hopewell burials, so it seems unique and particularly significant. Johnson (2002; 2019) estimated that Burial 1 was an adult male 30–40 years old at death.

Burial 2 was placed next to Burial 1 on the earthen platform, with around 100 copper beads in its left hand and a copper celt near its left foot (Fig. 11.2; Table

11.1). Johnson (2002, 224) estimates that Burial 2 was 14–19 years of age at death. Her analysis also estimates that this individual was male, although it was only based on femoral and humeral head diameters.

Burial 3

Burials 3 was placed under the southwestern portion of Mound 2 in a recessed stone-line crypt (Fig. 11.2). This burial was located to the southwest of Burials 4 and 5. All three burials appear to be closely related, based on their similar grave goods (Table 11.1). Burial 3 was interred with a conch shell cup, several thousand shell beads, two copper quadriconcave plates, a copper earspool in each hand, and a copper celt near her feet (Shetrone 1926, 23–5). Johnson (2002, 224–5) estimates that Burial 3 was a young woman, 20–25 years of age at death.

Burials 4 and 5

Burials 4 and 5 were placed directly on the lower floor under the southwestern extent of Mound 2. These burials were located to the northeast of Burial 3 and arrayed in a southwest to northeast alignment (Fig. 11.2). Burial 4 was located immediately southwest of Burial 5 with a conch shell cup, shell and pearl beads, a copper quadriconcave plate, and a copper earspool in each hand (Shetrone 1926, 25). Johnson (2002, 225–6) estimated Burial 4 to have been a young female, 20–25 years of age at death.

Burial 5 was located on the floor northeast of Burial 4 and interred with a conch shell cup, shell beads, a copper quadriconcave plate, a mussel shell spoon, a mica plate, and a copper earspool in each hand (Fig. 11.2; Table 11.1). Additionally, an isolated skull wearing a copper sagittal headplate was placed 10 in (25.4 cm) to the right of Burial 5's head, near the edge of the cache of blue-gray chert bifaces on the lower floor (Shetrone 1926, 25–7).

We consider Burial 5 to be an older adult but it is worth discussing the difficulties sexing and aging this individual. Accordingly, Shetrone (1926) estimated Burial 5 to be a very old man and noted the presence of extensive antemortem tooth loss. In contrast, Johnson (2002) estimates that Burial 5 was a female between 24 and 49 years old at death. However, the degree of antemortem tooth loss associated with this individual was pathological, which would have changed this person's food consumption. These changes undoubtedly altered this individual's mandibular and cranial shape, which complicates assessing Burial 5's sex because it was based, in part, on cranial morphology. Recent work has also suggested that it is difficult to use ectocranial suture closuring to accurately estimate the age of individuals over 50 years of age at death (Key *et al.* 1994). Given the absence of a detailed discussion of these issues (cf. Johnson 2002, 226–7), we adopt a conservative approach that estimates Burial 5 to be an indeterminate adult, who was likely quite old, given the extensive differential antemortem tooth loss. Yet it would be useful to reassess Burial 5's sex, age, and paleopathological profile in the future.[4]

The isolated skull interred with Burial 5 was estimated to be male and 35–45 years old at death (Johnson 2002; 2019). Moreover, Shetrone (1926, 27) identified cut marks on this isolated skull. This supports Johnson's (2002, 244) assessment that noted fine cut marks on this cranium's temporal and parietal bones, as well as on the right portion of its mandible. The cut marks and its depositional context support extensive postmortem manipulation and possibly its decapitated (cf. Johnson 2002; 2019; see also Shetrone 1926, 27).

Glimpses of a Middle Woodland cosmoscape

We argue that glimpses of a Middle Woodland cosmoscape can be drawn from the lower floor under Mound 2, analogous to the ephemeral images created in Navajo *'iikááh*/sandpaintings (*sensu* Berlo 2011, 2014; see also Newcomb and Reichard 1975). This Middle Woodland cosmoscape appears distinctly tiered given that the earthen platform with Burials 1 and 2 is evocative of the Above World, while the stone-lined recessed crypt with Burial 3 appears emblematic of the Beneath World. Conversely, Burials 4 and 5 were placed directly on the lower floor surface; a context that probably symbolizes the Middle World. These vertically differentiated contexts seem to correspond to the cosmologies documented for various historic Native American peoples (*sensu* Carr 2008; see also Reilly 2004; Lankford 2007a). Conversely, the extended processing of certain men's heads hints at dynamic dimensions, while linkages between the grave goods placed with these burials and regalia depicted on the Mound City, Statuette S278 suggests it was intertwined with Middle Woodland narratives.

Other aspects of the earthen platform with Burials 1 and 2 reinforce its connection to the Above World. For instance, this platform was constructed in the southeastern portion of this floor, which could be linked to the rising (or newly risen) Sun. Additionally, several conical depressions were positioned on the floor near the platform that contained fragments of dismantled ceremonial basin-shaped hearth(s) (i.e., ceremonial fires). Given the historic association between sacred fires and the Sun (Hudson 1976; 1984; Martin 2001; Koons 2016), we posit that this process of dismantling and interring pieces of broken hearth near this earthen platform expresses solar renewal or, in other words, the sun journey from birth/rebirth in the east (dawn) to its death in the west (dusk) (*sensu* Brown 2007a). Significantly, this burial group was the closest to the ceremonial basin-shaped hearth (i.e., a sacred fire) identified on this lower floor, positioned on the eastern edge of the lower cache of blue-gray bifaces (Fig. 11.2; Shetrone 1926). This mortuary context could also have masculine associations since Burial 1 and 2 were estimated to be male (Johnson 2002). Moreover, Burials 1 and 2 only have copper artifacts that appear to more closely link copper with the Above World, while Burials 3, 4, and 5 have both copper and shell artifacts with the latter symbolically associated with the Beneath World (Table 11.1). These connections could suggest that Middle Woodland peoples in southern Ohio associated men (or the masculine) with the Above World, while women (or the feminine) were more closely linked to the Beneath World.

Conversely, the placement of the head of Burial 1 in a pit associates it with a depth metaphor, which could express its loss and descent to the Beneath World. Additionally, the presence of a copper sagittal headplate at the top of the pit links Burial 1 to Mound City statuette S278, which portrays a figure wearing a sagittal headplate with falconoid imagery emblazon on his face (Giles 2019). Other Middle Woodland avian-anthropomorphic representation were also portrayed with (e.g., the Lankin Tablet) or as isolated heads (mica cutouts from Turner Mound 4) (Figs 11.4B and C). Of further note, are its parallels with how an archetypical hero – implicitly the Sun – loses his head to a Beneath World figure/character in certain Native American narratives, which Brown (2007a) links to the Late Woodland/ Mississippian Birdman theme (Fig. 11.5).

Typically, Hopewell copper sagittal headplates were worn on the heads (along the sagittal suture) of exclusively adult men (Carr 2005, 282–3), analogous to the portrayal on Mound City, statuette S278 (Fig. 11.3; Giles 2019). The shiny and reflectant qualities of this copper sagittal headplate were probably also important and it seems possible it was polished, given the striations visible on other copper plates from Hopewell Mound 25 (Seeman *et al.* 2019). Conversely, the form of the copper sagittal headplate might be an allusion to the path of the Sun across the sky dome. This linkage between the Sun's path, copper sagittal headplates, and certain men's heads could have been especially meaningful if Middle Woodland, Hopewell peoples believed that the human body (person) was a microcosm for the larger macrocosm, a common cross-cultural belief (cf. Wayman 1982; Ellen 1986; Giles 2010b; 2013 2019; 2021).

Burials 3–5 have different symbolic associations than Burials 1 and 2. For instance, they were arrayed in an arc under the southwestern portion of the floor under Mound 2, suggesting an association with the setting Sun. The southwest was also a direction often linked to the Path of Souls and the Beneath World (i.e., the Realm of the Dead) (*sensu* Lankford 2007b). This connection is reinforced by the placement of Burial 3 in a rock-lined recessed crypt emblematic of the Beneath World. The grave goods associated with Burials 3–5 seem illustrative of watery Beneath World wealth as well because they include shell and pearl beads, and conch shell cups (Table 11.1). The shell and pearl grave goods with Burials 3–5 appear particularly significant in comparison to Burials 1 and 2 which were only interred with copper artifacts (Table 11.1). These three burials might also associate the Beneath World more with femininity in the Middle Woodland cosmos because Burials 3 and 4 were women (Johnson 2002). Johnson (2002, 227) also estimated that Burial 5 was an older woman but the dental pathologies and the absence of a discussion of their impact on sex/age assessments prompts our hesitance.

Other aspects of Burials 3–5 point to narrative linkages with other ritual deposits and burial groups on the lower floor under Mound 2, as well. First, the placement of an isolated skull wearing a copper sagittal headplate to the east of Burial 5 appears connected to Burial 1 and Mound City, Statuette (S278). Extensive perimortem manipulation link Burial 1's head and the isolated cranium, placed next to Burial 5's head. Notable similarities also exist in the sex and age profile of Burial 1 and the isolated cranium (with Burial 5) that suggest their symbolic equation, since they were both men, roughly 30–45 years old at death (Table 11.1).

This seems a pivotal aspect of commonality – the loss of a mature man's head, closely associated with a copper sagittal headplate. Since statuette S278 depicts a mature male wearing a copper sagittal headplate with falconoid imagery emblazon on this face, we loosely equate these men with the Late Woodland/Mississippian Birdman that symbolically equates them with the solar cycles (dawn–birth/rebirth and dusk–death).

It is also intriguing that the isolated (possibly decapitated) head/skull of a mature adult man was placed with Burial 5 on the western edge of the cache of blue-gray chert bifaces (Fig. 11.2), since "the Pawnee imagined the Morning Star to be a warrior standing at dawn on a bed of glowing hot nodules of flint" (Hall 2012, 159–60; see also Chamberlain 1982, 57–8). Accordingly, in some mythic traditions, Morning Star was one of the sons of the Sun who reclaimed his father's head from the Beneath World and assumed his mantle/position (Brown 2007a). It is therefore possible that the isolated skull wearing a copper sagittal headplate (with Burial 5) should be envisioned as facing towards the dawn, symbolized by the puddled clay ceremonial hearth to its east (Fig. 11.2). Placing the cache directly west of the ceremonial puddled clay hearth could have similarly been visualized as heating up these blue-gray chert bifaces, which in turn symbolized different Middle Woodland communities in the Middle World. In this vein, our analysis of a sample of 172 bifaces from the caches with reflectance spectroscopy indicate that they were knapped from a variety of cherts from the St Genevieve, Upper St Louis, Vanport, and Zaleski formations (Giles *et al.* 2020). The bifaces were therefore not produced from chert that derives from one or a small number of localities, but rather resulted from the collaboration of many Middle Woodland communities from Illinois, Indiana, Ohio, Kentucky, and Tennessee. The bifaces (as gifts) might have materialized and memorialized the social bonds between various Middle Woodland communities and their relations with important other-than-human person(s).

In this context, Burial 5 was probably an important figure in this narrative and/or ceremonial event, since this individual was richly endowed with different grave goods and interred with the isolated skull wearing a copper sagittal headplate (Table 11.1). It also seems significant that Burial 5 was an older/elderly person with pathological tooth loss, physically in need of "renewal" (cf. Johnson 2002, 227; see also Shetrone 1926, 25). Yet the dead (e.g., the burials) were probably not the only actors in this ritual tableau or cosmoscape because its goal like many mortuary ceremonies was likely to enact healing and renewal (*sensu* Bloch and Parry 1982; Metcalf and Huntington 1991; Parker Pearson 1999). Another important goal could have possibly been the inheritance of different positions or ritual prerogatives; a process that is sometimes intertwined with and blessed by significant non-human persons (*sensu* Giles 2010a; 2010b).

A second connection is the placement of copper celts near the feet of Burials 2 and 3, which could suggest their analogical linkage. This analogical linkage is intriguing because Burial 2 is estimated to be a young adult male interred on the earthen platform with Burial 1, while Burial 3 is estimated to be a young female placed in the recessed crypt. This raises the question of why was it important for

Middle Woodland peoples to link these contexts? Wesley Bernardini and Chris Carr's (2005, 635–7) interpretation of Middle Woodland copper celts might offer an answer because they suggest that these objects could have been associated with the production of a "spirit canoe" that symbolized the journey to the Realm of the Dead or Beneath World. Accordingly, a journey via "spirit canoe" certainly seems appropriate if the burials below Mound 2 relate to a narrative about a descent from the Above World to the Beneath World. This journey could have been undertaken to reclaim the lost head of Burial 1, found in the pit dug above its shoulders.

A third linkage is that Burials 3, 4, and 5 were each interred with (at least) one copper quadriconcave plate; another piece of ceremonial regalia that was depicted on the Mound City statuette (S278). This connection suggests a narrative/iconographic linkage at the same time it highlights that the various pieces of regalia portrayed on Mound City statuette S278 had distinct associations. Copper quadriconcave plates appear to have a longer history than copper sagittal headplates in the Ohio Valley, since a potential example was found near the base of the Cresap Mound in West Virginia with a wooden slab dated to 2380±15 BP (ISGA-A 1832, cal BC 515–400 at 95.4% confidence) (McConaughy *et al.* 2014, 17). In comparison to copper sagittal headplates, the symbolic associations of copper quadriconcave plates seem different, as well, because these objects were placed with both male and female burials (Carr and Case 2005). Moreover, the copper quadriconcave plates, on the lower floor under Mound 2, appear more closely associated with women and contexts likely linked to the Beneath World and Middle World. For example, a copper quadriconcave plate was found under the left shoulder of Burial 3 in the stone lined recessed crypt, while a similar plate was placed under this female burial's hips (Table 11.1). Analogous copper quadriconcave plates were found under the heads of Burials 4 and 5. Given these associations, it is worth considering whether Middle Woodland narratives associated the origin of copper quadriconcave plates with a Beneath World journey or non-human personage, although this hypothesis requires a more robust analysis and considerably more evidence.

One way or another, the similar copper quadriconcave plates and sets of grave goods (e.g., conch shell cups, copper earspools, and shell beads) symbolically link Burials 3–5 (Table 11.1). These linkages and the spatial organization of these burials in a southwest to northeast array could suggest a continuous sequence of events that either began or ended with a journey to the Beneath World, as symbolized the stone lined crypt contained Burial 3. Our inclination is to see these burials as representing a narrative sequence where the Beneath World is visited in order to secure the lost head of Sun. This lost head is exemplified by 1) Burial 1's cranium, mandible and vertebrae found in the pit above his shoulders and 2) the isolated skull wearing a copper sagittal headplate interred with Burial 5 (Table 11.1; Shetrone 1926). Conversely, a journey between the Above and Beneath Worlds might be indicated by the copper celts, emblematic of a "spirit canoe" and journey (*sensu* Bernardini and Carr 2005, 635–7). Burials 4 and 5 were placed directly on the (lower) floor, which suggests (to us) a return to the Middle World. The narrative sequence could culminate with events associated with Burial 5, an older toothless individual, interred next to the isolated skull wearing a copper sagittal headplate that was located on the western edge of the (lower) cache of blue-gray chert bifaces (Fig. 11.2).

Yet considerable time separates historic Native American and Mississippian narratives from this Middle Woodland, Hopewell ceremonial context. Certain aspects of the Middle Woodland narratives that preceded historic Native American and Mississippian traditions were likely different and could reflect shifts in cultural values. For example, Middle Woodland narratives could have positioned women as playing pivotal roles in the renewal, rebirth, and continuity needed to perpetuate societies, as indicated by the prominent positions and grave goods with Burials 3, 4, and 5, based on Johnson's sex estimations (Table 11.1). Two of these three burials (i.e., Burials 3 and 4) were also women in their reproductive years, which could have been significant. In our opinion, these symbolic associations underlines women essential role in sexual (and social) reproduction, which could have been more highly valued by Middle Woodland peoples than later Mississippian groups. If women played a critical role in the narratives about [solar] death/rebirth during Middle Woodland period, then why did the ceremonial regimes of later groups remove or downplay this aspect? Perhaps, it was seen by men in certain elevated "sociopolitical" roles as making them subservient or derivative of women.

In this context, it seems significant that "chiefs" in historic Native American communities in Midwestern/Southeastern North America were often titled "Suns" (Hudson 1976). The connection between historic "chiefs" or "Suns" has not been emphasized in discussions of the Mississippian Birdman theme, but we contend it warrants further discussion and could have deep historical roots. Additionally, the alignment of certain Middle Woodland mounds, earthworks, and other features with astronomical phenomena (e.g., solstices, equinoxes, and lunar maximums) suggests that these communities attributed considerable ritual significance to them (cf. Aveni 2004; Romain 2005; 2015a; 2015b Hively and Horn 2013; 2019; Henry *et al.* 2020). The movement across the sky of celestial bodies (e.g., Sun, Moon, stars) were therefore an important dimension of Middle Woodland cosmoscapes, interwoven with their ritual practices and beliefs.

Conclusion

Glimpses of a tiered Middle Woodland cosmoscape can still be drawn the lower floor under Mound 2, while other aspects of the burials, grave goods, and ceremonial deposits on this floor could relate to a narrative about the death and rebirth of the Sun, akin to the later (Late Woodland and Mississippian) Birdman theme (Dye 2004; Brown 2007a; Brown and Dye 2007; King 2011; 2020; King and Reilly 2011). Given the cache of bifaces associated with this lower floor below Mound 2, we argue that this context was closely associated with capturing the attention and aid of important nonhuman or ancestral persons to enact healing, renewal, and overall wellbeing (Morrison 2000). Additionally, this lower floor was probably 'sacred' and assigned enhanced ontological weight (*sensu* Pavel 1981), which likely made it powerful, dangerous, and polluting. Yet these events were not forgotten by Middle Woodland peoples, although their material traces were erased from view. Instead, subsequent ceremonies built on these associations, since a second cache of blue gray bifaces were deposited on the subsequent floor. However, this upper floor was extensively disturbed prior to the 1920s, so its meaning is even more fleetingly ephemeral.

Notes

1 As Giles *et al.* (2020, 248–249) states, no absolute dates are available from Mound 2, but Ruhl's (1992) earspool seriation might clarify the site's chronology. The seriation of earspools from Mound 2 applies to its lower floor, since eight earspools were found placed in the hands of Burials 1, 3, 4, and 5 (Table 1). Ruhl's seriation indicates that Mounds 24 and 26 are older than the lower floor under Mound 2 and (Moorehead's) Mound 17. Conversely, Mound 25 has a wide temporal span encompassing these other periods. To provide a frame of reference, Mound 24 is a small mound in the main enclosure that covered at least ten burials with limited grave goods. Mound 26 was located inside the D-shaped enclosure with Mound 25 and contained numerous burials, two puddled clay hearths, and a cache (cf. Moorehead 1922; Shetrone 1926; Greber and Ruhl 1989; Lloyd 2002; Giles *et al.* 2020, 248–249).

2 Our perspective is similar to Carr's (2022) notion of Hopewell ritual dramas, although our emphasis is on how certain burials/ritual deposits can materialize collective (mythopoetic) representations.

3 The avimorph with falconoid supercilia on its head depicted on the Lankin A tablet has broader similarities to the figure represented on the Gaitskill clay tablet, as well as the avian-anthropomorphic effigy [tubular] pipe from the Adena Mound (Giles 2010b, 2020).

4 Another possibility would be for C. Johnson (2002, 2019) to discuss in more detail how the different sexing/aging attributes were assigned for Burial 5, which would lead to greater transparency.

References

Aveni, A. (2004) An assessment of studies in Hopewell astronomy. In *The Fort Ancient Earthworks: Prehistoric lifeways of the Hopewell culture in southwestern Ohio*, eds R. Connelly and B. Lepper, 243–57. Ohio Historical Society, Columbus OH.

Berlo, J. (2011) Navajo cosmoscapes – up, down, within. *American Art* 25, 10–13.

Berlo, J. (2014) Navajo sandpainting in the age of cross-cultural replication. *Art History: Journal of the Association of Art Historians* 37, 688–707.

Bernardini, W. and Carr, C. (2005) Hopewellian copper celts from Eastern North America: Their social and symbolic significance. In *Gathering Hopewell: Society, ritual, and ritual interaction*, eds C. Carr and D.T. Case, 624–47. Kluwer Academic/Plenum Publishers, New York.

Bloch, M. and Parry J. eds (1982) *Death and the Regeneration of Life*. Cambridge University Press, Cambridge.

Bold, R. (2020) Constructing cosmoscapes: Cosmological currents in conversation and contestation in contemporary Bolivia. *HAU: Journal of Ethnographic Theory* 10, 195–208.

Brown, J. (2004) Mound City and Issues in the developmental history of Hopewell Culture in the Ross County area of southern Ohio. In *Aboriginal Ritual and Economy in the Eastern Woodlands: Essays in memory of Howard Dalton Winters*, eds A.-M, Cantwell, L.A. Conrad and J.E. Reyman, 147–68. Center for American Archaeology, Kampsville IL.

Brown, J. (2007a) On the identity of the Birdman within Mississippian Period art and iconography. In *Ancient Objects and Sacred Realms: Interpretations of Mississippian iconography*, eds F.K. Reilly III and J. Garber, 56–106. University of Texas Press, Austin TX.

Brown, J. (2007b) Sequencing the Braden Style within Mississippian Period art and iconography. In *Ancient Objects and Sacred Realms: Interpretations of Mississippian iconography*, eds F.K. Reilly III and J. Garber, 213–45. University of Texas Press, Austin, TX.

Brown, J. (2017) *Mound City: The archaeology of a renown Ohio Hopewell mound center*. US Department of the Interior, National Park Service, Midwest Archeological Center OH.

Brown, J. and Dye D. (2007) Severed heads and scalplocks: Mississippian iconographic trophies. In *The Taking and Displaying of Human Body Part as Trophies by Amerindians*, eds R. Chacon and D. Dye, 278–98. Springer Press, New York.

Carr, C. (2005) The Tripartite ceremonial alliance among Scioto Hopewellian communities and the question of social ranking. In *Gathering Hopewell: Society, ritual, and ritual interaction*, eds C. Carr and D.T. Case, 258–338. Kluwer Academic/Plenum Publishers, New York.

Carr, C. (2008) Environmental setting, natural symbols, and subsistence. In *The Scioto Hopewell and their Neighbors. Biological documentation and cultural understanding*, eds D.T. Case and C. Carr, 41–100. Springer, New York.

Carr, C. (2022) *Being Scioto Hopewell Ritual Drama and Personhood in Cross-Cultural Perspective*. Springer, New York.

Carr, C. and Case, D.T. (2005) The nature of leadership in Ohio Hopewellian societies: Role segregation and the transformation from shamanism. In *Gathering Hopewell: Society, ritual, and ritual interaction*, eds C. Carr and D.T. Case, 177–237. Kluwer Academic/Plenum Publishers, New York.

Chamberlain, V.D. (1982) *When Stars Came Down to Earth: Cosmology of the Skidi Pawnee Indians of North America*. Ballena Press, Ramona CA.

Clay, R.B. (2002) Deconstructing the Woodland sequence from the heartland: A review of recent research directions in the Upper Ohio Valley. In *The Woodland Southeast*, eds D. Anderson and R. Mainfort, 162–84. University of Alabama Press, Tuscaloosa AL.

Dorsey, G. (1898) Clark's Works on the Hopewell Group, Ross County, Ohio, Part 1. Field Museum Library – Museum Archives, Chicago IL. [http://cdm17032.contentdm.oclc.org/cdm/compoundobject/collection/p17032coll2/id/155], accessed April 21, 2020

Dye, D. (2004) Art, ritual, and chiefly warfare in the Mississippian world. In *Hero, Hawk and Open Hand. American Indian art of the ancient Midwest and South*, ed R. Townsend and R. Sharp, 191–206. Yale University Press, New Haven CO.

Ellen, R. (1986) Microcosm, macrocosm and the Nuaulu house: concerning the reductionist fallacy as applied to metaphorical levels.' *Bijdragen tot de taal-, land-en volkenkunde* 142, 1–30.

Everhart, T. (2020) Scioto situations and the Steel Group monument assemblage. *Midcontinental Journal of Archaeology* 45, 269–89.

Giles, B. (2010a) Sacrificing complexity, renewal through Ohio Hopewell ritual. In *Ancient Complexities: New perspectives in pre-Columbian North America*, ed S. Alt, 128–97. University of Utah Press, Salt Lake City UT.

Giles, B. (2010b) The Ritual Mnemonics of Hopewell Symbols: An analysis of effigies and ceremonial regalia from Tremper, Mound City, and Hopewell. Unpublished Ph.D. Dissertation, State University of New York at Binghamton NY.

Giles, B. (2013) A contextual and iconographic reassessment of the headdress on Burial 11 from Hopewell Mound 25. *American Antiquity* 78, 502–19.

Giles, B. (2019) The genealogical connections between particular Hopewellian and Mississippian Avian motifs and themes. In *Encountering Hopewell in Ohio and Beyond*, eds B. Redmond, B. Ruby, and J. Burks, 231–64. University of Akron Press, Akron OH.

Giles, B. (2020) The emergence and importance of falconoid imagery during the Middle Woodland Period. In *Shamans, Priests, Practice, Belief: Archaeological examinations of religion and ritual in the Eastern Woodlands*, eds S. Carmody and C. Barrier, 75–92. University of Alabama Press, Tuscaloosa AL.

Giles, B., Rowe, B. and Parish R. (2020) An event-centered perspective on Mound 2 at the Hopewell earthworks. *Midcontinental Journal of Archaeology* 45, 243–68.

Greber, N. (1996) A commentary on the contexts and contents of large to small Ohio Hopewell deposits. In *A View from the Core: A synthesis of Ohio Hopewell archaeology*, ed. P. Pacheco, 150–73. Ohio Archaeological Council, Columbus OH.

Greber, N. and Ruhl, K. (1989) *The Hopewell Site: A contemporary analysis based on the work of Charles Willoughby.* Westview Press, Boulder CO and San Francisco CA.

Hall, R. (2012) Cores and flakes. In *The Life of Symbols*, eds M. Foster and L. Botscharow, 159–68. Routledge Press.

Hallowell, A.I. (1960) Ojibwa ontology, behavior, and world view. In *Culture in History: Essays in honor of Paul Radin,* ed S. Diamond, 19–52. Columbia University Press, New York.

Henry, E. and Miller, G.L. (2000) Toward a situational approach to understanding Middle Woodland societies in the North American midcontinent. *Midcontinental Journal of Archaeology* 45, 187–202.

Henry, E., Mickelson, A.M. and Mickelson, M.E. (2020) Documenting ceremonial situations and institutional change at Middle Woodland geometric enclosures in central Kentucky. *Midcontinental Journal of Archaeology* 45, 203–25.

Hively, R. and Horn, R. (2013) A new and extended case for lunar (and solar) astronomy at the Newark Earthworks. *Midcontinental Journal of Archaeology* 38, 83–118.

Hively, R. and Horn, R. (2019) Hopewell topography, geometry, and astronomy in the Hopewell Core. In *Encountering Hopewell in the Twenty-First Century, Ohio and Beyond*, eds B. Redmond, B. Ruby, and J. Burks, 117–53. University of Akron Press, Akron OH.

Hudson, C. (1976) *The Southeastern Indians.* University of Tennessee Press, Knoxville TN.

Hudson, C. (1984) *Elements of Southeastern Indian Religion.* Iconography of Religions, Section X: North America, Brill, Leiden.

Johnson, C. (2002) Culturally Modified Human Remains from the Hopewell Mound Group. Unpublished Ph.D. dissertation, Ohio State University, Columbus OH.

Johnson, C. (2019) More than skulls and mandibles: Culturally modified human remains from Woodland contexts in Ohio. In *Transforming the Dead: Culturally modified bone in the prehistoric Midwest*, eds E. Hargrave, S. Schermer, K. Hedman and R. Lillie, 61–78. University of Alabama Press, Tuscaloosa AL

Kan, S. (1989) *Symbolic Immortality: The Tlingit potlatch of the nineteenth century.* University of Washington Press, Seattle WA.

Keller, C. and Carr, C. (2005) Gender, roles, prestige, and ritual interaction across the Ohio, Mann, and Havana Hopewellian regions, as evidenced by ceramic figurines. In *Gathering Hopewell: Society, ritual, and ritual interaction*, eds C. Carr and D.T. Case, 428–62. Kluwer Academic/Plenum Publishers, New York.

Key, C., Aiello, L. and Molleson T. (1994) Cranial suture closure and its implications for age estimation. *International Journal of osteoarchaeology* 4, 193–207.

King, A. (2011) Iconography of the Hightower Region of eastern Tennessee and northern Georgia. In *Ancient Objects and Sacred Realms: Interpretations of Mississippian iconography,* eds F.K. Reilly III and J. Garber, 279–93. University of Texas Press, Austin TX.

King, A. (2020) The Cahokian diaspora, Etowah, and south Appalachian Mississippian. In *Cahokia in Context: Hegemony and diaspora*, eds C. McNutt and R. Parish, 352–65. University Press of Florida, Gainesville FL.

King, A. and Reilly, F.K. III (2011) Raptor imagery at Etowah: The raptor is the path to power. In *Ancient Objects and Sacred Realms: Interpretations of Mississippian iconography,* eds F.K. Reilly III and J. Garber, 313–20. University of Texas Press, Austin TX.

Knight, V.J. Jr., Brown, J. and Lankford, G. (2001) On the subject matter of Southeastern ceremonial complex art. *Southeastern Archaeology* 20, 129–41.

Koons, R. (2016) Dancing Breath: Ceremonial performance practice, environment and personhood in a Muskogee Creek Community. Unpublished Ph.D. Dissertation, UCLA – University of California, Los Angeles CA.

Lankford, G. (2007a) Some cosmological motifs in the Southeastern ceremonial complex. In *Ancient Objects and Sacred Realms*, eds F.K. Reilly and J. Garber, 8–38. University of Texas Press, Austin TX.

Lankford, G. (2007b) The "Path of Souls": Some death imagery in the Southeastern ceremonial complex. In *Ancient Objects and Sacred Realms,* eds F.K. Reilly and J. Garber, 174–212. University of Texas Press, Austin TX.

Latour, B. (1993) *We Have Never Been Modern.* Harvard University Press, Cambridge MA.

Lloyd, T. (2002) Mortuary Patterns, Social Organization, and Ideology at the Hopewell Site. Unpublished Ph.D. Dissertation, State University of New York at Albany NY.

Lynott, M. (2015) *Hopewell Ceremonial Landscapes of Ohio: More than mounds and geometric earthworks.* Oxbow Books, Oxford.

Martin, J. (2001) The Green Corn Ceremony of the Muskogees. In *Religions of the United States in Practice*, Vol. 1, ed. C. McDannell, 48–66. Princeton University Press, Princeton NJ.

Masco, J. (1995) "It is a strict law that bids us dance": Cosmologies, colonialism, death, and ritual authority in the Kwakwaka'wakw potlatch, 1849 to 1922. *Comparative Studies in Society and History* 37, 41–75.

McConaughy, M., Anderson, G. and Harding, D. (2014) A microscopic examination of materials adhering to two Early Woodland copper objects from West Virginia and Pennsylvania. *Archaeology of Eastern North America* 42, 15–24.

Metcalf, P. and Huntington, R. (1991) *Celebrations of Death: The anthropology of mortuary ritual.* Cambridge University Press, Cambridge.

Moorehead, W.K. (1922) *The Hopewell Mound Group of Ohio.* Field Museum of Natural History Publication, Chicago IL.

Morrison, K. (2000) The cosmos as intersubjective: Native American other-than-human persons. In *Indigenous Religions: A companion*, ed. G. Harvey, 23–36. Cassel, New York.

Newcomb, F.J. and Reichard, G.A. (1975) *Sandpaintings of the Navajo Shooting Chant.* Dover, New York.

Parezo, N. (1983) *Navajo Sandpainting: From religious act to commercial art.* University of Arizona Press, Tucson AZ.

Parker Pearson, M. (1999) *The Archaeology of Death and Burial.* Texas A&M University Press, College Station TX.

Pavel, T. (1981) Fiction and the ontological landscape. *Studies in 20th Century Literature* 6, 149–63.

Pederson Weinberger, J. (2006) Ohio Hopewell Earthworks: An examination of site use from non-mound space at the Hopewell Site. Unpublished Ph.D. Dissertation, Ohio State University, Columbus OH.

Penney, D. (1980) The Adena engraved tablets: A study of art prehistory. *Midcontinental Journal of Archaeology* 5, 3–38.

Reichel, E. (2012) The landscape in the cosmoscape, and sacred sites and species among the Tanimuka and Yukuna Amerindian tribes (north-west Amazon). In *Sacred Species and Sites: Advances in biocultural conservation*, eds G. Pungetti, G. Oviedo, and D. Hooke, 127–51. Cambridge University Press, Cambridge.

Reilly, F.K. III (2004) People of earth, people of sky: Visualizing the sacred in Native American art of the Mississippian Period. In *Hero, Hawk and Open Hand. American Indian art of the ancient Midwest and South*, eds R. Townsend and R. Sharp, 125–38. Yale University Press, New Haven CO.

Romain, W. (2005) Appendix 3.1, Summary report on the orientations and alignments of the Ohio Hopewell geometric enclosures. In *Gathering Hopewell: Society, ritual, and ritual interaction*, eds C. Carr and D.T. Case, 3A1–26. Kluwer Academic/Plenum Publishers, New York.

Romain, W. (2015a) Adena–Hopewell Earthworks and the Milky Way Path of Souls. In *Tracing the Relational: The archaeology of worlds, spirits, and temporalities*, eds B. Jacob Skousen and Meghan E. Buchanan, 54–82. University of Utah Press, Salt Lake City UT.

Romain, W. (2015b) *An Archaeology of the Sacred: Adena–Hopewell astronomy and landscape archaeology*. Ancient Earthworks Project, Olmsted Falls OH.

Ruby, B. (2019) Revealing ritual landscapes at the Hopewell Mound Group. In *Encountering Hopewell in Ohio and Beyond*, eds B. Redmond, Bret J. Ruby, and Jarrod Burks, 79–116. University of Akron Press, Akron OH.

Ruhl, K. (1992) Copper earspools from Ohio Hopewell sites. *Midcontinental Journal of Archaeology* 17, 46–79.

Seeman, M. (1979) *The Hopewell Interaction Sphere: The evidence of interregional trade and structural complexity*. Indiana Historical Society, Indianapolis IN.

Seeman, M. (2004) Hopewell art in Hopewell places. In *Hero, Hawk and Open Hand. American Indian art of the ancient Midwest and South,* eds R. Townsend and R. Sharp, 57–71 Yale University Press, New Haven CO.

Seeman, M., Nolan, K. and Hill, M. (2019) Copper as an essential and exotic Hopewell metal. *Journal of Archaeological Science: Reports* 24, 1095–1101.

Seguin, M. (1984) Lest there be no salmon: Symbols in traditional Tsimshian potlatch. In *The Tsimishian: Images of the past; views for the present*, ed. M. Seguin, 110–33, UBC Press, Vancouver.

Serres, M. and Latour, B. (1995) *Conversations on Science, Culture, and Time*. University of Michigan Press, Ann Abor MI.

Shetrone, H.C. (1926) Explorations of the Hopewell Group of prehistoric earthworks. *Ohio Archaeological and Historical Quarterly* 35, 1–227.

Smith, A. (1964) An Adena effigy pipe. *Ohio Archaeologist* 14, 26–7.

Smith, K. and Miller J. (2009) *Speaking with the Ancestors: Mississippian stone statuary of the Tennessee-Cumberland region*. University of Alabama Press, Tuscaloosa AL.

Squier, E.G. and Davis, E.H. (1848) *Ancient Monuments of the Mississippi Valley*. Smithsonian Books, Washington DC.

Thomas, C. (1888) *Burial Mounds of the Northern Sections of the United States*. Fifth annual report of the Bureau of Ethnology, 1883–1884, Smithsonian Institution, Washington DC.

Wayman, A. (1982) The human body as microcosm in India, Greek cosmology, and sixteenth-century Europe. *History of Religions* 22, 172–90.

Webb, W.S. and Baby, R. (1957) *The Adena People No. 2*. Ohio Historical Society, Columbus OH.

Willoughby, C. (1916) The art of the great earthwork builders of Ohio. *Annual Report of the Smithsonian Institute* 1916, 489–500. Smithsonian Institute, Washington DC.

12

Eternal performance: Mesoamerican and Mississippian tableaux in comparative perspective

David Freidel

Centering the World

When Linda Schele and I were preparing to write *Maya Cosmos* and I offered to draft a chapter on sacred space and community, what I now term landesque cosmography (Freidel, Rice, and Rich in prep.), Linda said I would have to be guided by the scholarship of her student Kent Reilly, with particular attention to his illumination of Olmec centering at La Venta and more generally in the corpus of incised celts (Reilly 1994). Indeed, Reilly's proofs regarding the layout of the four quarters and the center, the *quincunx* as Mesoamericanists term it, gave us the title and theme of Chapter 3 of our book. Reilly visualized two dimensional Olmec symbolic compositions, the great serpentine offerings at La Venta, the incised images of rulers framed by four motifs, in three dimensions, so that the four corner elements, sprouts or tree posts on the horizontal plane framed the central post, *axis mundi,* ruler, in the vertical plane (Freidel *et al.* 1993, fig. 3.7).

William Saturno (2009) and Karl Taube (Taube *et al.* 2010), applied Reilly's reasoning to their interpretation of the West Wall mural of the Pinturas Shrine at San Bartolo, Guatemala (Fig. 12.1) and demonstrated that a few centuries after the demise of La Venta the Preclassic lowland Maya were not only centering the world in the same fashion but also depicting it in two dimensions intended to be read as three, in the horizontal plane, as well as the vertical one.

The West Wall mural depicts four young lords letting blood with tree-branch spears each standing before one of four trees, each tree with a sacrificial offering on a tripod in front of it, from viewer's left a fish, a deer, and a bird. The fourth tree has a flower on the ground before it (Fig. 12.1B), possibly an allusion to a soul flower as a sacrifice as discussed below. Each tree has a Great Bird on top of it. Termed the Principal Bird Deity (Bardawil 1976), this majestic being has been associated with the Scarlet Macaw, and the Laughing Falcon, among other birds and it is a solar avatar and messenger, Mut Itzam, of the Old Man (Martin 2015) the creator Itzam (Helmke and Nielsen 2015; Bassie-Sweet and Hopkins 2021; Guernsey 2021; Neilson *et al.* 2021). The tree and the bird alighting upon it are a central theme of this essay. Following the four birds, trees, and offerings, a fifth Great Bird is descending from dark clouds, called forth by a dancing duck-billed person below. This bird comes to the center, but it is not alone: a Maize God stands before a center tree that has a realistic small bird on top. He is wielding a spear, but what he is piercing is now lost in a destroyed part of the mural. A fragment of mural from the East Wall shows a dead Great Bird on the waist belt of a young lord and another fragment shows the Great Bird with the face of the Old Man creator inside his maw. This visual tableau, the Maya equivalent of the Sistine Chapel Last Judgement in cosmic power (Karl Taube pers. comm. August 2021), is subject to ongoing interpretation, but certainly it was intended to be read in three dimensions.

Fig. 12.1. (opposite) A. Young Lords before the tripod sacrifices and the trees and birds, West Wall of the Pinturas Shrine; B. Trees and birds on the West Wall mural of the Pinturas Shrine (drawings: Heather Hurst with permission).

In his study of La Venta, among other Olmec centers, Reilly has applied this reading strategy to discern three dimensional tableaux in offerings and their spatial layout (Reilly 1994; 1996). In this essay, I will present some examples of such contextual readings thematically relating to the Great Bird and his Mississippian cognate birdmen (Brown 2021) from Early Classic settings in the lowland Maya sites of El Peru-Waka' in Peten, Yaxuna in Yucatan, and from Teotihuacan in highland Mexico as I am familiar with them and I think they bear comparative resonance with the Mississippian complex ritual deposits of Mound 72 and the Spiro Spirit Lodge, also of great interest to Kent Reilly and his colleagues (Reilly and Garber 2007; Brown *et al.* 2020; Singleton and Reilly 2020). The cultures of both Mesoamerica and North America materialized, and continue to materialize, their understandings of the cosmos guided by all-encompassing and transcendent narratives of creation and its mindful agents. In the cases at hand, the vertical nature of the cosmos was integrated by way of persons who could fly, bird beings, inviting application of Reilly's vision of the vertical dimension.

Dancing with the dead

Gillett Griffin in 1980 presided over a Princeton conference on the style and iconography of Classic Maya ceramics in which Michael Coe presented on the ideology of the Maya tomb. Subsequently published (Benson and Griffin 1988), this article was one of the first to propose what Mayanists call contextual analysis of complex ritual deposits. Coe (1988, 235) concluded "If my interpretation of the imagery on Classic Maya funerary pottery is correct they [ruling elite] like the Hero Twins, would be recycled into the heavenly world, to be worshiped by their descendants, by royal and noble lineages, and by the commoners". In 1966, Michael Coe and Elizabeth Benson had discerned that lords depicted standing with one heal raised were dancing. In 1990, Nikolai Grube (1992) provided the breakthrough decipherment of the verb to dance in Mayan glyphic *ak'ot*, and Linda Schele and I wrote about dance as cathartic performance in Maya Cosmos (Freidel *et al.* 1993). In the fall of 2007, Michelle Rich and I presented on eternal performance at the AAA Meetings (American Anthropological Association) and I identified the dance pose of Mutal King Yik'in Chan K'awiil in Tikal Burial

A
B

196. He was, in fact, dancing towards his large mosaic mirror, a scrying portal (Taube 1998).

In 2014, Andrew Scherer and his colleagues (Scherer *et al.* 2014) independently discovered the same pose in their study of individuals of more modest social status in the Classic Maya community of El Kinel in the Western Rivers region of the lowlands. They identified this as dance macabre. To anticipate comparison with Mississippian eternal performances, such as proposed by Jim Brown (2003) and Emerson and colleagues (2016) for the complex ritual deposits of Mound 72 at Cahokia, I discern in Burial 116, an adult male uniquely adorned with a multi-strand shell necklace and conch shell pendant not a person "thrown down or not completely dead" as bioarchaeologist Jeffrey Rose (1999, 64) is cited to have said (Emerson *et al.* 2016, 15), but rather a dancer in the pose of a chunky playing birdman descending from the heavens (Brown 2003, fig. 4). In this brief hopscotch, I intend to illustrate that Maya archaeology has moved decisively into the age of contextual, configurational analysis of mortuary settings. Scherer (2015) has published a monograph on rituals of body and soul, Vera Tiesler and Andrea Cucina (2006) have published an edited volume on King K'inich Janaab Pakal of Palenque practicing what Vera's European colleagues call archaeothanatology, and I have published another book with her, Cucina and Travis Stanton on burials at Yaxuna in Yucatan (Tiesler *et al.* 2017). James Fitzsimmons (2009) has published on the subject placing royal burials at Piedras Negras into a broader ideological context.

In his seminal definitional discussion of contextual analysis of eternal performance in archaeologically documented complex ritual deposits, James Brown (2003) described the great narrative creation stories manifest in the foundational Mound 72 interments at Cahokia. He and his colleagues (Brown *et al.* 2020) are now building on enduring iconographic patterns and ethnographic analogies/homologies (Knight 2013), contextual analyses of mortuary tableaux to show that at least in the most complex primary ritual deposits, like in the Spiro Spirit Lodge, one can discern eternal performance. I will propose at the end of this paper that this tableau at the western edge of the Mississippian world is linked in memory and intention, through heirloom artifacts, newly made artifacts, and their arrangements, to the Mound 72 tableau (Brown 2003) that helped found Cahokia as the sacred center of that world (Kelly and Brown 2020, 20–3). Such long-distance understandings of worlding are manifest in the tableaux I review at the lowland Maya cities of El Peru-Waka' in Peten, Guatemala, Yaxuna in Yucatan, and the highland Mexican metropolis of Teotihuacan.

Breath cups, crocodile trees, and bird mirrors

Most Maya complex ritual deposits are tombs focused on a deceased individual, although some are tableaux that include multiple interments. Maya royal tombs are generally masonry chambers with corbel-vaulted roofs set deeply within construction and sometimes into bedrock. There are occasional variants where tombs are essentially artificial caves cut into bedrock but these exceptions prove the rule. The rule is that tombs are like masonry palace and temple rooms, generally smaller, but often furnished with raised bench areas like such rooms. If there is a bench or throne dais in the chamber the principal individual is arranged on it. Words for tombs include *muk*, burial, and *naah*, house, but there are also more metaphorical allusions. *Chan Ch'een*, sky cave, is a trope for city center and could well reference both the rooms perched on top of high pyramids and tombs within these *witz*, which are human-made mountains.

White flower/seed container is another metaphor for tomb (Freidel and Guenter 2006). The as yet undeciphered logograph for container in this case is usually a lidded bowl or container but can be an open offering vessel. The white flower in question, *sak nikte'*, is usually identified as a species of *Plumeria*; the sweet fragrance of this five-petaled flower is notable and pervasive in the evening and likely connotes a sweet living breath. The usual way of writing *sak nikte'* in this trope has no literal flower depiction. White flower here actually refers to a kind of soul, one of several that Maya people, ancient and modern, recognize (Freidel *et al.* 1993) and scribes could write delicately of the death of a ruler by saying his white soul flower had faded, that is to say, his sweet breath had stopped (Taube 2004). This common container statement no doubt segues to the larger masonry corbel-vaulted container of his earthly remains.

The white flower container in question could take many forms as an artifact. The lidded ceramic drinking cup was perhaps the most common form, derived from more elaborate slab-footed tripod lidded cups fashionable in the 4th and 5th centuries during the Entrada and New Order era of the Teotihuacan lord Sihyaj K'ahk' (Freidel *et al.* 2007). One documented white flower container is a jade flower ear flare dating from this New Order era with the lidded bowl and open bowl glyphs inscribed on it (Adams 1999, 94), which can be glossed as the white flower container of the vassal king of the supreme warrior of the west Spearthrower Owl.

The lidded cup was elevated to masterwork in the Late Classic in the form of a wooden cup encrusted with jade mosaic with a portrait knob on the lid. Such cups were made for Tikal King Jasaw Chan K'awiil and his son Yik'in Chan K'awiil. The one in Burial 116 has a lid inscribed with a text identifying the cup as containing chocolate of the supreme warrior, presumably King Jasaw Chan K'awiil. The other was in the tomb of his son and has a personified flower stamen emerging from the cup and a "white" glyph as a pectoral (Freidel and Guenter 2006). In the case of the lidded drinking cup form, it is likely that the flowery soul was the sweet breath of the living king that regularly entered the cup when he drank from it (see Houston *et al.* 2006 for flowery breath). These special drinking cups were a variation on the festive ceramic drinking cups that Classic Maya famously used, particularly for chocolate beverage, and subsequently placed in burials. A portrait cup was made for Yuknoom Ch'een II, Kaanul king of the 7th century. He was at the height of his power in 672 when this cup was dedicated to one of his wives and to him (Prager 2004, 36). This cup was likely used as a container of breath and the power of speech, on the occasion of the calendar jubilee while the queen and king were living.

Many more modest examples of such lidded ceramic drinking cups with the head of the resurrected maize god, the god of royal spirit k'awiil, or the god huunal, literally paper of the royal crown (Freidel *et al.* 1993; Stuart 2012), can be found in the corpus of looted Maya art, no doubt taken from elite burials (Freidel and Guenter 2006). So, a white soul flower/seed container could be a tomb, the place where such soul containers were arranged. It could perhaps also be the cup container itself for the flowery breath of the living person, now deceased. In light of this proposed Maya trope of spirit breath going into drinking cups, it might be worth contemplating the assembly of Mississippian incised ritual shell drinking cups in the Spiro Spirit Lodge (Brown *et al.* 2020) as containers of the breath of the sages singing the stories incised on them, and perhaps also as a gathering of witnessing souls.

Underscoring the contextual significance of the drinking cups as soul receptacles in the Maya case, Juan Carlos Melendez discovered such an aggregation of four white soul flower cups in the royal tomb of a 6th century king at El Peru-Waka', Burial 37 (Fig. 12.1; see Chapter 6; Melendez 2019). These black burnished cups were arranged across the chest of the deceased, forming the crossbar of a cruciform World Tree and also outlines a sacred bundle of ancestral relics of the kind that Maya rulers display in stela portraiture – called the ceremonial bar. Generally, gods, ancestors, and ancestral bones manifest from such ceremonial bundles as depicted in carved stela portraits. The cups in this case had mismatched knob lids, from different sets. The cups might represent several different heirloomed souls. Polished red Spondylus shells, symbols of the womb of rebirth, defined the upright in this World Tree configuration.

A plate at the ruler's feet depicts the "precious pool maize plant" (Stuart 2006). That basal being, dubbed the "Waterlily Monster," is an upturned face on a horizontal line and it signals that the king should be read in the vertical dimension, standing as the cruciform World Tree maize god. The preserved three jade diadems of the king's crown on the traces of his skull are centered on one diadem depicting the maize god emerging from the crocodile tree, the ancient symbol of the royal *axis mundi* shown on the incised Olmec celt that Reilly used to show the vertical dimension. A pendant on the chest depicts the head of the cosmic crocodile face down, underscoring the king as emerging from the crocodile tree.

The Burial 37 ruler, King Chak Tok Ich'aak of Waka (Chapter 6; Melendez 2019), was a mirror conjuror and oracle as depicted on El Peru-Waka' Stela 44 (Kelly 2020; Navarro-Farr *et al.* 2021; Kelly and Freidel in prep.). In that portrait, he displays feather-tasseled mirrors, usually displayed on the back of the Great Bird, emerging from his bundle. In his tomb, his iron ore mosaic mirror, originally dark golden yellow, is above his head in a scatter of red Spondylus and green jade casting tokens. I suggest that this mirror of omens symbolizes the Great Bird (Nielsen *et al.* 2021, 304), whose back mirror and colorful feathers adorn the royal headdress – a Great Bird head-dress was worn by this king's predecessor on El Peru-Waka' Stela 9. In the Burial 37 tableau, I suggest that the Great Bird descends to the crocodile tree, a royal trope depicted on the Preclassic stelae of Izapa in Chiapas, Mexico (Guernsey 2020). In a Late Classic representation, the Great Bird also perches on the cruciform maize god plant on the Panel of the Foliated Cross at Palenque (Schele and Freidel 1990, fig. 6.12). In Burial 37, the postulated Great Bird is accompanied by a small white stone cup, probably a soul flower cup, and a mosaic jade mask, scrying instrument and insignia of the king's loyalty to the great power of his age, and the home of the jade craftsmen, Kaanul (Chapter 6; Melendez 2019).

Performing in the portals

As implied above, royal tombs were not resting places but places of active agency within liminal space like Mound 72 at Cahokia (Brown 2003) and the Spiro Spirit Lodge (Brown *et al.* 2020). Metaphors like *pib naah*, sweat lodge (Houston 1996), literally oven house, referenced interior chambers and subterranean chambers that were tomb-like and they were transformative, between the worlds of the living and the worlds of the gods and ancestors. The royal tombs archaeologists have discovered at El Peru-Waka' are all actively being studied from the vantage of the performances they convey. In general, Maya royal tombs can be studied in this fashion. Linda Schele and Peter Mathews (1998) have studied the famous tomb of Pakal of Palenque this way for example.

Vera Tiesler, who also studied the tomb of Pakal (Tiesler and Cucina 2006), along with Travis Stanton, invited me to participate in a monograph on the archaeothanatology of Yaxuna (Tiesler *et al.* 2017). I was tasked with first draft on the royal tombs, and I drew very heavily on the extraordinarily fine-grained bioarchaeological forensic and contextual analyses of my collaborators. The Selz Foundation Yaxuna Project (Stanton *et al.* 2010) discovered two royal tombs in the north acropolis of the site, Burials 23 and 24 (Suhler 1996; Suhler and Freidel 1998). Upon reflection, I have come to discern that Burial 24 is actually a Teotihuacan style burial/offering (Sugiyama 2014), rather than a royal tomb.

Burial 23 dates to around AD 400 and is an interment of a stranger king from south of Yaxuna (Tiesler *et al.* 2017, 190), probably from the Kaanul heartland in southeastern Quintana Roo. He was buried in majesty alone and bundled in a walled-off section of a vaulted subterranean corridor inside pyramid 6F-3. When Charles Suhler and I entered the tomb chamber it had many large rough stones in it. The tomb had been re-entered and those ritualists had created a tableau overlaying the original one created by the mourners. The original tableau included the king with his hands over his groin grasping a small bag of powerful jewels. These included three large jade beads, representing the hearth stones of creation, a jade profile of *Itz'at*, the word for sage, and a Spondylus pectoral depicting the young maize god. This was clearly a rebirth/resurrection tableau. The overlay tableau had construction fill rocks arranged as a clefted hill, leaving the bundle of the king exposed. It also had a small fire lit on a large water jar sherd on the southeast side of this effigy hill. Finally, it included on the southwest a set of divining tokens, small shells, a giant deer cowrie amulet, three manatee bones carved with knots and blades, one with a ceramic binder for this sacrificial tripod, a greenstone royal diadem jewel, and the snapped ceramic head from a white soul flower cup lid.

Fig. 12.2. Broken ceramic lid knob bearded head from a white soul flower cup lid placed in (royal tomb) Burial 23 in the north acropolis of Yaxuna.

This unique lid knob depicts a slack jawed severed head (Fig. 12.2). The face has a beard. The half-closed eyes are affirmation of this and the lolling tongue is clearly pierced, evidence of autosacrifice before death. The image also has a protruding snout and is adorned with a diadem with three beaded tassels. Previously I have identified the image as Akan (Tiesler *et al.* 2017, 194), a dangerous deity sometimes depicted cutting his own head off. However, Helmke and Nielsen (2015; Nielsen *et al.* 2021) have convinced me that this is the sacrificed Great Bird. They identify the descent and defeat of the Great Bird by heroes with blowguns as the means to royal access to his tree, an *axis mundi* source of wealth and power for an acceding ruler. In studying the iconography of the Great Bird in murals in the Tetitla complex at Teotihuacan and in Early Classic ceramic depictions, they have demonstrated that the bird is beheaded (Helmke and Nielsen 2015, fig. 7), and its head is displayed on an offering tripod such as was depicted in the Pinturas shrine and placed in the tableau in Burial 23 next to this artifact (Nielsen *et al.* 2021, fig. 12.8b). The severed head depicted on the Tetitla mural is nearly identical to the ceramic head placed in Burial 23 by Teotihuacan affiliated conquerors of Yaxuna (Tiesler *et al.* 2017). The Great Bird often wears the tasseled diadem found on this head. Finally, there is a flat long bone segment incised with a pictographic text that has at the top a foliated ajaw, now read by David Stuart (2012) as paper, as in the royal crown, followed by another ajaw glyph, followed by a profile skeletal raptor, possibly the Teotihuacan royal owl, followed by a segmented crown, called the *ko'haw*, Teotihuacan introduction into Maya country, followed by a hand with an axe. This is apparently a Teotihuacan inspired inscription (Tiesler *et al.* 2017, fig. 7.4).

Returning to Reilly's visual strategy of perceiving the third, vertical, dimension, the king in Burial 23 was positioned with his head facing west, normally associated with the descent of the Sun. But the king had painted plates at his head and feet, depicting him self-administering enemas, sprouting feathers, and flying. The celestial reference of these images is underscored by the conflation of his enemas with scorpion tails. The scorpion is associated with star patterns. This was likely part of the original tableau, for a set of special vessels, gutter-spouted warming cups, lidded containers, probably used for preparing enema potions, was concentrated in the northwestern corner of the tomb chamber. So, the king was conceived as flying west. This actually makes sense because he was embodying, in his original bundling and with ornate sprocketed Spondylus ear flares, the rising Sun of the east that brings the rains of summer, termed GI in Maya studies (Stuart 2012). That god is embodied by a cruciform tree on the Panel of the Cross at Palenque and has the Great Bird perched on top of it. The tripod overlay tableau with its sacrificed Great Bird severed head was placed next to the bundled king in his guise as the *axis mundi*. It links Burial 23 and its king to Burial 24, also discovered in 1993 in Structure 6F-4, the pyramid adjacent to Structure 6F-3.

Yaxuna Burial 24 is a complex burial/offering featuring 11 sacrificed individuals (Colour Pl. 12) (Suhler 1996; Stanton *et al.* 2010; Tiesler *et al.* 2017). The tomb, dating some years after Burial 23 in the early 5th century, contains Teotihuacan style ceramics and, like the burial offerings found at Teotihuacan (Sugiyama and Lopez-Lujan 2007), it is a tableau combining sacrifices with elaborate offerings. The bodies are arranged with women and children at the north end and a partially burnt bundled king at the south end. A bundled queen placed in the central-western side had a Teotihuacan style ceramic effigy of a pubescent female we identify as a moon goddess and a reference to the water (moon) goddess at Teotihuacan (Tiesler *et al.* 2017, 213). This masterwork young woman has the stepped mountain motif of Teotihuacan painted across her face and framing her mouth, source of prophecy of the speaking mountain (Helmke and Nielsen 2014). I identify this sacrificial tableau of people, with a broad northern base of children and women, the bundled queen in the middle, and a southern apex of the king's bundle, as an effigy mountain analogous to mountains composed of people in burial/offerings at Teotihuacan (Freidel *et al.* in prep). The bundled queen wore a shell and jade crown, linking her to the king and making of this mountain stack a female/male bundling. Next to the burnt shell segments and quetzal jade diadem of the king's crown adjacent to his partially cremated remains was a polychrome painted plate with the head of the king placed in it along with a bone stylus of the kind I believe was used for writing on waxed tablet surfaces (Freidel *et al.* 2016). The surface of the plate depicts a Scarlet Macaw impersonator. The Scarlet Macaw is an important avian source of the Great Bird, both in the Maya lowlands and in the art of Teotihuacan (there is a Sun Eagle person in the San Bartolo Murals (Zorich 2021), the falcon and owl are also possible sources). The bird man carries a turtle carapace drum, such as played by the maize god on the West Wall of the Pinturas Shrine at San Bartolo. We postulate that this is the Teotihuacan affiliated conqueror of Yaxuna. The bird man wears triple tails, an insignia of Teotihuacan warriors. So, the Great Bird in this tableau is not the sacrifice as in the overlay tableau of Burial 23, but the embodiment of resurrected rulership as outlined by Helmke and Nielsen (2015) in the cycle of defeat, sacrifice, and resurrection of the Great Bird as a royal crown at Teotihuacan. The conqueror placed a bundle of royal jewels in a jar in the floor of the ruined shrine at the summit of Str. 6F-4. In that bundle, he gathered the jade necklace beads, the ear and hair flares of jade and Spondylus, and the royal diadem jewels of the defeated king – including

Preclassic heirlooms – and placed on top of them all a jade owl diadem jewel with a mirror surface carved on the back of it, insignia of royal power at Teotihuacan (Headrick 2007). He symbolically sacrificed this bundle with a black andesite axe head carved into the figure of a deity. He chopped the axe into the mouth of the jar, breaking the rim, and left it there.

Burial 24 was not a typical Maya royal tomb of the Early Classic; it was a Teotihuacan style burial/offering tableau as seen in the dedicatory deposits of the Moon Pyramid at Teotihuacan discussed below (Sugiyama 2005; Sugiyama and Lopez-Lujan 2007). In the Entrada era following the rise of Teotihuacano Lord Sihyaj K'ahk' as conqueror of Tikal in AD 378, burial/offerings that combine royal interment in majesty with sacrificial tableaux occur in the Maya lowlands, Burial 10, the tomb of Yax Nuun Ahiin, the first explicitly Teotihuacan affiliated king of Tikal, being the exemplary case in point (Coe 1990). But Yaxuna Burial 24 is purely sacrificial, even as it includes sacrificed royals. I now turn to a brief consideration of two of the famous burial/offerings of Teotihuacan, Burials 2 and 6 of the Moon Pyramid, to show how Reilly's three dimensions work in that setting.

Reading burial/offerings at Teotihuacan

Tunneling into the Pyramid of the Moon, Saburo Sugiyama and his Mexican colleagues (Sugiyama and Cabreras Castro 2007; Sugiyama and Lopez-Lujan 2007) discovered uniquely complex ritual deposits interred as dedications in the sequent phases of expansion of this axial and anchoring pyramid. These date to the Early Classic period, at least a century before the Yaxuna burials. The Pyramid of the Moon is an effigy of Cerro Gordo, a great extinct volcano with a clearly clefted summit and field-nourishing springs as its base. The Pyramid of the Moon anchors the north–south axis of the city that extends northward on the Street of the Dead (Freidel *et al.* in prep.). Saburo and Nawa Sugiyama now identify the Pyramid of the Moon with the feminine divine, the Moon, the direction down, and water (N. Sugiyama 2014; S. Sugiyama 2017). They identify the Pyramid of the Sun with the male divine, the direction up, and fire. Clearly these archaeologists embrace the vertical third dimension as laid out in two dimensions (Freidel *et al.* in prep.).

Teotihuacan, while contemporary with Classic Maya civilization, is without written history. There are symbols that have been identified as mnemonic referents to words or ideas but they are not found used in actual inscriptions and they remain subject to iconographic rather than epigraphic interpretation. So, the iconography of its elaborate murals and the contextual analyses of ritual deposits are subject to ongoing interpretations. Suffice it to say that current consensus identifies a major goddess of the city associated with the Moon Pyramid and Cerro Gordo, currently called the water goddess (Robb 2017). Within the Pyramid of the Moon, the chambers termed Burials and more currently Burial/Offerings (there are other complex deposits termed offerings) are decisively not royal tombs but rather register cosmology in which royalty is alluded to tangentially and gods and divine animal counterparts responsible for sovereign power of the polity (registered in sacrifice) are foregrounded (Sugiyama and Lopez-Lujan 2007). They are dated at

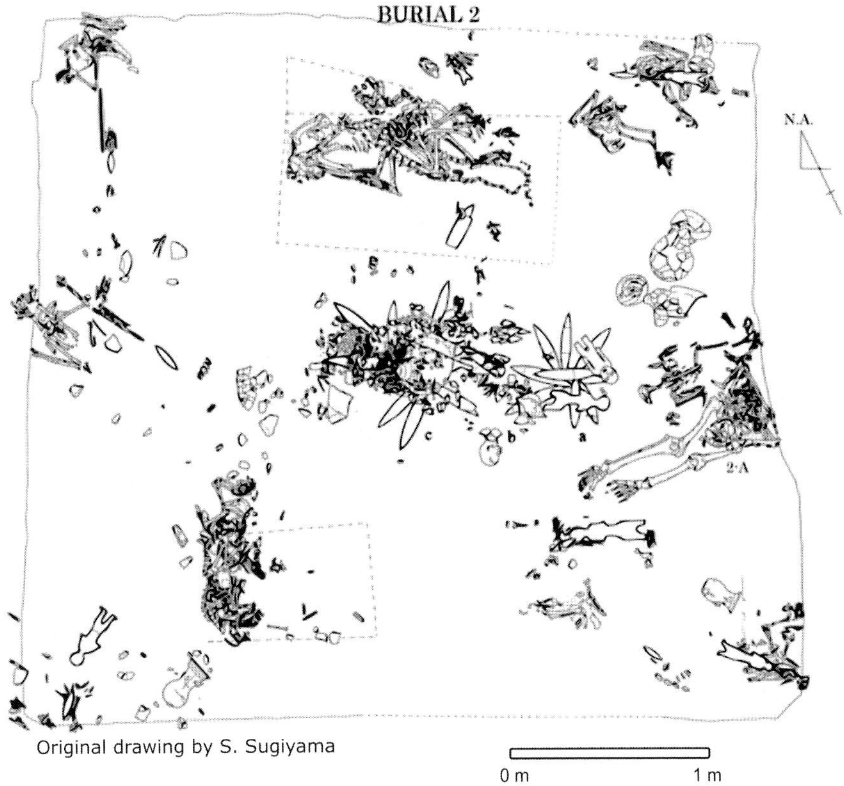

Fig. 12.3. Arranged burials and ritual deposits found in Burial 2, a complex horizontal tableaux, in the Pyramid of the Moon at Teotihuacan.

AD 250 (N. Sugiyama 2014; S. Sugiyama 2017), although the civic plan of the center was formalized by the end of the 3rd century (Sugiyama and Sugiyama 2021). I agree with Saburo and Nawa Sugiyama (Freidel *et al.* in prep.; N. Sugiyama 2014; S. Sugiyama 2017), that these Burials reference powerful animal incarnations of gods, felines, raptors, canids, and snakes, and the great water goddess associated with the Moon (Lopéz-Luján 2017). For purposes of this comparative essay, I will briefly and selectively interpret two of these complex horizontal tableaux in phase 4 of the pyramid, its affirmation as the foundation of the civic plan, Burial 2, at the base of the pyramid, and Burial 6 in its core, as they can be read with the vertical dimension and allude to birds, mirrors, the *axis mundi*, crocodiles, and male and female principals.

Burial 2 (Fig. 12.3) has many significant patterns but one is the quincuncial arrangement of black burnished water jars depicting the Storm God, clearly a declaration of the pyramid and its mountain as sources of summer rain as well as spring water (Sugiyama and Lopez-Lujan 2007). Along with the water jar, the center is marked by a large iron ore mosaic mirror, a portal (Taube 1992), here framed by nine large bifacial knives, stone feathers like the projectile points ornamenting the wings of the Great Bird in the San Bartolo mural depictions, among others (Taube *et al.* 2010, 31–2; Helmke and Nielsen 2015, 26). Recall that the bird is messenger of the creator and mirrors are the portals of the messages (Healey and Blainey 2007). In the vertical dimension, this is the Great Bird of prophecy as the zenith Sun. The number nine is half the number of the 20-day months in the approximate solar year of Mesoamerica and there is a second nimbus of nine knives directly east of this central one, so these are to be read together. The mirror has at its center, placed upright on the vertical axis, a large greenstone figure of a young female goddess (Sugiyama and Lopez-Lujan 2007) emerging from the portal. The goddess has pyrite mirror eyes and a stepped mountain crown: she is both the embodiment of the mirror portal and of the mountain; rising as the female aspect of the creator.

A golden eagle was placed next to the emerging goddess, a personification I suggest of the Great Bird represented by the knife wing feathers and mirror body, at the apex of a concentric frame of other birds on the edges of the offering. As Helmke and Nielsen (2015, fig. 5b) observe, a mural depiction of the Great Bird shows it to have a human face with the mouth framed by the stepped mountain like the goddess figure in Yaxuna Burial 24. It seems possible that this mural in room 15 of Zona 5A depicts the face of the goddess as she embodies the Great Bird, the source of wealth and power in the analyses of Helmke and Nielsen. The raptor bird head-dress of this Great Bird person is like that worn as a crown by the goddess in the Tepantitla Mural. The base of the vertical arrangement in Burial 2, on the northern side, had a stack of two cages holding live pumas. These represented the animal gods who rule in this water mountain (Sugiyama 2014) and were allowed to expire through asphyxiation so that their soul force would join the vital nature of the mountain.

A reading of the Burial 2 tableau east to west, from dawn to zenith of the Sun, to dusk, starts on the eastern side of the burial with a mature (ca. 50 years) foreign man adorned with ornaments and with his hands bound behind him. Very likely he also died of asphyxiation. Seated, he faces west towards a path formed by birds, golden eagle, falcon, owl (Sugiyama 2014), punctuated first by a nimbus of nine black knives framing a greenstone figure that is probably male, lacking breasts or vulva, and perhaps a deity like the female. This figure would seem to pair with the female to the west in the center forming together the solar year of 18 months. The foreign and evidently distinguished sacrificed man is the source of the path on which these birds and deities manifest. I would suggest that he is a mirror conjuror like the king of El Peru-Waka' discussed above and perhaps a royal captive. Burial 5 in the Moon Pyramid (Sugiyama and Lopez-Lujan 2007, fig. 8) had three seated individuals arranged around the seated greenstone figurine of a deity or elite personage. These seated sacrifices had royal insignia jewels of Maya style and their bone chemistry shows that they were from the Maya highlands. Burial 2 manifests the themes of *axis mundi*, birds of prophecy, wealth and power, the female and male principals of creation.

Burial 6 (Fig. 12.4), three-quarters of the way up inside of the fourth construction of the Moon Pyramid, is another very complex tableau and I will focus on a few select features of it relevant to the themes of this essay. The northern side of the tableau features ten headless sacrificed males. These form a rough triangle with its base on the north side, and I read this in the vertical dimension as an effigy mountain (Freidel *et al.* in prep.) on the premise that south is up, and north is down in the Teotihuacan cosmographic scheme (N. Sugiyama 2014; S. Sugiyama 2017). On the summit of this mountain of people there is another very large iron ore mosaic mirror. In this instance, the framing nimbus is composed of nine pairs of flaked bifaces – nine black obsidian undulating feathered serpents, and nine red obsidian flame/feathers – forming the 18 symbolic periods of the solar year. The red undulating knives that I identify as flame-feathers relate to many depictions of such objects on top of cropped feather-cartouched mirrors on tops of standards carried by high elite, possibly rulers, in Teotihuacan murals (Headrick 2003; Robb 2017). If I am right in this identification, then the red-feathered mirror in Burial 6 is perhaps symbolic of the Great Bird in its Scarlet Macaw aspect. A greenstone mosaic figure was on top of this mirror, mouth wide open and eyes staring, apparently originally standing like the goddess figure in Burial 2 (Sugiyama and Lopez-Lujan 2007, 143). This unique figure has no clear indications of gender, but I believe it depicts the same great goddess, but here as a version of the crocodile world tree (Freidel *et al.* in prep.). The head of this crocodile being, with protruding fanged maw, is likely depicted in the mosaic crown carried on the tail of the Feathered Serpent on the preserved western façade of the Feathered Serpent Pyramid (Sugiyama 2005). The composite image of the goddess on the Tepantitla mural includes a vertical stack of powerful elements, including a green faceted section of the upper face that is this crocodile aspect (Freidel *et al.* in prep.). Another reason to think this is the goddess is that the figure is flanked by two sacrificed males who are not decapitated and appear to be arranged as attendants, like the two attendants flanking the Tepantitla mural depiction of the goddess. While there is no comparable male figure as in Burial 2, this mosaic figure was accompanied by a large flaked black obsidian figure that might have served to convey duality. Finally, Burial 6 contained a total of 18 golden eagles, nine likely asphyxiated and nine from curated bird remains (Sugiyama 2014).

There are other themes in the Burials of Teotihuacan, and in the extraordinary offerings in the Sun Pyramid, the Feathered Serpent Pyramid, and elsewhere in the city, but the ones discussed here affirm what Saburo and Nawa Sugiyama and their colleagues have shown, which is that these tableaux are understandable and interpretable within the context of grand narratives of cosmology, in many respects reflective of pan-Mesoamerican world views. In his seminal discussion of the theory and method of analyzing tableaux in Mound 72 at Cahokia (Brown 2003) and in the Spirit Lodge of Spiro (Brown *et al.* 2020), James Brown and his many colleagues, including John Kelly (2003), Carol Diaz-Granados and colleagues (2015), shows how Mississippian tableaux can be discerned and interpreted. I end this essay with a brief consideration of reading such tableaux in the vertical dimension and how some of the themes of registered in Mesoamerican cosmology were likely shared at a deep and ancient level with North Americans.

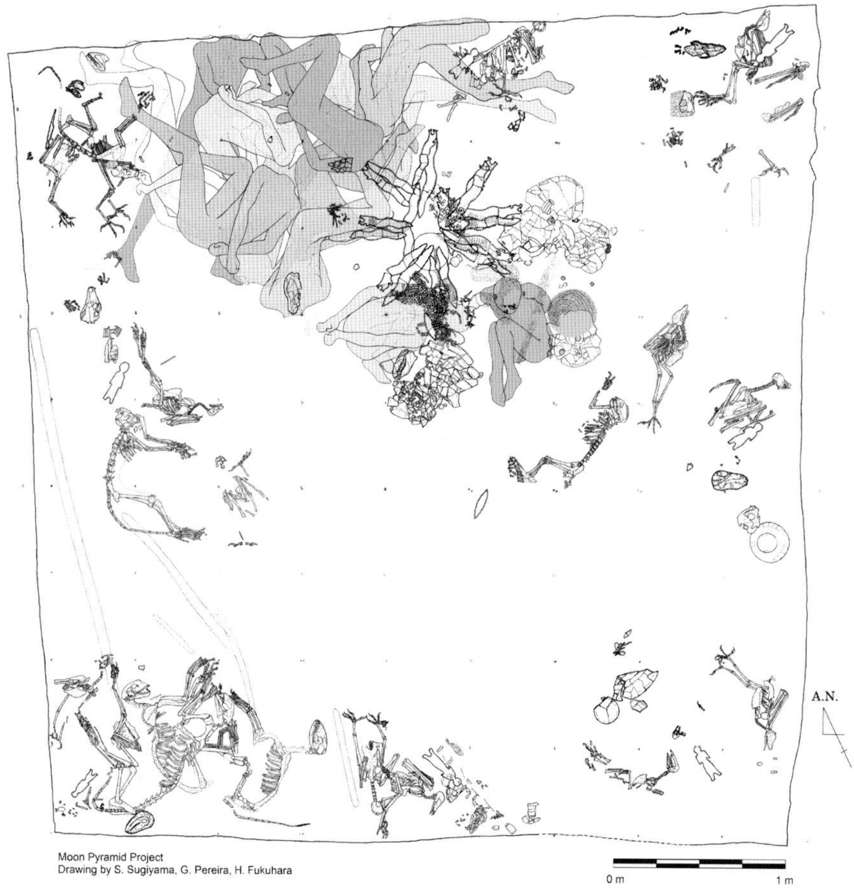

Fig. 12.4. Arranged burials and ritual deposits found in Burial 6, a complex horizontal tableaux, in the Pyramid of the Moon at Teotihuacan.

The Birdmen of Cahokia: The primary Mound 72 Tableau

> *When present as a group the birdmen are four in number; a fifth is sometimes present as in the instance of an engraved marine shell cup from Spiro. Each of the principal four represent a direction of the compass and a fifth operates from the center. Why use the center this way? My contention is that it represents the chief of the group of four.* (Brown 2021, 4)

Brown is describing the quincunx principal on a Braden (Eddyville variant) Style heirloom shell drinking cup from the Spirit Lodge of Spiro that he suggests originated at Cahokia, some two centuries before its placement in that tableau. In the course of his discussion of the birdmen, he describes these winged spirit beings as wafting breath and wind, storm, and rain, vital to agrarian peoples of the Mississippian world as they were to the Teotihuacanos with their Storm Gods. The centering principal of the cardinal quincunx is displayed in the founding civic center layout of Cahokia (Kelly and Brown 2020, 22) associated with an event in the early 11th century and the formation of a complex ritual deposit tableau in Mound 72 at the southern end of the south–north axis of the city. The proposed rapid establishment of the cosmic plan of Cahokia resonates with the rapid establishment of the cosmic plan of Teotihuacan (Sugiyama *et al.* 2021) and the offerings/burial tableaux evidently articulated and activated the collective consensus and affirmation of leadership vital to success in each case. These are instances of what James Brown and his colleagues (Brown *et al.* 2020, 112–13) term "eventful archaeology".

The vertical axis in the founding Mound 72 Sub 1 set of tableaux at Cahokia is clearly documented in the first massive post-hole (Fowler *et al.* 1999; Brown 2003; Kelly 2003; Emerson *et al.* 2016, fig. 2), manifestation of a tradition of massive cedar posts that were used to sight movement of celestial bodies, Sun, Moon and stars, with special focus on the solar and lunar cycles. To the west of this post, the leaders of this elaborate ritual placed in F101 a unique single sacrificed male adorned with a shell bead necklace and conch shell pendant. Brown described the pose of this individual as "akimbo" (2003, 95), but I think that the knee-up pose conforms well to his identification of his role as a birdman chunkey player as depicted on the Eddyville and St Mary's shell gorgets (Brown 2003, fig. 4). Moreover, the unusual face-down positioning of the body suggests that this birdman is descending from his world tree, like the Great Birds defeated by heroes in Mesoamerican narrative and depictions (Helmke and Nielsen 2015). The chunkey game tableaux continue in F102 on the far western side of this complex set of tableaux, framing the central featured interments in F101. In F102, an assembly of possible females (Emerson *et al.* 2016, 415) accompanying a concentration of chunkey stones and two offerings of projectile points, both elements of the ethnohistorically known practice of chunkey playing (Brown 2003; Emerson *et al.* 2016, fig. 4). Over the bodies of the assembled men and between the two offerings of projectile points was an oval offering of 72 liters of mica. Emerson *et al.* (2016, 20) propose that the mica and the females convey the Beneath World–Upper World dichotomy of the overall complex. Brown (pers. comm. January 2022) associates the mica with the Moon. I view every aspect of the offering design as intentional and see the oval layout of the mica, like the bird layout of the beaded burial discussed below, as intentional and representative of the ogee, a central symbol of the birdman seen in copper repoussé plate head-dress insignia and on the heirloom birdman pipe in the Spirit Lodge of Spiro. The ogee as an oval aperture is analogous to the Mesoamerican giant limpet shell *oyohualli* (wind jewel) pectoral introduced into the Maya lowlands at the time of the Teotihuacan inspired New Order. That power jewel is symbolic of the vulva and I suggest that the ogee is as well. It was not just a symbol: it was a living *pars pro toto* of a female being. The mica offering then could be a giant effigy ogee, representative of the feminine divine, called Earth Mother, an important feature of the Mound 72 offering according to Emerson and his colleagues (2016) and commensurate with the provisionally identified gender of several individuals in the assembly. When I corresponded with John Kelly about this identification and suggested that this vulva symbol might link with the post as a phallic symbol, he responded:

> *Here some thoughts about mica cache ogee. I generally assume that for American Indian sites, most everything especially those ritual acts are purposeful and thus have meaning. They also orient themselves to the four sacred directions and to the sky above and the earth/ water below. The Beaded Burial complex or Md 72 sub 1. was placed on a truncated surface to the west of the large Post, F 1. As David notes it is in a part a phallic symbolic and hence male, as well as, the mica cache ogee being indicative of the vagina and hence female. I know Carol and particularly Jim Duncan have discussed at length the ogee's depiction in their study of rock in Missouri. The vagina is not only indicative procreation but also birth. I wonder if the shiny mica while connected to the moon beams as suggested by Jim, might be seen as water. It might be seen as "breaking water" when the amniotic sac breaks. I'm not sure if this is the case of mother earth having given birth. It's interesting to note that the mound is placed in a low lying an area that was occasionally flooded especially late fall and into the spring.*
>
> *The beaded burial complex is roughly half between the Pole and Ogee. For some American Indian societies, a pole placed adjacent to a grave allows the deceased access to the milky way and the heavens above. Perhaps this would allow the beaded "falcon" effigy to take flight in the skies above* (pers. comm. David Freidel and James Brown February 7, 2022).

John Kelly perceives the third dimension in the Mound 72 tableaux, as do other experts on this subject (Brown 2003; Emerson *et al.* 2016). I would add that the projectile points are male, while the chunkey stones are female. Their conflation in F102 and in the chunkey game is not incidental as borne out by consideration of F101.

Turning to the F101 beaded burial, this is clearly central to the tableaux and has been subject to sustained discussion (Brown 2003; Emerson *et al.* 2016). Here is a young male and female laid together as a bundle - there is a second male–female mortuary bundle next to them to assure this identification (Emerson *et al.* 2016). They are pointed south and down on a massive bed of worked marine shell discs, objects in their quantity identified as symbolizing treasure or wealth. The offering clearly forms at the southern end the head of a raptor with a sharp beak facing east. To suggest that this is accidental, or incidental, is to belie all the clear evidence of intentionality in the Mound 72 deposits. This majestic bird of treasure is, like the mica ogee, a living flying being, which is facing south and down. Reading the tableaux east to west as I did in the case of Burial 2 of the Moon Pyramid, the vertical direction of his flight path is clearly descent, from the monumental post of F1, to the downward diving chunkey playing birdman, to the flying great bird of F101, to the mica ogee vulva of F102. It is the path of the Sun from zenith to dusk, very possibly implicating the Moon as suggested by James Brown. It is another manifestation of the saga of a legendary bird, here birdman of the enduring tales of North America. But in my view, it is also symbolic of bringing to the world of people a bundle representing the powers of the creators, a bifurcate, two headed bundle of male–female, the confluence of those creators. Such bifurcate bird personified powers were deeply ancient in North America and endured into the Mississippian era (Giles 2013). It was perhaps this male–female bundle brought to earth that established the allure of Cahokia (Brown and Kelly 2019).

The quincunx principle operates here, with single sacrificed individuals to the north and south of the beaded bundle framing the center with the more complex offerings to the east and west. The mass sacrifices of foreign young women that followed in Mound 72 (Koziol 2010) must have declared the truth of this event and the sovereign power of the rulers of Cahokia over all ethnicities and beliefs in the region. I propose that the birdman of Cahokia and this bifurcate bird bundle with its male-female principles are represented in the diorama, the complex tableau, of the Spiro Spirit Lodge and I complete this thought experiment essay with that reading.

The forked pole as creation bundle in the Spirit Lodge of Spiro

The Spirit Lodge was a deliberately made hollow chamber built around AD 1400 into and covered over with earlier mortuary remains interred in Craig Mound at Spiro (Brown *et al.* 2020). These experts in Mississippian culture call their reconstruction of the arranged materials placed in the Spirit Lodge a diorama. I have termed this kind of arrangement a tableau following existing literature in Mesoamerica but the meaning here is the same. There are historical and cultural connections between the Spirit Lodge diorama and the Mound 72 tableau discussed above. Brown (2021) describes a worn heirloom incised shell in Classic Braden Style cup from western array of more than 100 incised cups in the Spirit Lodge, Braden being the style of two and a half centuries earlier at Cahokia and elsewhere in the Mississippian world (Brown and Muller 2015, 118, with five heads depicting birdmen, including what he identifies as a central chief and he alludes to what Reilly has termed the quincunx formation. At the northern end of the north–south main axis of the diorama, the sages positioned a masterwork flint clay figure of the birdman. He wears a feathered cloak referencing the feathered arms of birdman dancers depicted on Braden Style coppers and shell gorgets, and the human head ear ornaments already in evidence in an early depiction in Picture Cave near Cahokia (*ibid.*, fig. 8.1; Duncan 2015). Finally, this birdman wears the ogee insignia on his forehead, the vaginal portal to the other world (*ibid.*, fig. 17.4). He is birdman, Morning Star in the reading of James Duncan, both male and female, like the beaded bird of Mound 72 with its male and female bundled individuals. At the apex of this axis, raised on the vertical, he is the head of a birdman bundle. This pipe figure was an heirloom from the glory days of Cahokia transported after centuries of reverent use to the western edge of the world.

The Spiro Spirit Lodge was a space enclosed by a circle of cedar posts, like the post circle that originally framed the massive F1 post in the Mound 72 tableau. At Spiro, these posts were angled inwards towards a center that was an open aperture at the top and the earthen walls of the Lodge were constructed over this conical design. So here there was no center post. The center is held by a special pale stone figure pipe of a female holding a maize cob and presiding over a petaca woven basket. There are flint clay pipe figures from greater Cahokia that depict female powers (Emerson and Jackson 1984), but this one is distinctive. The woven petacas in the Spirit Lodge diorama, surely made by women and representing female power, were arrayed on the eastern side on the central axis. Masterworks

(Horton 2020), these baskets contained regalia of spirit beings from all over the Mississippian world worn by ancestors and embodied spirit heroes. So, this central female, called Earth Mother (Brown *et al.* 2020), presided over the ability of humans to embody transcendent spirit.

Earth Mother is at the center of the *axis mundi*. To the south of her and at the southern edge of the Lodge is a human being, a bundled and revered skull. This is the plane of the world, inhabited by the people. They experience death, as symbolized by the vulture cleaning the bones of a deceased individual adjacent to the skull bundle. No human performing power can avoid it: embodied birdmen, the severed heads on the Braden heirloom drinking cup, experience sacrifice and death. But this axial pole path, human, Earth Mother, spirit birdman, points north on the pivot of the sky to resilience and soul rebirth led through the mud closed door of the Lodge by birdman (Diaz-Granados and Duncan 2015, 183). It is the male-female birdman pole, the bundle brought down from the north, the zenith sky, to found Cahokia. Here at the western edge of the world the birdman of Cahokia raised it again to return to the people in a time of dire need.

Alex Barker discerned the transfer of the birdman pole bundle in a narrative conveyed on incised shell drinking cups (Brown *et al.* 2020). These cups were incised in the Craig Style of Spiro and possibly made for the Spirit Lodge ceremonies. Like the Soul Flower cups of the Maya, they held the breath of the story singing sages. In Barker's reading, a forked pole is transferred from a spirit being, whose mouth forms an ogee, portal of the spirit world, to a human being whose mouth forms the cruciform that is the center of the human world. The series of cup scenes demonstrates that this forked pole is a bound duality, including a version of it that has a two-faced head, with a shaman's deer horns like the wood mask also placed in the Spirit Lodge. I suggest that this duality bundled forked pole is an expression of the two-headed male–female birdman bundle. This Janus bird image and idea very likely extended from the time of Hopewell to the founding of Cahokia and beyond (Giles 2013). The forked pole bundle is echoed in the forked rattles carried by birdman dancers on gorgets. The stone scepters assembled just south of the birdman pipe in the Spirit Lodge have profile beaks resembling raptors. These could be another form of the forked pole, the duality birdman bundle. Assembled where they were, they would symbolize the raising of the diorama north–south pole by the birdman embodying the figure, accompanied by arrows that fly and woodpecker axes that not only cleave heads but probably finish poles.

Concluding thoughts

Like all extraordinarily arranged offerings of the past discovered in the present, the Spirit Lodge of Spiro and Mound 72 of Cahokia will continue to be subject to analysis and debate. The same holds for the burial/offerings of the Classic Maya and people of Teotihuacan. What Kent Reilly discerned, and continues to see, is that these arrangements and depictions can be read in three dimensions as the people who made them intended. Contextual analysis of archaeological remains is a very well-established principal (Giles 2013) and reading in three dimensions brings study closer to the realities of the past. Archaeologists are beginning to attend seriously to the archaeology of the soul advocated by Robert Hall (1997). In such a perspective, like Omaha Man, the forked pole of the Spirit Lodge was a living bundle presence, in all its forms. Returned to human care, it persists in its many descendant incarnations.

References

Adams, R.E.W. (1999) *Río Azul: An ancient Maya City*, University of Oklahoma Press, Norman OK.

Bardawil, L.W. (1976) The principal bird deity in Maya Art: An iconographic study of form and meaning. In *Segunda Mesa Redonda de Palenque: The art, iconography and dinastic history of Palenque, part III*, eds M.G. Robertson, E.P. Benson, J.B. Carlson, M. Cohodas, M.F. de Molina, B. Fuente, P.T. Furst, G.G. Griffin, H. Hartung, G. Kubler, F.G. Lounsbury, A.R. Lhuillier, G.W. Pahl, D. Schávelzon and L. Schele, 195–209. Pre-Columbian Art Research Institute, San Francisco CA.

Bassie-Sweet, K. and Hopkins, N.A. (2021) Predatory birds of the Popol Vuh. In *The Myths of the Popol Vuh in Cosmology, Art and Ritual*, eds H. Moyes, A.J. Christenson and F. Sachse, 222–48. University Press of Colorado, Louisville CO.

Benson, E.P. and Griffin, G.G. eds (1988) *Maya Iconography*. Princeton University Press, Princeton NJ.

Brown, J.A. (2003) The Cahokia Mound 72–Sub 1 burials as collective representation. *Wisconsin Archaeologist* 84, 83–99.

Brown, J.A. (2021) On the centrality of bird-men in Cahokia religion. *Cahokian Spring 2021*, 3–5.

Brown, J.A. and Kelly, J.E. (2019) The allure of Cahokia as a sacred place in the eleventh century. In *Shaman, Priest, Practice, Belief, Materials of Ritual and Religion in Eastern North America*, eds S.B. Carmody and C.R. Barrier, 178–206. University of Alabama Press, Tuscaloosa AL.

Brown, J.A. and Muller, J., (2015) Tradition and horizons in Southeastern representation: Lessons from Picture Cave. In Diaz-Granados *et al.* (eds), 113–24.

Brown, J.A., Barker, A.W. and Sabo, G. III (2020) The Spirit Lodge, Spiro ritual and cosmic renewal. In Singleton and Reilly (eds), 92–113.

Coe, M.D. (1988) Ideology of the Maya tomb In Benson and Griffin (eds), 222–35.

Coe, M.D. (1990) *Excavations in the Great Plaza, North Terrace, and North Acropolis of Tikal: Tikal Report 14.3*. University Monograph 61, University Museum, University of Pennsylvania, Ephrata PA.

Diaz-Granados, C. and Duncan, J.R., (2015) Transmogrification, healing, and resurrection. In Diaz-Granados *et al.* (eds), 181–7.

Diaz-Granados, C., Duncan, J.R. and Reilly, F. K. III eds (2015) *Picture Cave, Unraveling the Mysteries of the Mississippian Cosmos*. University of Texas Press, Austin TX.

Duncan, J.R. (2015) Identifying the characters on the walls of Picture Cave, in Diaz-Granados *et al.* (eds), 209–36.

Emerson, T.E. and Jackson, D.K. (1984) *The BBB Motor Site*. American Bottom Archaeology, FAI–270 Site Report 6, University of Illinois Press, Urbana IL.

Emerson, T.E., Hedman, K.M., Hargrave, E.A., Cobb, D.E. and Thompson, A.R. (2016) Paradigms lost: Reconfiguring Cahokia's Mound 72 beaded burial. *American Antiquity* 81, 405–25.

Fitzsimmons, J.L. (2009) *Death and the Classic Maya Kings*, University of Texas Press, Austin TX.

Fowler, M., Rose, J., Vander Leest, B. and Ahler, S.R. eds (1999) *The Mound 72 Area: Dedicated and sacred space in early Cahokia*. Scientific Papers 54, Illinois State Museum, Springfield IL.

Freidel, D.A. and Guenter, S.P. (2006) Soul bundle caches, tombs, and cenotaphs: Creating the places of resurrection and accession, in Maya kingship. *In Sacred Bindings of the Cosmos: Ritual Acts of Bundling and Wrapping in Mesoamerica*, eds J. Guernsey and F.K. Reilly III, 59–79. Ancient America Special Publications 1, Boundary End Archaeology Research Center, Barnardsville NC.

Giles, B.T. (2013) A contextual and iconographic reassessment of the headdress on Burial 11 from Hopewell Mound 25. *American Antiquity* 78, 502–19.

Grube, N. (1992) Classic Maya dance. *Ancient Mesoamerica* 3, 201–18.

Guernsey, P. (2020) *Human figuration and fragmentation in Preclassic Mesoamerica: From figurines to sculpture.* Cambridge University Press, Cambridge.

Guernsey, P. (2021) Monuments in context. In *Ritual and Power in Stone: The performance of rulership in Mesoamerican Izapan Style art*, ed J. Guernsey and Schele, L. 119–42. Series in Maya and Pre-Columbian Studies, University of Texas Press, Austin TX.

Hall, R.L. (1997) *An Archaeology of the Soul, North American Indian Belief and Ritual.* University of Illinois Press, Urbana IL.

Headrick, A. (2003) Seeing through Sahagun: Observations on a Mesoamerican staff of office. *Mesoamerican Voices* 1, 23–40.

Headrick, A. (2007) *The Teotihuacan Trinity, the Sociopolitical Structure of an Ancient Mesoamerican City.* University of Texas Press, Austin TX.

Healy, P.F. and Blainey, M.G. (2007) Ancient Maya mosaic mirrors: Function, symbolism, and meaning. *Ancient Mesoamerica* 22, 229–44. [Doi:10.1017/S0956536111000241], accessed 5.16.22.

Helmke, C. and Nielsen, J. (2015) Defeat of the Great Bird and royal pageantry, a Mesoamerican myth in comparative perspective. *Comparative Mythology* 1, 23–60.

Horton, E. (2020) Sacred bundles in the Craig Mound Spirit Lodge at Spiro. In Singleton and Reilly (eds), 136–49.

Houston, S. (1996) Symbolic sweatbaths of the Maya: Architectural meaning in the Cross Group at Palenque, Mexico. *Latin American Antiquity* 7, 132–51.

Houston, S., Stuart, D. and Taube, K.A. eds (2006) *The Memory of Bones: Body, being and experience among the Classic Maya.* University of Texas Press, Austin TX.

Kelly, J.E. (2003) The context of the post pit and meaning of the Sacred Pole at the East St. Louis Mound Group. *Wisconsin Archaeologist* 1–2, 107–25.

Kelly, J.E. and Brown, J.A. (2020) In the beginning: Contextualizing Cahokia's emergence. In *Cahokia in Context: Hegemony and diaspora*, eds C. McNutt and R. Parish, 11–31. University Press of Florida, Gainesville FL.

Kelly, M.K. (2020) Documentación Epigráfica Durante la Temporada de Campo de 2019 al Sitio El Perú-Waka. In *Proyecto Arqueológico Waka', Informe No. 17. Temporada 2019*, eds J.C. Pérez Calderón, G. Pérez Robles, and D. Marken, 282–301. Unpublished report submitted to the Dirección General del Patrimonio Cultural y Natural, Guatemala City.

Knight, V.J. (2013) *Iconographic Method in New World Prehistory.* Cambridge University Press. New York.

Koziol, K.M. (2010) Violence, Symbols, and the Archaeological Record: A case study of Cahokia's Mound 72. Unpublished Ph.D. dissertation, State University of New York, Albany NY.

Lopéz-Luján, L. (2017) Life after Death in Teotihuacan: The Moon Plaza's Monoliths in Colonial and Modern Mexico in *Visual Culture of the Ancient Americas: Contemporary Perspectives*, eds A. Finegold and E. Hoobler, 59–90. University of Oklahoma Press, Norman.

Martin, S. (2015) The Old Man of the Maya universe: A unitary dimension to ancient Maya religion. *Maya Archaeology* 3, 186–227.

Melendez, J.C. (2019) A Contextual and Technological Study of Ancient Maya Greenstone Mosaic Masks. Ph.D. dissertation, Washington University in St Louis MI. [https://openscholarship.wustl.edu/art_sci_etds/1929/], accessed February 27, 2022.

Navarro-Farr, O., Pérez Robles, G., Pérez Calderón, J., Menéndez Bolaños, E., Patterson, E., Eppich, K. and Kelly, M. (2021) Burial 61 at El Perú-Waka's Structure M13-1. Latin *American Antiquity* 32(1), 188–200. doi:10.1017/laq.2020.99.

Nielsen, J., Taube, K., Helmke, C. and Escobedo, H. (2021) Blowgunners and the Great Bird at Teotihuacan: Mesoamerican myths in a comparative perspective. In *The Myths of the Popol Vuh in Cosmology, Art and Ritual*, eds H. Moyes, A. Christenson and F. Sachse, 295–314. University Press of Colorado, Boulder CO.

Prager, C.M. (2002) Die Inschriften von Pusilha: Epigraphische Analyse und Rekonstruktion der Geschichte einer klassischen MayaStätte. Unpublished M.A. thesis, Philosophischen Fakultät, Rheinischen Friedrich-WilhelmsUniversität zu Bonn, Bonn.

Prager, C. (2004) A Classic Maya Ceramic Vessel from the Calakmul Region in the Museum zu Allerheiligen, Schaffhausen, Switzerland. *Human Mosaic* 35, 31–40.

Reilly, F.K. III (1994) Visions to Another World: Art, Shamanism, and Political Power in Middle Formative Mesoamerica. Unpublished Ph.D. dissertation, University of Texas, Austin TX.

Reilly, F.K. III (1996) Middle Formative origins of the Mesoamerican ritual act of bundling. In *Sacred Bindings of the Cosmos: Ritual Acts of Bundling and Wrapping in Ancient Mesoamerica*, eds J. Guernsey and F.K. Reilly III, 13–34. Ancient America Special Publication 1, Boundary End Archaeology Research Center, Barnardsville NC.

Reilly, F.K. III and Looper, M. (2002) Women(men) and men(women): Classic Maya rulers and the third gender. In *Ancient Maya Women*, ed. T. Ardren, 171–202. Altamira Press, Walnut Creek CA.

Reilly, F.K. III and Garber, J.F. eds (2007) *Ancient Objects and Sacred Realms: Interpretations of Mississippian iconography.* University of Texas Press, Austin TX.

Robb, M.M. (2017) *Teotihuacan: City of water, city of fire.* Fine Arts Museums of San Francisco and University of California Press, San Francisco CA.

Rose, J.C. (1999) Mortuary data and analysis. In *The Mound 72 Area: Dedicated and sacred space in early Cahokia*, eds M.L. Fowler, J.C. Rose, B. Vander Leest and S.R. Ahler, 63–82. Illinois State Museum Reports of Investigations 54, Illinois State Museum, Springfield IL.

Saturno, W. (2009) Centering the kingdom, centering the king: Maya creation and legitimization at San Bartolo. In *The Art of Urbanism: How Mesoamerican kingdoms represented themselves in architecture and imagery*, eds W.L. Fash and L.L. Luján, 111–34. Dumbarton Oaks Research Library and Collection, Washington DC.

Schele, L. and Freidel, D.A. (1990) *A Forest of Kings: The untold story of the ancient Maya.* William Morrow & Co., New York.

Schele, L. and Mathews, P. (1998) *The Code of Kings: The language of seven sacred Maya temples and tombs.* Scribner, New York.

Scherer, A.K. (2015) *Mortuary Landscapes of the Classic Maya: Rituals of body and Soul.* University of Texas Press, Austin TX.

Scherer, A.K., Golden, C., Prera, A.L.A. and Robles, G.P. (2014) Danse macabre: Death, community and kingdom at El Kinel, Guatemala. in *The Bioarchaeology of Space and Place: Ideology, power and meaning in Maya mortuary contexts*, ed. G.D. Wrobel, 193–224. Springer, New York.

Singleton, E.D. and Reilly, F.K. eds (2020) *Recovering Ancient Spiro: Native American art, ritual, and cosmic renewal.* National Cowboy and Western Heritage Museum, Oklahoma City OK.

Stanton, T.W., Freidel D.A., Suhler, C.K., Ardren, T., Ambrosino, J.N., Shaw, J.M. and Bennett, S. (2010) *Excavations at Yaxuna, Yucatan, Mexico (1986-1996).* British Archaeological Report S2056, Archaeopress, Oxford.

Stuart, D. (2006) *The Palenque Mythology: Inscriptions from the Cross Group at Palenque.* Sourcebook for The 2006 Maya Meetings, Department of Art and Art History, University of Texas, Austin TX.

Stuart, D. (2012) The name of paper: The mythology of crowning and royal nomenclature on Palenque's Palace Tablet. In *Maya Archaeology* 2, eds C. Golden, S. Houston and J.

Skidmore. Precolumbia Mesoweb Press, San Francisco CA. [http://www.mesoweb.com/articles/stuart/Stuart2012-lores.pdf], accessed February 27, 2022.

Sugiyama, N. (2014) Animals and Sacred Mountains: How ritualized performances materialized state -ideologies at Teotihuacan, Mexico. Unpublished Ph.D. Dissertation, Department of Anthropology, Harvard University, Cambridge MA.

Sugiyama, N., Sugiyama, S., Catignani, T., Chase, A.S.Z. and Fernandez-Diaz, J.C. (2021) Humans as geomorphic agents: Lidar detection of the past, present and future of the Teotihuacan Valley, Mexico. *Plos One* 16, e0257550. [https://doi.org/10.1371/journal.pone.0257550], accessed February 27, 2022.

Sugiyama, S. (2005) *Human Sacrifice, Militarism, and Rulership: Materialization of state ideology at the Feathered Serpent Pyramid, Teotihuacan.* Cambridge University Press, Cambridge.

Sugiyama, S. (2017) Teotihuacan: Planned city with cosmic pyramids. In Robb (ed.), 28–37.

Sugiyama, S. and Cabreras Castro, R.C. (2007) The Moon Pyramid Project and the Teotihuacan State Polity, a brief summary of the 1998–2004 excavations. *Ancient Mesoamerica* 18, 109–25.

Sugiyama, S. and Lopéz-Luján, L. (2007) Dedicatory burial/offering complexes at the Moon Pyramid, Teotihuacan, a preliminary report of 1998–2004 explorations. *Ancient Mesoamerica* 18, 127–46.

Sugiyama, S. and Sugiyama, N. (2021) Monumental Cityscape and Polity at Teotihuacan in *Mesoamerican Archaeology: Theory and Practice*, eds J. Hendon, L. Overholtzer, and R. Joyce, 98–128. John Wiley & Sons, Hoboken.

Suhler, C.K. (1996) Excavations at the North Acropolis Yaxuna, Yucatan, Mexico. Unpublished Ph.D. dissertation, Southern Methodist University, Dallas TX.

Suhler, C.K. and Freidel, D.A. (1998) Life and death in a Maya war zone. *Archaeology* 51, 28–34.

Taube (1992) *The Major Gods of Ancient Yucatan.* Studies in Pre-Columbian Art & Archaeology 32, Dumbarton Oaks Research Library and Collection, Washington DC.

Taube, K. (1998) The Jade hearth: Centrality, rulership, and the Classic Maya temple. In *Function and Meaning in Classic Maya Architecture*, ed S.D. Houston, 427–78. Dumbarton Oaks, Washington DC.

Taube, K. (2004) Flower Mountain: Concepts of life, beauty, and paradise among the Classic Maya. *RES: Anthropology and Aesthetics* 45, 69–98.

Taube, K.A., Saturno, W.A., Stuart, D. and Hurst, H. (2010) *The Murals of San Bartolo, El Petén, Guatemala; Informe preliminar de la temporada 2005.* Ancient America 10, Boundary End Archaeology Research Center, Barnardsville NC.

Tiesler, V. and Cucina, A. eds (2006) *Janaab' Pakal of Palenque.* University of Arizona Press, Tucson AZ.

Tiesler, V., Cucina, A., and Freidel, D. (2017) *Before Kukulkán: Bioarchaeology of Maya Life, Death, and Identity at Classic Period Yaxuná.* University of Arizona Press, Tuscon.

Zorich, Z. (2021) Piecing together Maya creation stories. *Archaeology*, Nov.–Dec., 32–7.

Part 3

Cosmoscapes in perspective

13

Final thoughts on the archaeologies of cosmoscapes

Shawn P. Lambert, J. Grant Stauffer, and Bretton T. Giles

This book presents a broad, kaleidoscopic range of case studies to illustrate the complex and recursive entanglements that people, non-human agents, objects, places, images, landscapes, and natural resources have with one another and how they interact and animate cosmological worlds. Additionally, the case studies illustrate how the meanings associated with certain objects and places inevitably become fused with social, political, economic, and religious processes (i.e., experiential place-making) in the reiterative creation of cosmoscapes. As a result, cosmoscapes reflect worlding practices or, in other words, how communities frame and situate cosmological engagements between human and non-human agents in different places and times. The ways communities select/shape certain bodies, objects, and spaces as models of the broader cosmos (or relationally – macrocosm) constitute a significant aspect of these practices that highlights the relevance of perspective and scale (Crumley and Marquardt 1987; 1990). Conversely, the manner in which cosmoscapes, as ontologically charged landscapes, change and transform mirroring peoples' religious perspectives leads to other intriguing research trajectories, such as how and why did past communities alter and deconstruct features of prior cosmoscapes. Object worlds, places, and landscapes also played active roles in mediating and transforming cosmoscapes, as well as shaping past experiences, interpretations, and identities. Cosmoscapes, then, become a wellspring for expressing everyday practices and ritual traditions.

Archaeologists, anthropologists, and scholars in other disciplines have become increasingly interested in how people enroll different cosmological currents in creating particular cosmoscapes and worlding practices. For example, Bold's (2020) ethnographic work uses an ontological framework to understand newly formed, non-linear cosmoscapes that emerged due to significant cosmopolitical movements in the Kaata community of contemporary highland Bolivia. For the Kaata people, conflicts and corresponding changes emerge from the importance of maintaining ritual relationships with their animate mountainous landscape versus the modern capitalistic acquisition of wealth. A different perspective on cosmoscapes as everchanging landscapes is present by Giles *et al.* (Chapter 11). Their work employs ethnographic, archaeological, and iconographic evidence to assess how Mound 2 at the Hopewell Site offers a glimpse of how Middle Woodland cosmoscapes emphasized continual motion and could have been modeled on cosmological (celestial) cycles. Important here is that cosmoscapes are influenced by the ebbs and flows of different historical trajectories and need constant maintenance. In this spirit, cosmoscapes can be transitory, ephemeral, and might have only existed, been enacted, and/or "destroyed" during ceremonial activities. The creation and short lives of the mythopoetic images created in Navajo sandpaintings, which are destroyed shortly after they are made, represent another pertinent example (Berlo 2011; 2014). In contrast, certain objects probably solidified and created complex multitemporal representations of past peoples' cosmoscapes by incorporating anachronistic features with contemporary ones, like the presence of both stingray spines and bone awls, respectively, as tools of autosacrifice on the Aztec Calendar Stone (Headrick, Chapter 7). This variability lends itself to the ways that the contributors in this volume mobilize multiple types of evidence including, material culture in controlled archaeological and historical contexts, written documents, and ethnographic and ethnohistorical literature, to observe and study the complexity of past peoples' cosmoscapes.

Complexity of cosmoscapes

An important aspect that several contributors to this volume communicate is that the ways in which people incorporate the world around them to construct cosmoscapes is not a linear or universal process. The nature and character of a singular cosmoscape can vary considerably, possessing both volatile and stabilizing components that had to be balanced by human and non-human agents. Likewise, the temporality of cosmoscapes can be equally variable and was likely perceived by past peoples in multifaceted ways. As a consequence, the dynamic creation and recreation of cosmoscapes involves negotiations among peoples whose knowledge of the cosmos can be common knowledge or carefully controlled, protected esoterica restricted to select knowledge keepers. For instance, multiple chapters vibrantly illustrate cases where cosmoscapes were materialized as portable objects or certain spaces were carefully constructed to mirror and create cosmologically charged places.

Specific individuals, groups, and sometimes entire communities use and negotiate how certain places and objects are employed to enact different aspects of their cosmoscape. In Chapter 4, Lambert focuses on how ritual practitioners incorporated Arkansas polychrome ceramic vessels, imagery, and hallucinogenic plants to (re)negotiate how their cosmoscapes were constructed and communicated with non-human beings during altered states of consciousness. The use of hallucinogenic plants and ceramic vessels to evoke altered states of consciousness was probably restricted to the ritual practitioners that partook in these ceremonial activities. The broader community, who did not share in the altered states, may or may not have had a holistic understanding of parts of this cosmoscape. Thus, knowledge of cosmoscapes can be esoteric in nature and controlled by specific people in power. We know that in some late pre-Columbian societies, like the Caddo along the Red River valley, communities spatially constructed their settlements to situate ritual specialists, who wielded the knowledge to communicate with agents in their cosmoscapes, on the periphery of the community. Sabo (2012) has argued that this was an intentional act by the community because ritual practitioners' powerful medicine was dangerous and represented too many risks for them to live within the settlement.

In other instances, representational materializations of the cosmos appear to have had a more egalitarian distribution in certain communities. For instance, Azar and Steponaitis (Chapter 2) examine Late Mississippian rim-effigy bowls from the Central Mississippi Valley (CMV). They argued based on the vessels' iconographic structure, that Late Mississippian communities throughout the CMV – regardless of social of status – may have utilized rim-effigy bowls during rituals that emphasized the structure and wholeness of the cosmos. Similarly, Mersmann and Stauffer (Chapter 8) emphasize that the Cahokia community reaffirmed the knowledge and meaning of their cosmoscape collectively through shared knowledge. These Cahokian cosmoscapes were negotiated through prescribed communal ritual experiences that the entire community engaged in through positioning and centering posts. Knowledge of cosmoscapes can therefore be controlled by a few individuals (see also Chapter 7) or meshed with and/or maintained by an entire community.

Cosmoscapes are also uncertain and can need to be renegotiated, balancing past practices and traditions with the emergence of novel perspectives. Their meanings can wax and wane as new practices, human and non-human agents, objects, places, beliefs, and narratives become intertwined. For instance, some aspects of a cosmoscape can be selectively adopted, while other parts are actively forgotten because they do not align with a group's cosmological worldview. For example, Ramey Incised vessels from Cahokia have been hypothesized to have acted as cosmograms "through which Cahokians attempted to frame relationships among different social groups and the broader cosmos" (Friberg 2018, 39; see also Pauketat and Emerson 1991). Mississippian groups that were socially and politically interconnected with Cahokia adopted the production and use of Ramey Incised vessels but made them meaningful in localized ways. Friberg (2018) noted significant iconographic variation between Cahokia and surrounding Mississippian communities which, she argues, illustrates that these groups actively perceived the composition and structure of cosmoscapes differently than Cahokians. Melendez *et al.* (Chapter 6) also emphasize understanding the varied nature of cosmoscapes in their analysis of Maya greenstone mosaic face masks. Broadly speaking, they argue that these masks served as mnemonic devices through which human and non-human agents communicated, which may have overly homogenized their meanings. Melendez *et al.* also contend that these mosaic masks and other mosaic features manifested different animals like snakes, turtles, birds, bats, or crocodiles. When incorporating a theoretical framework, like cosmoscapes, researchers need to be aware that members of smaller scale societies (e.g., primary mound center and peripheral settlements) or large scale regional polities (e.g., Cahokia or Tikal) did not passively adopt a religious worldview. Instead, cosmoscapes were embodied and materialized in the various ways communities used objects, places, and landscapes, and that intersectionality continually resituated how they understood and defined their world.

Equally, cosmoscapes can be intertwined in complex, multifaceted ways with various temporalities and the experience of time. Accordingly, certain cycles provide temporal frameworks for life, such as the daily path of Sun across the sky, the "year" marked by the changing seasons, the phases of the Moon, and the movement of other celestial bodies (Aveni 2002). These temporal cycles interdigitate with linear time in complex ways leading to considerable variability in how people experience various intervals (cf. Gell 1992; Munn 1992). Moreover, various peoples' belief systems and objects can also profoundly alter the way time is perceived and experienced, with clocks and the modern formal segmentation of time being compelling, pervasive examples (Postill 2002; Eriksen 2004; Pels 2015). In this vein, Headrick (Chapter 7) examines the Aztec Calendar Stone and its ritual associations with solar and other temporal cycles, as well as how it marked specific events of the past, present, and future in ways that re-affirmed religious and political cosmoscapes. Furthermore, she explores how the Calendar Stone was a receptacle for sacrificial offering, such as hearts and blood, including autosacrifices of blood from the ruling elite. This example is useful in illustrating how ideologies can reinforce the importance of ruling (Aztec) elites with their very blood sacrifices (i.e., autosacrifices) to the Calendar Stone were believed to be essential in maintaining cosmic balance and controlling time.

Navajo sandpaintings are another example of a cosmoscape in which time, space, and meaning are complexly interwoven. These ceremonies do not produce art in the Western sense, but animate diagrams created in multisensory ritual contexts that document the "constant motion of an animate and dynamically symmetrical universe" (Berlo 2011, 12; see also Johnson 2019). Navajo sandpaintings or *'iikááh* are intended to invite the *Diyin Dine'é* (Gods or "holy" [non-human] persons) to the event and induce their aid in healing the recipient, as well as instilling communal well-being (Berlo 2014, 690). In this context, Navajo cosmoscapes manifest a layered sense of time because the (contemporary) sandpaintings illustrate how the *Diyin Dine'é* created images at the beginning of time from the ephemeral material of the universe (Berlo 2014, 690–1). Ephemeral events depicted with ephemeral materials (as microcosms representative of the larger macrocosm) that disappear into the wind and desert provide glimpses of Navajo (*Dine'é*) cosmoscapes. Hence, Navajo sandpaintings are worlding ceremonies *par excellence* that bring together the *Dine'é* and *Diyin Dine'é* in their shared mountainous homeland, and another example of how temporality can be densely interwoven with nonwestern cosmoscapes.

Objects as cosmoscapes – the ontological turn

The first section of the book (Chapters 2–7) explores how objects influence and engage with humans and non-human agents that, together, afford the people who use these objects the ability to conjure and engage with cosmoscapes. Part of the motivation for this approach comes from the ontological turn in anthropology and archaeology, which consist of a range of approaches related to peoples' perception and beliefs about reality, and their actual ontological commitments (cf. Alberti and Marshall 2009; Olsen 2010; Alberti 2013; 2016a; 2016b; Alberti *et al.* 2011; Kohn 2015; Skousen and Buchanan 2015; Baltus and Baires 2017; Harris and Cipolla 2017; Harrison-Buck and Hendon 2018). Accordingly, the ontological turn and object centered approaches have had considerable influence on archaeological theory in the last decade (Harris and Cipolla 2017), which has prompted scholars to reconsider how objects influence (and communicate information about) people, landscapes, and the creation of realities (i.e., worlding practices) (Gosden 2005; Olsen 2010).

Given this volume's focus, its contributors address how and why certain objects are considered to represent, manifest, and/or otherwise materialize aspects of past peoples' cosmoscapes, or in other words their "overarching models and templates for the shape and scope of the cosmos" (Reichel 2012, 136–7). The answers to this question illustrate considerable complexity and diversity (see above), but they also shed light on how fundamentally different perspectives on certain objects can exist. For example, archaeological narratives have often characterized various ceramic vessels as dead, culturally inert objects that have no value other than their temporal and diagnostic power. Yet Azar and Steponaitis (Chapter 2) explore how rim-effigy bowls from the CMV might have served as cosmoscapes for Late Mississippian communities that manifested the structure and wholeness of the cosmos, while their ritual use could have been essential in preparing and consuming various foods and herbal medicines, including hallucinogens and stimulants. Lambert (Chapter 4) similarly analyzes how ritual practitioners used certain polychrome ceramic vessels from the Arkansas River Valley (ARV) to process and consume hallucinogenic ritual beverages, produced with Datura, to induce altered states of consciousness that provided specialized knowledge and a heightened awareness of the connections between the people, places, and things of the universe. Cosmoscape approaches therefore ask and answer meaningful questions concerning: how and why groups symbolically charge certain objects; the ways these objects were used and influenced the lives of people; and how certain symbolically charged objects influence the practices, traditions, and historical trajectories of communities.

Objects that manifest cosmoscapes can also gain or lose ritual power through the way in which they are treated and especially the offering/sacrifices made to them. For example, Maya stelae that served as extensions of the rulers they portrayed were given offerings, including royal bloodletting, when unwrapped/unbundled during calendric rites. In turn, the way these stelae were often subsequently mutilated (after the death of the ruler) indicates the perceived importance/power they continued to have to Maya peoples (Stuart 1996). Commensurately, the royal autosacrifices, hearts, and other blood offerings made to the Aztec Calendar Stone were almost certainly considered to enhance its power (Headrick, Chapter 7). Abundant other examples can also be referenced, such as how Iroquois False Face masks, each believed to house a distinct spirit, are fed cornmeal and offered tobacco to make them more amiable, while their status increases with age (Niesyto 2020). Likewise, the long-term use of pipes to smoke tobacco and other ritual substances probably empowered them in analogous ways, as exemplified by how communities often curated, retooled, and/or tried to fix them. In this vein, Zedeño (2008, 368) observes that origin ("pedigree"), age, and complexity of the ceremonial bundles (comprised of ordered sets of objects) made by North American Plains people was related to their relative power, as well. These examples raise the question of whether the Cahokia style flint clay figurines analyzed by Boles (Chapter 3) (as well as other figurines and statuettes from the Eastern United States) could have functioned as extensions of certain important, in this case non-human, persons that were given various offerings like tobacco, gaining and/or losing power through their treatment. Equally, we would be remiss in not noting how the symbolism of many of these objects appears closely related to bodies, which could pertain to how cross-culturally the human body is a common microcosm (cf. Wayman 1982; Ellen 1986; Henry 2003).

The ritual power and corresponding danger/pollution associated with these cosmologically charged objects in the ancient Americas is likely linked to why they were often ritually broken, "killed," and buried, removing them from circulation. Yet some contributors in this volume have challenged the notion that cosmologically charged objects are passive once they were deposited in the ground. Moreover, they assert that these deposited objects do not become inactive and, rather, may become more cosmologically animated, like the greenstone face masks discussed Melendez *et al.* (Chapter 6) or the Tunican ceremonial bottles assessed by Dye and Toney (Chapter 5). Understanding how objects influence cosmoscapes (i.e., how we construct our identities with animated things) is to know how material culture affects worlding practices, which has relevance today.

Building on this insight, Chapters 2–7 urge readers to consider another ontological move – the possibility that objects can model, evoke, and/or literally become multiple worlds. Once again, ceremonial pots and bottles can serve as useful examples because Azar and Steponaitis (Chapter 2) and Lambert (Chapter 4) illustrate how particular ceramic vessels' form and imagery can mirror their cosmos. Moreover, CMV rim-effigy bowls model various beings on their rims in ways that likely represented the Earth Disk, while the bodies of these bowls and their contents symbolized the Underworld. In Azar and Steponaitis's words, these rim-effigy bowls can therefore be "interpreted as miniature *cosmoscapes*" or, in another sense, a multiplicity of worlds. Various other objects that manifest cosmoscapes can often be interpreted in similar ways.

Non-Western ontologies further prompt us to consider how some cultures think of certain things and non-human agents as animate persons (Morrison 2000; Olsen 2010). In these ontologies, the "boundaries between persons, animals, and 'inanimate' things are often quite permeable" and *animistic* perspectives can be useful for understanding human–object–non-human–environmental relationships (Harris and Cipolla 2017, 181). As Zedeño (2009, 408) explains, "animism is part of a worldview that recognizes a life force or soul in things". In these frameworks, certain objects are animate (non-human) persons that can be as influential as (human) persons and are considered to have their own desires, appetites, thoughts, and histories. The identification and contextualization of these animate objects has considerable interpretive potential for understanding past peoples worlding practices and especially their cosmoscapes, which can be seen in many chapters in this volume. For example, the movement or migration of certain objects, like Cahokia-style flint clay female figurines, can be perceived as influencing other people and places. As Boles (Chapter 3) argues, these female figurines might have literally taken on the role of Earth Mother, an important ancestral creatrix recognized in Native American cosmologies, who migrates to influence other cultural groups.

Overall, each contributor to the Objects as Cosmoscapes section incorporates other ways of seeing past people lifeworlds and their worlding practices. These chapters also illustrate how the ontological turn has prompted scholars to incorporate more diverse perspectives that challenge western ontologies, including taken-for-granted distinctions between the natural and the cultural, the mental and the material, and other persistent dualisms. Additionally, future analyses that assess how changes in the ways objects were modeled as cosmoscapes by past peoples could contribute to understanding how their ontologies subtly shifted through time or were marked by drastic ruptures.

Cosmoscapes as place-making

The second section of the book (Chapters 8–12) is dedicated to exploring how landscapes, settlements, and architectures manifest cosmoscapes in whole or in part, as well as the agents that inhabit them. As ontological landscapes, larger scale cosmoscapes result from complex worlding practices that encode lifeworlds with complex analogies that richly saturate places with meaning, reveal the omnipresence of animating forces, and characterize (or invite the participation of) important non-human persons (Pavel 1981, 152; Morrison 2000; Reilly 2004; Lankford 2007; Zedeño 2009; Berlo 2011; 2014; Bold 2020). Like the objects that materialize cosmoscapes, materializations of cosmoscapes on landscapes illustrate a mixture of stability and volatility that was likely carefully managed by past communities for the sake of balance. The complex interplay of these forces resulted in temporal changes that affected how certain places were modeled as cosmoscapes, and these worlding practices that were far from static. Indeed, the shifting arrangements of constructed spaces probably marked corresponding changes in perspective that played out in tempos ranging from the staccato to legato. Negotiations among distinct communities often dictated the tempos in which these cosmoscapes were created and recreated, not unlike the potent objects examined in the Objects as Cosmoscapes section. Consequently, the places examined as cosmoscapes exhibit palimpsestic qualities that are well-known among other archaeological landscapes (Sauer 1926; Ingold 1993; Cosgrove 1998; Lewis and Stout 1998; Boyea 1999; Skaanes 2021).

Pre-Columbian peoples perceived, imagined, and iteratively (re)created their cosmoscapes by employing knowledge rooted in animistic and analogistic beliefs, often constructing new knowledge in the process. At the scales of houses, settlements, and physiographic regions, communities frequently constructed overlapping and nested microcosms within a perceived macrocosm, which implemented their animistic and analogic perspectives (*sensu* Ellen 1982, 2). For example, the observed arrangements of center posts at the Cahokia site (see Mersmann and Stauffer, Chapter 8) and superimposed mortuary contexts under Mound 2 at the Hopewell Site (Giles *et al.*, Chapter 11) materialize sequences of eventful emplacements that articulated cosmological knowledge with the proper ordering (and possibly disposal) of potent objects in particular spaces. In their final forms, both the Cahokia Site and Mound 2 materialize microcosms that reflect the identities and beliefs of their creators. Duncan and Diaz-Granados (Chapter 9) also present how the pictographs of the Picture Cave manifest a microcosm that both visualizes the pantheon of human and non-human agents in Native American lore and demonstrates how their organization within the cave space corresponds with their ideal placement within the macrocosm, highlighting the critical importance of oral traditions in the process.

Just as objects can evoke or become multiple worlds, cosmoscapes are instilled with and conversely offer *genus loci* to those that build and occupy them, as places within physical landscapes or architectural features that often exist as worlds in-and-of-themselves with unique qualities. Moreover, interconnections between potent spaces were often established during these eventful constructions, as demonstrated by ancient Maya, Dhegiha-Siouan, and Caddoan speaking peoples who incorporated portals into their mortuary programs (Duncan and Diaz-Granados, Chapter 9; Freidel, Chapter 12). The compositional depictions of human and non-human figures emerging from pots in the iconographic imagery of Eastern Woodland engraved shell gorgets suggest that such portals existed both as portable objects and as physical places, as the chapters throughout our volume attest (Brain and Phillips 1996). Much like how plains bundles "embod[ied] the corpus of ecological and cosmological knowledge needed to survive" (Zedeño 2008, 362), these places and contexts provided the avenues and dwelling spaces that humans and other-than-human-persons relied upon to access their proper niches in the cosmos and channel suprasensible forces through creative acts (Knight 1989, 284; Chappell 2002; Cobb and King 2005; Buchanan and Skousen 2015).

Knowledge of venerated ancestors, non-human agents, and animate powers that specifically identify (or reside in) particular places attest to the fluid nature of their qualities and often outline specific behaviors that facilitate passage through the permeable boundaries between them with the aid of iconographic depictions (*sensu* Reilly 2004; Olsen 2010; Harris and Cipolla 2017). In other cases, this knowledge probably sanctioned how certain spaces must remain inaccessible and contained (*sensu* Mills 2008; Payne 2010; Cobb 2022), possibly by covering some of them with mounds (Giles *et al.*, Chapter 11; Knight 1989; Miller 2015). The encasement of raptorial imagery and purposefully arranged burials within Mound 2 at the Hopewell Site, therefore, can be considered a sealed microcosm.

There are also cases where non-human agents occupying a cosmoscape possess qualities that defy human attempts to organize them in the manners exemplified by Picture Cave or the Craig Mound at Spiro (see Lambert 2018; Brown *et al.* 2020). Martin's (Chapter 10) study attests to this by drawing connections between Earth Mother depictions and tornadic forces observed in nature, suggesting that crafting imitations was perhaps the only viable strategy for recording knowledge about the transformative capabilities of nonhuman agents. Altogether, these contributions collectively reinforce that cosmoscapes, as places, offered ancient cultures both the means of concentrating special qualities in sanctified spaces and the ability to impose their own qualities on them by carefully structuring eventful spaces.

Yet it is important not to create artificial boundaries between how pre-Columbian peoples modeled objects and spaces as cosmoscapes. For example, the scale and materiality of Maya stelae and the Aztec Calendar bridge these categories, illustrating how certain large objects played active roles in pre-Columbian place making and worlding practices. Similarly, the careful wrapping and unwrapping of Maya stelae illustrates their close association with more portable ritual bundles (Guernsey and Reilly 2006; Stuart 1997). So, while it has been analytically useful to separate how pre-Columbian peoples crafted Objects as Cosmoscapes from Cosmoscapes as Place-Making, these worlding practices were intertwined for many (if not most) communities.

Concluding remarks

We focus in our concluding remarks on how pre-Columbian peoples were able to interact and engage with (and possibly manipulate) cosmological forces and beings through the ways that they modeled various objects and places into cosmoscapes. In this vein, Crumley and Marquardt (1990, 73–4) discuss how "specific models of reality are conceived, negotiated among human groups and applied at specific scales" while Ashmore (2004, 262–3) notes that scale activates and "shapes social actions in multiple ways." Accordingly, the choices pre-Columbian peoples made about what scale or size-various cosmoscapes should be created had clear ramifications for how communities used and interacted with them. For instance, portable, hand-held objects (e.g., ceramic bottles or bowls) or ones that can be worn (e.g., the greenstone masks) could be used and manipulated in quite different ways than buildings, earthworks, poles, or Maya stelae.

This difference recalls discussions of how miniaturism/miniaturization can be used to create or allow access to alternate worlds, as well as the way it can facilitate more intimate interactions and a sense of control (Bailey 2005). The most detailed theoretical discussions of miniaturism/miniaturization in archaeology have often been pursued as part of the interpretation of figurines (cf. Bailey 2005; Foxhall 2015; Alberti 2016a; 2016b; Insoll 2017; Martin and Langin-Hooper 2018; Langin-Hooper 2020), but these ideas seem equally pertinent to how various objects manifested cosmoscapes. But differences might exist too because of how some objects, like certain ceremonial bottles and bowls, were used to attain altered states of consciousness through the consumption of the hallucinogens, stimulants, and other medicines they contained (Azar and Steponaitis, Chapter 2; Lambert, Chapter 4).

Conversely, the way larger scale cosmoscapes were modeled by pre-Columbian peoples as features of landscapes, settlements, and architectures allow them to be incorporated into ritual regimes and ceremonies in quite different ways. Discussions related to how the movement into, within, and through various places, as well as how they were inhabited by human and non-human agents, seems quite relevant to past experiences of these pre-Columbian cosmoscapes. In this context, another useful example is Howey and O'Shea's (2006) analysis of how the Mide origin myth of Bear's Journey can be linked to the layout of Late Prehistoric earthen enclosures in northern Michigan. Yet drastically different experiences were created by the moving into and through Picture Cave and other similar subterranean caverns, which underlines their variability (Duncan and Diaz-Granados, Chapter 9). Equally, the way certain places were created to highlight celestial alignments/ events illustrates how temporal and spatial scales were often carefully modeled and articulated by pre-Columbian peoples (Pauketat 2013; Henry *et al.* 2020).

To return full circle, it is startling and impressive how many colorful threads appear to be interwoven in complex ways to create pre-Columbian peoples' cosmoscapes. These cosmoscapes can be visualized as composed of rich arrays of patterns with a multiplicity of centers discernable at different scales. The diversity, complexity, and characteristics of these pre-Columbian worlding practices provides a robust challenge to western ontological dualisms, especially the partition of lifeworlds and realities into distinct natural and cultural domains. Similarly, how animistic and analogic perspectives informed the ways that pre-Columbian peoples modeled objects and places into cosmoscapes constitutes a useful archaeological research trajectory.

References

Alberti, B. (2013) Archaeology after Interpretation. In *Archaeology after Interpretation: Returning materials to archaeological theory*, eds B. Alberti, A.M. Jones and J. Pollard, 37–42. Routledge, New York.

Alberti, B. (2016) Archaeologies of ontology. *Annual Review of Anthropology* 45, 163–79.

Alberti, B. and Marshall, Y. (2009) Animating archaeology: Local theories and conceptually open-ended methodologies', *Cambridge Archaeological Journal* 19, 344–356.

Alberti, B., Fowles, S., Holbraad, M., Marshall, Y., and Witmore, C. (2011) "Worlds otherwise" archaeology, anthropology, and ontological difference. *Current Anthropology* 52, 896–912.

Ashmore, W. (2004) Social archaeologies of landscape. In *A Companion to Social Archaeology*, eds L. Meskell and R.W. Preucel, 255–71. Chichester, Wiley.

Aveni, A. (2002) *Empires of Time: Calendars, clocks, and cultures* (rev. edn). University Press of Colorado, Boulder CO.

Bailey, D. (2005). *Prehistoric Figurines: Representation and corporeality in the Neolithic*. Routledge, New York.

Baltus, M. and Baires, S. eds (2017) *Relational Engagements of the Indigenous Americas: Alterity, ontology, and shifting paradigms.* Lexington Books, Lexington KY.

Berlo, J.C. (2011) Navajo cosmoscapes – up, down, within. *American Art* 25, 10–13.

Berlo, J.C. (2014) Navajo sandpainting in the age of cross-cultural replication. *Art History: Journal of the Association of Art Historians* 37, 688–707.

Bold, R. (2020) Constructing cosmoscapes: Cosmological currents in conversation and contestation in contemporary Bolivia. *HAU: Journal of Ethnographic Theory* 10, 195–208.

Boyea, A. (1999) Native American music and curriculum: Controversies and cultural issues. *Philosophy of Music Education Review* 7, 105–17.

Brain, J. and Phillips, P. (1996) *Shell Gorgets: Styles of the late prehistoric and protohistoric Southeast*. Peabody Museum Press, Cambridge MA.

Brown, J.A., Barker, A.W. and Sabo, G. III. (2020) The Spirit Lodge, Spiro ritual, and cosmic renewal. In *Recovering Ancient Spiro: Native American art, ritual, and cosmic renewal*, eds E. Singleton and F.K. Reilly III, 92–112. National Cowboy and Western Heritage Museum, Oklahoma City OK.

Buchanan, M.E. and Skousen, B.J. (2015) *Tracing the Relational: The archaeology of worlds, spirits, and temporalities*. University of Utah Press, Salt Lake City UT.

Chappell, S.A. (2002) *Cahokia: Mirror of the cosmos*. University of Chicago Press, Chicago IL.

Cobb, C.R. (2022). Landscapes of forgetting and structural silence in the American Southeast. *American Anthropologist* 124, 90–103.

Cobb, C.R. and King, A. (2005) Re-inventing Mississippian tradition at Etowah, Georgia. *Journal of Archaeological Method and Theory* 12, 167–92.

Cosgrove, D.E. (1998) *Social Formation and Symbolic Landscape*. University of Wisconsin Press, Madison WI.

Crumley, C.L. and Marquardt, W.H. (1987) Regional dynamics in Burgundy. In *Regional Dynamics: Burgundian landscapes in historical perspective*, eds C.L. Crumley and W.H. Marquardt, 609–23. Academic Press, San Diego CA.

Crumley, C.L. and Marquardt, W.H. (1990) Landscape: A unifying concept in regional analysis. In *Interpreting Space: GIS and archaeology*, eds K.M.S. Allen, S.W. Green and E.B.W. Zubrow, 73–9, Taylor and Francis, New York.

Ellen, R. (1986) Microcosm, macrocosm and the Nuaulu house: Concerning the reductionist fallacy as applied to metaphorical levels. *Bijdragen tot de taal-, land-en volkenkunde* 142, 1–30.

Eriksen, T.H. (2004) *What is Anthropology?* Pluto Press, London.

Foxhall, L. (2015) Introduction: miniaturization. *World Archaeology* 47, 1–5.

Friberg, C.M. (2018) Cosmic negotiations: Cahokian religion and Ramey Incised pottery in the northern hinterland. *Southeastern Archaeology* 37, 39–57.

Gell, A. (1992) *The Anthropology of Time: Cultural constructions of temporal maps and images*. Routledge, New York.

Gosden, C. (2005) What do objects want? *Journal of Archaeological Method and Theory* 12, 193–211.

Guernsey, J. and Reilly, F.K. III (2006) Introduction. In *Sacred Bindings of the Cosmos: Ritual acts of bundling and wrapping in ancient Mesoamerica*, eds J. Guernsey and F.K. Reilly III, 1–12. Ancient America Special Publication 1, Boundary End Archaeology Research Center, Barnardsville NC.

Harris, O.J.T. and Cipolla, C.N. (2017) *Archaeological Theory in the New Millennium: Introducing current perspectives*. Routledge, New York.

Harrison-Buck, E. and Hendon, J.A. eds (2018) *Relational Identities and Other-than-human Agency in Archaeology*. University Press of Colorado, Boulder CO.

Henry, E.R., Mickelson, A.M. and Mickelson, M.E. (2020) Documenting ceremonial situations and institutional change at Middle Woodland geometric enclosures in central Kentucky. *Midcontinental Journal of Archaeology* 45, 203–25.

Henry, J. (2003) Macrocosm/microcosm. In *The History of Science and Religion in the Western Tradition: An encyclopedia*, ed G.B. Ferngren, 418–24. Routledge New York.

Howey, M.C. and O'Shea, J.M. (2006). Bear's journey and the study of ritual in archaeology. *American Antiquity* 71, 261–82.

Ingold, T. (1993) The temporality of landscape. *World Archaeology* 25, 152–4.

Insoll, T. ed (2017) *The Oxford Handbook of Prehistoric Figurines*. Oxford University Press, Oxford.

Johnson, A.F. (2019) Documenting the multisensory and ephemeral: Navajo Chantway singers and the troubles of a "science" of ceremonialism. *Journal of the History of the Behavioral Sciences* 55, 230–51.

Knight, V.J. Jr. (1989) Symbolism of Mississippian mMounds. In *Powhatan's Mantle: Indians in the colonial Southeast*, eds P.H. Wood, G.A. Waselkov and M.T. Hatley, 297–291. University of Nebraska Press, Lincoln NE.

Kohn, E. (2015) Anthropology of ontologies. *Annual Review of Anthropology* 44, 311–27.

Lambert, S.P. (2018) Addressing the cosmological significance of a pot: A search for cosmological structure in the Craig Mound. *Caddo Archaeological Journal* 28, 21–37.

Langin-Hooper, S. M. (2020). *Figurines in Hellenistic Babylonia: Miniaturization and cultural hybridity*. Cambridge University Press, Cambridge.

Lankford, G.E. (2007) The "Path of Souls": Some death imagery in the Southeastern ceremonial complex. In *Ancient Objects and Sacred Realms: Interpretations of Mississippian iconography*, eds F.K. Reilly III and J.F. Garber, 174–12. University of Texas Press, Austin TX.

Lewis, R.B. and Stout, C. eds (1998) *Mississippian Towns and Sacred Spaces: Searching for an architectural grammar*. University of Alabama Press, Tuscaloosa AL.

Martin, S.R. and Langin-Hooper, S.M. eds (2018) *The Tiny and the Fragmented: Miniature, broken, or otherwise incomplete objects in the ancient world*. Oxford University Press, Oxford.

Miller, J. (2015) *Ancestral Mounds: Vitality and volatility of Native America*. University of Nebraska Press, Lincoln NE.

Mills, B. J. (2008) Remembering while forgetting: depositional practices and social memory at Chaco. In *Memory Work: Archaeologies of material practices*, eds R.M. Van Dyke and S.E. Alcock, 81–108. Blackwell, New York.

Morrison, K.M. (2000) The cosmos as intersubjective: Native American other-than-human persons. In *Indigenous Religions: A companion*, ed G. Harvey, 23–36. Cassel, New York.

Munn, N. D. (1992) The cultural anthropology of time: A critical essay. *Annual Review of Anthropology* 21, 93–123.

Niesyto, J. (2020) Medicine masks of the Iroquois people as revealed by the False Faces Society. *Studia Etnologiczne i Antropologiczne* 20, 1–20.

Olsen, B. (2010) *In Defense of Things: Archaeology and the ontology of objects*. AltaMira, Lanham MD.

Pauketat, T.R. (2013) *An Archaeology of the Cosmos: Rethinking agency and religion in ancient America*, Routledge, New York.

Pauketat, T.R. and Emerson, T.E. (1991) The Ideology of authority and the power of the pot. *American Anthropologist* 93, 919–41.

Pavel, T.G. (1981) Fiction and the ontological landscape. *Studies in 20th Century Literature* 6, 149–63.

Payne, C. (2010) The disposal of heirlooms and the end of memory at Lake Jackson. Unpublished paper presented at the annual meeting of the Society of American Archaeology, St Louis MI.

Pels, P. (2015) Modern times: Seven steps toward an anthropology of the future. *Current Anthropology* 56(6), 779–96.

Postill, J. (2002) Clock and calendar time: a missing anthropological problem. *Time & Society* 11, 251–70.

Reichel, E. (2012) The landscape in the cosmoscape, and sacred sites and species among the Tanimuka and Yukuna Amerindian tribes (north-west Amazon). In *Sacred Species and Sites: Advances in biocultural conservation*, eds G. Pungetti, G. Oviedo and D. Hooke, 127–51. Cambridge University Press, Cambridge.

Reilly, F.K. III (2004) People of earth, people of sky: Visualizing the sacred in Native American art of the Mississippian Period. In *Hero, Hawk, and Open Hand: American Indian art of the ancient Midwest and South*, eds R.F. Townsend and R.V. Sharp, 125–38. Yale University Press, New Haven CO.

Sabo, G. III (2012) The Terán Map and Caddo cosmology. In *The Archaeology of the Caddo*, eds T.K. Perttula and C.P. Walker, 431–47. University of Nebraska Press, Lincoln NE.

Sauer, C. (1926) Recent developments in cultural geography. In *Recent Developments in the Social Sciences*, ed. E.C. Hayes, 154–212. L.P. Lippincott, Philadelphia PA and London.

Skaanes, T. (2021) Mapping materiality – social relations with objects and landscapes. In *Mapping the Unmappable?* ed. U. Dieckmann, 223–60. Transcript Press, Bielefeld.

Skousen, B.J. and Buchanan, M.E. (2015) Advancing an archaeology of movements and relationships. In *Tracing the Relational. The Archaeology of Worlds, Spirits, and Temporalities*, eds M.E. Buchanan and B.J. Skousen, 1–19. University Utah Press, Salt Lake City UT.

Stuart, D. (1996) Kings of stone: A consideration of stelae in ancient Maya ritual and representation. *RES: Anthropology and Aesthetics* 29, 148–71.

Wayman, A. (1982) The human body as microcosm in India, Greek cosmology, and sixteenth-century Europe. *History of Religions* 22, 172–90.

Zedeño, M.N. (2008) Bundled worlds: The roles and interactions of complex objects from the North American Plains. *Journal of Archaeological Method and Theory* 15, 362–78.

Zedeño, M.N. (2009) Animating by association: Index objects and relational taxonomies. *Cambridge Archaeological Journal* 19, 407–17.